AFRICAN ISSUES

Zimbabwe's Land Reform

AFRICAN ISSUES

AFRICAN ISSUES

Zimbabwe's Land Reform

Myths & Realities

IAN SCOONES
NELSON MARONGWE
BLASIO MAVEDZENGE
JACOB MAHENEHENE
FELIX MURIMBARIMBA
CHRISPEN SUKUME

JC JAMES CURREY

WEAVER
PRESS

JACANA MEDIA

James Currey
is an imprint of
Boydell & Brewer Ltd
PO Box 9, Woodbridge
Suffolk IP12 3DF

and of

Boydell & Brewer Inc.
668 Mt Hope Avenue
Rochester, NY 14620, USA
www.boydellandbrewer.com
www.jamescurrey.com

Weaver Press
Box A1922
Avondale, Harare
Zimbabwe
www.weaverpresszimbabwe.com

Jacana Media (Pty) Ltd
10 Orange Street
Sunnyside, Auckland Park 2092
South Africa
www.jacana.co.za

First published 2010

1 2 3 4 5 14 13 12 11 10

British Library Cataloguing in Publication Data

Zimbabwe's land reform: myths and realities. -- (African issues)
1. Land reform--Zimbabwe--History--21st century.
I. Series II. Scoones, Ian.
333.3'16891'090511-dc22

ISBN 978-1-84701-024-7 (James Currey paper)
ISBN 978-1-77922-110-0 (Weaver Press paper)
ISBN 978-1-77009-985-2 (Jacana paper)

The publisher has no responsibility for the continued existence or accuracy of URLs for external or
third-party internet websites referred to in this book, and does not guarantee that any content on
such websites is, or will remain, accurate or appropriate.

This publication is printed on acid-free paper
Typeset by
forzalibro designs, Cape Town
in 9/11 Melior with Optima display

Printed and bound in Great Britain by
CPI Antony Rowe, Chippenham and Eastbourne

This is an important, exciting and hugely impressive study which throws original light on the impacts of Zimbabwe's controversial Fast Track Land Reform Programme in one province, Masvingo. It makes a major contribution to our understanding of these complex events, moving away from standard myths and stereotypes to paint a rich and nuanced picture. It is without doubt a major contribution to scholarship which deserves to be widely read. *Robin Palmer, Mokoro Ltd, Oxford; formerly Global Land Adviser, Oxfam GB*

This book represents arguably the most comprehensive empirical evidence challenging the popular myths that Zimbabwe's land reform has been a total failure, attributed to political cronyism and lack of investment. The book will be most instructive for South Africa and Namibia as they ponder a way forward with their own land reform challenges. *Mandivamba Rukuni, Professor and Director, Wisdom Afrika Leadership Academy; formerly Chair, Commission of Inquiry into Zimbabwe's Land Tenure Systems*

This book is a comprehensive assessment of the nature of agrarian change during the last decade. It captures the diverse range of real life responses of newly resettled family farms and the new small to medium scale commercial farmers to changing commodity and financial markets within the new agrarian landscape, during a period of economic distress. *Sam Moyo, Professor and Director, African Institute for Agrarian Studies, Harare*

This important study presents compelling evidence that the accepted view that land reform in Zimbabwe has been a total disaster is inaccurate and highly misleading. It breaks new ground in its exploration of livelihood dynamics and the complexities of social differentiation within redistributive land reform. It is likely to influence both scholarship and emerging policy frameworks in the 'new' Zimbabwe. *Ben Cousins, Research Chair on Poverty, Land and Agrarian Studies, University of the Western Cape*

Whatever you thought about the land issue in Zimbabwe, be prepared to change your mind. Events in Zimbabwe since 2000 have been so coloured by superficial media reporting and obscured by strident political posturing that little attention has been directed to what has become of the thousands of families that received land following the occupations. Despite the unevenness of outcomes to date, they have succeeded in establishing a base for themselves as serious producers with the capacity to contribute significantly to Zimbabwe's agricultural economy. *Bill Kinsey, Professor, Ruzivo Trust and Free University Amsterdam*

This fascinating study critically engages with a question being posed across Africa, as well as other regions: is small-scale agriculture doomed, as conventional ideas about development trajectories posit, or does it have a role that would be productive and equitable in a globalised world? *Pauline Peters, Professor, Center for International Development, Harvard University*

Controversy over the Mugabe regime, not least the consequences of its 'fast-track' land reform since 2000, too often generates more heat than light. This makes all the more important sound, well-grounded empirical research as reported in this study of agrarian change in the first decade of land reform in Masvingo Province. The design of the research, how it was conducted, its findings, the sensitivity and illumination of their interpretation and the authors' ability to connect Zimbabwean specificities with wider literatures and debates, make for an outstanding contribution. This book is as innovative and valuable as it was necessary. *Henry Bernstein, Professor of Development Studies in the University of London at the School of Oriental and African Studies*

This is an excellent book on the political economy of land reform and livelihoods in Zimbabwe that radically alters the boundary of existing knowledge on this highly controversial issue. The relevance of this study goes far beyond Zimbabwe: anyone interested in understanding the relationship between land, political power and rural livelihoods should read this book. *Saturnino M. Borras Jr., Canada Research Chair in Development International Development Studies, Saint Mary's University, Halifax*

Much of Zimbabwe's land reform policy since 2000 was unwise, cruel or corrupt. Yet beneficiaries responded by using land and labour, and producing output, in different ways from the big pre-reform farms. Both casual and official observers missed this, reinforcing myths of unredeemed failure. The authors' careful fieldwork, in 400 farms over nine years, provides a powerful and reasoned alternative narrative. *Michael Lipton, Research Professor, University of Sussex*

This book is essential reading for those who wish to go deeper into the complexities and often unexpected outcomes of Zimbabwe's post-2000 land reform. It provides a richly detailed and eloquent examination of a radically altering agrarian landscape in a highly contested environment. *Amanda Hammar, Professor in African Studies, University of Copenhagen*

This is an important book that injects substantial new empirical material into controversies over land reform in Zimbabwe. It is bound to stimulate new debate and become a prime point of reference and is essential reading for policy makers and academics concerned with agrarian intervention in southern Africa. *JoAnn McGregor, Department of Geography, University College London.*

This book gives us a detailed picture of the restructuring of the agricultural economy and the diversity in people's livelihoods that land reform brought to the province of Masvingo. It is a picture that defies generalisation, encompassing an extraordinary mix of shifting strategies, successes and failures. *Jocelyn Alexander, Professor of Commonwealth Studies, University of Oxford*

In this book, the pervasive views that Zimbabwe's land reform has been a disaster, causing food shortage, cutting off investment and benefiting only a coterie of 'cronies' are subject to the scrutiny of in-depth surveys over time, and on that basis dismissed as 'myths'. Material for an evidence-based verdict is now to hand, and very welcome. *Lionel Cliffe, Emeritus Professor, University of Leeds*

This book is required reading for all interested in going beyond the rhetoric and media headlines of the controversial land reforms in Zimbabwe. *Admos Chimhowu, Institute for Development Policy and Management, University of Manchester*

At last – a book that stretches across all the common-place myths and polarisations by delivering thorough empirical research and critical analysis to reveal the changing complexities, potentialities and pitfalls of Zimbabwe's dramatic agrarian reform. Highly focused, detailed, yet accessible and provocative, positive but uncompromising, this is a must-read for anyone concerned with land and livelihoods in Zimbabwe, the region and beyond. *Joost Fontein, Department of Anthropology and Centre of African Studies, University of Edinburgh*

CONTENTS

LIST OF FIGURES, TABLES & BOXES

FIGURES

TABLES

BOXES

PREFACE & ACKNOWLEDGEMENTS

The research reported in this book has been undertaken in Masvingo province since 2000, first under the auspices of the 'Sustainable Livelihoods in Southern Africa' project, and subsequently focusing on livestock as an extension to the 'Crop-Livestock Integration' project, both supported by the UK Department for International Development and coordinated by the Institute of Development Studies (IDS) at the University of Sussex. The main fieldwork, from 2006, was undertaken as part of the regional 'Livelihoods after Land Reform in Southern Africa' project (www.lalr.org.za) which was coordinated by Professor Ben Cousins at the Institute for Poverty, Land and Agrarian Studies at the University of the Western Cape and funded by the UK Economic and Social Research Council and Department for International Development ESRC/ DFID Joint Scheme for Research on International Development (Poverty Alleviation) (Grant No. RES-167-25-0037), and involved studies in Namibia, South Africa and Zimbabwe.

The Livelihoods after Land Reform project research team in Zimbabwe was led by Dr Nelson Marongwe, an urban and rural planner, of the Centre for Applied Social Sciences Trust in Harare. He has been supported by Professor Ian Scoones, originally an agricultural ecologist, based at IDS, and Dr Chrispen Sukume, an agricultural economist from the University of Zimbabwe. The Masvingo province field team was led by B.Z. Mavedezenge, formerly the regional team leader of the Farming Systems Research Unit (FSRU) of the Department for Research and Specialist Services in the Ministry of Agriculture, but now of the Agritex (agricultural extension) department in Masvingo. He is also an A1 resettlement farmer in the province. He worked with Felix Murmibarimba, formerly also of FSRU and then Agritex, but now a full-time A2 sugar cane farmer in Hippo Valley, and Jacob Mahenehene, who farms in the communal areas near Chikombedzi, as well as having a new resettlement plot in an informal site in Mwenezi district. Dr William Wolmer, formerly of IDS, was a key member of the team until 2006, and his pick-up truck continued to keep the field team moving thereafter. We were assisted in the field by: Joice Zivhu, Vimbai Museva, Mr Tagarira, Mrs Matura, Wilfred Sorofo, Rodgers Ndikudze, Virimai Madzivire,

Ushoma Senzeni, Mjurindi Taru, Christopher Shangurai, Trust Chaputsira, James Todhlana, Onias Magweregwede and Edmore Makovere. Tafadzwa Mavedzenge in Masvingo and Herbert Ntuli and Emmanuel Ziyenga at the University of Zimbabwe helped with data input and further data analysis was carried out by Alvaro Pascual Martinez at IDS. Thanks are also due to Maggie Klousia at IDS who helped wih the references and Murray McCartney of Weaver Press, who edited the manuscript.

The research team came from very different backgrounds, with different experiences, outlooks and political persuasions. It made for an interesting, but productive, dynamic. We were always there to challenge each other's assumptions and biases, but what held the group together was the commitment to explore the empirical realities on the ground, and root our analysis and policy recommendations in such solid evidence. In this effort we have been helped by many others. In particular, we have had enormous support from those in the field, both farmers and officials. The period of study has not been easy for anyone in Zimbabwe, and research was especially difficult at times for both logistical and political reasons. Farmers in our study areas spent large amounts of their time sharing their experiences and answering our seemingly endless questions. Quotes have been anonymised in the text with an initial. In addition, we have had continued support from Ministry of Agriculture officials in Masvingo province and most notably N. Pambirei, the Provincial Agricultural Extension Officer, who over many years has been a great supporter of research in the province, as well as a highly astute commentator on and reviewer of our work.

We would also like to acknowledge the support of the Livelihoods after Land Reform reference group, including Jun Borras, Johann Kirsten, Sam Moyo, Robin Palmer and Cheryl Walker. The book has substantially improved thanks to careful reviews from Ben Cousins, JoAnn McGregor, Sam Moyo and Robin Palmer. This is only one of a number of field-based studies looking at what happened following land reform in Zimbabwe. We have benefited enormously from collegial discussions and interactions with other researchers working in other parts of the country, including colleagues at the African Institute for Agrarian Studies, led by Sam Moyo, and Prosper Matondi and colleagues at the Centre for Rural Development and the Ruzivo Trust.

There is of course no single story of Zimbabwe's land reform. Some have dismissed our findings as being 'not representative' or 'exceptional'. In a strict statistical sense, case-studies are always such. However, the findings reported in this book very much echo those from other researchers in most areas outside the very highly capitalised farming areas of the Highveld. This was where the greatest disruption to commercial farming took place; where the largest concentration of high-level, politically-driven land grabbing happened and where the concentrations of election violence, particularly in 2008, were. Important research has taken place in these areas, notably a concentrated effort in Mazowe district. By contrast, the story of resettlement elsewhere in the country is less well documented, and certainly has not appeared in most media or academic representations of this period. We argue therefore that the Masvingo story told in this book is more generally representative of the geographical majority of the country beyond the Highveld.

Our work has been guided by empirical findings from the ground. In many cases these have been surprising, and difficult to take on board. As researchers we were continually challenged. As a team we had many heated discussions about the meanings and implications of our data. Those of us exposed regularly to the international, especially British, media found it hard to match what we heard on the TV and radio and read in the newspapers with what we were finding on the ground. Those of us who lived in Harare were surprised to find the situation very different further away from the capital. And those of us who were resettled farmers ourselves were fascinated to find the diversity of experiences and outcomes across the different sites in the province.

We hope that you, as the reader of this book, will be equally engaged, intrigued and challenged by the story of Zimbabwe's land reform in Masvingo province.

Harare, Masvingo, Hippo Valley, Chikombedzi and Brighton

ACRONYMS & LOCAL TERMS

A1	Smallholder farming settlement (villagised or self-contained)
A2	Small-scale commercial farming settlement type
ACP	African Caribbean and Pacific countries
Agritex	Agricultural extension service, Ministry of Agriculture
AIAS	African Institute for Agrarian Studies, Harare
ANC	African National Congress of South Africa
ARDA	Agriculture and Rural Development Authority
AREX	Agricultural extension service, Ministry of Agriculture
ASPEF	Agricultural Sector Productivity Enhancement Facility
BIPPA	Bilateral Investment Promotion and Protection Agreement
CADEC	Catholic Development Commission
CAMPFIRE	Communal Area Management Programme for Indigenous Resources
CBZ	Commercial Bank of Zimbabwe
CFU	Commercial Farmers Union
Chimurenga	Revolutionary struggle
CIO	Central Intelligence Organisation
CSC	Cold Story Company (formerly Commission)
CV	Coefficient of Variation
DA	District Administrator
DTZ	Development Trust of Zimbabwe
ESAP	Economic Structural Adjustment Programme
EU	European Union
FCTZ	Farm Community Trust of Zimbabwe
FMD	Foot and Mouth Disease
FSI	FSI Holdings Ltd, agricultural company
FTLRP	Fast Track Land Reform Programme
GAPWUZ	General Agricultural Plantation Workers Union of Zimbabwe
GDP	Gross Domestic Product
GIS	Government Input Scheme
GMB	Grain Marketing Board
Humwe	Work party
Hurudza	Successful farmer
ICFU	Indigenous Commercial Farmers Union
IFAD	International Fund for Agricultural Development
IMF	International Monetary Fund

JAG	Justice for Agriculture
Jambanja	Period of chaos, confusion, violence
JOC	Joint Operations Command
Kuronzera	Loaning (of cattle)
Lobola	Bridewealth
Maheu	Non-alcoholic grain drink
MDC	Movement for Democratic Change (Tsvangirai and Mutambara factions)
Miombo	Woodland type dominated by Julbernadia and Bracystegia spp.
NFAZ	National Farmers Association of Zimbabwe
NGO	Non-government Organisation
Nyimo	Bambara nuts
Operation Maguta	Command agriculture/input support programme
Operation Murambatsvina	Clean up the filth operation
PSF	Productive Sector Facility
PLAAS	Institute for Poverty, Land and Agrarian Studies, Cape Town
RBZ	Reserve Bank of Zimbabwe
Sabhuku	Village headman
SACU	Southern African Customs Union
SADC	Southern African Development Community
SD	Standard deviation
SG	Success Group
Svikiro	Spirit medium
SWAPO	South West African People's Organisation of Namibia
UNDP	United Nations Development Programme
Vlei	Wetland
ZANU-PF	Zimbabwe African National Union – Patriotic Front
ZAPU	Zimbabwe African People's Union
ZESA	Zimbabwe Electricity Supply Authority
ZFU	Zimbabwe Farmers Union
ZimVac	Zimbabwe Vulnerability Assessment Committee
ZNLWA	Zimbabwe National Liberation War Veterans Association
ZRHDS	Zimbabwe Rural Household Dynamics Study
ZUM	Zimbabwe Unity Movement

1

Livelihoods & Land Reform in Zimbabwe

1.1 Land reform in Zimbabwe: myths and realities

From early 2000, headlines around the world reported the invasion of Zimbabwe's largely white-owned commercial farms in dramatic terms. This was 'Mugabe's land grab', with an 'unruly', 'violent mob' of war veterans looting and destroying property across the country. They were supported by Mugabe's 'thugs', and the political and security apparatus of the state. Stories of violence, displacement and loss were reported, alongside accusations of 'wanton environmental destruction'. Images of race were never far away, and the struggle between black land invaders and white commercial farmers was played out on TV screens internationally. Zimbabwe, it was claimed, had been turned from 'bread basket' to 'basket case'. Stark contrasts were presented between violent nationalism and sovereignty, and democratic freedom, the rule of law and development. Zimbabwe's subsequent economic collapse and widespread food insecurity were attributed to the 'chaotic' land reform, where property and human rights were violated and successful commercial farming had been transformed into underutilised plots run by 'political cronies' with no knowledge of or interest in farming.[1]

But the story is far more complex than the generalisations of the media headlines.[2] This book looks at the realities behind the headlines, and tries to tackle some of the oft-repeated myths about Zimbabwe's land reform with a hard look at empirical data. Our aim is not to deny what has happened, including some appalling violations and abuses. However, there is an enormous amount of confusion, misinformation and misunderstanding about what happened to whom, where and with what consequences over the last decade, and a more nuanced story urgently needs to be told. In large part misconceptions repeatedly arise because

[1] See the many reports in the archive on www.zimbabwesituation.com from March 2000.
[2] There is a growing genre of Zimababwe literature, mixing biography with popular political commentary, including for example Buckle (2001), Blair (2002), Harrison (2006), among many others, as well as a documentary feature film ('Mugabe and the White African') and an extraordinary array of material on YouTube, blogs and websites.

of a simple lack of solid, field-level data. This book aims to fill this gap by providing insights from 16 different sites and some 400 households, situated along a transect of contrasting agroecological conditions in Masvingo province.

In the last decade, there have been major changes in the rural landscape of Zimbabwe, with some radical reconfiguration of land, production, economy and livelihoods. But the implications of this are often not clear. It is too early to draw up a definitive balance sheet on Zimbabwe's land reform, but there have been benefits and opportunities as well as costs, challenges and pitfalls. Why is this assessment important? It is important for Zimbabwe, as land remains – as it always has been – a highly emotive and political issue. At Independence in 1980, Zimbabwe inherited a highly skewed ownership pattern, with around 42% of the country owned by some 6,000 large-scale farmers, most of whom were white (Palmer, 1990; Stoneman, 1988, 2000). This commercial agricultural sector dominated the formal agricultural economy, contributing 75% of total agricultural output and 96% of sales. Advanced technologies and effective management resulted in high yields, with maize for example averaging 4.2 tonnes per hectare. The commercial sector also employed a significant workforce, about a third of formal sector employment and around 250,000 people (Bratton, 1994a: 71). The liberation war of the 1970s was fought over land, and ZANU-PF, the nationalist ruling party since 1980,[3] always emphasised the continued racialised pattern of land-ownership, especially at election time (Alexander, 2006). The land reforms since 2000 have been a focus of intense debate, reflecting highly divided opinions about the future of the country (Hammar et al., 2003). As Robin Palmer concluded in 1977: 'the most acute and difficult question confronting the first ... Government of ... Zimbabwe, whatever its ideological hue, will be that of land, bedevilled by its past use as a political and economic weapon by the whites, and by the consequent mythologies to which this has given rise. The problem will not be an easy one to resolve' (quoted in Palmer, 1990: 164).

For southern Africa more broadly, the experience of Zimbabwe has highlighted one potential path for countries unable or unwilling to deal with the unequal inheritance of apartheid or colonialism (Bond, 2000; Bond and Manyama, 2002). The spectre of land invasions destabilising an economy and the wider social and political system has sent shockwaves through the region (Lahiff and Cousins, 2001; Cousins, 2003; Goebel, 2005a). Equally, the alternatives to an agricultural sector reliant almost exclusively on large-scale commercial farms, and the potential of a more equitably distributed, small-scale production system have highlighted the possibility of alternative rural development options (Cousins, 2007).

The Zimbabwe case also offers some important insights into wider international discussions about agrarian futures, and the potential for redistributive land reform based (largely) on a smallholder model. Many thought that, with neoliberal, market-based policy prescriptions centred on the 'Washington consensus', radical and redistributive land reform

---

[3]   A 'unity' accord was signed between ZANU and ZAPU in 1987 following the Gukurahundi massacres in Matabeland (http://en.wikipedia.org/wiki/Zimbabwe_African_People's_Union).

was off the agenda (Lipton, 1993). So-called 'new wave' land reform, based on principles of willing-buyer and willing-seller land reform, was deemed acceptable as contributing to poverty reduction objectives (Deininger and Binswanger, 1999; Deininger, 1999; World Bank, 2003), but a land reform based on a major restructuring of the agrarian economy and patterns of ownership was just not expected. The Zimbabwe experience is in many respects unprecedented, and deserves special scrutiny for the broader lessons it reveals. For, as Michael Lipton (2009) points out, land reform is both unfinished business and alive and well, and remains a hot debate across the world (Borras et al., 2008; Akram-Lodhi et al., 2009).

The future role of agriculture in African development is also a much-debated topic in policy circles, as witnessed by the flurry of major reports on the subject in recent years (IAASTD, 2008; World Bank, 2008). Many foresee a 'new African green revolution' based on the flourishing of smallholder agriculture (Johnson et al., 2003),[4] with land reform often seen as a critical precondition. Others envisage a process of 're-peasanti-sation' which fosters local economic growth based on locally-controlled production systems (van der Ploeg, 2009). Still others view the advocacy for small-scale agricultural solutions as naïve and populist, pointing to the competitive advantages of large-scale, 'modern', commercial agriculture in the context of globalisation (Collier, 2008) and the on-going patterns of de-agrarianisation and livelihood diversification across Africa (Bryceson and Jamal, 1997; Bryceson et al., 2000; Ellis, 2000).

These are debates which we return to throughout the book. Needless to say, many issues are not resolved by the lessons from Zimbabwe. However, the empirical material from Masvingo province does offer some important insights, charting a way forward which in many important respects challenges the myths generated by the stereotypical views presented in media and other commentaries.

1.2 A new agrarian structure

Today Zimbabwe has a radically altered agrarian structure. In 1980, over 15m ha was devoted to large-scale commercial farming, comprising around 6,000 farmers, nearly all of them white. This fell to around 12m ha by 1999, in part through a modest, but in many ways successful, land reform and resettlement programme (Table 1.2). Today, there are still 5m ha under large-scale farming, some of it in very large holdings (such as the 350,000 ha Nuanetsi ranch in Masvingo province). There are perhaps only 2-300 white-owned commercial farmers still operating, with most having been displaced, along with a substantial number of farm workers. Most land today is under small-scale farming, either as communal areas or resettlement. Estimates vary, but around 7m ha have been taken over through the Fast Track Land Reform Programme (FTLRP) since 2000. This book describes this process in detail, and the way land units of different sizes were created, based on two broad models (A1, small-scale farming, either in villagised arrangements or

---

4   http://www.agra-alliance.org/.

Table 1.1 National land distribution pattern

Land category	1980 Area (million ha)	1980 % of total land area	2000 Area (million ha)	2000 % of total land area	2010 Area (million ha)	2010 % of total land area
Communal areas	16.4	42%	16.4	42%	16.4	42%
Old resettlement	0.0	0%	3.5	9%	3.5	9%
New resettlement: A1	0.0	0%	0.0	0%	4.1	11%
New resettlement: A2	0.0	0%	0.0	0%	3.5	9%
Small-scale commercial farms	1.4	4%	1.4	4%	1.4	4%
Large-scale commercial farms	15.5	40%	11.7	30%	3.4*	9%
State farms	0.5	1%	0.7	2%	0.7	2%
Urban land	0.2	1%	0.3	1%	0.3	1%
National parks and forest land	5.1	13%	5.1	13%	5.1	13%
Unallocated land	0.0	0%	0.0	0%	0.7	2%
Total	39.1	100%	39.1	100%	39.1	100%

Source: Moyo (2009, and pers. comm, May 2010) (derived from various government sources)
* includes all large commercial farms, agro-industrial estate farms, church/trust farms, BIPPA farms and conservancies

as self-contained plots and A2, small- and medium-scale commercial farms). While, as we will show, there is much variation and blurring of boundaries, the overall pattern of land distribution and agrarian structure has changed beyond recognition as Tables 1.1-1.3 show.[5]

Some important questions emerge. Has the dualistic pattern of the past – with two contrasting sectors, one involving a large number of small-scale farms and one involving fewer large-scale farms – disappeared, or is it re-emerging in new forms, simply with a deracialisation of ownership patterns? Where do the agro-industrial farms, estates, plantations and conservancies, many left untouched by the land reform, fit within the overall picture? With many more small-scale farms across the country, and crucially in higher potential areas, will this provide the basis for a new agrarian dynamic, promoting growth and development, or will the larger-scale farms still remain the backbone of the formal agricultural economy? How will the new configuration of land units of different sizes and orientations articulate with each other? Will this result in conflict or are there potentials for synergy?

In Zimbabwe today policy-makers must grapple with such difficult questions. There have been some major shifts in production, with certain commodities – such as tobacco, beef, horticulture and tea/coffee, seen by some as the mainstay of Zimbabwe's agricultural economy – being particularly badly affected by land reform, while others, such as cotton, traditionally a smallholder crop, have been less affected (Moyo, 2009). Food production, particularly maize, has been down in most years compared to 1990s averages (see Chapter 7) due to the dislocations of land reform and the establishment of new farms, as well as poor input supply and repeated drought. Food imports and emergency relief have occurred each year since 2000, although the 2009 maize harvest was estimated at 1.24m tonnes, reducing the need for emergency measures.[6]

The displacement of around 150,000 permanent farm-worker households, formerly resident and working on the large-scale commercial farms, along with a comparable number of temporary workers, many of them women, is another major policy challenge; relatively few, particularly in the Highveld areas, have been accommodated by the land reform (Chapter 6). While the majority of new farms have benefited land-poor or landless smallholders, some elites – notably politicians and those in the security services – have taken advantage of the situation to grab large tracts of land (and the associated infrastructure), often holding multiple farms under different names. The need for a transparent land audit which redresses these imbalances and restores legitimacy to the reform process is a top policy priority. Equally, there are no easy solutions to the question of compensation for those who lost farms through land occupation and compulsory acquisition.

---

[5] Data on land distribution is of course much disputed, and difficult to get hold of. Statistics of this sort should be taken with a large health warning therefore, although it is the broad trends and contrasts that are important.

[6] http://www.reliefweb.int/rw/rwb.nsf/db900sid/STRI-7SHRJS?OpenDocument.

Table 1.2 Emerging agrarian structure: estimated landholdings (2007)

Farm categories	Farms/households		Area held		Average farm size (ha)
	No (000s)	%	Ha (millions)	%	
Smallholder farms					
Communal	1,100,000	82.1%	16.4	51.8%	15
Old resettlement	72,000	5.4%	3.7	11.7%	51
A1	140,866	10.5%	4.236	13.4%	40
Sub-total	1,312,866	98.0%	24.34	76.9%	20
Medium-scale farms					
Old small-scale commercial farms	8,000	0.6%	1.4	4.4%	175
Small A2	14,072	1.1%	1.0	3.2%	71
Sub-total	22,072	1.6%	2.4	7.6%	
Large-scale farms					
Large A2	1,500	0.1%	0.9	2.8%	600
Black large-scale commercial farms	1,440	0.1%	0.9	2.8%	625
White large-scale commercial farms	725	0.1%	1.5	4.7%	2034
Sub-total	3,729	0.3%	3.3	10.5%	889
Agro-industrial farms and Conservancies					
Companies/trusts	753	0.1%	1	3.2%	1522
Parastatals	143	0.0%	0.6	1.9%	3922
Sub-total	896	0.1%	1.6	5.1%	2722
Total	1,339,563	100.0%	31.7	100.0%	

Source: Adapted from Moyo (2009)

1.3 Challenging myths about Zimbabwe's land reform

In order to address these major policy challenges, there must be sound, well-grounded empirical research. This book aims to answer the apparently simple question: what happened to different people's livelihoods once they acquired land through the land reform? Of course, the question is not simple: there are many interacting factors that have influenced such livelihood trajectories. Unravelling this complexity required a multi-disciplinary approach based on a longitudinal study that has now stretched in some sites in our study sample over the period from land invasion in 2000 to the end of 2009 (Chapter 2).

Zimbabwe's land reform has been a constant focus of international

Table 1.3 FTLRP: extent and distribution in 2008

Province	A1			A2		
	Farms	Area (ha)	Households	Farms	Area (ha)	Households
Manicaland	223	215,427	12,309	258	102,215	1,232
Mashonaland Central	243	568,197	16,853	342	259,489	2,434
Mashonaland East	384	437,269	17,731	349	314,233	4,703
Mashonaland West	476	811,033	28,435	592	873,111	4,460
Masvingo	248	750,563	33,197	155	341,000	1,351
Matabeleland North	281	520,214	9,394	88	259,659	421
Matabeleland South	151	383,140	10,812	194	288,324	765
Midlands	282	451,242	17,044	317	243,611	1,019
Total	2,288	4,137,085	145,775	2,295	2,681,642	16,386

Source: Ministry of Lands and Rural Resettlment (quoted by Rukuni et al., 2009)

media attention, and much academic and editorial commentary besides. Numerous reports, newspaper op-eds and consultancy documents have offered opinions about what to do. What is noticeable about most of these, is their almost complete lack of empirical data. The result is the generation of a series of oft-repeated 'myths' – simple ways of explaining the world, which may have only a tenuous basis in fact – which have gained the status of 'truth'.

Such myths serve political purposes, too. By offering a simple storyline they suggest an explanation for complex events, and thus the possibility of coping with uncertainty, radical change and deep complexity in ways that articulate with media commentary, academic generalisation or blueprint policy prescriptions (Roe, 1991). Such narratives, and the myths they perpetuate, do not of course come from nowhere: they are constructed by particular people, and are always positioned in a wider political arena. Thus in the tense and highly divided political situation that has characterised Zimbabwe over the last decade or more, the ideological positions and political commitments of different narrations of events, processes and potential outcomes are often very evident. This does not mean that evidence is not brought to bear, but that it is necessarily selective and positioned, and, as in other policy areas, particularly those which are highly contested, is always socially and politically constructed (Jasanoff and Wynne, 1998). This is not to argue for a relativist position, rather that knowledge is always co-constructed, and its personal, institutional and political location matters (Keeley and Scoones, 2003). We argue that recognising the creation of myths and their portrayal through policy narratives is an important first step in unpacking the complexity of Zimbabwe's land reform story. We are also at pains to offer the empirical evidence in ways that allow broader interpretations; perhaps different to the ones that we end up with. This richer, more differentiated empirical base will hopefully provide the platform for more informed debate as Zimbabwe moves forward.

The debate about land reform, even following the emergence of an inclusive political settlement in early 2009, remains highly charged, and is informed more by ideological persuasion and political affiliation than any reference to the situation on the ground. As the donor agencies and NGOs are gradually persuaded to re-engage, they suffer the same problems. For nearly a decade, donors have not interacted with the government in any substantive, day-to-day way. Officials – whether from government, NGOs or donor agencies – have rarely been to the rural areas, and if so only on flying visits and almost certainly never to the new resettlement areas. Donor-initiated research efforts have been few, and have focused on short-term emergency relief rather than long-term strategic development challenges. In many respects this paucity of data, only slowly being rectified a decade on, is at the heart of the problem, and is one of the main reasons why myths – and their associated policy narratives – persist.

In this book we challenge the following five myths through the examination of the field data from Masvingo province:

• Myth 1: Zimbabwean land reform has been a total failure
• Myth 2: The beneficiaries of Zimbabwean land reform have been largely political 'cronies'
• Myth 3: There is no investment in the new resettlements
• Myth 4: Agriculture is in complete ruins, creating chronic food insecurity
• Myth 5: The rural economy has collapsed

Some have accused us of picking straw people, setting them up just to knock them down. We dispute this charge. All of these myths have been repeated many times, in many places. There are others we could have added, and which we will touch on in various parts of the book relating, for example, to changing patterns of farm labour, environmental destruction and land tenure (Moyo, 2009). All five will be recognisable to anyone who has followed the Zimbabwe debate. Sometimes they are stated very baldly, sometimes more subtly, but the overall thrust is the same: Zimbabwe's land reform has been a disaster, and future interventions must address the catastrophe. By challenging these myths, and suggesting alternative policy narratives, we do not want to fall into the trap of offering an unjustifiably positive picture. We want instead to present the story as we have observed it on the ground: warts and all.

Each of these myths – and associated policy narratives – of course has deeper roots, with strong historical precedents. The biased lenses through which the recent land reform experience has been viewed can be traced to a variety of sources. Most striking is the strong technocratic vision of the 'viability' of agriculture, with the dominant model being one based on a commercial farm. Small farms, even if accepted as part of the mix, are expected to function like 'small, big farms', rather than as enterprises which are part of a wider livelihood portfolio

(Cousins and Scoones, 2010). This bias towards a commercial or mixed farm model is rooted in the long experience of technocratic planning from the Rhodesian era through Independence (Wolmer and Scoones, 2000). The dualistic agricultural economy – separating small-scale (read backward, inefficient and in need of 'development') and large-scale farming (read modern, efficient and forward-looking) has deep roots in people's understanding of what a successful agricultural economy should look like (Drinkwater, 1991; Alexander, 2006). Anything that deviates from this model is deemed a failure.

This long-standing bias – deeply embedded in political, economic and technical thinking in southern Africa more broadly – is compounded by further biases introduced from standard economic analysis of farm production. Most economic assessments of production, inputs, labour, capital investment and returns are based on standardised measures, again usually derived from a large-scale commercial model. These systematically miss the complexities found on most small-scale farms, and artificially separate farm production from wider livelihoods. Thus, for example, a focus on marketed output through formal channels misses the array of barter, exchange and informal – sometimes illegal – transactions that go on (Chapter 7). In the same way, a focus on employed labour avoids an assessment of the different informal arrangements for acquiring labour – through family links, communal arrangements, exchanges and other informal systems (Chapter 6). And a focus on farm-based production of crops and livestock misses the array of non-farm harvesting of wild products and natural resources, as well as the potential for adding value to produce through selling cooked foods, brewing grains for beer and so on (Chapter 8). Simple metrics and standard measures do not capture this complexity, and often grossly underestimate the value of total output, and the livelihood implications of this for smallholder settings.

As people established themselves on the new farms, a large range of livelihood pathways became evident. Different people, with different assets, different connections and different ambitions were able to do very different things with the land. What happened on the new land is also highly dependent on the wider livelihood portfolios of individuals and households. For those with businesses or jobs in town, prospects are quite different from those without. Similarly, some have maintained land and homes in former communal areas, and operate a split household, moving people and assets between sites. Such a strategy is quite different from those who abandoned old homes and set up afresh in the new resettlements. This wide diversity of livelihood strategies reflects the experience of informal resettlement and 'squatting' in districts like Gokwe and Hurungwe since the 1980s, where numerous communal area residents from the densely-populated areas of Masvingo and Midlands provinces transferred to new lands (Nyambara, 2001a; Chimhowu, 2002; Chimhowu and Hulme, 2006).

The new resettlement land, therefore, carries with it quite different meanings for different people. For some it is a source of private accumulation, a useful asset as part of a wider range of activities; for others it is the first time they have had productive land and is their main source of livelihood; for others it is a source of security for later in life or for their children; and for others still it has particular symbolic value, an achievement from long-term political struggle. Constructions of 'success', 'viability' and 'impact' therefore vary significantly in the new resettlements, and may not tally with those in the minds of the technocrats and planners. For them, the new situation is wholly new. As the head of the Masvingo provincial agriculture department commented in 2006: 'This is a wholly new situation, we just don't know our new clients'. As a result, technical recommendations will have to be tailored to such a new setting, requiring in turn a rather fundamental rethink of definitions and framings of success and viability.

Thus, while myths have understandable origins, they can be open to empirical challenge. This is the aim of this book. Each of the chapters addresses the five myths in different ways. Chapter 3 looks at the different beneficiaries of land reform, while Chapters 2 and 10 look at different measures of 'impact' and 'success'. Chapter 4 looks at investments, and Chapter 5 at agricultural and livestock production. Chapters 7 and 10 in turn look at the wider rural economy. Together, as discussed in the final chapter, the findings add up to a fundamental questioning of these myths, and the policy narratives that they generate.

1.4 Livelihoods and land reform

How does Zimbabwe's recent experience relate to the wider debates about land reform and development? In important respects, Zimbabwe's land reform is distinctive, having involved the dismantling of functioning large-scale, commercial farming operations and the transfer to small-scale agricultural 'peasant' production, rather than the nationalisation or land-to-the-tiller distribution of pre-capitalist forms of landed property as part of a longer-term transition to capitalism (Bernstein, 2004). This does not negate the importance of the Zimbabwe experience, particularly in the context of the former settler migrant labour economies of southern Africa, but it does suggest different questions about the ability of smallholder farming to generate alternative trajectories of economic development, based on a particular form of small-scale farm production and 'accumulation from below' (Cousins, 2010).

There has been much heated debate on the relationships between land reform and livelihoods.[7] Those who make the case for land reform on the basis of economic efficiency and poverty reduction, argue that smallholder farming is both efficient and productive, and support for redistributive reform can reverse urban and industrialisation biases (Lipton, 2009). The economic argument often centres on the so-called inverse relationship which posits that, due to the reduction of transactions costs especially over the supervision of farm labour, small-scale family farming results in higher returns than large-scale capitalist farming (Berry and Cline, 1979; Carter, 1985; Binswanger et al., 1995). Others present a more political case, arguing that transfer to small-scale peasant production is not only efficient, but also socially just (Griffin

7   It is beyond the scope of this book to provide a comprehensive review of this vast literature, but see Lipton (2009), Akram-Lodhi and Kay (2009), Akram-Lodhi et al. (2007) for recent helpful overviews from different perspectives.

et al., 2002, 2004). An approach advocating a smallholder-led approach has been central to land reform and development initiatives, from the 1950s (World Bank, 1975; FAO, 1979; United Nations, 1951) to the present (IFAD, 2001; World Bank, 2003), under a variety of guises: from state-driven land reform focused on enforcing land size ceilings via a state-run land authority to more market-centred approaches, emphasising market-based incentives including land taxation (World Bank, 2003). While there has been a furious debate about the pros and cons of each, including equally damning indictments of state-focused approaches (Deininger, 1999) and willing-seller, willing-buyer principles and market-based reform (Borras, 2003), all agree that land reform needs ideally to be beneficiary-led, state-supported and economic productivity enhancing (Borras et al., 2007), as well as reducing poverty and inequality (Binswanger et al., 1995). Through providing access to land, reforms can increase the asset base of the poor, providing new streams of income from farming – or in some cases from renting or selling the land. A transition from a few large farms to multiple small farms can also increase the demand for labour, benefiting farm workers' livelihoods. In addition, small farms managed by poorer people tend to use more locally-sourced input supply and services, and so non-farm income rises. Finally, there can be economy-wide effects, as deep land inequality can hamper growth and so improvements in livelihoods (Lipton, 2009).

However, others argue that what is dubbed a 'populist' (neoclassical or otherwise) position runs against any historical analysis which inevitably sees the triumph of capitalist agrarian relations over subsistence-oriented peasant production systems (Byres, 2004). A variety of paths to agrarian transition are envisaged, echoing different historical experiences, but support for land reform focused on smallholder production is seen as misguided (Bernstein, 2010). For example, Sender and Johnson (2003), commenting on South Africa, argue strongly that large-scale commercial agriculture provides the most productive and efficient option under conditions of globalisation, while redistributive land reform is doomed to failure, resulting in the inevitable impoverishment of so-called 'beneficiaries'. While this is perhaps an extreme position, distorted by what Bernstein (2004: 207) calls the 'Western Cape effect', the argument that, given the changing nature of agri-food systems under globalisation, large-scale options where scale efficiencies, market connections and capalistion are necessary, is an important one. Further, Bernstein (2004: 221) argues that, under such conditions, a new agrarian question must be posed, one focused on questions of labour and 'rooted in crises of employment, and manifested in struggles over, and for, land to secure some part of its reproduction needs'. Under conditions of insecure employment and a growth in informal, survival-focused livelihood activity, where people must make a living across urban and rural spaces, combining agriculture with non-farm employment (both wage-based and self-employed), there is often a crisis of employment facing people, rather than a simple, classic agrarian crisis.

Redistributive land reform thus must be seen in relation to these dynamics of labour and the processes of differentiation that they entail (Hart, 2002). Under contemporary livelihood conditions in Africa, and certainly in Zimbabwe, differentiation occurs across intersecting lines of class, gender, age and ethnicity. A key question arises: what are the dynamics of differentiation, and what lines of social difference help us understand the patterns and processes unfolding following land reform? For some, Zimbabwe's land reform can be seen in terms of a classic peasant-focused transformation, led by peasants – where capital and labour are combined within the household – with processes of differentiation leading to 'rich', 'middle' and 'poor' peasants. But a more nuanced analysis would highlight the diverse class interests and different patterns of accumulation involved (Moyo, 2009; Cousins, 2010). A sophisticated, differentiatied and nuanced analysis is required, where there is a great diversity in livelihood outcomes and transitions occurring, linked to a variety of alliances, allegiances and styles of accumulation.

In the Zimbabwe context, Bush and Cliffe (1984) and Cousins et al. (1992), all offered cautions against applying simplistic categorisations, given the diversity of livelihood strategies and class positions. These cautions apply as much today. In the new resettlements, petty commodity producers can be seen alongside worker-peasants, semi-proletarians and an emergent petty bourgeoisie (Moyo and Yeros, 2005). As we discuss in Chapter 10, class is only one axis of differentiation, and tensions between genders, generations and ethnic groups are equally evident, reflected in the complex cultural politics of processes of agrarian change, where different identities, identifications and senses of belonging are represented.

How then should we conceptualise the relationships between land and livelihoods in Zimbabwe? What is the future for agrarian livelihoods following land reform? Does land redistribution, primarily to small-scale producers, only prolong the transition to capitalist agriculture, leaving an increasing number of people impoverished, reliant on informal, fragile and insecure livelihoods from diverse sources, or can redistributive land reform result in a revitalisation of agriculture as the primary motor of growth and employment in ways that were prevented by the colonial inheritance?

In this book we reflect on four perspectives, each offering a different diagnosis, with different implications for how we understand the role of redistributive land reform and its prospects. First, there are those, like Bryceson et al. (2000) and Ellis (2000), among others (e.g. Ashley and Maxwell, 2001), who argue that, across Africa, a long-term process of movement out of agriculture is occurring and that investment in smallholder agriculture makes less sense than supporting exits from agriculture and the growth of alternative livelihoods, including those in rural areas. This position reflects one strand in the long-running debate about how agriculture and industry relate to each other in developing economies. For such agriculture-pessimists, redistributive land reform, based on a smallholder model, makes little sense beyond temporary welfare relief, unless combined with a very substantial investment in off-farm enterprise development, with firm links to urban areas. Under this scenario, positive growth linkages would be created which would allow the transformation of the agricultural sector to larger-scale enterprises as in Brazil or Thailand, which are assumed to be more productive and efficient (Collier, 2008).

Second, as discussed above, an argument based on an historical analysis of political economy is forwarded by Marxist analysts who argue that smallholder farming will only persist if in the interests of capital, and will be swept aside as capitalism develops (Bernstein, 2010). They point to the globalisation of agri-food systems and the assumed efficiencies of large-scale commercial farming and argue that such forms of capitalist agriculture will inevitably win out (Sender and Johnson, 2003). The remnants of small-scale agriculture are, it is argued, simply forms of labour self-exploitation and the growth of off-farm diversification a consequence of the increased proletarianisation of the countryside, and a sign of desperation as self-sufficient peasant livelihoods are undermined (Bernstein, 2004). For such analysts, redistributive land reform, based on 'land-to-the-tiller' reforms, and the creation of multiple smallholdings from large capitalist farms runs against the direction of history and the forces of capitalism. Such forms of redistributive land reform are therefore often a (neoclassical) populist fantasy, based on an idealised notion of small-scale agriculture (Byres, 2004).

Others argue that smallholder agriculture is a transitory stage, but one that is critical if economic growth and industrial transformation are to occur (Kydd et al., 2004; Dorward et al., 2004). Here a series of 'stages' are suggested in an assumed progressive development trajectory. Smallholder agriculture is seen as efficient and growth-oriented, based on the assumptions of an 'inverse relationship' between land size and productivity, and so should be supported. Such an evolutionary model is encapsulated in the World Bank's 2008 World Development Report on agriculture, with transitions expected between agriculture-based, transitional and urbanising economies (World Bank, 2008). A market-led, technology-supported 'green revolution' is envisaged for the smallholder sector, one which will provide wide benefits and foster economic growth, even in more marginal areas (Fan et al., 2000; Lipton, 2005). In such arguments, redistributive land reform, based on a smallholder model, is seen as a precondition for successful take-off of smallholder agriculture, along with market reforms, infrastructure support and input supply (Lipton, 2009). In this view, land reform can help reverse the marginalisation of smallholder agriculture and put smallholders centre-stage in agricultural policy.

A different view argues that a focus on smallholder agricultural production, local markets and the growth of community-based agri-food systems presents an alternative, centred on peasant systems of agriculture (van der Ploeg, 2009). Such a position is highly critical of what is seen as the neoliberal, market-oriented stance, which does nothing to counter the injustices of globalisation and corporatisation of agri-food systems (Weis, 2007), and proposes an alternative 'peasant way', most vocally through the Via Campesina movement (Borras and Franco, 2010). Such advocates argue that there is no inevitability about the elimination of smallholder agriculture-based livelihoods. Instead, processes of globalisation, corporatisation and commodification must be resisted, and an alternative re-imagined, based on local resources and economies. In this argument, redistributive land reform is a central element of such transformation, with peasant movements providing the lead (Rosset et al., 2006).

Thus, depending on the diagnosis, and the political commitments associated with the analysis, very different views emerge about the relationship between land and livelihoods. We need to ask: What are the possible agrarian futures for Zimbabwe's countryside and its people? What are the potentials and pitfalls, and how should we assess Zimbabwe's post-2000 land reform ten years on? Do any of these themes in the literature (or indeed combinations of them) reflect the Zimbabwe experience? In this book we adopt an empirical stance, one that is at the outset agnostic to the diversity of theoretical positions adopted in the literature. At the end of the book, we come to some tentative conclusions, and make the case for a disaggregated and differentiated perspective on agrarian change, one that acknowledges the primary importance of context. This highlights how many of the dynamics emphasised by different strands of literature are, in fact, unfolding in parallel. While this does not prevent us from suggesting some ways forward for policy, it certainly emphasises the need for caution and the avoidance of generalisation. In challenging the myths that have surrounded Zimbabwe's land reform, we want to avoid creating new ones, and keep our analysis and prescriptions firmly based in the realities on the ground.

1.5 Land reform in Zimbabwe: setting the scene

How then has the link between land and livelihoods been thought about in Zimbabwe? This section offers a brief review of the experience of land reform and resettlement since independence in 1980.[8] This sets the scene for the period from 2000, the main subject of this book.

The early 1980s
The 1979 Lancaster House agreement set the terms for all land reform policy in the first ten years of Zimbabwe's Independence. The British agreed that they should contribute to land purchase, and £20m was pledged in 1980. All acknowledged that land reform had to be a central plank of post-Independence policy, but options were severely constrained. The limitations on compulsory acquisition through the 'willing seller, willing buyer' approach, with full compensation in foreign exchange, meant that any resettlement was going to be slow and expensive. According to Robin Palmer, Lancaster House was a 'crucial capitulation' (1990: 166). No major agrarian reform was on the cards; this was all going to be 'carefully planned', designed to increase 'farming efficiency'. A dualistic structure of the farming sector was not open to question (Cliffe, 1986).

During this period, the new government played by the rules, keen to gain international confidence and encourage 'reconciliation' with the white farming community. White farmers were seen as a 'protected species' (Palmer, 1990: 167) for much of the early 1980s. The first Minister of Agriculture (1980-85, and briefly deputy in the 1990s) was Dennis Norman, past president of the Rhodesian National Farmers Union. The

---

[8]   Much of this section is based on Lahiff and Scoones (2000). A much richer and more comprehensive treatment, with greater historical depth, is offered by Alexander (2006). For indispensible overviews of agricultural policy more broadly, see Rukuni and Eicher (1994) and Rukuni et al. (2006).

well-organised and well-resourced Commercial Farmers Union (CFU) had very good access to government, and a considerable amount of influence on policy development, price setting, and (behind-the-scenes) land reform policy (Herbst, 1990; Poulton et al., 2002).

This did not prevent the government setting a number of increasingly ambitious targets for resettlement: 18,000 households in 1980, 54,000 in 1982 and 162,000 two years later. This latter figure remained the benchmark against which the 'failure' of the 1980s resettlement programme has been judged by critics. The government saw the resettlement programme as necessary to 'neutralise a looming crisis of expectation on the part of a land hungry population' (Zimbabwe, 1981: 124). Resettlement was seen as a political imperative which would create stability and so promote economic growth. By 1989 some 52,000 households had been resettled on 2.7m ha, with some 16% of commercial farmland purchased. By 1996 around 71,000 families had been resettled, 93% on village-based schemes (Bratton, 1994a; Moyo, 2000a).

Drawing on its long history of technocratic land use planning and rural intervention, land reform in Zimbabwe was seen in terms of resettlement 'schemes', of which a number of models were developed in the early 1980s. While the cooperative Model B schemes were the ideologically-preferred options of the new government, most were resettled in the Model A village schemes. These were designed by planners in the Ministry of Agriculture and bore a striking resemblance to the earlier plans central to the Native Land Husbandry Act of the 1950s. The assumptions embedded in the technical models 'left unchallenged colonial myths about African farmers as subsistence oriented and inefficient, in contrast to market oriented European farmers' (Alexander, 1994: 331). The appropriation of the same technical arguments used as the core of Rhodesian policy approaches was unquestioned. A series of commissions in the early 1980s reinforced this, notably the Riddell Commission of 1980 and Chavanduka Commission of 1982. While recognising the importance of land reform, both made the case for rational planning and an emphasis on sound land husbandry, highlighting the supposed ills of the communal areas – communal tenure, overstocking, soil erosion, poor land use, populated by part-time farmers not committed to climbing the ladder to full commercial enterprises.

During the 1980s plenty of land was made available for sale under the willing-seller arrangements. However, this often represented only the marginal sections of larger properties, as farmers retained their productive core. Particularly as farming enterprises shifted from extensive production of maize or cattle to high-value activities such as horticulture or tourism, the need for large land areas decreased. As confidence returned, the economy grew and the government continued to provide significant support to the commercial sector, and land prices escalated. The government did not buy all the land available, however. During the 1980s around 1m ha changed hands on the private market, with many of the new black elite buying into land.

The slow-down: the mid-1980s
It was clear by the mid-1980s that the great plans for mass resettlement were not going to happen, and for a number of reasons. Initially, the

'target beneficiaries' for resettlement were largely resource-poor farmers in the existing communal areas, returning war veterans and those
displaced by the war. Very often these people had few assets of their
own and found it difficult to get started in new resettlement areas, particularly when the models assumed an ability to farm a relatively large
plot full-time. The idea was to transform the poor, 'backward', 'inefficient' farmer from the 'reserves' into a full-time farmer who followed all
the recommendations stipulated by the planners and extensionists. But
incentives to join resettlement schemes were not high. Plots were offered
on a permit basis, requiring strict adherence to rules. Being under the
direct administration of the Ministry of Lands and under the control
of the resettlement officer, settlers had no form of representation, not
being part of the District Councils. A 1983 government report noted:
'The resettlement process discourages spontaneity in settlements and
fights against attempts at reversion back to traditional methods of agriculture .... Resettlement can never be about extending the boundaries
of existing communal areas ... creating new power bases for the restora-
tion of traditional authorities, such as chiefs, headmen etc.' (quoted in
Alexander, 1994: 334).

The drought of 1982-84 also highlighted the issue of food security as
a central policy imperative, given the huge investment of government in
food relief and rehabilitation. Sceptics argued that resettlement could
jeopardise the food security of the country if the commercial sector was
in any way affected. The great early successes in communal area production – dubbed Zimbabwe's 'green revolution' (Rukuni, 1994b; Eicher,
1995; Rohrbach, 1989) – were also seen as an example of why a focus
on support to existing, successful communal area farmers might be a
better strategy than moving people to poorly supported resettlement
areas. This was officially encapsulated in plans for communal land
reorganisation from 1985 (Brand, 1994). This of course had a political
dimension too, as the communal area reorganisation was to be centred
on new administrative structures – village and ward development committees (Mutiza-Mangizwa and Helmsing, 1991; Wekwete, 1991).

Combined with the budgetary, administrative and logistical difficulties faced by the resettlement programme, a new narrative emerged
which suggested that resettlement was not after all a route to a major
restructuring of the agricultural economy, but was merely a social welfare sideline; useful for political purposes but little else. This suited
an increasingly diverse range of actors – the large-scale commercial
farmers, the new black farm-owning elite who were cashing in on land
purchases, the National Farming Association of Zimbabwe (NFAZ) who
represented the better-off communal area farmers keen on increased
service provision in their home areas, the Ministry of Finance, the
implementing ministries who were getting overwhelmed by the task,
and the donors – and especially the British, who were lukewarm about
being involved in land reform anyway (Palmer, 1990; Moore, 2003).

But this impasse in the formal resettlement programme did not prevent land hunger increasing, and demands being made. Stories of the
hard work, poor conditions and insecure permit system had filtered
back to the communal areas by this time. Many decided this was not for
them. Instead people adopted more informal options – poaching, squat-

ting, and rural-rural migration – especially to Gokwe and the Zambezi valley during much of the 1980s (Nyambara, 2001b).

The late 1980s
With the approaching end of the Lancaster House constitutional arrangement, land was once again on the political and policy agenda. Questions were asked about why, nearly ten years after Independence, so little had been done.

The British government commissioned an evaluation of the resettlement programme in 1988 (Cusworth and Walker, 1988; Cusworth, 2000) which was very upbeat. While commenting on the lack of attention to service provision, the lack of a gender focus and the inadequate response in parallel communal area development initiatives, the report assessed the achievements of the resettlement programme on technical and economic grounds. A 21% internal rate of return was proclaimed for Model A schemes. The report was favourably received by both the British and Zimbabwean governments, and Britain's aid programme seemed ready to support the idea of a major new commitment to land reform.

But as 1990 approached, the debate shifted. Robin Palmer noted at the time that there was '[e]very sign that the British government is striving behind the scenes to perpetuate Lancaster House beyond April 1990 and so prevent significant land reform from taking place' (1990: 163-4). In the lead-up to the 1990 elections Joshua Nkomo highlighted the land issue in a number of high-profile interventions, including an address to the CFU. Mugabe picked this up and land became (as before) a core issue for the election, with the usual racial, anti-British slant. As never before, the now unified ZANU-PF government was under threat and the land card had to be played hard. Corruption scandals, economic challenges and the threat of a new political party, ZUM, were all key issues.

A new policy agenda was developed for the post-Lancaster House era. This included the abandonment of the willing seller, willing buyer principle in favour of the option of compulsory acquisition with compensation based on the original purchase price and value of permanent improvements. New incentives for the release of land were to be added, including a land tax, ceilings on land area ownership, restrictions on multiple ownership and penalties for absentee landholders. A 1990 conference recommended the setting up of a Land Commission to look at the whole issue thoroughly. But, with the election over and duly won, a shift back to a technocratic framing quickly occurred. The early 1990s saw the combination of another major drought period (1991-2) which had devastating effects on the agricultural economy (and cost the government a lot of money in drought relief and grain imports) and the advent of the economic structural adjustment programme (ESAP) from 1991. Being seen in a favourable light by the World Bank and International Monetary Fund was vital for the successful negotiation of loans. Financial and political stability was all, and land reform of any sort might rock the boat. A neoliberal, export-oriented, free-market agenda was firmly adopted by the core ministries of government (Brett, 2005). Broader reform of agrarian structures (and biases against nationalisation or compulsory acquisition by the state) was off the policy agenda (Moyo, 2000a).

This is not to say that the World Bank were (or are) against land reform. The Zimbabwe World Bank Agricultural Sector Memorandum of 1991 made a strong case for continued land reform and a shift in approach (World Bank, 1991). Around this time the debate on what to do about land reform in South Africa was hotting up, and the World Bank were heavily involved there too (Binswanger and Deininger, 1993). However, technical policy advice often conflicted with the that of economists in charge of loan portfolios. The compromise saw redistributive land reform as a social welfare complement to hard-nosed economic reform, and the major strand of land reform became the creation of a new entrepreneurial class of small-scale farmers, assisted in their endeavours to acquire land through market-assisted mechanisms. Rather than a wholesale reform, a market-friendly, neoliberal option could still be advocated, without offending the agenda based on market liberalisation, modernisation and trickle-down effects of growth (Moyo, 2000b). A market-assisted approach supported by the international donor community was thus acceptable to a key local constituency made up of the new elite: the large farmer unions, banks and financial interests, NGOs and others keen on providing support services as part of donor-funded projects, and the elites who could speculate on land markets (Moyo, 2000a, b).

Land reform did not go off the policy agenda altogether during this period, but it had to be seen to be compatible with economic reforms, and despite the continued political rhetoric (usually focused most intensely around election periods), the policy approach shifted significantly. Land reform and resettlement was seen as key in the Second Five-Year National Plan of 1991; in 1992 a Land Acquisition Act was passed to support the post Lancaster House policy consensus; and also in 1992 the President commissioned a wide consultation on land tenure policy. The report concluded that resettlement and land reform were necessary, but new conditions must apply to settlers (less restrictions, leasehold options etc.), and that this must be combined with an overhaul of land administration in the communal areas, involving the creation of village assemblies and the reinstatement of some powers of chiefs and headmen (Rukuni, 1994a).

Despite the flow of policy proclamations, however, little happened on the ground in this period. Only 20,000 households were resettled between 1990 and 1996. This suited many. Land became available to government which it duly rented out at nominal rents to key political officials, civil servants, army personnel and others. Government continued to blame the slow pace of implementation on the lack of funds, as well as technical, legal and bureaucratic delays. Others less keen on the resettlement programme highlighted a range of apparent costs – potential production losses, market confidence and stability and unemployment knock-on effects. Few evaluations looked at the positive gains made (and the opportunity costs of not doing anything), and a broadly negative view emerged about resettlement in policy debate.

It was only by the late 1990s that results began to emerge from the long-term monitoring of resettlement households by the Zimbabwe Rural Household Dynamics Study (ZRHDS), led by Bill Kinsey. Contrary to his earlier commentaries which offered rather pessimistic prognoses (Kinsey, 1983), the long-term panel data was significantly more positive (Kinsey, 1999, 2003). For example, the research showed showed how resettled farmers' real income had more than doubled over the period between 1982-3 and 1994-5, and had also become less variable. Although some of the findings were later qualified (Gunning et al., 2000; Hoogeveen and Kinsey, 2001; Deininger et al., 2004), the bottom-line message remained the same: resettlement had been much more successful across a variety of criteria than many pessimists had predicted, and it took time for such benefits to be realised. These positive findings were also echoed in other studies (e.g. Harts-Broekhuis and Huisman, 2001; Robilliard et al., 2001).

Despite the bad press, resettlement schemes and settler beneficiaries were apparently doing rather well. Households had higher incomes, lower income variability and more evenly distributed incomes (although higher childhood malnutrition) than their (near) equivalents in the communal areas (Kinsey, 1999). Kinsey and colleagues argued that these (mostly) positive results emerged after a time lag, with an establishment phase where people got organised, gained access to services and accumulated productive assets (Kinsey, 2003; Owens et al., 2003). Success was not just the result of efficient production, although this helped, but also about social organisation, institution building and coordinated post-settlement support.

Throughout the 1990s broad economic and livelihood changes altered the nature of the land-livelihoods question too. The boundaries between different land types, and changes in uses and tenure regimes, had been in considerable flux for some time. This accelerated in the 1990s particularly because of the responses to structural adjustment and drought, which forced both commercial and communal farmers to switch strategies. The concentration of commercial farmers on high-value export commodities accelerated in the 1990s, resulting in large parts of farms previously used for extensive cropping or ranching no longer being used (Moyo, 2000b). For nearby communal area farmers, this allowed new deals to be struck – for grazing, for wood collection, and even sometimes for cultivation. These were often informal arrangements made with farmers, and persisted 'in the spirit of neighbourliness', or 'to keep the peace'. Such investments in social relationships often paid off later. Boundaries between communal and state land were also becoming more blurred, as resource sharing schemes (e.g. with the Forestry Commission), CAMPFIRE arrangements and others became popular. Communal lands were also becoming 'privatised' by the introduction of joint venture tourism arrangements through CAMPFIRE in communal areas (Hill, 1994; Hughes, 2003), and the penetration of commercial companies operating outgrower and contract farming schemes (Moyo, 2000b). Alongside these more formalised arrangements, the illegal, covert practices of poaching, stealing and squatting persisted (Nyambara, 2001b). But all combined to make the spatial distinctions, so embedded on the minds of Zimbabweans and the maps that describe the land uses and designations of the country, less concrete. Land reform (including tenure reform) was ongoing, but often outside the formal policy process, and often unnoticed by policymakers.

The new land reform programme: 1997-98
This status quo came to a sudden halt in 1997. This was a crucial year in a number of respects. A new opposition party – the Movement for Democratic Change (MDC) – was launched, emerging out of the largely urban-based trade union movement, but with substantial backing from white, large-scale commercial farmers and white-owned businesses, with Morgan Tsvangarai at its head (Raftopoulos, 2006a). In the same year, the government was forced to make substantial unbudgeted payments to war veterans who were demanding compensation for their role in the liberation war. The National Liberation War Veterans Association (ZNLWA) was to become a key actor in subsequent events, but its hold on government – and ZANU-PF in particular – became apparent from 1997 (Raftopoulos, 2009).

In November 1997, under the powers of the Land Acquisition Act, the government engaged in a sweeping designation of 1,471 farms. The criteria for listing were: multiple and absentee ownership, dereliction or underutilisation and whether the farm bordered a communal area. These were of course controversial and open to interpretation (Moyo, 1998). By 1998, 510 farms were degazetted on the basis of incorrect assignation. A further 841 were challenged in the courts, with only 85 being uncontested. In November 1998 acquisition orders were signed for 926 farms. This was a radical departure from past policy, and signaled a shift in political thinking. The net result was clear: with government now prepared to designate and compulsorily acquire land for resettlement, redistributive land reform was firmly back on the agenda.

The programme was officially focused on two target groups (a shift encapsulated after 1990 in the new land policy): poor, landless rural farmers from the communal areas, and potential entrepreneurial farmers (with appropriate qualifications, including college training and Master Farmer certificates). The process of listing, delisting and court wrangles became highly contentious, time consuming and politically charged. For some, this was all a means of diverting attention from rising discontent with the government and party, centred on economic mismanagement, corruption and unpopular – although highly lucrative for the political-military elite involved - foreign forays in the Democratic Republic of Congo (Raftopoulos and Mlambo, 2009; Bond, 2007).

Media comment and donor disquiet fed into a growing apprehension amongst would-be investors, both domestic and foreign. The result was much uncertainty, and a growing lack of trust in the government's policy approach. Yet much of this concern was not based on any insight into the hard facts. For example, 'white farms' being expropriated at this stage were in the main owned in multiple units by large companies, often with South African connections, and around 50% of the large-scale farming area was multiply owned. But such arguments did not convince the sceptics. There was widespread concern that a recommitment to the land reform programme would upset the political and economic stability that Zimbabwe had achieved in the past decade. The commercial farming lobby, together with an increasingly important black elite now engaged in farming, urged caution. The Indigenous Commercial Farmers Union, representing black, large-scale farmers, urged a 'clear demarcation between subsistence level resettlement models intended mainly for the alleviation of poverty in communal areas and commercial settlement models whose main aim is produce nationally strategic agricultural products on a business basis' (ICFU, 1998: 1). The note went on to make the case for an emphasis on the commercial, business model through farm settlement schemes open to 'well identified and qualified farmers' (1998: 9). It offered a prescient warning about other threats to the viability of new land reform efforts: 'Precautions should be taken against allowing those with ill-begotten wealth or corrupt intention from entrenching their selfish will on the vulnerable process of land reform ... if no adequate planning, financial and institutional support are put in place, the noble resettlement cause can plunge the nation into a social and economic disaster that will be more difficult to correct than the present situation. It will serve no one to blame indigenous farmers and new settlers for failure because of inadequate planning and support' (1998: 1, 13).

Realising that new government initiatives were imminent, the CFU also offered options. Emphasising again the importance of commercial agriculture to the economic prosperity and stability of the country, David Hasluck, the then CFU President, argued for the inclusion of the CFU in land reform, belatedly offering 1.5m ha immediately for the resettlement programme. The Union further offered financing, extension and skill training support to new indigenous commercial farmers. However, concerns were raised about issues of fair compensation, the importance of retaining freehold title deeds and the employment of the current commercial farming workforce of 327,000 people (Hasluck, 1998).

Behind the scenes, other discussions were going on. The Shivji Commission was established to rethink the land reform programme, and some careful diplomatic manoeuvering brought together a number of different stakeholders (Shivji et al., 1998). Within government this resulted in the creation of a new land reform proposal (Zimbabwe, 1998) – the Land Reform and Resettlement Programme, Phase II (Policy Framework and Project Document) which was presented to a donor conference in late 1998. This saw a sea-change in opinion. The World Bank came on board, with a commitment of US$5m for a Learning and Innovation project linked to the main land reform strategy, and a number of other donors committed funds. The Phase II document had many familiar elements; a number of the recurrent justifications were repeated: communal areas are overpopulated and environmentally degraded; an efficient, rational structure for the small-scale agricultural sector is needed; smallholder production has great potentials and colonial legacies of land alienation must be rectified. The objectives were to acquire 5m ha for redistribution to 91,000 families, youths graduating from agricultural colleges and others with demonstrable experience in agriculture. The programme, it was claimed, would contribute to GDP by increasing the number of commercialised small-scale farmers using formerly underutilised land, and, through careful planning, it would result in environmentally sustainable use. Critically, such a policy, it was argued, would 'increase the conditions for sustainable peace and social stability by removing imbalances of land ownership' in the country (Zimbabwe 1998: 3).

At its core, it was once again a technical set of proposals, based on past models, and with a particular, long-standing vision of viability based on small-scale, commericalised farming. A series of model plans for resettlement were presented, including a village model (A1), a village ranch model (three tier), a self-contained, small-scale commercial farming model (A2) and an irrigation scheme model, each with an ideal layout proposed. These model plans were of course drawn – if not directly copied – from earlier schemes dating back many decades. In the project document, the poor past performance of resettlement is put down to the usual list of problems: failure to relieve communal area pressures; lack of progress on communal area reorganisation; inappropriate targeting (initially to the resource poor who could not make much of the potentials); the permit system resulting in insecurity; restrictions on land subdivision; the failure to implement a land tax; inadequate support services; lack of professional capacity and poor inter-ministerial coordination. Plans for deregulation of subdivision rules were laid out, and maximum farm sizes by natural region were specified. This would form the basis for a graded land tax system and a Land Tax Bill was passed to Cabinet. All looked set for moving forward, nearly 20 years after Independence.

However, there was reticence about paying for land acquisition, and ongoing political tensions between Mugabe and the new British government affected diplomatic interactions. In late 1998 the signing of acquisition orders for 2m ha sent shock-waves through the diplomatic and aid communities. Despite the fact that the government followed the 'fair market value' approach to compulsory acquisition, some saw this as an aggressive act. The IMF threatened to withhold a tranche of new payments due in early 1999. Events, however, took another turn in the following months, and the Phase II plan quickly unravelled.

Jambanja: *War veterans, land invasions and elections, 1999-2000*

From 1999, in the midst of political confusion and intense debate generated by the constitutional referendum and in the run-up to the much delayed 2000 elections, land invasions started across the country (Moyo, 2001). Sometimes these were spontaneous efforts involving only local people, sometimes they were organised by networks of war veterans, and sometimes they involved the government and security forces. This is not the place to give a full account of this *jambanja* period,[9] but it set in train a process of radical land reform, and a reconfiguration of the rural landscape in ways that could not have been imagined even a year before.

Competing visions of what land was for and what land reform should be about were played out. In parallel to the technical view focused on the commercial viability of the agricultural sector, other visions of the resettlement programme emerged, including claims for restitution of 'ancestral lands', compensation for war veterans and wider social and equity goals linked to a radical restructuring of the agrarian economy. Each suggested in turn different framings of land reform, and the neat

---

9   See Chaumba et al. (2003a,b); Marongwe (2003, 2009); Hammar et al. (2003); Willems (2004); Masiiwa (2004); Moyo and Yeros (2005); Sadomba (2008) for diverse views.

if uneasy consensus struck the previous year around a commercially-driven smallholder sector, linked to a reduced but still significant large-scale commercial farm sector, was undone.

There remains much academic dispute as to whether this was a 'peasant-led movement', emerging from below and facilitated by war veterans and the landless, motivated by a genuine desire to achieve the promises of the liberation war and so create a new 'democratic revolution' (Moyo and Yeros, 2005; Sadomba, 2008), or one orchestrated from the top in a desperate attempt by a political elite to maintain power which resulted in extreme violations of rights and precipitated economic collapse (Moore, 2003; Hammar et al., 2003). David Moore (2004) has characterised this schism among left-leaning academic commentators as between 'patriotic agrarianists' and 'critical cosmopolitans', and all sides of the debate have aired their views, often coming to much more accommodating positions along the way.[10]

As with so much in contemporary discussion, a two-sided debate, based on often simplistic generalisations and limited empirical data, is insufficient to capture the complexities on the ground. As discussed further in Chapters 2 and 9, and reflected in a growing array of field-based studies, it is simply impossible to say whether the events of 1999-2000 were the result of a ground-up social protest movement which took hold, or whether the process was set up and manipulated by ZANU-PF. As subsequent chapters show, each farm 'invasion' had a different character: different origins, different people involved and different forms of external support. In most settings there were several phases, too, stretching over weeks or months. Spontaneous gatherings of people may have initiated an occupation of a farm, but subsequent organisation may have been facilitated by war veterans who established base camps and became base commanders, sometimes with support from the state, including transport, tents and food supplied by the security services. As Chapter 9 shows, the story of *jambanja* – this notorious period of invasion, occupation, associated with chaos and confusion – is complex, and generalisations, even within a province like Masvingo, are impossible to make.

Whatever their origins, the land invasions took on a symbolic character in the political debate around the elections of 2000 (and subsequently in 2005 and 2008), with Mugabe and elements of ZANU-PF supporting them. The war veterans, through the Zimbabwe National Liberation War Veterans Association (ZNLWVA), had the party in a political stranglehold. The international press commentary was condemning, most western governments showed disapproval, and international aid agencies put programmes on hold; the British government was especially vocal in its condemnation of Mugabe and his tactics. With international loans seriously overdue, the government was digging itself into a political position with potentially dire economic consequences.

Land invasions escalated in early 2000, with over 1,000 commercial farms (out of around 4,000 in the country) 'invaded' by the time the elections were finally held in late June. With the continued rhetoric

---

[10] See Raftopoulos (2003, 2006b); Moyo (2001, 2004); Moyo and Yeros (2005, 2007); Mamdani (2008); Raftopoulos and Mlambo (2009), among others.

emerging from the President about the need for radical land reform, political support for the invasions continued after the elections. The last act performed by the outgoing parliament on 6 April 2000 was to amend the constitution to allow for more rapid land reform (Presidential Powers (Temporary Measures) (Land Acquisition) Regulations, 2000). The 1992 Land Acquisition Act was subsequently amended in May. These changes allowed the government to pay for land improvements only.

On 15 July, minister Joseph Msika announced the Fast Track Land Reform Programme (FTLRP) which was to start immediately on 804 gazetted farms.[11] On 31 July he announced the identification of additional farms for the 'programme'; rather than the 804 gazetted on 2 July, a total of 3,041 would be acquired. Rather than returning to the proposals of 1998, these appeared to have been torn up; the political rhetoric of land seizure, normally left only to election periods, had been carried on into the post-election period. With the Presidential elections due in 2002, and local elections due before then, the technical debates were now well off the agenda and the policy processes became dominated by political calculations and whims.

Fast track: reasserting order?
Attempts to retrospectively impose a legislative framework and policy on the confusion of the *jambanja* period were less than convincing. The rapidly-concocted FTLRP in turn confirmed elements of the earlier Phase II plans, including the distinction between A1 and A2, as well as maximum farm sizes by type of farm and agroecological region (Zimbabwe, 2001). Large targets for land acquisition were set and were then significantly exceeded as land invasions continued. Beneficiary selection was no longer focusing on skilled, well-resourced entrepreneurial farmers, but was responding to local circumstance, and particularly popular political pressure to offer poorer people land (UNDP, 2002; Utete, 2003; Sachikonye, 2003b; Masiiwa, 2004; Marongwe, 2003; Moyo, 2009). The new resettlements were not the neatly socially-engineered, planned compositions of their predecessors, but the result of complex local political contingency and circumstance (Chaumba et al., 2003b) The losers, as a result, were usually farm workers who had been working on the former commercial farms, people associated with the opposition political party and the old and infirm (often the poorest) living in the communal areas who were unable to join the invasions (Moyo, 2001; Sachikonye, 2003a).

Data about beneficiary numbers and remaining large-scale farms remain uncertain. ZANU-PF has tended to exaggerate the scale of its achievements while the MDC, the CFU and many external media generally underestimate the total number of white commercial farmers still farming. Beyond the numbers game there has been much criticism of the implementation of the programme. For example, the UNDP criticised the scale and limited support of the land reform, highlighting a lack of participation and poor transparency (UNDP, 2002), while the World Bank (2006) suggested ways of boosting support to resettlement areas in order to improve the agricultural economy more generally.

---

[11] http://news.bbc.co.uk/1/hi/world/africa/834486.htm.

The uncertainty and confusion have resulted in diverse and varied outcomes on the ground, as subsequent chapters will show. The end result was that those on the resettlements – either physically or as absentee landholders – were a very mixed group, ranging from the extreme poor to elites (Chaumba et al., 2003b; Marongwe, 2009). Most farmers, whether in A1 or A2 schemes, had settled without basic infrastructure or resources. With the withdrawal of external donor support and the collapse of the economy due to the flight of capital, there was little state support to new settlers. On the new resettlements, the period since 2000 has been far from easy. The devastating droughts of 2001 and 2002 meant production was minimal in the first years, and the challenges of clearing land, establishing basic infrastructure and raising capital for investment were significant.

Since the land invasions there has been a significant amount of retrospective planning of the resettlements (Chaumba et al., 2003a). By mid 2001 pegging teams were being sent out to lay out villages and demarcate fields and grazing areas. Rapid revisions of farm sizes had to be made as more people demanding land had to be accommodated. During the last few years, there has been a tense to-and-fro between the technocrats who were reasserting their authority and the politicians who continued to use the offer of new land as part of their political capital and as a form of patronage. Thus technical definitions of farm size, appropriate land use and business viability rubbed up with political expediency and processes of local political accommodation. Thus, in any area, some so-called A1 farms are larger than some A2 farms, with significant numbers of both being smaller than what was deemed the 'viable' economic size for that particular natural region, as more people were squeezed in. In many places, disputes and uncertainties persist about the status of settlements, with some areas still being 'informal', having not yet received any certificates of occupancy from the government even after the extensive land auditing process of recent years. Informal settlements rarely follow the standard technical models at all, having been settled spontaneously during the invasion period with a wide variety of settlement and land use patterns. Alongside this variety of smallholdings, very large farms do still persist, sometimes held by their former owners, sometimes having been taken over by a politically well-connected 'new' farmer. Although now formally designated A2 farms, these operations are often of a very different scale.

Economic chaos and electoral violence

Zimbabwe's economic decline started in the late 1990s, precipitated by the failed policies of structural adjustment, combined with a potent mix of economic mismanagement, foreign military and mining extraction adventures in the Democratic Republic of Congo, and growing corruption amongst the political, security and business elites (Moore, 2001; Bond and Manyama, 2002; Davies, 2005). However, the economic problems of the 1990s were nothing to what followed. Some identify the starting point of the economic meltdown as 'Black Friday' of 14 November 1997 (UNDP, 2008). On that date, the Zimbabwe dollar crashed against major currencies, a move that was triggered by the government's unbudgeted payment of gratuities to the country's war veterans. The extended period of economic crisis that followed over the next 12 years severely damaged public and private sector capacity, as well as eroding the country's human capital base. As international finance was removed, the government shifted to a cash budget and began printing money. The formal economy collapsed and salaries became worthless. A UNDP report commented: 'The crisis years have seen the severe weakening of the country's middle class, as many either dropped below the national poverty line, or have been forced to emigrate ...' (2008: 4). More people have fallen into deep poverty, with the Poverty Assessment Study Survey (PASS II) of 2003 showing that 72% of the population was living below the Total Consumption Poverty Line compared to 55% in 1995 (Zimbabwe 1998, 2006). The cumulative effect of the deepening economic melt-down fundamentally affected rural livelihoods and the wider political economy.

As people settled on the land, cleared new fields and started production, the effects of the wider economic troubles began to have an impact. With the collapse of the exchange rate, and the multiple devaluations of the Zimbabwe dollar, combined with ever-increasing inflation, the formal economy was under severe stress. Operation Murambatsvina ('clean up the filth') caused added disruption in 2005, displacing many informal businesses, particularly in the urban areas (Potts, 2006a, 2008). Inflation accelerated through 2006, and by February 2007 Zimbabwe was officially experiencing hyperinflation, with prices rising more than 50% every month. This continued through 2007 and 2008, with inflation peaking at 231m% towards the end of 2008 (Chimhowu, 2009). Such inflation wiped out the value of any cash resources, including salaries and all savings. Financial transactions were difficult, and barter arrangements became more common. There were huge uncertainties, with overnight devaluations or massive inflation hikes disrupting any business plan. The result was sporadic scarcity of products, exacerbated by an extensive black market trade in virtually everything. According to the UNDP report: 'Zimbabwe's inflation is fundamentally caused by excess government expenditure, financed by the printing of money in an economy with a real GDP that has been declining for the last 10 years. Money supply growth has been completely decoupled from economic growth, the inevitable result being continued and accelerating inflation' (2008: 13). Figure 1.1 presents trends in two key statistics since 1980: per capita GDP and agriculture value added. With economic conditions deteriorating before 2000, this was exacerbated by the collapse of large-scale commercial agriculture's contribution to the formal economy.

With increasingly desperate attempts to tame 'the casino economy' by the Reserve Bank governor, Gideon Gono,[12] government resorted increasingly to price controls and regulations. These were implemented with force, often with the backing of the security services and police, but were largely ineffectual. While they emptied the shops of goods, and drove many agricultural commodity markets underground, they did nothing to stem the collapse of the economy. By 2008, the government was broke, and most businesses were unable to function. Statistics

[12]   http://www.gideongono.com/index.php for the 'official' website.

Figure 1.1 Economic trends since Independence

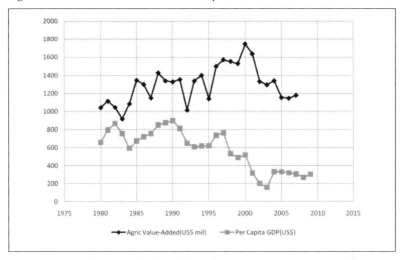

Sources: UN database for agricultural value added; IMF database for per capita GDP

vary, but by some estimates Zimbabwe's formal GDP declined by 40% between 2000 and 2008 (Bracking and Sachikonye, 2008; Coltart, 2008). The existence of parallel markets for everything – from cash to fuel to food – meant that there was increasing scope for speculation, dealing and trading on differentials in price and patterns of availability. With monetary valuation so arbitrary, those with foreign exchange could buy up businesses or commodities and trade them. Corruption and collusion were rampant, with business people working hand-in-hand with Reserve Bank officials, politicians and security service personnel. Some made fortunes through the rentier economy, and benefited substantially from the economic chaos unleashed (Davies, 2005).

However, most ordinary people suffered. The collapse in state services was almost complete by 2008; only those able to afford private payment, usually in foreign exchange, were able to access education or health services, for example. In the resettlement areas, the consequences were significant too. The Zimbabwean economy is highly integrated, with remittances supporting agriculture and agriculture supporting urban populations. As Chapter 10 shows, the hoped-for economic linkages that might have emerged from the growth of a new agricultural economy often failed to arise. Instead, business people who had earlier been eager to provide services in the resettlement areas – shops, bars, butcheries, transport services, grinding mills etc. – closed up shop, unable to run their businesses in the crazy economic conditions of the time.

Instead, across the country, a 'second economy' emerged. This existed in the shadows, was often illegal, and was rooted in a burgeoning black market based on barter transactions and dealing in foreign currency (Chapter 7). Of course this was in fact the main economy at this time: everyone participated, and indeed had to. But those in charge of regulating it – at border posts, in markets and at the road blocks – had plenty of opportunity for extracting rents. Police, youth militia, the army, health officials and local government officers all demanded a cut, taxing the second economy at source. While the fiscal crisis assumed catastrophic proportions in the formal economy, the informal economy thrived.

2008 was probably the low point of the period since 2000. This combined the peak of the economic crisis with a series of highly contested parliamentary and presidential elections. As the power of ZANU-PF waned, violence was unleashed and came to a peak before the second presidential run-off election. The ruling party fared badly in both contests, including in places which party officials had assumed were stalwart support bases for ZANU-PF. To secure a win for President Mugabe in the second round, voters who had dared to cast their vote in favour of the MDC and Tsvangirai earlier were punished. Compulsory rallies and all-night political education meetings were held, and those accused of having opposition sympathies were beaten, or worse. The notorious youth militias, established by the late Border Gezi some years before, were mobilised. For modest payments they terrorised populations and ensured that people toed the line.

The concentrations of violence were in Mashonaland East and West provinces. Out of 2,168 cases of violence documented by independent observers, however, only 33 were recorded in Masvingo province, and none of these were in the study sites.[13] As Table 1.4 shows, across Masvingo only Masvingo Central (including Masvingo town) had voted for the MDC-T in the 2000 and 2005 elections. All other constituencies showed continued support for ZANU-PF, with those in the south of our study area in Chiredzi and Mwenezi districts showing overwhelming support for ZANU-PF.

In 2008, this changed, but not as dramatically as in other parts of the country. The electoral choice of the Gutu rural voters was seen as a betrayal, and substantial intimidation, if not much recorded violence, took place in the lead-up to the June presidential elections. In other areas, it is largely solid ZANU-PF territory, although intense fights continue within the party over different factions' control of the province. The lack of extreme and brutal violence probably reflected the confidence the party had in the electoral outcome. Although substantial numbers of people voted for the MDC, ZANU-PF held sway.

The inclusive government: a new start?
For several months during 2008, the country was in meltdown – economically and politically. Fear and uncertainty ruled, and no one could move freely (certainly this research was suspended for this period). No one knew what the outcome would be. Stalemate between the parties prevailed despite intensive attempts at a compromise political settlement. So it was to everyone's great surprise and relief that on 15 September 2008 a 'Global Political Agreement' was signed, paving the way for an inclusive government which was eventually established in February 2009.

For some this was a compromise too far. How could ZANU-PF, in large part the architects of the recent chaos, and the MDC work together? For

---

13 http://www.sokwanele.com/map/electionviolence.

Table 1.4 Parliamentary election results (% of votes): 2000, 2005, 2008 for selected Masvingo constituencies (expanded in 2008) for MDC-Tsvangirai and ZANU-PF (MDC wins shaded).

Year	2000		2005		2008	
Constituency	MDC-T	ZANU PF	MDC-T	ZANU PF	MDC-T	ZANU PF
Gutu North	34.5	62.7	21.4	76.2	53.7	46.2
Gutu South	28.4	49.2	45.5	53.9	51.3	31.7
Gutu Central					57.3	42.7
Gutu East					54.8	40.7
Gutu West					35.4	43.3
Masvingo Central	59.8	38.7	48.9	48.0	46.4	45.3
Masvingo North	44	49.6	33.5	64.3	43.0	46.4
Masvingo South	26.7	73.3	19.3	77.3	35.0	60.2
Masvingo West					46.6	42.5
Chiredzi North	44.8	52.5	26.0	67.7	12.5	85.9
Chiredzi South	34.1	61.7	27.9	64.0	25.6	59.7
Chiredzi East					24.8	61.1
Chiredzi West					51.9	37.6
Mwenezi	6.7	80.6	11.8	84.4		
Mwenezi East					19.4	75.9
Mwenezi West					11.1	88.8
Province	33.2	58.9	30.8	65.7	41.2	52.3

Sources: www.zimbabwesituation.com/results.html; www.kubatana.net/html/archive/elec/050331parlres. asp?sector=ELEC; www.sokwanele.com/election2008/results2008

others it was the only solution – pragmatism had to override anything else. The inclusive government's time in office has not been plain sailing. An inordinately cumbersome compromise has meant that there are over 40 ministers, with some ministries having political masters from both parties overseeing them. Without any budgets, most ministries are hampered, and have been able to do less than planned. But there have been bright points. The violence that characterised 2008 has subsided if not disappeared, and with the dollarisation of the economy and the abandoning of the Zimbabwe dollar as a currency, inflation was dealt with at a stroke, declining from astronomical figures to single digits in a matter of days. Donors and the large financial institutions continue to be sceptical, and a set of stringent conditions are being applied before any formal reengagement with the government is permitted, but the mood music has improved, and many hope that progress will be gradual but consistent.

Not surprisingly one of the main policy items in the inclusive government's in-tray is the land issue. None of the political parties has a clear strategy in this regard, and policy documents are couched in generalities, often obscuring fundamental debates about what the future should be, in respect, for example, of the future of 'commercial agriculture' or the status of land tenure in the rural areas. The Global Political Agreement[14] outlines the challenges for land reform in Article V. This recognised that 'colonial racist land-ownership patterns established during the colonial conquest of Zimbabwe and largely maintained in the post independence period were not only unsustainable, but against the national interest, equity and justice', and accepted the irreversibility of land acquisitions and redistributions in recent years. The parties in turn agreed to conduct a land audit, to ensure that all Zimbabweans shall be considered for allocation of land; to ensure security of tenure for all landholders; and to call on the UK government to support compensation payments and work together, with external financing, to restore full productivity of the land.

This is clearly a big agenda. None of these issues are going to be easily resolved. While a land audit, for example, appears to be a simple technical task, it is far from this, as senior politically-connected figures continue to hold land in contravention of specified rules. Land grabbing continues sporadically, including in Masvingo, with several farmers evicted in the period since February 2009,[15] despite earlier assurances that they were secure. Compensation, too, remains a thorny issue, with the British government – ever since the infamous letter from Clare Short[16] – refusing to accept responsibility. And getting agricultural production back on track will mean investments in infrastructure, inputs and support services that a bankrupt government cannot afford. With the donor agencies remaining very tentative about engaging with the new inclusive government, moving forward will be slow and painful.

1.6 Conclusion

The story that this book tells is a complex and controversial one. The question of land in Zimbabwe has long been a hot political topic, but this

[14] http://www.kubatana.net/html/archive/demgg/080915agreement.asp?sector=OPIN.

[15] See 'Farm invasions escalate', April 1 2009, http://www.zimbabwesituation.com/apr1_2009.html#Z2; 'Farmer demands $2.1m for farm', April 11 2009, http://www.zimbabwesituation.com/apr11_2009.html#Z7. But settlers on black-owned farms were also being evicted too, http://www.zimbabwesituation.com/nov12a_2009.html#Z6 and http://www.zimbabwesituation.com/feb26_2010.html#Z11.

[16] In 1997 Clare Short was the minister responsible for international development in the new Labour government. The letter can be read in full at http://maravi.blogspot.com/2007/03/zimbabwe-claire-shorts-letter-nov-5th.html. Peter Freeman offers an astute perspective on these events (http://www.thezimbabwean.co.uk/200710249564/opinion-analysis/the-british-role-in-land-reform.html). For a recent British position, see http://www.royalafricansociety.org/images/stories/pdf_files/aappg_report_land_in_zimbabwe.pdf.

has become acutely so in the period since 2000. In the intense debates that have surrounded Zimbabwe's land reform, both internationally and within Zimbabwe, many myths have been created. Academic and policy debate has rarely been grounded in empirical analysis. The aim of this book is to redress this imbalance, and focus on ground-level, field realities. Our aim is to chart a way forward, and not dwell excessively on the interpretations of past events. This chapter's brief history of land and agrarian reform has aimed to situate our study in its wider context, both in relation to academic debates about land reform and livelihoods, and in terms of the policy debates about agrarian change and development. The next chapters move to a more focused empirical treatment, zeroing in on the changing livelihoods of people who gained land in Masvingo province.

This book is intended as a modest contribution to the rebuilding of Zimbabwe. Through solid evidence from the field, we hope to illuminate some fairly basic questions: who got the land, what did people do with it, and what are the implications for broader development options? We hope that a more informed understanding will help direct the type of support and define the form of policies required in appropriate ways. To this end, Chapter 11 provides a ten-point agenda for the way forward. The rest of the book explores the experiences on the ground over the decade from 2000 across the Masvingo study sites. We start in Chapter 2 by offering an overview of the study areas, data sources and research methodology. We then move to looking at the establishment of the new resettlements in Masvingo province, and the livelihood transitions that have resulted from land reform since 2000.

2

Land Reform
in Masvingo Province

2.1 Introduction

Fast track land reform presented people with new land on a massive scale. It was a radical departure from past experiences, both in terms of methods of acquisition and the selection of beneficiaries. This chapter introduces the Masvingo province context, the study areas and the methodologies used in the research. The distinctive patterns of Masvingo's new agrarian structure are explored, including the relationships between new smallholder areas (under A1 schemes), small-scale commercial farms (under A2 schemes) and remaining large-scale farms, estates and conservancies. The process of acquiring land – through land occupations, formal administrative processes and via patronage connections – is examined across the case-studies, showing the diverse array of processes at play.

In the latter part of the chapter, we look at how the land was taken, the motivations of the new settlers, who got the land and the socio-economic composition of new resettlements. We ask also how different the new resettlements are from what went before and what the emerging patterns of social differentiation, class formation and agrarian relations are. For example, are the A2 schemes simply scaled-down versions of larger commercial farms or something different? Are the A1 schemes extensions of communal areas, or do they replicate patterns seen in the old resettlement schemes from the 1980s? These are important questions for policy: do we have to re-imagine our recommendations for a very new set-up, or will old models and routines suffice, adapted to the new situation?

2.2 Land reform in Masvingo province

What has land reform since 2000 meant in Masvingo province? Table 2.1 offers the official data on fast-track resettlement, showing the extent of change that has occurred. This was not land reform at the margins; this was a major transformation in agrarian structure and relations.

Table 2.1 Overview of land distribution in Masvingo province, 2009

Category	Area (ha)	% of Total
A1	1,195,564	21.1%
A2	371,520	6.5%
Old Resettlement	440,163	7.8%
Communal area	2,116,450	37.4%
Gonarezhou National Park	505,300	8.9%
Remaining large-scale farms (white owned)	44,724	0.8%
Other (indigenous-owned, large-scale farms, small-scale farms, state farms etc.)	982,879	17.5%
Total	5,656,600	100.0%

Source: Compiled from various sources, including Masvingo Land Department data, 2009

Data are difficult to get hold of and often inconsistent, and the situation has been very fast-moving with official statistics not covering contested areas and new invasions. However, Tables 2.1 and 2.2 give an overview. The majority of land resettlement has been under the A1 smallholder model. This involves both 'villagised' (village settlement and communal grazing) and 'self-contained' systems (separate plots). Other land has been allocated under the A2 model which is aimed at more commercial operations.

In 2000, Masvingo province had a total of 623 large-scale commercial farms, covering 2.1m ha. Ownership of these farms was varied. They were indigenously-owned, white-owned, church-owned (especially the Reformed Church in Zimbabwe, Apostlic Faith Mission, Zion Christian Church, African Independent Churches and the Catholic Church) and state institutions (especially the Agricultural Rural Development Authority (ARDA) and the Cold Storage Company). By 2009, a total of 176 farms (28% of the farms in the province), with an area of 371,520 hectares, were acquired under the A2 model. A further 244 farms (1,195,564 ha) were acquired under the A1 model. In terms of area, 23.7% of the acquired land was allocated to A2 farmers and 76.3% to A1 farmers. A total of 1,169 and 32,597 settlers benefited under the A2 and A1 schemes respectively. The number of official, recorded land reform beneficiaries (certainly an underestimate) for Masvingo is 33,766 households – over 200,000 people – occupying over 1.5m ha. In addition, Masvingo has a large number of informal settlements not registered under the fast-track programme. We denote these as 'informal' schemes. Most are constituted as village settlements with individual farm plots and communal grazing. Around 8,500 households are currently settled in this way on large-scale farms, with perhaps 6,000 of these concentrated in the Nuanetsi ranch area.

Table 2.2 Fast track resettlement in Masvingo province, 2009

Scheme type	Settlement patterns	Gutu	Masvingo	Chiredzi	Mwenezi	Province
A1 villagised and self-contained	Total farms settled	83	56	33	72	244
	Total area (ha)	154,522	70,455	248,176	722,411	1,195,564
	Total settlers	5,479	3,209	11,155	12,754	32,597
	Average area /settler (ha)	28.2	21.9	22.2	56.6	36.7
A2	Total farms settled	18	21	73	64	176
	Total area (ha)	58,281	27,755	73,927	211,557	371,520
	Total settlers	179	372	672	372	1,169
	Average area/ settler(ha)	326	75	110	569	318

Source: Compiled from Lands Department data (2009)

2.3 Wider changes: land and politics in Masvingo

The redistribution of 28% of the total land area in the province to A1 and A2 schemes is certainly considerable, but substantial areas of land were, at least initially, left untouched by the land occupations and the FTLRP, and remained as estates, conservancies and large-scale farm units. In order to understand the wider agrarian structure, and the relationships between different types of land use and ownership arrangements, we must situate the study of what happened on the A1 and A2 schemes in this broader context.

Areas not affected by the land redistribution included, for example, 27 large-scale commercial farms left in the hands of the original owners. Although the situation remains changeable, with evictions occurring during 2009 and 2010,[1] white-owned, large-scale farms do still exist in Masvingo province, even if in most cases other properties owned by the same individual were taken. Their livelihoods and security has, however, been tenuous, with a continuous threat of arbitrary dispossession. While many former large-scale farmers have abandoned farming operations, others have persisted against the odds. Some have diversified operations, particularly moving into transport, import-export and agricultural processing. New deals have had to be struck with new neighbours on the resettlement schemes, and securing alliances with key officials is always important. Away from the limelight, many new arrangements have been made – involving, for example, sharing grazing

[1] In 2009, for example, three farms (3,000 ha) in Gutu, seven farms (18,400 ha) in Masvingo and ten farms (22,900 ha) in Mwenezi district were acquired. Some of these farms were under BIPPAs.

resources, operating joint wildlife hunting enterprises or engaging in marketing support for new farmers.

As discussed in Chapter 1, there was a peak in insecurity and associated evictions around the 2008 elections. But, unlike the earlier land invasions, these largely involved land grabs by elites. This has caused deep divisions between factions of ZANU-PF within the province. For example, Mr N in Chiredzi district was ordered by the court to vacate his crocodile farm to make way for a senior police officer. The trial magistrate, himself a beneficiary of land reform, ordered N to remove his 8,000 crocodiles by February 2010. However, the high-profile case saw the former governor of Masvingo and a party politburo member testify against the eviction on the grounds that he was a highly productive cane and crocodile farmer. ZANU-PF structures in the province were against the eviction. These efforts were, however, unsuccessful, paving the way for the determined Senior Assistant Commissioner from Matabeleland North province to move on to the farm.[2] Further north in our study area, several farmers were evicted during 2008 and 2009, including Johannes Nel, a dairy farmer from Gutu area and John Bolland, a stock breeder from Masvingo district.[3] Farms under Bilateral Promotion and Protection Agreements (BIPPAs), owned by foreign nationals, were not immune either. For example, the owner of Chikore farm offered his farm to the resettlement programme, except for a ten-hectare plot where he was running a prosperous flower export business. The farm was then subdivided and eleven A1 beneficiaries moved onto the land and established self-contained plots. The whole farm was later allocated to the now late Mrs M, wife of a senior minister in the ZANU-PF government. The war veteran settlers refused to vacate the farm, and a struggle ensued. After Mrs M's death, the farm was allocated to the minister who was appointed the heir of her estate. As with a number of senior officials, he is well known to hold a number of farms, registered under children and other relatives.[4]

Some farms were acquired as part of the FTLRP, but were redistributed as whole units. Across the province, a total of 58 farms (111,330 ha) were allocated in this way according to official figures. One property deserves special mention. The vast Nuanetsi ranch, covering 376,994 ha, owned by the Development Trust of Zimbabwe (DTZ) on behalf of Joshua Nkomo's estate, remained largely intact, although there were land invasions along the northern area (represented by one of our 'informal' study sites, Uswaushava). The DTZ offered 150,000 ha for official settlement, with 54,000 ha going to 1,205 A2 beneficiaries. About 25 of the A2 farmers went into cattle ranching, with the remaining 100 engaging in crop production under irrigation. Around 6,500 households were allocated plots ranging in size from 0.5 to 10 ha under the A1 model (Utete, 2003). New farmers were allocated grazing blocs by the Trust and there

2   http://www.thezimbabwetimes.com/nov6b-2009.html.

3   Ex-MP Defies Court Orders Over Farm Occupation http://www.zimbabwesituation.com/oct 26a_2008.html#Z7; Masvingo farmer abducted, assaulted http://www.zimbabwesituation. com/mar17a_2009.html#Z2; http://www.swradioafrica.com/news170309/masvingofarmer 170309.htm; 'Farm invasions escalate' http://www.zimbabwesituation.com/apr1_2009. html#Z2.

4   Zimbabwe, A2 Land Audit Report 2006: 56.

were also lease grazing arrangements with white ranchers whose land had been taken in other areas. No one is ready to admit the numbers of ranch cattle moved to the Nuanetsi ranch, but they run into the thousands. Nuanetsi remains a controversial area, given investments by the notorious Billy Rautenbach, a fugitive Zimbabwean businessman with very strong connections with the ZANU-PF elite,[5] and both official and informal resettlements are under threat due to his investment plans (see below). More land under Nuanetsi Ranch was being opened for irrigation development, including by a Chinese company that had cleared 1,000 ha in 2004.

A substantial proportion of the lowveld citrus and sugar estates at Triangle, Hippo Valley and Mkwasine also remained under the original ownership structure, although in the sugar estates outgrower plots were redistributed as part of land reform as A2 farms (again including one of our study sites at Hippo Valley).[6] At Mkwasine, 3,871 ha of the 4,880 ha were allocated under the FTLRP, leaving only about 442 ha to the estate. Hippo Valley Estate was less targeted, with most of the land taken being that of outgrowers who bought the farms from the estate in the 1960s. Hippo Valley estate still has 19,917 ha of cane land. Triangle Limited was largely unaffected, and still has 21,553 ha of land (Sierevogel et al., 2007). The challenges of sugar production following land reform are discussed in detail in Chapter 5. This is an important sector of the national economy, providing substantial in-flows of foreign currency. In 2005, it represented 1.4% of GDP, realising US$65m. The lowveld sugar industry provides direct employment to around 25,000 workers, and indirectly to possibly more than 125,000 people. Since 2000 there has been a decline in sugar production, from 570,000 tonnes in 2002 to 290,000 tonnes in 2008-09.[7] The industry has had massive historic investments in establishing the estates, irrigation systems and dams, and continues to have strong backing from the state and donors, notably the European Union.

The lowveld area of the province also includes some of the most significant wildlife and conservation areas in the country (Wolmer, 2007). These have been of major economic importance, through tourism, hunting and game farming. The conservation lobby has been exploring how land reform and wildlife might mix, and a range of policy proposals have been tabled.[8] A substantial area of the lowveld is also envisaged as part of the Great Limpopo Transfrontier Park, involving Mozambique, South Africa and Zimbabwe. While an agreement has been signed by political leaders in all three countries, implementation has been slow, certainly on the Zimbabwe side. However, plans are still on the table, and, if seen

---

5   See various news articles: http://www.zimbabwemetro.com/news/rautebach%E2%80% 99s-links-to-zanu-pf-reap-rewards-for-him-and-misery-for-25-families-on-nuanetsi-ranch/; http://allafrica.com/stories/200910261325.html; http://www.zimbabwesituation.com/nov15_ 2009.html#Z8; http://www.theindependent.co.zw.local/24785-party-bigwigs-locked-in-nuanet si-ranch-turf-war; http://www.thezimbabwetimes.com/?p=26384; http://en.wikipedia.org/wiki/ Billy_Rautenbach; http://www.thezimbabwean.co.uk/2010010927709sunday-top-stories/nkomo -orders-war-vets-off-nuanetsi.html.
6   http://www.huletts.co.za/au/introduction.asp.
7   http://ec.europa.eu/europeaid/documents/aap/2009/af_aap_2009_sugar_zwe.pdf.
8   http://www.limpopo-tp.net/.

through, these would have major ramifications for land reform benefi-ciaries in our Mwenezi sites in particular (Wolmer et al., 2004).

One of the most important developments in wildlife and land use since the 1990s has been the establishment of conservancies in the lowveld. These linked contiguous properties, often formerly cattle ranches, to allow game to move freely across a wide area, allowing the stocking of high-value species and the establishment of a range of lucrative hunting and tourism facilities. They included the Save Valley, with 26 properties measuring 338,000 ha, the Chiredzi River Conservancy (12 properties; 89,482 ha), the Bubiana Conservancy (7 properties; 127,546 ha) which straddles Masvingo and Matabeleland South and the Malilangwe Con-servancy Trust. Most of the properties of Save Valley Conservancy were initially retained, although there were some incursions along the edges. For instance, Chigwere Ranch was excised from the Conservancy and allocated to A1 farmers who immediately went into cotton production in the 2000-01 agricultural season. Conservancies were supposed to be awarded 25-year leases, and wildlife-based land reform was touted as a complementary activity (Wolmer, 2007). However, during 2009 the ownership of conservancy areas was contested by political elites want-ing to grab what they perceive as valuable assets. Under the pretence of an 'indigenisation' drive, a number of top officials have been presented as new business partners to the existing owners.[9]

The national parks estate, most notably Gonarezhou National Park in the south-east, was also largely left untouched, except for one high-pro-file invasion by the Chitsa people (Chaumba et al., 2003b). Some 16,000 ha of the park were occupied by over 700 families from Chitsa commu-nity. Plots were pegged and allocated to them by the then Governor of Masvingo Province. Whereas there is a cabinet decision that the Chitsa people move out of the Park, this has not yet been effected. Meanwhile, efforts to relocate the communities continue to be stalled by political considerations amid allegations that the settlers were engaged in poach-ing wildlife (Mombeshora and Le Bel, 2009). Outside the parks estate some state and parastatal land was transferred as part of the FTLRP, but much has remained under the control of such organisations as ARDA and the CSC. The future of such land is unclear.

Unofficial settlements are very prevalent in Masvingo, as already mentioned. Fuelled by factionalism and other politically motivated in-fighting, the Utete Report noted that 28 properties measuring 466,448 ha were informally occupied in the province. A total of 8,505 households are involved, 88% of which are located in Chiredzi district alone. This includes the Uswaushava 'informal' settlement study site, part of this research.

Thus areas redistributed as part of the FTLRP represent one part of a larger jigsaw, and their futures are bound up with what happens else-where – and particularly the political struggles over land and resources within Masvingo. It is this wider land politics that will determine the long-term future of the new resettlements and the livelihoods of the new settlers. These themes will be returned to at the end of the book. Now we turn to the focus of the study, and the main subject of the rest of

9   http://www.independent.co.uk/news/world/africa/safari-operators-enraged-as-zanupf-rewards-the-faithful-with-stolen-share-of-lucrative-trade-1786869.html.

this book: what happened to people when they got new land following the land reform?

2.4 The Masvingo study: sites and methods

In order to capture the range of experiences and dynamics in the new resettlement areas, we chose four research clusters – along a north-south agroecological gradient across the province. These were:

- Gutu – Region III;[10] wetter; poor sandy soils, former ranching area
- Masvingo – Region III/IV; poor sandy soils, former ranching (and tobacco) area
- Chiredzi – Region IV/V – heavy soils, dry/mopane, former ranching and wildlife
- Mwenezi – Region V – heavy soils, very dry, former ranching/wildlife areas

The location of the clusters in Masvingo province is shown in Figure 2.1, and a profile of each is provided in Table 2.3.

Figure 2.2 offers a picture of the changing rainfall patterns over the period of study from three functioning meteorological stations across the province, from Buffalo Range (near the Chiredzi cluster) to Bikita (near the Gutu cluster) between 2000 and 2008. Our sites span a greater range than this, with the Mwenezi cluster being drier than Buffalo Range (average annual rainfall over this period of 520mm, coefficient of variation (c.v.), 33%) and the Gutu cluster often being wetter than Bikita (average rainfall 1102mm, with a c.v. of 21%). Masvingo town is comparable to the Masvingo cluster, with an average rainfall of 746mm (c.v., 28%). The drought seasons of 2000-01 to 2001-02 and 2004-05 are evident from the data, as are the higher rainfall years of 2003-04, 2005-06 and 2007-08. 2008-09 surpassed even these figures, and the season was especially good, given the distribution of rainfall through the season in all sites.

As Table 2.4 shows, most of the sites were formerly cattle ranches and were first settled in 2000. The research has tracked their fortunes since 2004-5, and in a few cases since 2000-01. Through retrospective analysis, we have built up a detailed understanding of the stories of 16 sites, made up of around 400 households, over the ten years since the land was resettled. This offers a unique insight into the dynamics of land reform in its first decade.

The fieldwork over the past decade has involved a combination of qualitative and quantitative data collection, involving intensive engagement with a relatively small number of sites over an extended period. Such longitudinal household analysis is essential for gaining insights into the different phases of resettlement – from establishment to invest-

---

[10] In Zimbabwe, five agroecological 'natural regions' are recognised (and some sub-divisions), with Natural Region I having the highest agricultural potential, while Natural Region V is the driest, supposedly only suitable for cattle ranching (Vincent and Thomas, 1961).

Figure 2.1 Map of Masvingo province, showing study areas

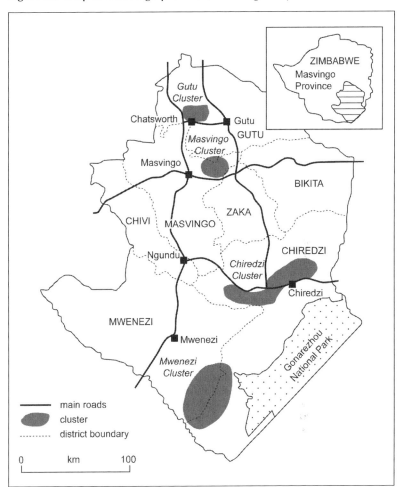

ment to production (Kinsey, 2003), and the dynamics of household fortunes over time. Analysis has taken place at a number of scales: detailed individual testimonies, life histories, household surveys, broader scheme-level assessments and investigations at the wider district and provincial levels.

Piecing together the story told in this book has involved a number of specific activities. A first activity across all sites was the drawing of a site map by settlers themselves. These indicated settlement patterns, arable land, water sources and other services. The exercise was conducted at the introductory meeting held at each site. This linked with key informant interviews on the history of the site, particularly the period of invasion and how this unfolded. The first quantitative data

Table 2.3 Cluster profiles

Cluster	Gutu	Masvingo	Chiredzi	Mwenezi
Soil type	Sandy	Sandy loams, clay loams, red loams	Red clay loams dominant soil type. Patches of sandy and gravel soil found. Sodic patches	Black basalts prevalent. Red soils cover 25% of area
Vegetation type	Miombo woodland: Julbernadia globiflora, Brachystegia spiciformis, Parinari curatelifolia	Acacia thorn veld, plus Dichrostachyis cinerea and Ziziphus mucronata	Colophospermum mopane woodland, with Acacia and Combretum spp.	Colophospermum mopane woodland, with Acacia and Combretum spp.
Former land uses	Cattle ranching	Cattle ranching	Cattle ranching, sugar production, cotton, game ranching, veterinary quarantine	Cattle ranching
Adjacent commercial centres	Chatsworth business centre	Madakuchekwa business centre	Hippo valley estate	Chikombedzi Business Centre
Distant commercial centres	Gutu Mupandawana Growth Point Masvingo Town	Mazare Business Centre Masvingo town	Triangle Town Chiredzi Town Ngundu growth point	Chiredzi Town

Source: Authors.

Figure 2.2 Rainfall patterns in Masvingo province

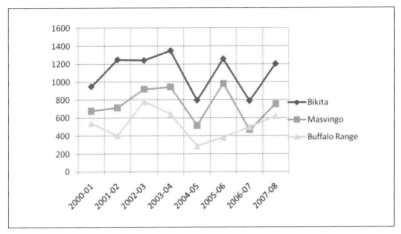

Source: Department of Meteorological Services, Harare

collection was a census of all 400 households during 2006; this was followed up for new sites in 2007, building on earlier work in some sites in 2004-05. This collected basic data on household assets and activities. Using livestock ownership as the key variable, a stratified sample was drawn up in each of the sites. A total of 16 households were sampled in sites where the total population was larger than this; in other cases (notably in the A2 sites) all households were included in the sample. This sample (N=177) has been the focus for more detailed data collection on a range variables using a questionnaire survey during 2007-08, as well as annual assessments of agricultural production (for all years since settlement).

To complement the census and survey data a ranking exercise was carried out in all sites in order to get insights into local understandings of social and economic differentiation, and notions of livelihood 'success'. With a group of key informants, this explored how settlers themselves ranked households on the site according to a composite idea of 'success'. The discussions then explored the criteria used. At a later stage of analysis, the three 'success groups' (denoted throughout the book as SG1-3, with SG1 being the most 'successful'), and various quantitative criteria derived from the survey and census data, were related. In addition, we undertook 120 detailed household biographical interviews examining people's own perceptions and strategies, as well as a focus on intra-household dynamics, and especially the gender and age differentiation of livelihood pathways. These were selected from the household sample, and so represented a range of households across success groups.

At the broader level, a number of focused studies deepened the analysis. For example, an economic linkages analysis was carried out for all sites, qualitatively tracing linkage effects from new resettlement outwards to the wider economy. This included an enterprise audit, looking at new enterprises established since resettlement, as well as the closure

Table 2.4 Site profiles

Cluster	Farm name	Area ha	Former Owner	Year Settled	Previous land use	Resettlement Model	No. of settlers
Gutu	Northdale	2,832	H. Jovner (Gambinga)	2002	Cattle ranching	A2	12
	Lonely A village 2	1,355	C Erasmus	2000	Cattle ranching	A1 villagised	30
	Clare	1,493	C. Erasmus	2000	Cattle ranching	A1 self-contained	43
Masvingo	Wondedzo Extension	1,285	George Hartley	2000	Cattle ranching	A1 self-contained	39
	Wondedzo Wares	1,286	George Hartley	2000	Cattle ranching	A1 villagised	64
	Sanangwe	689	O. Khan	2000	Cattle ranching	A1 villagised	54 official 37 unofficial
	Bompst	933	HG & PD Swart (Pvt) Ltd	2002	Cattle ranching	A2	4
Chiredzi	Hippo Valley Farm 3	120	White outgrowers	2002	Cane production	A2	14
	Uswaushava Village 7b and 8	Section of Nuanetsi ranch	DTZ	2000	Cattle ranching	Informal	Village 7b= 20 Village 8 =37
	Fair Range (2 sites)	341	Mapanza Estate	2002	Cattle ranching	A2	4+11
Mwenezi	Turf	n.d.	G. Viljoen	2000	Cattle ranching & wildlife	Informal	26
	Asveld	n.d.	J. Edwards	2000	Cattle ranching & wildlife	A2	14
	Edenvale (2 sites)	9,900	C. Schimper	2000	Cattle ranching & wildlife	A1 villagised	13+11

Source: Ministry of Lands and Audit reports. There is no area data (n.d.) for some sites as these were sub-divisions of larger properties. 'Informal' refers to sites, settled as villages, which are not officially recognised under the FTLRP, with no offer letters issued

of old ones. In each site detailed case-studies on social, political and institutional change were also undertaken. These explored the emerging relationships of authority, including issues of land administration and tenure.

This was not an easy time to undertake fieldwork in rural Zimbabwe. However, strong local connections and good relationships with people in all of the study areas have allowed for continuity and engagement in data collection. Subsequent chapters examine the different dimensions of livelihoods, but before moving to this analysis, we need to get to grips with who the new settlers are – where they came from, how they got the land, what their motivations were, as well as their socio-economic profiles. As will be shown in Chapter 3, the composition of the new resettlements is strikingly different from nearby communal or old resettlement areas, and of course very different from the former large-scale commercial farms which they replaced.

Table 2.5 offers a broad socio-economic profile of the study sites, based on a sampled survey carried out in 2007-08. This provides an aggregate insight into key household characteristics and livelihood assets, which subsequent chapters will elaborate on.

2.5 Taking the land: the process of land reform

There is no single story of the process of land reform across our sites. Each was different. But understanding what happened when land was taken is critically important for understanding what happened next. Some land was taken with a struggle; sometimes, though rarely in our cases, involving violence. Sometimes the former owner stayed on, or nearby, and relations were at least cordial with the new settlers; in other cases the owner and family fled, taking with them what they could and destroying what was left. In some cases, land occupations were led by organised groups of war veterans, with back-up from the state; in others it was groups of villagers from nearby communal lands who occupied the land. On some occasions farm workers were involved in – or even led – the land occupations; on others they were excluded and left the area. Sometimes the land was occupied for extended periods, without any state intervention, formal planning or even recognition; in other cases the state was soon on the scene, demarcating plots and issuing offer letters.[11] In some instances – for A2 farms in particular – land was allocated through a formal application process, where business plans were submitted and assessed; in other cases people arrived without going through any recognised procedure and were given land as part of patronage deals.

All of these dynamics – and more – occurred in our case-study sites. There has been much debate in the academic literature on the so-called *jambanja* period and its underlying political dynamics (see Chapter 1). The period from 1999 to 2001 was tumultuous, confusing and highly context-specific. As Moyo (2001) points out there were numerous localised and contradictory waves of land occupation. As the central state increas-

[11] Offer letters were issued by the Ministry of Lands as permits to occupy.

Table 2.5 A socio-economic profile of the study sites

Cluster	Gutu			Masvingo			Chiredzi		Mwenezi		
Scheme type	A1 self-contained	A1 villagised	A2	A1 self-contained	A1 villagised	A2	Informal	A2	A1 villagised	A1 informal	A2
Age of household head	39	34	43	36	40	43	37	46	n.d.	33	44
Educational level of household head	Form 2	Form 2	Form 3 or higher	Form 2	Form 2	Form 3 or higher	Grade 7	Form 3 or higher	Grade 7	Grade 7	Form 2
Land holding (ha)	35.5	4.0	232.1	33.0	3.9	167.0	6.2	39.1	7.9	8.0	868.7
Area cropped (ha)	5.6	3.1	6.6	8.4	3.4	n.d.	4.6	16.8	3.6	4.0	0.5
Cattle owned (nos)	6.9	5.4	25.2	11.9	4.4	11.7	4.4	14.8	4.7	4.9	60.3
Maize output in 2006 kg	2,790	2,627	3,133	7,385	3,140	65,000	2,256	2,582	449	104	n.d
Sales (GMB and local) in kg in 2006	1,310	1,157	896	5,283	1,766	54,563	378	1,357	104	0	n.d
% owning a scotch cart	32%	24%	20%	68%	63%	75%	40%	33%	55%	50%	64%
House type (% with tin/ asbestos roof)	43%	40%	25%	45%	44%	100%	42%	78%	96%	100%	100%
% receiving remittance	44%	39%	15%	n.d.	23%	0%	21%	28%	44%	52%	64%

Source: Survey data, 2007–08 (n.d. means no data available, or not applicable)

ingly lost authority and control, new sources of authority emerged. In the rural areas, base commanders – usually war veterans (or collaborators in the liberation war in some way[12]) – who led the invasions became key figures. They often had connections with the ZNLWA, and thus to the District Land Committee, which, although formally chaired by the District Administrator, was in most instances effectively controlled by war veteran leaders. As the FTLRP became formalised, agricultural extension officials and Lands Department officers also became significant players, as they were able to provide offer letters to the new land occupiers, and began to plan – and replan (Chapter 9) – the occupied areas. Political intervention was also important, but this again came from many directions – from the Provincial Governor's office, from the President's Office, from the ZANU-PF party structures or from powerful individuals with connections to party and security organs. These groupings, often represented as singular (as 'ZANU-PF' or 'the state-security apparatus' for instance), were often in conflict, and there was much dispute between different groups. In the Masvingo context for example, the long-running divisions within ZANU-PF factions continued to be played out in this period, with different groups allied to the Governor (then Josias Hungwe) and the then Vice President, Simon Muzenda.

The role of war veterans was certainly crucial in the *jambanja* period. For example, on 29 November 2000 Comrade Hunzvi, then Chairman of the ZNLWVA, addressed people at the Chief's Hall in Masvingo town and urged them to go and invade farms. News of invasions spread in different ways and from different sources through MPs, political meetings, radio, press, TV and word-of-mouth. War veterans were deployed as area and base commanders with disciplinary and land distribution powers across the province. They played only a minor role in the A2 resettlement process, however. Invasion was officially prohibited on these farms, which were designated by government to mimic the commercial production models of departed white commercial farmers.

Each invasion had its own particular character and history, and the wider political factionalism was also reflected in divisions within the war veterans. As discussed in Chapter 9, there was a shifting mix of forms of authority – some 'official', some 'unofficial'; some 'traditional', some 'modern'; some more 'political', some more 'technocratic'. What prevailed in a particular place was highly contingent on circumstance and context, and there was much blurring of boundaries and local contestation of authority and legitimacy. The politics of land in this period was therefore not straightforward. Any simple generalisation is almost certainly untrue for a range of particular settings. For this reason, we start with the empirical particularities and avoid making any wider, sweeping generalisations about political motivations and dynamics. It was the particular circumstances prevailing on a particular farm that is important, for it is these that have affected people's livelihood pathways over the following decade. The following paragraphs offer a brief summary of the diverse stories of land acquisition across the case-studies. In some sites in Chiredzi district, we were present during the occupa-

---

[12]   See McGregor (2002), Kriger (2003, 2006) and Fontein (2006a) for historical and political assessments of the role of war veterans – and the diversity of this category.

tions and got a first-hand insight into the emerging dynamics (Chaumba et al., 2003a, b; see Chapter 9); for other sites the stories are reconstructed from discussions held in 2004-05. The following section offers an overview of the processes of land invasion, occupation and allocation in each our study sites.

GUTU CLUSTER

Clare farm
The farm was invaded in October 2000, led by Comrade TM and Mr M from Gutu. They had previously led a group to Bath farm, but had left that area to come to Clare where they had hoped to get large plots. On arrival they pegged huge plots, with the base commander getting an even larger portion. In this area, farm workers did not join the invasion. They mostly fled to the nearby communal areas, although a few joined the villagised resettlements at Southdale. Soon after establishing the base camp, the invaders approached the farm owner, Mr E, and asked him to drive his cattle to the other side of the Chatsworth-Masvingo road, so they could plant crops. He ignored their request, so the land occupiers launched 'Operation Gariraioko', and drove the cattle themselves to the farmer's yard. The white farmer called the police, but they did not intervene. In January 2001, Ministry of Lands officers arrived to peg the land. Instead of 25 large plots envisaged by the occupation group, 42 plots were allocated to farmers, with two being left near a dam. The District Administrator came and allocated land first to the land invaders and then, drawing bottle tops from a hat, allocated land to others who had come from nearby areas with their councillors. District Development Fund (DDF) tractors were sent in March to help clear land, and one hectare was cleared on each plot. Some of the plots were not even occupied by this stage, and it was only later that new farmers, chosen by the District Land Committee, joined the original invaders on the land. In 2002, the base commander, Comrade TM, died, and a new leader was nominated. By 2003, farmers started investing in permanent houses, and other family members, cattle and equipment were brought to the area.

Lonely farm
The farm was first invaded at the end of 1999 by a small group, led by Comrades M and G from Gutu. Nearby Bath farm was the base camp. In 2000 more people came and they started building shacks and pegging plots. They cleared land and planted, but the crops were destroyed by the farm owner's cattle. The invaders requested food from the farm owner, Mr E, and they were given meat. This made many ill, and the land occupiers accused Mr E of poisoning them. Mr E was happy to live together with the invaders, and tried to make a plan with them. However, Mrs E was very against the idea, and racially abused the occupiers, saying, 'I don't want to live with kaffirs on my farm.' She later accused the farm occupier leader, Mr V, of rustling cattle and called the police, although the case was never heard. In 2001, government officials repegged the land, providing offer letters. The temporary huts were destroyed, people were moved to the new village areas, and new structures were developed. Disputes continued with the former owner, particularly as cattle destroyed the crops. In 2001, the settlers led an operation to contain the cattle of the former owner; all were driven to the homestead area and several killed. The settlers also took

an electric motor. *Accusations between the new settlers and Mr and Mrs E continued, with the farm workers being sent at night to search for meat in the new settlers' homes. None was ever found and in time the disputes abated, with the former owners retreating to their homestead area and reducing their cattle herd.*

Northdale farm
This was invaded in 2000, led by a Comrade M from Gutu. Eleven invaders established a base at the farm compound. The farm had previously had a dairy, but the former owner retreated to Gweru and removed the electricity transformer and destroyed the dairy and other farm infrastructure to prevent the invaders using it. Under the fast-track programme the farm was designated an A2 farm and plots were applied for by a number of people. Some of the invaders got plots, but most went to outsiders, including senior officials. Those who were well-connected could choose their plots at the offices in town using aerial photographs. Settlement was slow in Northdale, and it was only in 2004-05 that people started establishing permanent structures. Up to this time a portion of the farm, including the homestead and dam area, was retained for the former owner, although he was not resident and the place was managed by workers. In the end this was taken by a high-ranking government official who took over the homestead and farm, with the workers now transferring to the new owner.

MASVINGO CLUSTER

Wondedzo farms
At the end of 1999, PC was working on Wondedzo farms as a general hand. A war veteran and colleague approached him and he agreed to join the land occupations. Each day he would wake up and pretend that he was repairing the fence, when in fact he was busy with other occupiers establishing 'bases' at the farm. In the company of war veterans they went back to the communal areas and moved from door to door, asking those who wanted land to come and join them. About 30 people came. Once on the plot, people were not allowed to go back home. The white farmer only discovered the occupation of his farm when the base had been established and structures built. Some of the occupiers had already started fishing from his dam. One of the land occupiers was caught and beaten. The white farmer had skirmishes with one of the ZANU-PF politicians from Gutu district. When they asked him to sell meat, he said, 'I don't sell beef to ZANU-PF.' When the beating incident occurred, the land occupiers wanted to hit back, forcing him to withdraw to Masvingo. By this time, informal pegging of stands and plots had started. PC had already moved from the farm accommodation to the 'base'. Occupation of farms had spread in the area, encouraged by rousng speeches by Cormrade Hunzwi. Another group led by Comrade B, a war veteran, was also coming to occupy the farm with people from the Nemamwa area. The numbers of land occupiers swelled. There were now over 200 in the base camp, and not enough land. As base commander, Comrade B decided to establish criteria for who would get self-contained plots in Wondedzo Extension and who would join the villages of Wondedzo Wares. He pretended to go to the District Administrator to consult, and then announced that it was only those with at least ten cattle and a roll of wire who could join the self-contained scheme. These spurious criteria

were then used to split the group, with most of the war veterans associated with Comrade B and some of PC's group taking up self-contained plots. At this point, the government was called and AREX (agricultural extension) became involved in pegging. All but 15 at the base camp got some land, but many were very small portions. Comrade B later became sabhuku (headman) and chair of the Committee of Seven.

Sanangwe farm

In 2000, Comrade M, a war veteran, led the invasion into Sanangwe farm. They established a base camp near Mr K's homestead, inviting people from nearby communal areas to join. They requested land from K and started to survey the area. K did not respond and in the meantime bribed the police to come and intimidate the settlers. This had no impact, and the land occupiers continued clearing land in the areas they had demarcated. However, this was not the end of the story. K encouraged a group of settlers from nearby Sandrift farm who had acquired land earlier under the government resettlement programme to come to Sanangwe and help him evict the invaders. A major confrontation arose, resulting in one death and several serious assaults. The Sanangwe invaders retaliated and went to Sandrift and destroyed crops in the fields. In the end a settlement was negotiated and the Sandrift farmers retreated. People then started clearing land and establishing homes in earnest. But it was not easy. Due to the lack of clean water, a major diarrohea outbreak occurred in 2001, and K's cattle, which were still on the farm, kept destroying crops. There was another problem on the horizon for the Sanangwe settlers: a further group, led by two other war veterans, was invading the same farm from the south. These new invaders were confronted by Comrade M and the core group of occupiers who then left for another farm. Comrade M sadly passed away soon after this, but he remains a hero of the area. In 2002 the area was repegged and people were given offer letters. However, there were more problems in store. The District Administrator settled another 37 households in the grazing area of Sanangwe scheme, making it very crowded, now with a total of 91 households resident on a small 600 ha farm. The original occupiers have complained endlessly since, but to no avail, and conflicts between the groups have been on-going (see Chapter 9). Conflicts also exist with nearby A2 and A1 self-contained farmers. One Sanangwe farmer complained: 'They hire us to plough for them, but then accuse us of poach grazing. These people are similar to whites. They have land they are not using, but do not want others to use it.'

Uswaushava

In June 2000 two war veterans, AC and ZM, established a base camp on the edge of Nuanetsi ranch, adjacent to the Ngundu-Chiredzi road. Comrade ZM, 'Kid', became the base commander, bringing people who had earlier been displaced by a nearby dam development. More and more people joined them, and under the direction of the war veteran leaders, land was allocated in six-hectare pieces. The area however did not come under the fast-track policy and the government refused to issue the new settlers with offer letters. In order to attract attention, in 2001 the settlers blocked the main road, setting brushwood on fire. The occupation lasted a whole day, with promises being made by the government and senior politicians that the situation would be sorted out. More people arrived in the area and further land was cleared. A primary school was built out of poles and mud, and a secondary school was planned. But still, despite continued assurances, there were no offer letters forthcoming. Later the charismatic base commander passed away, and a leadership vacuum emerged. Without the strident, radical voice, challenges to the settlers' tenure security from the Nuanetsi ranch owners (and later others – see Chapter 1) increased.

Hippo Valley

Applications to the Ministry of Lands for sugar plots were made in 2000; in 2001 successful applicants were issued with offer letters, and in 2002 new settler farmers were asked to report to the agricultural extension offices in Chiredzi town. They were then shown their new plots. The former white farm owners at first tried to resist acquisition through legal battles, and when litigation failed some resorted to vandalisation of production infrastructure. In Hippo Valley Sugar Estate, centre-pivots and electric motors were deliberately damaged or removed by departing farmers. Initially all white farmers were offered one of the A2 plots, usually linked to the homestead. However, disputes continued to rage, particularly over the harvesting of the cane crop in 2002. The former owners argued it was their crop, and that the new settlers had no right to use it. War veterans tried to solve the disputes, but on occasions violence erupted. In the end, the government agreed that it was the former owners who should harvest. For the following season, formal transfer agreements were made for the use of water, electricity; the new farmers began investing in the land, and the Chiredzi Sugar Cane Farmers Association was formed to oversee the process. Disputes continued with the mill owners over payments and supply of services. The former owners continued to argue that the occupations were illegal, and that new settlers should not be paid. It took several years for these disputes to subside. Some white farmers left, while others accepted the new arrangements and further disputes occurred in some areas.[13]

Fair Range

In these farms, formerly part of Mapanza Estates, a similar process of land allocation took place under the FTLRP. Applicants were allocated A2 plots in 2002. Some new settlers moved onto their plots, but disputes with the former owners disrupted settlement. The former owners sent hired thugs to try and chase the new settlers away. A number of them were assaulted, and the police were called. Later the army arrived to restore order. It was only in 2003-04 when land clearing and planting really took off, but serious droughts struck the crops, along with erratic electricity affecting attempts at irrigation.

MWENEZI CLUSTER

Edenvale

A group from Chikombedzi area decided to invade Edenvale Ranch having heard news of the land invasions on the radio. The local MP, Mr B, was encouraging land occupations. The farm workers were very loyal to their employer and tried to resist, but the invaders soon established a base camp, and started erecting temporary structures. Many people now started arriving from nearby communal lands. At one stage there was a confrontation between a group

---

13 http://www.zimbabwesituation.com/nov24_2006.html#Z7.

of youths and the farm workers. The police were called and some invaders were put behind bars for a few days. The war veterans motivated the local people and funds were raised to pay the fines, and secure their release. The farm owner suggested areas for the invaders to establish fields and homes in an attempt to reduce the tensions. However, in a neighbouring area invaders destroyed the safari lodge on the farm as the farmer was not offering any land. The dispute escalated, with farm workers being armed. A major fight occurred and two people were killed. The farm committee on Edenvale started allocating large areas of land in self-contained units. However, later the Ministry of Lands came and smaller plots of arable land were given as part of a villagised scheme, and in 2002 offer letters were issued to the settlers.

Turf Ranch

In 2000, HM led people from Makanani area under Chief Gezani to the farms. He had first surveyed the area on his bicycle and identified a number of farms. He then called some friends, including JC, a war veteran, to come to the area. He went first to Asveld and encountered the farm owner, JE. HM explained he had come to take the land. JE laughed, and said, 'this place is dry. If you have pipes for irrigation then come, but otherwise you cannot live here.' They then moved to Sheba where a base camp was established. Women and children remained here, and supplies were ferried from the communal areas in scotch carts, sufficient for a few days at a time. On 3 May, HM travelled south and eventually found what he described as 'the promised land' at Turf Ranch. This was, he said, 'the place where milk and honey flows'. He returned to his home area and invited others to join him. He was not a war veteran, but had heard about the invasions in other places. The original farm owner, Mr G, had passed away and his wife was visiting her other farm in Mhangura. Within a week, the farm occupiers had finished building temporary structures, and had met with J, the farm manager. This was a cordial meeting, and he drove them round the farm in his pick-up. The first sites they were shown were rocky and barren, but then they found an area with good, deep basalt soils. They started clearing land and establishing homes. Within three months, cattle were being brought to the new area. Eventually three villages were established with a total of 114 households. They invested in building their own community structures, including a large multi-denominational church, a school and a number of wells. The farm manager started selling his bosses' cattle and eventually ran away to South Africa during 2000. Mrs. G left for Mhangura, and the Turf farm was fully occupied. The settlers continued to have running battles with a neighbouring rancher, a white man, who left poisoned bait which killed their dogs. This prevented them from both hunting, and chasing wild animals from their fields. Despite much lobbying (Chapter 9), they still remain without offer letters.

Asveld Ranch

This ranch had been scouted by HM and his colleagues, but the white farm owner, JE, had persuaded them to leave. Other invaders came later, and negotiated with the owner, who allocated them plots. At the same time the farm had been designated an A2 scheme. A number of people from the local area applied for plots at the encouragement of the local agricultural extension worker. Very few were successful, and most plots were allocated to those from outside. This generated resentment among the local people, who regarded this as a Shangaan area. Some of the invaders however stayed; a few received offer letters, while others remained waiting. The white owner carried on in the area for some time, and made arrangements with the new settlers. However, with ten other settlers also occupying the farm, he had to scale down his ranching operation, reducing his herd from 1,500 to around 250 and laying off 23 workers, retaining only seven. A joint-venture arrangement for hunting was established, and a new safari business emerged. Deals with the new settlers around water supplies and veterinary care were also forged, but there was a high turnover of settlers at the farm, with many of the original ones leaving because of the harsh environment and long distances to the nearest markets. In May 2009 JE was evicted, retreating to his other home and coffee farm in Chipinge as his plot was taken over by a senior official. In March 2009, 189 cattle were sold, and a further 120 were sold in May before his departure.

2.6 Motivations and ambitions

What motivated people to take the land? Although politics came into it, there were other motivations and broader ambitions. Joining the land invasions and establishing new farms was not easy. This was a tough time for many. No one quite knew what would happen next, and whether the land would become theirs. The prospect of retaliation by the existing landowner was always present, and complex stand-offs and tense negotiations ensued. Conditions were harsh, as people camped out in the farms – in some cases for months. Support systems were necessary, and relatives brought food, blankets and other resources. In some cases, there was back-up from the state, but this was often sporadic and came only later, following the original invasion. As more and more people joined the invasions, there was competition between invading groups, often resulting in disputes over control of a particular farm. There were also challenges among the leadership, as different people claimed authority, often beyond the original war veterans who led the occupations, and splits emerged within the committee structures. Negotiations with traditional leaders, spirit mediums and others created further claims on authority and control, as discussed in Chapter 9. Establishing new fields and homesteads was no simple task. The new resettlements had previously been ranches, often with scattered irrigated plots near farm houses, so land had to be cleared from scratch. Cutting and clearing was hard work, and before the rains came in earnest shelters had to be constructed using poles, mud and thatch. Ploughing and planting under such conditions was not easy, and new social arrangements for production, marketing and service support had to be established. Settlers often came from different places – from across nearby communal areas and beyond – and new communities had to be formed. New church congregations and cooperative groups were established and schooling arrangements for children had to be worked out. All of this took much hard work and effort and a patient investment in the building of good social relations.

Joining the land reform, then, especially for the A1 areas, was not easy. Why would people leave their communal homes and take up such a challenge? What motivated them? And what ambitions for the future did they have? To understand who the new people are on the new land, answering such questions is a vital step. Throughout the book are a series of case-studies showing a range of experiences. We collected 120 such stories, but all stories are different. Many identify the problems of their previous lives in the communal areas: the lack of land, the low productivity of the soil, the absence of good grazing. Some point to social problems in previous areas: disputes with neighbours, family problems or accusations of witchcraft. Others had left jobs, now no longer paying a living wage, and argued that abandoning the job and seeking an alternative livelihood in farming was the only option. The opportunities of resettlement highlighted by the new settlers were diverse too. All identify the availability of land for ploughing and grazing, as well as the good soils. Some, and particularly women, point to the emancipatory potentials of joining a new community, away from abusive husbands or families and escaping accusations and marginalisation. Others looked to a future offering the potential for handing down land to the next generation or sharing it among large, polygamous families. Others offer a more politicised argument, saying that getting the land was part of the promise of independence and what they had struggled for during the liberation war, and so only now could they say that they were free. Some echo the ZANU-PF slogan, 'the land is the economy, the economy is the land', and argue that now they were going to be really able to contribute to the wider economy and the growth of Zimbabwe as productive farmers. Others point to their existing skills that had been underutilised in their former lives: training in agriculture for example now could be put to good use.

The list could go on. But, despite the hardships and challenges, the commitment to a future in the new resettlements was tangible and inspiring, particularly among the A1 farmers interviewed. A2 farmers were rather different, as they did not by and large occupy their new farms, but were allocated them, either through formal administrative process or through patronage connections. Most continued in their jobs, and many remain absentee landholders. The challenges of the economy prevented substantial investment in their farms, and many were holding on to their land for the future, often as a retirement option as their pensions had been wiped out by inflation. A sense of having a farm as part of a new, aspirant middle-class ambition was evident too. Everyone now could be a 'yeoman farmer', and join an elite group, echoing the Purchase Area farmers of the colonial era (Cheater, 1982; Shutt, 1997). Some, as subsequent chapters show, have seriously invested in their new farms, and despite all odds, have made a go of it, with great plans for the future.

2.7 Who got the land?

Table 2.6 summarises the categories of settlers in the study areas by scheme type. The focus here is on the dominant occupation of the

Table 2.6 Settler profile across schemes (% of households)

	A1 villagised	A1 self-contained	Informal	A2	Total
'Ordinary': from other rural areas	59.9	39.2	69.7	12.2	49.9
'Ordinary': from urban areas	9.4	18.9	22.6	43.8	18.3
Civil servant	12.5	28.3	3.8	26.3	16.5
Security services	3.6	5.4	3.8	1.8	3.7
Business person	3.1	8.2	0	10.5	4.8
Former farm worker	11.5	0	0	5.3	6.7
N	192	74	53	57	376

Source: Census data, 2007 (N=376)

household head prior to getting the land.[14] Overall, 49.9% were farmers from other rural areas, almost exclusively from nearby communal lands (with three cases across all sites from old resettlement areas and one from a small-scale farming area). Other groups included those who were living in urban areas (18.3%) (unemployed or in low-paid jobs in regional towns, growth points and mines), former farm workers (6.7%), civil servants (16.5%), employees of the security services (3.7%) and business people (4.8%). These categories of course overlap. Employees of the security services (army, police, Central Intelligence Organisation) are of course civil servants, but are worth identifying separately due to their role in important patronage networks. Many, across all categories, will have had homes and plots in the communal areas, but this was not, at the time of land occupation, their primary occupation or place of residence.

The distribution of these categories varies by scheme type. The first two categories are those who were classified as 'ordinary' beneficiaries (as defined in the various government audits, i.e. not members of the other categories, and largely asset and income poor). This group made up 92% of the sample in the informal schemes, 69% in A1 villagised schemes, 58% in A1 self-contained schemes and 56% in A2 schemes.

[14] Zimbabwean households are hugely diverse, with a variety of intra-household arrangements, especially given the absence of (often) men participating in off-farm employment. Women are thus very often *de facto* household heads, managing day-to-day affairs, but nevertheless absent males are usually recognised as the formal head. Patrilocal household establishment means that women generally move to the husband's family's area on marriage, although with resettlement such traditions are only being established now. HIV/AIDS has also reconfigured household structures, with the deaths of parents and the creation of child-headed households led by orphans (Foster et al., 1997). Female-headed households exist where the husband has died or where the couple have divorced. In this study we took the household head to be the one recognised by the members of the household.

Civil servants constituted 24.6% and 25.9% of beneficiaries in A2 and
A1 self-contained schemes, dropping to 3.5% in the informal schemes
and 11.9% in the A1 villagised schemes. Civil servants sought plots
in the A2 and A1 schemes where plot sizes are larger, while shunning
the informal schemes. They are particular evident in the sugar plots
(around 30% were central or local government employees). In particular, because of their qualifications and connections, a number of
agricultural extension officers were allocated sugar plots. The pattern is however different with employees in the security ministries.
As a powerful group, one would expect these to dominate in the A1
self-contained and A2 schemes. However, they constitute 4.9% of the
settlers in A1 self-contained, 3.5% in the A1 villagised and informal
schemes, and only 1.6% in the A2 schemes. This reflects the diversity
of people within this category – from senior army generals to the most
junior police officer. Business people constitute 7.4% of beneficiaries in
A1 self-contained schemes, 6% in villagised schemes, 9.8% in the A2
schemes and are missing in the informal schemes. Former farm-workers
make a surprise inclusion in the A2 schemes, making up 4.9% of the
settlers compared to 10.9% in the A1 villagised schemes.

Across all of these categories are 'war veterans', but they account for
only 8.8% of the total. As already discussed, such a status was a key
factor in the land occupations and land allocation processes. But the
label represents another loose and contested categorisation, reflecting
multiple, competing affiliations (Sadomba, 2008). Most are linked to
the ZNLWA, and may have been guerrilla fighters in the liberation war,
collaborators or political detainees. Table 2.7 explains who the war veterans are in relation to the other categories. Nearly all were men, but
most were, prior to land invasions, farming in the communal areas, a
few were living in town (notably those in the A2 farms), while some
were civil servants (often from local government offices), business
people and employees in the security services. Sloppy analysis that
refers to war veterans as a singular group is clearly inadequate. Many
indeed had long dropped their 'war veteran' identity and had been poor
small-scale farmers in the communal areas for 20 years since the end of
the liberation war.

2.8 Land reform as a gendered process

The process of land reform is inevitably highly gendered. Various
studies both in Zimbabwe and in southern Africa more widely have
highlighted these dimensions (O'Laughlin, 1998; Goebel, 2005a, b). In
what particular ways have gendered relations affected the land reform
process in our study sites?

First, and most obviously, men and women have been allocated land
in their own right (with their names on offer letters, for example) highly
unequally. The proportion of women who benefited from land reform in
this way is small. For the overall A2 allocations in Masvingo province,
women constituted only about 13% of the total according to the 2007
Provincial A2 Land Audit. Similar patterns are observed in the study
sites. Based on the census data, female-headed households constitute

Table 2.7 Distribution of war veterans by origins and scheme type (%)

	A1 villagised	A1 self-contained	Informal	A2
Ordinary (from rural and urban areas)	100.0	53.8	75.0	60.0
Civil servant	0.0	38.5	25.0	0.0
Security services	0.0	7.7	0.0	20.0
Business person	0.0	0.0	0.0	20.0
% of total population in scheme type	5.7	16.2	9.4	8.8

Source: Census data, 2007 (N=376)

12% of the total sample, with 8% of A2 beneficiaries being women, compared to 14% in A1 villagised, 13% in A1 self contained and 15% in the informal schemes.

Competition for plots was pronounced in A2 schemes, and a substantial number of allocations were on the basis of patronage, rather than technical qualification or need. Women lost out in these processes, due to a lack of formal qualifications and particularly a lack of access to male-dominated patronage networks. By contrast, women were able to join the land occupations freely, and were warmly welcomed. While they often took on highly gendered roles in the base camps (including cooking, collecting firewood and water), and were rarely in top leadership positions, independent women (often widows or divorcees) were allocated land alongside men. In many cases women were given committee roles, often as treasurer or secretary, given their perceived trustworthiness and competence. For other women, gendered domestic obligations in the communal area home – notably looking after the home and children – meant that they could not join the land occupations. However, they often took on an important, and well-recognised, supportive role, in providing back-up to the base camps and occupation groups.

Table 2.8 also shows the pattern of replacement when ownership was transferred. What is interesting to note is the larger proportion of women gaining access to land through this process from 2000 to 2008 than gained access in the first instance (except in the informal settlements). Although allocation is still dominated by men, women – especially in the A2 schemes – are inheriting land or getting it reallocated to them. The patterns observed reflect in large part the legal status of women as landholders in Zimbabwe. While formal legal systems have changed, the *de facto* situation is that 'traditional' or 'customary' systems of land allocation, universally overseen by men (as headmen or chiefs), favours the allocation of land to men. In the new resettlements however, as Chapter 9 discusses in detail, patterns of authority are much contested and in flux, and the power of traditional leaders is perhaps not as great as it is in the communal areas. Thus differences in authority structures may go some way to explaining the differences in subsequent land allocations in our study sites.

Table 2.8 Land allocation by gender

	A1 Villagised	A1 Self-contained	Informal	A2	Total
Total plots	177	81	82	52	392
% male owned	86	87	85	94	88
% female owned	14	13	15	8	12
% female replacements following exit	33	22	0	50	26

Source: Census data, 2007 (N=392)

The following cases highlight the diversity of circumstances by which women have gained access to land in the new resettlements.

GUTU CLUSTER
Two widows, Mrs B and Mrs P, survived by selling vegetables and fruits at the bus rank in Gutu Mupandawana Growth Point. When land invasions began they joined others and got land in Lonely farm. One still owns land, but the other surrendered her plot to a relative. Women are not discriminated against, says Mrs B. Since invasion, Mrs T has been the treasurer in Lonely's Committee of Seven. Mrs B is the secretary of the committee and responsible for scheme administration, while Mrs P is an ordinary committee member. In addition, many women hold posts in cooperative gardens and burial clubs. In nearby Clare farm, four widows hold land in their own right. Mrs M, headmistress of a local primary school, joined Clare already widowed. She used her car to transport war veterans to bases and meetings.

MASVINGO CLUSTER
Nine women owned own land in Sanangwe A1 villagised scheme at the beginning, but only five remain after others died. Three Sanangwe women were in the Committee of Seven, but this was disbanded by the sabhuku when he assumed authority. In Wondedzo self-contained scheme, one woman, a school teacher, owns land. Six women got land in Wondedzo A1 villagised scheme; one is secretary and two are committee members. In Bompst A2 scheme, Mrs. M deserted the plot after her husband, a former Masvingo headmaster, died.

CHIREDZI CLUSTER
Four women own land in Uswaushava Village 8. 'I came in 2000,' said O, aged 44 years. 'I am a widow. I had the chance to fend for my children. I cleared the land with the help of my child.' O is the kraal head's policeperson. In Uswaushava Village 7B four women own land. One is the chairperson of the local ZANU-PF Women's League. In Hippo Valley A2 farms, Mrs V, who is employed by Heifer International, owns land in her own right. Mrs M and Mrs M now own land inherited from their late husbands.

MWENEZI CLUSTER
In Edenvale A1 scheme, Mrs KM is in a polygamous marriage with two other wives. She is mother to seven children. The other wives stay elsewhere; one at BJB ranch, where the household was allocated another plot, one at Machindu in the communal areas. The husband stays at BJB ranch and visits the other

wives occasionally. Mrs KM was motivated to seek land by the desire to secure a piece of land for her only son. Mrs K was given a plot which was registered in her own name, but she later decided to give it to her son. In Asveld A2 farm, EM owns plot 8 where she built a good house. She has 121 cattle. Her husband owns a plot in nearby Sheba Ranch.

The gendered dimensions of land reform do not stop at who has been formally allocated land; intra-household gender dynamics are also critical to understanding how men and women have benefited from land reform. These aspects are discussed throughout the rest of the book, but it is worth highlighting a few recurrent dimensions here. Gendered divisions of labour within households are important in understanding overall livelihood strategies. While most of the data for this study has been collected at the household level – defined as a group 'cooking from the same pot'[15] – activities are very often highly gendered. This applies to agricultural production (Chapter 5), where women and men may focus on particular crops or patches of land; investment foci, where for example women and men may acquire different types of livestock species on their own account (Chapter 5); and off-farm income earning, where again activities are highly gendered (Chapter 8). While different resources and income streams are individualised, and there is of course much negotiating and bargaining within households over priorities, claims and access, there is also much cooperation – in farming, in looking after children and in managing a range of other activities. In this sense, a household in rural Zimbabwe is a useful unit of analysis, as many production, reproduction and accumulation processes occur at this scale.

2.9 Conclusion

Masvingo has experienced a fundamental shift in agrarian structure, with major implications for livelihoods and the agricultural economy. While the northern half of the province reflects a pattern seen across much of the country, with the most of land formerly under large-scale commercial farming (mostly as cattle ranches) taken for land reform, the southern lowveld areas have retained large blocs of land under state, private estate or individual control. Here a different agrarian structure has emerged, with its own agrarian relations and politics. The relationships – economic, social and political – between the new resettlements, the old communal areas and the remaining large-scale farming, estate and conservancy areas will fundamentally affect the future pattern of development in the province. There are many potentials, as we will discuss later in the book, for significant linkages and synergies, but there is also much scope for conflict.

[15] See O'Laughlin (1998) and Guyer and Peters (1987), among many others, for extensive discussions of the challenges of defining a 'household' in African contexts. In Zimbabwe, households are more recognisable than in other places, but in some cases – such as with polygamous arrangements in different sites or where orphan-headed households are linked to others – the boundaries are sometimes difficult to define. In this study, we relied people's own definitions, and then traced connections outwards to other locations.

Focusing on the land that has been redistributed – in A1 and A2 schemes, in the informal settlements and the variants within these categories – we observe a new composition of people in these areas. Previously inhabited by a single farm owner and family (sometimes only a farm manager) together with a limited number of workers (see Chapter 6), today they are populated by many new people. The composition of land reform beneficiaries is highly varied. The claim that the land reform was dominated by politically well-connected 'cronies' is simply untrue. Nor are war veterans a dominant group. Although many took leadership roles during the land invasions, the majority came from rural backgrounds where they had been farming in the communal areas. While some civil servants and business people are members of the elite, many are not. Teachers, extension workers and small-scale entrepreneurs have joined the land reform, adding new skills and capacities. And farm workers too have been important beneficiaries; while some were displaced, many joined the invasions, and some were central to their organisation.

The next chapter provides a more a detailed examination of the new people on the new land, and the implications this has for livelihood opportunities and change.

3

New Land,
New People,
New Livelihoods

3.1 Introduction

The new settlers are certainly a very diverse group, as Chapter 2 has explained. What, then, are the key characteristics of these people, and how successful have they been in forging livelihoods on new land? A number of descriptors of the population are examined in this chapter, including demographic structure, educational levels, agricultural training and religion and church affiliation. But things are not static. There is much movement on and off the new settlements and within households as people come and go. This chapter examines this dynamic, exploring how the new land is acting as a magnet attracting new people, each in search of new livelihood options.

The land reform has generated a number of livelihood transitions, as people have moved homes and occupations. Who is doing well, who is doing less well and why? This chapter looks at the results of the 'success ranking' introduced in Chapter 2, and examines some of the key features that have resulted in livelihoods improving or declining following land reform.

3.2 Livelihood success

A wide range of work has attempted to elaborate livelihood patterns and dynamics in Zimbabwe. Most has focused on the communal areas, dating from the classic studies of Weinrich (1975) to the large corpus of post-independence research (Scoones et al., 1996; Cavendish, 2000; Chimhowu, 2002; Campbell et al., 1997a, 2002; Bird and Shepherd, 2003; Scoones and Wolmer, 2002, 2003; Frost et al., 2007). Important work was also carried out on livelihood changes in the post-Independence resettlement areas (Kinsey et al., 1998; Kinsey, 1999). All of this has shown how livelihoods are highly differentiated, and that they change over time, in response to demographic, ecological, economic and other factors.

But what of the new resettlements? Here the work has been more scanty. Research by the African Institute for Agrarian Studies has surveyed a number of sites across six districts and offered an important snapshot of conditions on the ground (Moyo, 2009). Other work has focused on in-depth assessments in Matabeleland (Bulimamangwe) and Mashonaland (Mazowe) (Matondi et al., forthcoming). A range of other case-studies have examined particular dimensions of livelihoods.[1] But none of these has offered a comprehensive insight into livelihood patterns and changes over time.

To get an idea of this new socio-economic diversity a series of ranking exercises were undertaken. The methodology used was a version of 'wealth ranking' (Grandin, 1988; Scoones, 1995), whereby all members of the scheme were ranked according to locally-defined criteria of success. In each case a small group of settlers (usually between two and five) was assembled – local community leaders, base commanders, councillors or members of the Committee of Seven. Attempts were made to include both men and women in each group, and in all cases the informants had to know the whole community. The ranking workshop would start with a discussion of 'success' on the resettlement, aimed at eliciting criteria of livelihood success and generating discussion. Using the list of all households on the scheme (developed for the earlier census work, but updated as necessary), cards with each of the names of the households were produced. These were sorted into groups. Different ranking workshops resulted in different numbers of groups, but most chose three (successful, middling and not successful), with approximately similar numbers of households allocated to each. As each household was ranked, a profile was presented justifying the allocation to different ranks. This allowed for the further development of 'success' criteria, and thus a rationale for each of the success groups. The ranking workshops also provided an opportunity to discuss 'exits' from the scheme, and the reasons for this.

Throughout the book, three 'success groups' (denoted SG) are used as a basis for differentiating households within schemes. While each site offered a unique insight into 'success', there were important commonalities. Success ranks in each site correlated with a range of quantitative indicators, including asset ownership, income earning activities, agricultural production and sales (see Chapter 10). But 'success' is clearly more than just such household level indicators. Relationships between success groups were also an important part of all the discussions, and offered important insights into the emerging patterns of social and economic differentiation. As Chapter 10 explores in detail, by looking at the different livelihood strategies linked to different success groups, the beginnings of a livelihood typology can be developed. In order to gain insights into livelihood change the ranking data was in turn related to the 120 detailed biographies of individuals and households. These allowed for further assessment of how people came to be more or less successful over time, as well as their aspirations and ambitions for the future.

Table 3.1 offers a summary of the main criteria used in each of the rankings. There are of course biases in the criteria used, reflecting the composition of the informants. Some emphasised farming – and crop sales through formal channels – while others emphasised the broader

[1] http://www.lalr.org.za/zimbabwe/zimbabwe-working-papers-1.

off-farm portfolio of activities. Some highlighted assets and material aspects, while others pointed to wider issues, such as ill-health, deaths in the family, connection to social networks, membership of churches or the existence of an alcohol abuse problem. Presence or absence on the plot and the implications for adequate supervision of labour was frequently mentioned.

3.3 Livelihood transitions: patterns of success

The following section offers more qualitative insights from a selection of the 120 biographies. The quotes capture some of the motivations for getting involved in the land invasions, the struggles that have followed and the hopes and fears for the future. The cases are ordered by success group (SG) to give a flavour of the range of livelihood transitions involved.

SUCCESS GROUP 1 — DOING WELL, IMPROVING

FV, Lonely Farm (A1 villagised)
I was born in Gutu in 1950, and am a father of nine children. My previous home was in Serima nearby, and I have kept that home and field. I have a small engine for irrigation which is moved between my two farms. I irrigate maize, wheat, rice, beans, vegetables and fruit trees. At my Serima home I have seven wells and two small dams. At my new farm I have already dug two deep wells, and am planning more. My main reason for transferring to Lonely was to gain access to good grazing for livestock. In Serima it is very crowded, and the livestock suffer in the dry season. My wife trades vegetables from our plot. We also have a good trade in green mealies and other crops. Some of my children are now grown up and send us remittances as both cash and groceries. Two of my sons are teachers and two are builders. With the good grazing our animals are thriving. The cows are producing new calves every year, and we have plentiful milk supplies.

SM, Edenvale (A1 villagised)
I was born in Mahungu, Mateke Hills in 1941. We were evicted from the area in 1963 to make room for white commercial farms. In 1976 the war of liberation started. Some people were herded into 'keeps', others went to Triangle. I remained in the bush and continued tilling land with a gun slung on my back until the ceasefire in 1979. I was in the people's militia doing surveillance and reporting to guerilla bases. After the war I farmed poor land in the communal areas. During the land invasions I was in charge of a number of groups. I have married three wives and, although some of my older children have left, I have plenty of labour on the farm. Since we arrived here, six of my sons have married and got land in the resettlement. My role in the land invasions was recognised with a large area, as well as giving my sons land. With a large family you must think of the future. We have spent a lot of time clearing fields. We grow a range of local sorghum varieties. My wives make and sell ilala palm trays, while some of my sons are border jumpers. One son is a gunner who works with safari hunters based in Chiredzi. He is well paid, has a car and assists us. I keep four orphans left by my late daughter. I had just a few cattle before coming here,

Table 3.1 Success ranking criteria – quotes from the ranking discussions

District	Site	SG1	SG2	SG3
Gutu	A1 Lonely	Have cattle, implements. Good farmers. Sell to Grain Marketing Board (GMB). Good home.	Some assets. Good home. Suffered deaths, illness. Sometimes absent. Get remittances from formal jobs.	Limited assets. Illness, deaths affected households. Informal off-farm activities (e.g. border jumping). Often absent from plot.
	A1 Clare	Sell maize to GMB regularly. Real farmers. Good supervision and management of workers. Good home, many houses. Work very hard. Other activities – irrigation, horticulture, chicken business	Professionals, some with jobs. Remittances important. Have assets for farming, but often absent. Problems of management.	Old age, ill health. Trying, but few assets. Lack of labour. Absentees show lack of commitment.
	A2 Northdale	Have assets and capital. Investing in farm. Have connections. Crop farming, with irrigation. Many workers who are paid.	Absent. Some are farming, but limited success. Low levels of investment. Some cattle.	No crops. Cattle kept by workers.
Masvingo	A1 Sanangwe	Good farmers. Sales to GMB. Full granary. Draught animals plentiful. Remittances from children. Good houses.	Problems with draught power. Lack of cattle. Stay at plot, but struggling.	Family problems (deaths). Absentees, with workers or other relatives holding the plot. Land conflicts common.
	A1 Wondedzo Wares	Good home, plenty of cattle. Good yields.	Building up assets, but lack of draught power and labour. Some in formal jobs, but limited incomes.	No draught power. Absent. Relatives and workers at the plot. Health problems and labour shortages.
	A1 Wondedzo Extension	Adequate equipment, including carts, etc. Sell maize to GMB regularly. Granary full. Multiple cash generating crops – maize, soy bean, sugar beans, groundnuts.	Built decent homes. Adequate resources, but not committed. Off farm work and remittances significant. Absenteeism means lack of supervision/control of workers.	No resources for farming. Male head absent. Lack of planning, skills and knowledge of farming.
	A2 Bompst	Substantial investments in irrigated farming. Off-farm businesses support farm operations. Well connected. Good homes. Many workers.	Fenced plot, dryland farming. Workers well managed. Good homes. Car and other assets plentiful.	Limited capital assets and investment resources. Reliant on other businesses. Farming suffering.

District	Site	SG1	SG2	SG3
Chiredzi	Informal Uswaushava 7B	Hard workers, hire labour. Sufficient farm implements and livestock. Enough draught. Good houses. Mostly present at plot.	Insufficient labour; lack of resources for hiring. Average home. Draught power shortages.	Poor farmers. Rely on piece jobs and border jumping. Young people, often absent, or older widows and widowers.
	Informal Uswaushava 8	Sell to GMB and cotton companies. Present at farms. Older. Have cattle, carts, barrows etc.	Trying, but few implements and other resources. Few cattle, so draught power shortages. Mostly younger. No GMB sales.	Struggling. Limited agriculture, few livestock. Assisted by others for draught, food. Widows, makorokoza or employed on sugar estates.
	A2 Fair Range 1	Plentiful assets. Well connected. Beneficiary of mechanisation scheme. Pays workers well. Irrigation.	Have assets, but illness a problem.	Deaths, leaving only workers with cattle.
	A2 Fair Range 2	Equipment and transport present. Irrigated farming. Mostly resident on the plot. Good relations with workers. Older.	Equipment is there, but mostly farmer's family is absent. Supervision problems with labour.	Some cattle. Mostly not resident. Limited production.
	A2 Hippo Valley	Nearly all have full set of equipment (tractor, periloader etc.). Tonnage high. Stays at farm. Good labour supervision and business management.	Problems with equipment, access to water for irrigation. Work hard. Those who are absent rely on workers and hired managers.	No equipment. Low tonnage.

District	Site	SG1	SG2	SG3
Mwenezi	A1 Edenvale 11	Have cattle, scotch carts and other farm equipment. Get good yields, even in drought. Large (polygamous) families with plentiful labour. Good links with old homes in communal lands. Remittances from children in South Africa important.	Straddling. Keeping home in communal lands. Investments in new resettlements only tentative. Poor crops, limited assets.	Neglected plots. Often absent.
	A1 Edenvale 3	Livestock, scotch carts and other assets. Full granaries. Remittances from children in South Africa important. Older.	Hard working with some cattle. But often reliant on SG1 parents for draught, etc.	Off farm work, less focus on farming. Limited assets. Illness and labour problems.
	Informal Turf	Assets are there. Remittances from South Africa important. Large households with labour. Successful crop production.	Farming improving. Investing in plot and accumulating assets. Often male absent working away. Remittances being sent home.	No or few cattle. Reliant on remittances. Deaths and illness have had major impacts.
	A2 Asveld	Many cattle. Jobs elsewhere. Good connections. Workers paid and reliable. Regular visits to the plot. Good business management.	Few cattle, but making an effort. Fewer workers.	Absent. Struggling. Not paying workers.

Source: Discussions at success rankings

but now I have 18. We are happier here at the resettlement. There is more land, plots are larger and there is no overcrowding. Last season I got very good yields, and filled two granaries with sorghum. Following resettlement, there is now a future for my family, and my sons will have land.

MR – Uswaushava (Informal)
I was born in 1955 in Razi area of Chivi South. I have two wives and eight children. I worked for a long time in various jobs. My first, from 1973, was at Hippo Valley estate doing general work. Then I worked in at Triangle as a tractor driver. I joined the liberation war in 1978, and after Independence I returned to work at Mkwasine estate to work in the garage. Later, I transferred to Ngundu where I managed a carpentry shop. Despite being employed all this time, my life didn't improve much. We had some land in Chivi, but it was small and not productive. For this reason I joined the land invasions and got six hectares which is now cleared. I have been growing cotton and maize, and getting good harvests. My cattle herd has expanded significantly due to the good grazing. There are problems though. There are no clinics or shops in the area, and rainfall is always erratic. But on my new land I can improve my life much better than when I was employed.

EG, Wondedzo Extension (A1 self-contained)
We came to this place in 2000, coming from Buhera communal area. We came looking for land, as our original home area was very crowded. Since coming we have had much better crop production than we had before. We have learned a lot, and developed skills in producing soya beans and sugar beans that earn good cash. I must get water from my neighbours, as we do not have a well. When we get maize we buy cattle. One tonne of maize allows us to buy a cow. My husband is retired and we work the farm together. He used to be a police officer and later worked at a store in town. We have five children: four boys and a girl. I also look after two orphans, the children of my brother who passed away. Before, we had no cattle and little farm equipment. We now have cattle, and are able to sell up to eight litres of milk per day in Masvingo. In the future, we have plans to dig a well, so that water supplies are close by and we can irrigate a garden.

AW, Clare Farm (A1 self-contained)
I was born in Gutu in 1946. I came here in 2000, and now my cattle numbers have increased to 21. It is very good grazing here, compared to where we came from. The main reasons for leaving Gutu was to find bigger lands for farming, as well as grazing for livestock. For a long time the whites had used our forefathers' land while we lived in cramped Gutu. Now we can make use of this land ourselves. We maintain links with our old home, and especially in drought times we supply food to our relatives. I have seven children, ranging from the age of 30 to 11. My eldest son is a panel beater in Gutu, while my daughters are a nurse and and a butchery assistant, both working locally. Their salaries are low these days, and we all must rely on the farm. I have cleared a large area on my 30-hectare plot, and have been farming around nine hectares each year. In 2005, I got nearly 200 bags of maize, sold both locally and to the GMB. Sales of crops have allowed me to buy a scotch cart (in 2006), a cultivator (in 2004) and a wheelbarrow (in 2003). As well as the family's help on the farm, I hire labour, but usually only on a temporary basis. My wife brews beer from our

finger millet crop. This brings some extra cash to the home. We enjoy farming at our new plot.

SR – Wondedzo Extension (A1 self-contained)
Before, I was a shoemaker and builder, based in Zvishavane and later Masvingo. Until now I never carried out farming, and concentrated only on my trade. This provided a good income and I established a home in Mpandawanda Growth Point in Gutu. I was one of six boys and got a very small portion of land in the communal areas. I applied for peri-urban plots, but never succeeded. My business kept me going. I have three girls and four boys, two of whom are still at school. I moved to full-time farming in 2004. Before that I lived in Masvingo carrying out my business, and my wife ran the farm. But farming is hard work and needs everyone there. We now are really working to develop the farm and have cleared ten hectares in the 28-hectare plot. I have dug a small dam for watering animals, invested in a well and things are really coming up. Now I have eleven cattle, when before I had none. I have also new farm equipment such as ploughs, scotch cart and so on. We have had good yields, and I have managed to sell, as well as sending food to my parents in Gutu communal area. I am now doing farming as a business – not just subsistence. After the farming season is over, I usually go to South Africa and Botswana and do small jobs such as building and fencing homesteads. I am now vice-chair of the Wondedzo scheme development committee, and in charge of organising people, and trying to get assistance. I have great hope for farming. I now have something my children can inherit.

FM, Hippo Valley (A2 sugar outgrower)
I was born in 1956 in Gutu district and grew up on my parent's small-scale farm in Gutu South. Both my parents had Master Farmer certificates. They were also teachers by profession. I am a diploma holder in agriculture and was employed by the Ministry of Agriculture in research and extension for 40 years from 1976. I married in 1986. My wife grew up at her father's small-scale farm in Masvingo district. She trained in secretarial work. We have three children: two daughters and a son. The eldest is studying for a degree, while the others are still at school. My wife and I have a passion for agriculture. For years we have been doing market gardening from our backyard at our house in Ngundu, Chivi. Profits have been good and have kept our family going, especially when government salaries were so poor. When land reform came I applied for a sugar plot. I am excited about irrigated agriculture and have been using my horticultural knowledge on my plot, converting some of the cane area to vegetable production.

SUCCESS GROUP 2 – GETTING ON, BUT WITH POTENTIAL
JM, Lonely Farm (A1 villagised)
I was born in Gutu in 1979. I am married and have one child. In Gutu I had very little land to farm. It was not a good life for a young family. We had to rely on others. In 2000, I decided to join the invasion groups. Before I had no cattle, but now I own five head, all purchased through farming. I have also managed to buy a plough. Now I help my family back in Gutu during drought years with food, and I send cash for my young brothers to pay for school fees. All of this is from our hard work. I have cleared four hectares of land and I employ two workers on the farm, who stay with us. My wife has a vegetable garden and

sells tomatoes and onions locally. She also has a small business selling second-hand clothes. The new land has transformed our lives.

OB, Sanangwe (A1 villagised)
I was born in 1965 in Gutu district. I worked for four years as a temporary teacher in Gokwe, then came to Masvingo to study electrical engineering at the polytechnic. I also had a job in town to pay for my studies. When fast track came I really wanted to get a portion of land. I eventually did in 2002, and I have four hectares. Currently there is one person at the plot, a worker. He manages the farm, but I visit every week. My wife is a teacher, and we stay in town where I work too. Our two sons, aged 15 and 9, are at school, and our youngest daughter is only two. My focus is on production, but the problems are late delivery of inputs and lack of tractors to hire. I do not have the farm assets – for example I have no cattle – but I want to invest in the land. So far, we have just started, but we are getting 40 or 50 bags of maize each year, and selling regularly to the GMB. My plans are ambitious, but without support from the government it is going to be difficult to improve. All the inputs are distributed to the people who are living at their plots, but what about those of us in town?

MM – Turf Ranch (Informal)
I was born in 1956 in Makhanani communal land. I worked for ten years as a herd boy and got a beast in payment. This became the foundation of my life. Its offspring paid lobola (bridewealth), and I was able to marry. In my old home there were very poor soils, and the place was so overcrowded. Here the soil is first class, and there is underground water. I have dug a well at my homestead, and my dream is to start irrigating. We keep in good touch with those from our previous home. When there are ceremonies, we brew beer together. I have a few cattle myself but I also look after others' animals as part of a sharing agreement. In addition to agriculture, we have a number of other activities. For example, I sometimes do some small-scale hunting in the area. I also sometimes do part-time piecework jobs on the nearby plots: maintaining fences for example. The pay is poor, but at least it is something. My wife makes mats and baskets and also does gardening and sells the vegetables. However, her main business is selling milk. Mrs M explains: 'I make a deal with farm workers on nearby farms, and purchase the milk which they are selling – usually without the knowledge of the plot owner. I can make a real profit in a single day.

RC Wondedzo Extension (A1 self-contained)
We came from Masvingo town. We did not have land before 2000. We had tried to get land in Bikita, but failed. Now our family is growing: we have five children, and we need to feed them. My husband left his job in 1998. He had been an administrator working for the army since Independence. We managed to build a decent house in Masvingo, and owned a car. Two daughters are working in South Africa and one son is a teacher. I am a dressmaker and can make money from sewing. Since settlement we have acquired a range of farm equipment, including a scotch cart, ploughs, a harrow and a cultivator. We have seven cattle and three goats. We want to build a large house at the farm, and purchase a tractor from our farm produce.

DN – Fair Range (A2)
I am now 60 years old, and I come from the Gonakudzingwa small-scale farming

area where my father had a plot. I have a general dealer business at Chany-enga Business Centre near Chikombedzi. I am a member of the Agrodealers Association of Zimbabwe, and a member of the Dairy Association in the new resettlement areas. I settled here in 2003 with an offer letter. I am married and have two sons and one daughter. It was my interest in livestock production that encouraged me to apply for a farm under the fast track programme. My plot is 66 hectares in size, but I have only cleared ten so far. I am irrigating a portion, but otherwise I keep my livestock. I now have 12 cattle and 35 goats. These are sold sometimes in Chiredzi. I live at the farm with my wife and one son and daughter who are still schooling. We hire workers on a temporary basis. I have been unwell recently, so it is mostly my wife who does the work. Farming like this is my dream, and if I get the resources I plan to develop the farm.

SUCCESS GROUP 3 – ASSET POOR, OFTEN STRUGGLING

CM, Lonely Farm (A1 villagised)
I was born in 1974 in Gutu communal land. I was allocated one hectare by my father when I got married. We now have three children, all boys with the oldest being nine. I used to own two cattle, but they died in 2000. I mostly relied on my father. In 2000, I joined my father in the land invasions and came to Lonely farm. My brothers took over the farm in Gutu. The linkages with our old home area are strong, as people come and work in the cropping season on our new farms. They are paid with food. Since my father has cattle and equipment, he helps me out. But I must work on his farm in return as he is old. We work closely together. I have managed good yields, getting 30 or 40 bags, even in the drought years. My biggest problem is lack of draught power and labour. We are very happy about our new lands. The soils are good, and if we work hard we will build good houses and increase our livestock herds.

AG – Edenvale (A1 villagised)
I was born in 1966, the daughter of headman Gezani. I was married to a busi-nessman in Chikombedzi, but he passed away. I suffered a lot bringing up my children following the death of my husband. Most of the cattle were distributed to his other wives, and I had very little. However, the few animals I got paved the way for a new life. The land reform programme was a great boost, and I soon joined the land invasions. My old home is still nearby, and I keep good connections. But I have worked hard on my new land and cleared six hectares. Rain is the biggest problem in this area, but I have good soils and have been getting good crops. These can pay for school fees for my two daughters. I now have my own place. I am free from others and can do my own farming.

SK – Edenvale (A1 villagised)
I was born in 1984, and my father was an immigrant who came from Malawi, and was a farm worker. My father had many sons by different wives, but there was no land for me. Instead I tried to find work. I first worked at Plot D16 look-ing after cattle. Then I got a job at Whitehead's farm, but the work was tough and the pay poor. When I heard of the land invasions, I quickly joined. My wife has had two children. Life is not easy on the resettlements. In our previous place we used to get help from the World Food Programme. They don't come here. There was also an irrigation scheme there, which helped a lot. In the resettlement areas I only get anything if it rains. But the move to resettlement

has been good overall. We now have land, and I have managed to get a buy a few goats from the crops sold so far.

EM – Wondedzo Extension (A1 self-contained)
I have married two wives, each now with one young child. I am also staying with three brothers and a sister. There was no land for me at my home area, so resettlement was a good option. When we came to this place we had nothing. We now have one donkey and one goat, and I have bought a bicycle too. We now produce good crops, and we can send food to our relatives at our original home. I also do some clay pot making which gives a bit of extra money. Now we eat well and have better clothes. In the future I want to become a Master Farmer, and help my young brothers and sister go to school.

PP, Northdale (A2)
I live in town where I work for the Vehicle Inspection Department. I have three houses in Masvingo, but I was keen to have a farm. I do not have any connections to the rural areas, as I have always been in town. So in 2000 I applied for land and got my plot at Northdale. It is 278 hectares in size, but is not yet developed. I have not had the resources. I have five cattle on the plot and have cleared six hectares. We have employed some temporary labour to farm, but the yields have been poor. Last year I did not plant anything, as I could not get hold of inputs and there are so many animals that come and destroy the crops. My eldest daughter stays at the plot and manages the farm. She grows a few vegetables and does some trading in the area. I stay with my wife and younger children who go to school in Masvingo. Hopefully in the future the farm will take off.

What can we learn from these cases? People have moved to new land for a variety of reasons, and from many places. While most transferred from communal areas, others had poorly-paid jobs in town and were interested in improving their livelihoods through farming. Some have invested full-time in farming, others are continuing with off-farm livelihoods or with multiple rural homes. For some, new land is an investment for future generations, while for others it is an important source of accumulation today. Some see the immediate benefits in terms of food or income; for others the major gain is an escape from oppressive relationships elsewhere.

3.4 Household characteristics

The following sections illustrate this diversity further, looking at a range of characteristics defining the new settlers, ranging from demographic patterns to educational and training qualifications to church affiliations.

Demographic patterns
The age distribution of household heads – defined as the adult household member who is accepted as in charge, even if not resident – is presented in Table 3.2. For A1 self-contained schemes, the dominant groups are

Table 3.2 Age of household head by scheme type (%)

	A1 villagised	A1 self-contained	Informal	A2
Years 21 to 30	15.0	4.0	30.2	0.0
Years 31 to 40	24.5	45.9	24.5	16.7
Years 41 to 50	37.7	39.3	18.9	48.1
Years 51 to 60	16.8	5.4	11.3	18.5
Years 61 or more	6.0	5.4	15.1	16.7

Source: Survey, 2007-08 (N=177)

Table 3.3: Educational achievement of household head by scheme type (%)

	A1 villagised	A1 self-contained	Informal	A2
None	9.4	0.0	17.0	5.2
Grade 7	45.8	28.4	43.4	3.4
Form 2	38.0	62.2	37.7	25.9
Form 3 or higher	6.8	9.4	1.9	65.5

Source: Census data, 2007 (N=400)

those in the 31-40 and 41-50 cohorts, which make up 46% and 39% of the sample. A similar pattern obtains in the A1 villagised schemes, with 24% in the 31-40 cohort and 38% in the 41-50 cohort. Patterns are different in the informal schemes with 21-30 being the largest cohort (24%). Younger people, it seems, ended up in the informal schemes; perhaps because of their willingness to take risks, and possibly as they did not have the connections to allow access to other scheme types. For all the A2 schemes, the dominant group is older – 41-50 – and constitutes 48% of the sample. As with other A2 farmers, A1 cane farmers in Hippo Valley are concentrated in the higher age groups, with almost half of them aged 51 years and above.

Overall, the profile is one of a young population, with household heads being considerably younger than those in old resettlement and communal areas. In Kinsey's 1997 sample survey (1999: 185), the average age of the household head in the resettlement areas was 56, and that in the communal area sample was 53.

Educational levels
Table 3.3 summarises the educational characteristics of the household heads. The proportion of those with no education is highest in informal schemes at 17%, compared to 5.2% in the A2 and 9.4% in A1 villagised schemes. The bulk of the settlers in A1 villagised and A1 self-contained reached Form 2 (secondary school). In the informal schemes, the biggest group is that with Grade 7 (end of primary schooling), at 43.4%.

Table 3.4 Agricultural training of household head by scheme type (%)

	A1 villagised	A1 self-contained	Informal	A2
Master Farmer	11.2	17.6	7.5	46.5
Agricultural professional	0.0	1.3	0.0	5.2
No training	88.8	81.1	92.5	48.3

Source: Census data, 2007 (N=400)

A2 schemes have settlers with higher educational levels than all the other schemes, with 65.5% of the settlers having attained Form 3 or more. Generally, there is high literacy among the new settlers, with educational achievements better on average than those in the communal areas and in the pre-2000 resettlement areas. For example, Kinsey (1999:185) recorded on average only about five years of education in both resettlement and communal area household heads, while Campbell et al. (2002: 27) noted that less than 20% of sample households had gone beyond primary education in nearby Chivi communal area. As we discuss in subsequent chapters, the relatively high levels of educational achievement of the new settlers is potentially important in influencing their livelihood strategies, and the form of support they are offered.

Agricultural training
The most common type of agricultural training is the Master Farmer Certificate (Table 3.4). The A2 schemes have more certificate holders than other schemes, at 46.5%. 5.2% of A2 settlers have formal further training in agriculture, and among the cane plot holders, 31% of the settlers fall in this category.

Although the majority of new settlers do not have formal training in agriculture, there is a significant minority who do. This is an important base to build on, and many such individuals have been actively involved in supporting others as they establish their new farms. In a number of our sites, the agricultural extension department, Agritex, has started new Master Farmer training courses, and the response has reportedly been substantial.

Religion and church affiliation
Religion and church affiliation have emerged as a vital component in the construction of social relations and networks on the new resettlements (Chapter 9). These play an important role in shaping the outcomes of resettlement in terms of agricultural production, access to inputs and productive assets. Church affiliation has been an important source of labour, as settlers have contributed pooled labour based on it. As Table 3.5 shows, the dominant church affiliations of household heads were Anglicans, Catholics, Zionists and a variety of evangelical and pentecostal churches. While not always the case, most households follow a similar church. Especially among the smaller new churches, these

Table 3.5 Church affiliation of household head by scheme type (%)

	A1 villagised	A1 self-contained	Informal	A2
Anglican	35.1	17.6	11.8	7.3
Catholic	29.2	50.0	0.0	25.4
Reformed Church in Zimbabwe	2.4	8.1	0.0	0.0
Zionist	19	18.9	54.9	10.9
Apostolic Faith Ministries	5.4	0.0	0.0	7.3
Other evangelical and pentecostal churches	8.9	5.4	33.3	49.1

Source: Survey, 2007-08 (N=177)

connections have been important for contributions of labour, draught power and other resources. This has been especially significant when people are ill or infirm (Chapter 9).

Comparing the profile of people in the Masvingo study sites with nearby communal areas or old resettlements overall, we find a younger (on A1 sites), more educated (with the exception of informal schemes) and better trained (especially in A2 sites) group of people. Religious affiliation is more diverse, often reflecting the wide range of places of origin. In different ways, these factors all have important implications for livelihoods on the new resettlements, as subsequent chapters will discuss.

3.4 Movement into and out of the resettlement schemes

The data presented above represented a snapshot (largely based on surveys in 2007 and 2008), but it is important to recognise that the population on the new resettlements has not been fixed. Since 2000 we have observed a substantial turnover of people within households, as well as exits and entries of new households. Births and deaths have combined with migration to produce a continuous reshuffling of people and households.

New household members: the magnet effect
Bill Kinsey and colleagues' work on the old resettlement areas has demonstrated that they act as 'magnets', attracting people who seek to cash in on the benefits (Gunning et al., 2000; Deininger et al., 2004), with an average household size of around ten being recorded in the resettlements compared to 6.5 in the communal areas (Hoogeveen and Kinsey, 2001: 133).[2] Resettlements act as social safety nets, distributing benefits to larger groups of people.

---

[2]   Studies in Chivi communal area record household size ranging from an average of 6.5 (Campbell et al., 2002: 26) to 7.2 (Scoones et al., 1996: 16), although with ranges between one and 36.

Table 3.6 Household sizes and composition at settlement

	A1 villagised	A1 self-contained	A2	Informal
Males in original household	2.20	2.10	2.53	2.85
Females in original household	2.04	1.27	1.29	2.55
Total original household size	4.24	3.37	3.82	5.40

Source: Survey data, 2007-08 (N=177)

Our surveys show that there was a significant movement of people into and out of the resettlement schemes, although not, as yet, as dramatic as seen in the 1980s and 1990s in the old resettlements. At settlement, the 177 households in the household sub-sample across the study sites had 748 people; the average household size (of resident members on the new plot) was 4.2 people per household, with a range from one to 18. Table 3.6. shows relatively low household sizes, reflecting the early stage of settlement (prior to subsequent influx) and the young demographic profile of the population.

Across the schemes an average of 2.8 new people were added to each household over the period from 2000-01 to 2007-08. In the A1 villagised schemes there are three main reasons for this. The largest addition is that of children born since resettlement (24%), followed by marriages by sons (21%) and children accompanying new-entry parents (19%). For the A1 self-contained schemes, the factors are the same, but their relative contribution is different. Children accompanying new-entry parents is the most dominant (31%), compared to sons marrying-in (18%) and children born in the family (17%). Other reasons included the return of retired or retrenched household members, the return of household members on divorce, the taking on of children born out of wedlock, new workers becoming resident at the plot, relatives settling at the plot and children coming to attend school. The pattern is different for the informal schemes. Here more than half of the new entries are children born into the family, reflecting the younger demographic composition of the households. The second most important influx is children joining their new-entry parents (15%), followed by relatives settling on the plot (12%) and women marrying into the household (10%).

For the A2 schemes, the dominant factors are different again. More people have moved onto A2 schemes to work, and these constitute 46% of the new entries. The movement of children accompanying new-entry parents accounts for 26%, and children born in the family 13%. A good number of the new entries are relatives who came to settle on the newly-acquired plots. For the A2 and self-contained schemes, 4% of the new entries fell in this category, compared to 12% for informal and A1 villagised schemes. Some of the relatives originally came on a social visit, such as extending condolences following death in a family, while others had come to take care of an ill person. In the end, the social visits were transformed into permanent moves.

Another common factor explaining new entries relates to children born out of wedlock who came to join the families. The percentage was 4% in the informal, A1 villagised and A1 self-contained settlements, and 2% in the A2 schemes. Resettlement was seen as providing more livelihood opportunities, encouraging children born outside marriage to join their fathers on the new plots. Such children could as well have been born during the *jambanja* period when husbands, as the first group of household members to occupy and settle on the farms, were temporarily separated from their wives. The wives only followed later, with children coming to attend school at later stages, once facilities were established.

Exits: leaving the plot
Outward movement from resettlement schemes occurred in two main forms. The first was the withdrawal of entire households. This was studied through scheme-based exit surveys where numbers and reasons for exits were ascertained. The second was the movement of individual members. Whereas new entries were often associated with children, outward movement was more connected to the movement of adults. On average 1.2 people left the remaining sample households in the period from 2000-01 to 2007-08, a pattern which did not vary significantly across site and scheme type. The dominant exits were women who left for their husband's homes on marriage, followed by those (mostly men) taking up employment or seeking jobs. Other reasons included death, schooling and movement away to stay with relatives.

Over the period from settlement to 2007-08, 20% of households who originally established homes had left. The main reasons for the dissolving of a household was death (46% of 78 such exits), finding farming difficult (18%), tenure insecurity (lack of an offer letter) (15%) and domestic problems (8%). Other reasons included expulsion, movement to another plot on another scheme and community disputes. Below we look at the reasons for all full household exits since 2000 from two very different schemes: an A1 self-contained scheme in Gutu cluster and an A2 scheme in Mwenezi cluster.

The ward councillor from Clare A1 self-contained scheme provided the reasons for the six exits from the total of 41 plots on the farm:

> AM went to South Africa. He never did anything here. Once he cut a small piece of land, but no real farming. There were no real structures, just a temporary shelter. A worker operated from his home in the communal land nearby. He doesn't come here any more, and the plot was reallocated.

> M is now late, but the plot was taken over by his son, Machokoto.

> MM tried to establish a farm, but she did not manage anything. She had no resources. She gave up and returned to the communal areas. There is a new person there now, allocated by the District Lands Committee.

> TM got land because his father was the base commander. However, he is just a boy. He went to Chiadzwa [to look for diamonds – see Chapter 8], but was chased by the army helicopters. He returned and stays at the plot, but lives with his mother.

OZ is now late. He was ill for a long time, and passed away last year. His wife left for their old home.

CM is in Harare working. His wife came with a step-son who is now holding the plot. Since he is Mai M's son, the plot cannot be taken, as she was so important in the land invasions.

MM is absent in Harare. A brother is a caretaker there, but not much is happening.

As Mr S explained, there are very different reasons for leaving: death, jobs elsewhere, or having too few resources to make a go of the new plot. Reallocations occur through lineage inheritance and through both the local scheme committee and the District Lands Committee. In some cases land which is not being used is not reallocated and remains empty. A range of reasons are offered for this, including political connections and commitments to the scheme from the land invasion period.

There were very different dynamics in the Asveld A2 scheme and a much more substantial turnover across the 14 plots. Local informants explained the changes on the six plots where exits had occurred:

BGM left the plot when he failed to secure loans to buy heifers under the Cold Storage Company scheme. 'A2 plots are for people with money', he explained. He moved to an A1 villagised plot where he also had land.

MM left when a subsequent invasion took place. He was competing for the same land and water with another war veteran. He was however later usurped by another claimant who arrived with an offer letter. 'If you have connections in the ministry, you get a letter. They are ignoring the war veterans', he complained. He decided to return to his communal home.

FM had an offer letter, but abandoned the place when he failed to find water. He hired well diggers but they failed in three different locations. He later invaded Chikwara ranch, and moved his cattle and goats there.

LC moved from Edenvale A1 resettlement to Asveld in the hope of getting larger lands. But the distances were too great. He has now returned to Edenvale where he stays with a junior wife, while the senior wives stay at the original home in Pfumari in the communal areas.

JM has returned to the communal areas, and has an irrigated plot where he grows wheat and maize.

In this case, tenure insecurity, administrative confusion over offer letters, lack of transport and shortage of water all combined to encourage exits. And, in the more fluid context of Mwenezi district, many had other options, with smaller, more manageable A1 farms in addition.

Thus a variety of reasons explain the turnover of households in the resettlements. In most cases death resulted in transfers to others – either through inheritance or through new allocations. However, many other reasons for turnover exist: some only planned to stay temporarily (for hunting, for example); others suffered setbacks and a lack of assets to get new livelihoods moving; others got into conflicts in their new communities and others simply longed for the stability, familiarity, social connections, friendships and the peace of their communal area homes. We discuss in more depth patterns of inheritance and transfer of land in Chapter 9, but as people left there were always others ready to take their place, and often much competition for plots.

3.5 Conclusion

The new lands have attracted new people and created new livelihoods, but they are in flux and static snapshots are insufficient to explain livelihood trajectories. Patterns of 'success' are highly varied across households and schemes, with some people and households improving their livelihoods over time, while others' fortunes decline. Despite this diversity of experience, for those who have remained there is a near universal recognition that gaining access to land has improved people's lot. The new land is recognised as a valuable resource: 'Land is what we fought for. Our relatives died for this land... Now we must make use of it', argued one settler. In the eyes of those who have moved onto the new land, and contrary to the views often propagated, the land reform has been far from an unmitigated disaster.

There is much movement on and off the schemes, and not everyone has continued on the land, but the net movement inwards reflects the 'magnet effect'. As a consequence, while more people benefit from the new resettlements and the 'decongestion' aims of the resettlement policy are progressively achieved, the livelihood benefits have to be shared with more people, making individual gains more limited.

Overall, the new resettlements are populated by younger, more educated people with a greater diversity of backgrounds, professional skills and connections than their neighbours in the communal areas and old resettlements. This suggests important questions about the agrarian future, and its implications for class dynamics, forms of accumulation and wider economic development opportunities.

As we have noted, the new resettlements are not just made up of A2 plots modelled on large commercial farms, and nor are the A1 schemes simply replicas of the communal areas. A very different dynamic has emerged with fundamental implications for the future. In the following chapters we explore the patterns of investment made by the new settlers, and their achievements in crop and livestock production and off-farm earnings, before concluding with an assessment of the implications of Zimbabwe's land reform.

4

Investing
in the Land

4.1 Introduction

One of the recurrent myths about Zimbabwe's land reform is that investment has been insignificant in the new resettlements: the land lies idle,
people are not committed to farming and infrastructure is destroyed,
neglected or non-existent. Perceptions of a lack of order and poor tenure
security have further contributed to the view that investment has been
negligible. This is far from the case. Certainly, unstable macroeconomic
factors until 2009 undermined opportunities for capital investment,
but impressive investments have been made in clearing the land, in
livestock, in equipment, in transport and in housing. Issues of tenure
insecurity, contrary to the conventional wisdom, do not seem to have
undermined investment, except in some particular cases. Questions of
environmental sustainability do remain a concern, however, although
considerable tree planting, soil conservation and water resource development have taken place. Overall, we argue, the scale of investment
carried out by people themselves, and without significant support from
government or aid agencies, is substantial, and provides firm foundations for the future.

While it is easy to dismiss the myth of minimal investment, a set of
bigger, and rather more interesting, questions arise, however. Who is
investing, and in what? Where are investment resources coming from?
This chapter looks at some of these questions, offering data on assets
and investment and an analysis of differentiated patterns across households, scheme types and sites. Of particular interest is the longer-term
dynamics of investment and accumulation by new settlers, and the
implications this has for livelihoods and agrarian change in the future,
a theme we return to in Chapter 10.

4.2 Assets and investments

In order to understand investment in relation to patterns of social and
economic differentiation, the data in this section is analysed in relation

77

to the three 'success groups' (SG) identified in Chapter 3, allowing us to explore whether there are distinct patterns across households, and how this affects wider socio-economic changes within and across schemes.

Land clearance
Newly settled farmers had to navigate a host of challenges to get established in their new surroundings. In most sites, the farms had previously been used for extensive cattle ranching. For those wishing to embark on arable agriculture this entailed substantial investment in clearing the land to establish fields. Other new farmers did not have the draught power for tillage purposes as they were new to farming or the new farms were too far from original homes to move key assets.

Table 4.1 Amount of land cleared by 2008

Scheme type	Area cleared (ha)
A1 villagised	6.8
A1 self-contained	13.3
A2	23.7
Informal	6.8

Source: Survey data, 2007-08

Table 4.1 shows the pattern of clearing and subsequent use for cropping. Clearing started in most sites in 2001-2 and continued over the subsequent years. Households in scheme types with larger land areas – notably A2 and A1 self-contained – have cleared larger areas, and are generally cultivating more of the land. There were exceptions, however. In Chiredzi cluster, for example, many A2 case-study households were on sugar plots and did not have to invest in land clearing, as they inherited fully cleared plots, and in the A2 scheme at Asveld ranch in Mwenezi very limited land was cleared as ranching remained the preferred land use. Average land areas being cultivated by 2007-08 ranged from 2.6 ha (in Lonely Farm A1 scheme in Gutu) to 52 ha in the Bompst A2 scheme in Masvingo cluster.

Overall, a substantial amount of land has been cleared across the study area in a short space of time. By 2008, for those who had cleared some land, an average of 11ha per plot had been cleared, most being cultivated (see Table 5.4). This is significantly more than occurred in the old resettlements where by 1997 an average of 3.7ha was being planted (Hoogeven and Kinsey, 2001: 131), as well as in nearby Chivi communal area where average field areas of 2.4ha (Campbell et al., 2002:24) and 5.5ha (Scoones et al., 1996:16) have been recorded. Most clearing has been done by hand, with only a few A2 farmers using mechanical means. Taking an average cost of hiring labour to clear land – including clearing bush and destumping – of US$50 per hectare,[1] this represents an average investment in land clearance of US$385 per household (including those who cleared none).

---

[1] Average price in 2009, although it varies in relation to tree densities.

Figure 4.1 House qualities by scheme type

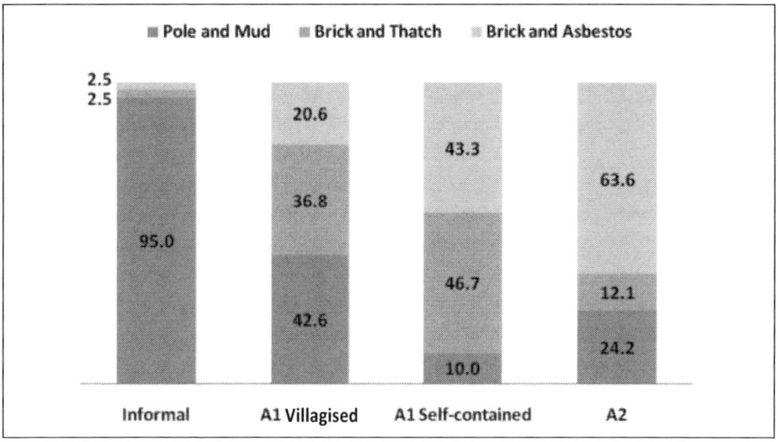

Source: Census data, 2007 (N=400)

Housing infrastructure

Given that many of the farms across the province were cattle ranches prior to land reform there was little housing infrastructure to inherit, and people largely had to start from scratch. Figure 4.1 shows the distribution of housing quality of the main house by scheme type. The informal settlement schemes have 95% of main houses constructed of pole and mud. Settlers explained that this was in part due to lack of offer letters. By contrast, other schemes, with most households having such letters, have much more improved housing and roofing, with A1 self-contained and A2 sites having the highest proportion. A1 villagised sites continue to have a large proportion of pole and mud housing (42.6%), although much of this is in the Chiredzi cluster where Shangaan traditional housing predominates. 24% of A2 main homes were pole and mud, indicating a low level of investment in around a quarter of A2 plots, where only workers, if anyone, is resident.

The pattern of investment in housing infrastructure also correlates with success group. Thus in the A1 self-contained schemes, 73% of SG1 households have brick with asbestos/iron roofing as their main house. This declines to 35% in A1 villagised sites, although this is higher than for SG2 (17%) and SG3 (5%) households in these schemes. By contrast, pole and mud houses exist across all success groups in both A1 scheme types. They only represent 9-11% of main houses in A1 self-contained sites, while in A1 villagised sites they account for 69% of SG3 households, 39% of SG2 households and 27% of SG3 households.

In sum, over the seven years from settlement to the 2007 census a considerable investment in housing infrastructure occurred. By comparison, in a long-settled neighbouring communal area only 35% of households had metal or absbestos roofing in 1999-2000 (Campbell et al., 2002: 24). While some housing is basic and made from local products, much has required the purchase of roofing and other materials. All households had some structures on their plots by 2007, and many had

Table 4.2: Changes in the holdings of cattle (owned cattle plus loaned in): at settlement and 2007-08

Scheme Type	Success Group	% households with cattle at settlement	% households with cattle in 2007-08	% households with cattle under care of other resettled farmers
A1 Villagised	1	85.2	85.2	4.5
	2	45.8	58.3	0.0
	3	35.3	47.1	6.3
A1 Self-contained	1	81.8	81.8	0.0
	2	33.3	88.9	11.1
	3	30.0	50.0	0.0
A2	1	90.0	80.0	10.0
	2	76.5	68.8	0.0
	3	71.4	57.1	0.0
Informal	1	84.6	100.0	46.2
	2	57.1	80.0	0.0
	3	0.0	16.7	0.0

Source: Survey data, 2007-08 (N=177)

between three and five structures, including kitchens, granaries and other huts. Across the 177 households in the survey sample a total of 89 brick structures with asbestos/iron roofing, 232 brick structures with thatch and 236 structures made from pole and mud were constructed. Given average building costs (including both labour and materials),[2] this amounts to a total investment of US$631 per household.

Cattle
Table 4.2 shows changes in cattle holdings between settlement and 2007-08. Among SG2 and SG3 households in both the A1 villagised and A1 self-contained schemes there has been significant expansion of the proportion of households holding cattle, while for SG1 households the proportion (if not the numbers) remained more static. For SG3, the proportion holding cattle rose from 35.3% to 47.1% in A1 villagised schemes, and from 30% to 50% in A1 self-contained schemes. Some of these increases are due to accumulation through purchases of new animals, but most has been through natural growth, due to good grazing conditions (Chapter 5). In addition, cattle holdings have increased through an influx of animals as part of sharing (*kuronzera*) arrange-

---

[2]   There are three categories of building quality (brick house with asbestos roof, windows door etc; a brick house with a thatched roof, windows, door etc. and a mud and pole house with a thatched roof). For different categories of building there are different construction/ materials costs. For a house the average 2009 US$ prices are $450, $300 and $80; for a kitchen $350, $200 and $80 and for a granary $200, $150 and $40.

ments. For example, across SG2 households, 55% of households kept other people's cattle at their plots. Similarly, 46% of households in SG1 in the informal schemes have cattle under the care of other resettled farmers in the area. Once again, the pattern on the A2 plots is different. All success groups witnessed declines in the proportion of households holding cattle, reflecting the high incidence of cattle rustling and disease on the A2 schemes.

As Chapter 5 explores in more depth, investment in cattle has been significant. There has been substantial accumulation across success groups in A1 and informal schemes. The proportion of people with access to cattle is today higher than in the nearby communal areas, where herd sizes average around 3.5 and the percentage of households owning cattle is around 60% (Scoones et al., 1996: 16; Campbell et al., 2002:24). The A2 schemes, however, show another pattern, with less accumulation, and in some cases significant losses. Across the schemes there has been a net increase of 344 cattle in the household sample since settlement. Taking an average replacement cost of $315,[3] this amounts to an accumulation of value of US$612 on average per household.

Farm equipment
Figure 4.2 shows the ownership of ox-ploughs at settlement and in 2008. Across all scheme types and success groups, ox-plough ownership has increased since settlement.[4] As expected, SG1 households are more likely to own ox-ploughs than other groups.

A similarly differentiated pattern is shown for the ownership of cultivators. Cultivators are owned by a smaller group. These are expensive and not vital pieces of equipment, and acquisitions have been concentrated among SG1 and SG2 households. For example, for SG1 households in A1 villagised, A1 self-contained and A2 schemes, percentage ownership levels have risen from 22%, 46% and 20% to 50%, 55% and 30% respectively.

There has also been an increase in the ownership of scotch carts across scheme types and success groups (Figure 4.3).[5] Particularly significant investments occurred among SG1 households in the informal schemes, where ownership increased from 46% to 84%. The importance of transport in the new resettlements of Uswaushava and Turf, allowing farmers to transport crops to markets, is reflected in these acquisitions. However, not all have managed to invest. Across the schemes very few SG3 household own a scotch cart. However, the overall increases in scotch cart ownership among both SG1 and SG2 households have wider benefits, as those without are able to borrow or hire.

[3]   US$ replacement cost prices in late 2009 are listed here. The average cost of cattle (taking account of herd composition observed in the study areas – see Chapter 5) is: Adult cow (45%; US$325), Heifer (17%; US$275), Oxen (18%; US$425), Bull (3%; US$550), Calf (15%; $175)
[4]   In the early 1990s in Chivi communal area, plough ownership ranged from 100% of households with draught power and 38% of households without draught, averaging 69% (Scoones et al., 1996:16).
[5]   Ownership levels in Chivi communal area, for example, were between 30% and 40% in 1999-2000 (Campbell et al., 2002: 24); higher than levels at settlement, but significantly lower than levels eight years later.

Figure 4.2 Ox ploughs

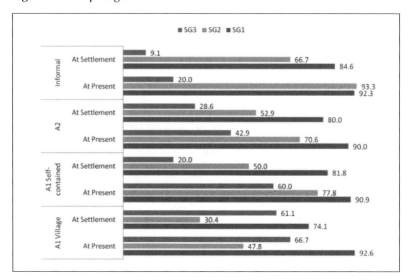

Figure 4.3 Scotch cart ownership

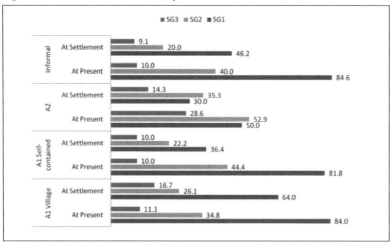

The Hippo Valley A2 cane farmers have shown equal determination in the acquisition of productive assets (Table 4.3). More than half of the farmers now own a tractor. While a few of these were part of generous loan schemes (Chapter 5), most were purchased, and are witness to the serious commitment to farming shown by many new settlers.

Across schemes and success groups, investment in equipment for farming has been significant. While there have been some loan schemes for equipment (Chapter 5), most farmers in our sample did not benefit from them. Instead, they have used whatever resources they had – from

Table 4.3 Investment in productive assets by cane farmers

Farm Assets	At settlement %	At present %
Tractors	20.0	51.4
Ploughs	11.4	31.4
Harrows	5.4	8.6
Knapsack	28.6	62.9
Boom spray	2.9	5.7

Source: Survey data, 2007-08 (N=35)

farming, remittances or off-farm work – to invest in productive assets. This pattern of accumulation has been differentiated, with those in SG1 and SG2 acquiring more. But with all assets the greater availability of equipment, transport or cattle means that there are wider, collective benefits through sharing, borrowing and hiring arrangements.

Taking each of these farm assets in turn, what is the overall value of the investments? Since settlement, 48 ploughs, 22 cultivators and 33 scotch carts have been acquired across the 177 households in the sample. Using 2009 prices,[6] this amounts to an average investment of US$198 per household.

Transport
One of the biggest challenges in new resettlement areas is the lack of public transport. The decline in the economy forced many transport operators to withdraw their services in the rural areas. For many of the newly settled areas, no public transport was ever provided. At Sanangwe, for example, people had to travel 15km to the nearest bus stop. At Wondedzo Extension, all public transport passing through the area was withdrawn, and people were walking 4km to the Masvingo-Mutare highway. In the same way, the Edenvale scheme has no shops or clinics and the settlers had to walk 16km to Chikombedzi. Investment in the means of transport – bicycles, cars and trucks – has therefore been a priority across the study sites.

Bicycles were owned by a significant proportion of SG1 and SG2 households (between 46% and 64%). New investment has been largest among SG3 households. For example, in A1 self-contained and A1 villagised schemes the bicycle ownership rose among SG3 households from 30% to 50% and 28% to 44%. Not surprisingly, patterns of car ownership are more differentiated. No households in the informal schemes own cars. By contrast, A2 farmers increased the ownership of cars across all success groups. For instance, no SG3 houseolds owned cars at settlement, but this increased to 14% by 2007-08. Equally, 65% of SG2 households in A2 schemes had cars by 2007-08, compared to 30% at settlement.

[6] Replacement costs in 2009 were: a cultivator, $220; a plough, $150; and a scotch cart, $700.

Table 4.4 Gardens, irrigation and domestic water sources

	A1 self-contained	A1 villagised	A2	Informal
% households with home garden	44.6	20.8	29.8	5.3
% households with garden elsewhere	39.2	4.1	40.4	77.3
% households with irrigated plot	1.4	1.2	47.3	0.0
% households main water source communal well or borehole	31.3	72.0	26.3	98.7
% households with main water source river or dam	4.1	8.9	5.3	0.0
% households with engine or windmill pump	2.7	0.0	36.8	0.0
% households with main water source own well/borehole	62.2	19.0	31.6	1.3

Source: Census, 2007 (N=400)

In the survey sample (N=177) a total of 29 bicycles and 17 cars/trucks were purchased by 2008. At 2009 average values,[7] this would amount to a total investment of US$150 per household on average.

Water and sanitation
When the land was taken there was little water and sanitation infrastructure, although the former ranches occasionally had some small-scale irrigation near the main farm house, which also had running water and toilet facilities. Elsewhere there were scattered cattle troughs, possibly a dip and sometimes some small dams. In other words, the infrastructure was not set up for settlement. As a result the new settlers have had to invest substantially in the development of water and sanitation facilities across the schemes. In the absence of external support, this has almost exclusively been done through the settlers' own efforts.

The investments have been substantial. By 2008, 38.4% of the study sample had invested in constructing toilets at their homesteads, made

[7] In 2009 the cost of a bicycle was US$115, a second-hand car US$1,000 and a small truck US$1,750, although prices varied widely depending on age, quality, etc.

from a range of materials. While lack of cement and external support impeded progress, people showed a real determination to improve their sanitation facilities. A total of 68 toilets had been built across the study sample by 2008. Taking an average cost of construction (both labour and materials),[8] this amounts to an average investment of US$77 per household.

Gardening is a critical part of agricultural systems in the new resettlements. But gardens need creating, and fencing and water sources are required. Table 4.4 shows the pattern of investment in gardens – both at the homestead and away from the home – as well as the sources of water. Across the sample, 67 gardens have been constructed. Assuming that all were fenced with brushwood and the cost of fencing is approximately US$50 per 100m,[9] the average investment in garden fencing would be US$29 per household.

The digging of wells has also been an important investment across the study sites. Most of these are unprotected, open wells, although some people have dug deep wells or contracted borehole digging companies. Wells and boreholes are generally owned and maintained by the plot holder, although neighbours may gain some access. Other public sources of water (such as dams and rivers) are important too. Focusing just on private wells and boreholes, a total of 70 have been constructed since settlement across our sample of 177 households. Assuming the cost of construction is US$200 per well, this amounts to an average investment of US$79 per household.

In addition to these investments at a household level, others have occurred at the community level. These are equally impressive. Across our study sites, schools, churches, markets and other structures have been built. In Turf ranch, for example, a large multi-denominational church was built out of poles, mud and thatch, while in Uswaushava, thousands of bricks were burned to build a school. These investments are even more difficult to value, but are significant, and again are evidence of the commitment of new settlers to improving their areas.

Trees and natural resources
The planting of trees and the adoption of soil conservation measures is another important facet of people's investment in the land. As Table 4.5 shows, a surprising number of people had planted trees, most of them fruit trees. Although fewer had invested in conservation measures, no one denied their importance.

It is difficult to value these type of investments, but assessments of the economic value of trees (Campbell et al., 1997b; Luckert and Campbell, 2002) and soil conservation (Bishop, 1995) suggest that these are significant if a wider notion of value, beyond direct uses, is taken.

---

[8]   The digging and building of an average pit latrine was estimated to cost US$200 in 2009. A similar price was estimated for digging an unlined, unsealed well of average depth. Both figures vary depending on the type of soil, depth of the water table, etc.

[9]   These 67 gardens covered 98,827 square metres. Assuming all gardens were square and the same size, this would require a total of 10,278m of fencing. Not all gardens were fenced with brushwood; some were fenced with wire (mostly removed from farm boundaries).

The value of investments

Aggregating the estimates above – rough as they are – we get a picture of the scale of investment in the decade since settlement (Table 4.6).

If we add in farm labour, livestock, farm inputs and community-level investments, the totals would be higher. While state investment in the new resettlements has been very low, and that of donors and aid agencies effectively zero, settlers themselves have been investing on an impressive scale. If this pattern is replicated across the province, where a total of 33,766 new A1 and A2 households exist according to official figures, this adds to a total of US$73m of investment on this sub-set of items (and $US18.3m more if we add in the estimated 8,500 informal settlers). To put this into perspective, the total overseas development aid to Zimbabwe averaged US$289.6m per annum over the period 1999-2008, of which an average of $49.7m per annum was from the UK.[10] The myth that there is no investment on the new resettlements can thus be safely dismissed. And significantly, this is coming from sources often not acknowledged or recognised.

4.3 Investment and security of tenure

What of the link between tenure security and investment (Barrows and Roth, 1990)? As Chapter 9 discusses in more depth, there is much policy discussion around forms of tenure, with strong arguments being made in favour of formalising tenure arrangements in order to encourage increases in investment. The data from our study sites are ambiguous. The standard argument runs that, without formal tenure security – ideally through freehold, if not through leases – then investment will not happen.[11] This does not seem to be the case. Investment is happening on all sites under a range of tenure arrangements, including the informal settlements, with houses being built, wells being dug, fields cleared and ploughed and herds accumulated. The most intensive investments appear to be happening in the A1 farms and not in the A2 areas, the reverse of what would be predicted if tenure (in)security was the main factor driving investment. Most settlers feel that tenure is secure enough and the likelihood of land being taken away again is small. This is a political judgement based on a trust in the state's commitment to the irreversibility of the land reform – a commitment that has now been made by all political parties. Some settlers in the informal settlements in Ushwaushava in particular cited tenure insecurity as a factor in the exit of a particular household (see Chapter 3), but there were always other factors too, including the harshness of the conditions and the lack of facilities.

However, all would agree that some basic policy clarity is needed. If offer letters are transferred into formal permits, then, settlers argue,

[10] See http://www.reliefweb.int/rw/rwb.nsf/db900sid/SKEA-83VJ2R?OpenDocument/ (page 24).
[11] Richardson (2005, 2007), for example, argues the lack of firm property rights explains Zimbabwe's agricultural decline; although see the rebuttal by Andersson (2007).

Table 4.5 Planting of trees and building conservation measures

District/ Cluster	Scheme Type	Percent of households that planted trees	Percent of households that invested in soil conservation (including contour ridges and protecting waterways)
Gutu	A1 villagised	70.6%	26.7%
	A1 self-contained	93.3%	15.8%
	A2	57.1%	16.3%
Masvingo	A1 villagised	87.1%	80.2%
	A1 self-contained	80.0%	58.4%
	A2	0.0%	50.0%
Chiredzi	A2	52.9%	71.5%
	Informal	85.2%	100.0%
Mwenezi	A1 villagised	17.6%	37.5%
	A2	100.0%	25.0%
	Informal	36.4%	18.2%

Source: Survey data, 2007-08.

Table 4.6 Average investments since settlement per household

Focus of investment	Average per household (US$)
Land clearance	385
Housing/buildings	631
Cattle	612
Farm equipment	198
Transport	150
Toilets	77
Garden fencing	29
Wells	79
Total	US$2161

this may allow them to acquire finance. But the relationship between the form of administrative arrangement guaranteeing tenure and agricultural finance is not always so clear. Again, the conventional thinking posits that, with more secure forms of tenure (with freehold as the gold standard), then finance will flow. In the past this had been the basis for the private financing of the large-scale commercial sector. But with finance dried up, or hyperinflation making it impossible to function, this was no longer the case during much of the last decade. Instead, other routes were used to gain financing, often through political connection and forms of patronage. Thus the state financing schemes over the past period have been notoriously poor in targeting appropriate beneficiaries, leading to huge wastage and substantial political patronage. In the new fiscal environment, this occurs less, but will the banks and finance institutions return to supporting the agricultural sector now that economic stability has at least partially returned? The situation is unclear. Hopefully, guarantees will be established to allow lenders to finance settlers in the resettlement areas on the basis of offer letters, permits and leases. This will help boost the already considerable investment in the new resettlements and allow the under-capitalised A2 enterprises in particular to take off.

4.4 Sustainability and investment

There have been many complaints that the fast-track land reform has resulted in the destruction of the natural environment. For example, the number of veld fires expanded massively following settlement, there was extensive hunting of game in the new areas, trees were cut to create fields and charcoal was manufactured in large quantities. Add to this the damage done by alluvial gold panning, and the tales of environmental degradation are substantial (Marongwe, 2002; Elliot et al. 2006; Fox et al. 2006).

There is much truth in these claims. As fields and settlement sites have been cleared, much previously forested land has been removed and transformed into arable areas. These are not devoid of trees – indeed they can be characterised as indigenous orchards, given the prevalence of fruit trees (cf. Wilson, 1989) – but the overall tree biomass has declined considerably. Cleared trees and shrubs were often burned, creating pollution and further fire hazards. With a very high fire load because of plentiful grass and limited grazing, veld fires were common in the early years of settlement. If fires caught at the height of the dry season they could sweep across vast swathes of land. With the opportunities for charcoal production created by land clearance, some people established small businesses, including labourers on A2 farms in need of supplementing their meagre or non-existent salaries. Through such trade more land was cleared to meet the demand for charcoal in towns and nearby settlements.

In the early period of resettlement, particularly in areas which had previously been uninhabited and had substantial wildlife populations, there were many opportunities for hunting. Most of this was of small game for local consumption, but a trade in biltong built up in the some of the lowveld sites, and some hunters developed their trapping techniques to capture larger game such as giraffe, and even buffalo and elephant. With the collapse of capacity in the Parks authorities, the more adventurous hunters expanded their operations into the national parks, cutting fences and poaching game. On the resettlement areas themselves the availability of easily hunted game soon declined, as land was cleared, but there remain some who still rely almost exclusively on illegal hunting for their livelihoods (Chapter 8). This rapid extraction of resources also happened with fish in small dams. With poor control and uncertain ownership, some dams were emptied of fish stocks in weeks. In one case the dam was drained and the whole stock harvested; in others sacks and fine nets were used.

Alluvial gold panning has long been banned in Zimbabwe under environmental regulations that prevent the digging up of river banks. Getting permits to undertake small-scale mining operations is notoriously difficult, and anything valuable is usually captured by those with power and influence. Unregulated gold panning can cause major erosion in riverine areas, resulting in substantial erosion and downstream deposition with the silting of dams and pools. This has been well documented in many parts of the country (Maponga and Ngorima 2003).[12] In the study areas, the sort of intensive alluvial panning seen in Manicaland, for example, is not evident, but there is undoubted reason for concern.

Clearly in the longer term many such practices are unsustainable. But the argument that land reform has caused untold environmental destruction and should be reversed has to be tempered. What constitutes environmental degradation or not depends on what users want from the resource in question (Abel and Blaikie, 1989). Clearing land for agriculture can only be construed as degradation if the woodland that it replaces is deemed to be more valuable. Of course, the new agricultural land use must demonstrate that it can sustain its value and effective conservation practices must be applied to ensure its sustainability, but the fact that trees are removed and burnt through land clearance should not necessarily be seen as unsustainable. The same might apply to hunting. A rapid culling of wild animals may reduce crop damage and, in the case of larger animals, danger to humans in newly resettled areas, and could be seen as advantageous, as long as the wildlife resource is not regarded as important for the future. In the national parks area, where preservation is the main objective, hunting is appropriately seen as negative, but this may not be the case elsewhere. As for gold panning, this gets a universally bad press, and without sensible measures to counteract erosion the negative impacts can be high. But this need not be the case, if a more regulated approach to gold panning, accepting its importance as a livelihood resource, was countenanced.

As Chapter 9 discusses, authority over land and resources is still in flux. No one quite knows who is in charge and this varies between places and over time. Effective natural resource management based on the regulated use of common property resources requires institutions that can manage use, preventing negative impacts and assuring sustainability.

---

12 http://allafrica.com/stories/200907200050.html.

Traditional institutions in the communal areas allow for this to some extent (Fortmann and Nhira 1993; Mukamuri et al., 2009), creating rules for inclusion and exclusion from a resource and for levels of extraction. But such local institutions need to be facilitated by others, whether technical or local government officials. Given the vacuum of power and authority and much uncertainty about institutional arrangements in the new resettlements, opportunities for effective common property resource management are only now emerging. As discussed in Chapter 9 also, the often proposed alternative of imposing individual title and specified ownership/leasehold on such common property resources is not much of an answer. Some resources have already become effectively privatised, where *de facto* private ownership operates over trees and fruits, for example, inside new homestead boundaries or within fields. In the A2 and A1 self-contained sites such fixed boundaries may be vigorously defended, with all resources within a fenced area being regarded as private. But, very often, such areas are not defendable, and given the relatively low value of resources – grass, fruit trees, small game, for example – it probably does not make sense to attempt to exclude others.

4.5 Straddling livelihoods: multiple locations for investment

One important dimension of the process of investment is the link with former homes, mostly in the communal areas. As households established new homes in the resettlements, old homes were often retained, at least for a while. This allowed people to spread risks and hedge bets. In terms of investment patterns, choices had to be made about where to focus: how much was the new settlement to be built up, what types of buildings should be constructed, where should effort be invested in farming, where should the cattle be kept? These were all issues that households across the study sites had to confront, particularly in the A1 areas.

A variety of factors influence the degree to which straddling livelihoods across sites was feasible. Most obviously, location was a factor, as moving between distant homes was not practical. Histories of settlement were important too. When groups of people occupied new land together, strong connections with relatives in the former home area have been retained. Demography is also significant, with younger households in the new resettlements maintaining links with their parents in the communal lands, often making use of their equipment, cattle and other resources in the establishment phase. For very large polygamous households, the original households sometimes split, with different groups living in either the communal land or the new resettlement areas. Connections with former homes are not just about production, labour and assets, but also about social relations. Social gatherings, including funerals and church functions, are important factors binding people together. People are often moving between the resettlement and communal areas attending funerals. Churches of the appropriate denomination are not always present in the new resettlements and some travel back to their communal homes to attend church. These ties keep communities connected, and are important for the processes of investment discussed above.

In 2008, 31% of households across the sample had land in the communal areas. Only three people were still farming their communal area land by 2008, with a further three employing a worker and another three leaving it fallow. There were at least seven cases of repossession by headmen in the communal areas as a result of the departure of the household. Most land had been handed over to relatives, including children (72% of cases). Table 4.7 shows the proportion of households keeping livestock in their original homes by scheme type and success group. By 2008 most livestock had been transferred to the new resettlements, with the notable exception of a number of A2 households. These included cane farmers who found it difficult to keep cattle in their new plots, but also others who had insufficient fencing or herding labour to keep animals safely, especially when the new owners themselves were absent. Comparing these figures for 2008 with data collected in 2005, there is evidence of the continued transfer of resources to the new resettlements. The increases in cattle numbers noted above reflect this transfer, as well as births and purchases. As homes became established and fields cleared, people and animals moved to the new resettlements on a more permanent basis. This reflected growing confidence in the new resettlement areas as places where people could stay long term. While at the beginning, people thought that a sudden change of political environment might result in the reversal of the land reform, as time went on and a consensus was established that land reform was not reversible, people accepted that it was a long-term proposition, even on the informal sites, without offer letters or government approval.

4.6 Conclusion

Over the last decade there has been considerable investment of labour and capital on the new land. This has been unevenly spread, with diverse consequences for livelihoods. Similar patterns are observed to the investment seen in 1980s resettlements, where increases of livestock numbers (Kinsey et al., 1998), investment in farm equipment (Kinsey, 2003) and significant expansions of areas cultivated (Hoogeven and Kinsey, 2001) were seen. In the new resettlements the rates and levels of investment are generally higher than seen from the 1980s in the old resettlements, and certainly higher than in households in nearby communal areas (Scoones, et al., 1996; Campbell et al., 2002).

Across our study sites, the success stories of the land reform are centred on SG1 and SG2 households, especially in the A1 sites. These people have been able to invest in getting agricultural production going, they have accumulated herds, they have built housing infrastructure, wells and toilets and purchased equipment. Given the hardships that have existed in Zimbabwe in this period, with a combination of economic collapse and political turmoil, let alone the recurrent droughts and the continuing scourge of HIV/AIDS, there has been unquestionably an upward livelihood trajectory for these households. Those in SG3,

Table 4.7 Keeping livestock in original homes

Scheme Type	Success Group	% households with goats at original homes	% households with sheep at original homes	% households with cattle at original homes	% households with chickens at original homes
A1 villagised	1	8.3	4.2	4.3	8.00
	2	4.3	0.0	4.3	4.4
	3	0.0	0.0	11.8	0.0
A1 self-contained	1	0.0	0.0	0.0	9.1
	2	0.0	0.0	11.1	0.0
	3	10.0	0.0	20.0	0.0
A2	1	10.0	0.0	20.0	20.0
	2	25.0	6.7	37.5	6.7
	3	14.3	0.0	28.6	0.0
Informal	1	7.7	0.0	7.7	0.0
	2	0.0	0.0	13.3	0.0
	3	0.0	0.0	0.0	9.1

Source: Survey data, 2007-08.

however, have fared less well. Despite evidence of investment, there have been setbacks too. These have largely occurred through misfortunes such as deaths and illness in the family. For the A2 farmers there has been a greater mix of success and failure. A number of them have invested substantially in their new enterprises, but always with mixed returns. The last decade has not been the moment for establishing new businesses of any sort, and certainly not in the farming sector, with limited financing and other forms of support. Yet, despite this, some have made a go of it, and managed to get things moving. Others, by contrast, have not, and there is little going on on their farms, with the land being held for better times.

As we discuss further in Chapter 10, the successes of A1 and informal settlers – and particularly a significant group of 'middle farmers' – could be described in terms of 'accumulation from below' (Neocosmas, 1993; Cousins, 2010): local investment and local gains through small-scale petty commodity production. Limited capital availability has prevented the emergence of a significant capitalist class of farmer – whether on the A2 or A1 self-contained sites. But this may be only temporary, and patterns of investment by some – and emerging labour relations (Chapter 6) – suggest evidence of an emergent group of capitalist producer (Chapter 10). As discussed further in Chapter 11, how these different forms of production interact will be important for the next period of agrarian transformation in Zimbabwe.

The lessons of the past decade must not be ignored. Despite the challenges, small-scale producers on the A1 and informal schemes acquired land and invested substanitally. The subsequent chapters explore some of the key elements of the overall livelihood system – both on- and off-farm – and in so doing tease out some of the details of investment dynamics introduced here.

5

The New Farmers | Agricultural & Livestock Production

5.1 Introduction

Farming is central to most people's livelihoods on the new resettlements. The much-repeated narrative is that Zimbabwean agricultural production has collapsed, with disastrous consequences. How does this simplistic picture relate to the reality on the ground? And what are the challenges faced? The story is highly differentiated – between and within households, as well as across sites and schemes. In this chapter we ask: how have different people fared, and what are the implications for broader processes of change? Can agricultural and livestock production provide a firm basis for livelihood improvement and economic growth following land reform? What are the challenges and implications for policy? These are big questions and can only be touched on here. However, in the following sections we attempt to give a flavour of the challenges faced and opportunities realised across the sites in Masvingo.

Early in our study, we carried out a ranking exercise exploring constraints to production on the new resettlements with around 75 people across the sites. Informants – a mix of rich and poor, men and women – were remarkably uniform in their answers. In 2004, the top four constraints identified were: lack of rain; shortages of draught power; pest and diseases of crops; poor soil fertility and a lack of fertiliser supplies.[1] This is a familiar list. Although having extensive land areas, the new farmers were facing similar problems to those experienced in the communal areas. Yet in the post-2000 period, these were exacerbated by a combination of policy distortions, failures of input supply and service support and drought. This chapter explores how these factors interlinked, and how they affected different producers in different places for different crops.

---

[1] Others were (in rank order) distance to markets/transport; seed supply; wild animal damage; labour supply; equipment acess; vandalism/theft (of fences) and shortage of dipping chemicals.

5.2 Diverse farming systems

In earlier chapters, we have introduced the different resettlement scheme types: A1 (villagised and self-contained), informal (essentially a village-type arrangement, but not formally planned) and A2 (a self-contained plot of a larger size). However, the reality on the ground does not conform to the neat plans laid out by government programmes. For example, smaller A2 and larger A1 self-contained plots are very similar, while A1 villagised and informal settlements are comparable. Arrangements vary between clusters across our study sample, with larger areas allocated in the drier south, although the standard farm size ceilings are not adhered to. The particular events surrounding land occupation and subsequent planning also had a big impact, upsetting any attempt at formulaic planning, as schemes accommodated more or less people, depending on the circumstances (Chapter 2).

Across our study sites there is a wide range of farming systems. Most are variants on mixed, crop-livestock farming (Wolmer et al., 2002) – some with communal grazing (such as the villagised schemes, but also in practice most self-contained and A2 schemes, currently without fencing). Across the schemes, even in the A2 sites outside the sugar cane estates, there has been little specialisation. New farmers have preferred to hedge their bets with a wide portfolio of agricultural activities, complementing the diversity of non-farm livelihood options (Chapter 8). As we discuss below, cropping and livestock production systems show high levels of diversity.

However, within households there is often some specialisation. This is often highly gendered, with women, for example, focusing particularly on gardening and the production of vegetables, groundnuts and bambara nuts, while men focus on the outfields and maize production. Similarly, women may specialise in goats and chickens, while men focus on the cattle. This results in a gendered division of labour and potential competition over resource allocations within the household. With limited external inputs supplied by the government or bought from remittances, for example, where will these be applied, and who decides? The answer depends on the household make-up and dynamic. With men sometimes working away, 'traditional' roles may be abandoned and women make the decisions, while in other cases, a more classic 'patriarchal' arrangement predominates.

The relative importance of livestock versus cropping, and the type of cropping practices, therefore varies enormously. There are agroecological dimensions to this, with more reliance on livestock in the drier south. However, across the sites, despite the formal mapping of land suitability and natural regions (cf. Vincent and Thomas, 1961), crop farming is an important part of livelihood strategies across the sites. Even in the A2 ranch at Asveld and the neighbouring A1 informal settlement at Turf in the far south, where rainfall averages around 400mm per annum, some gardening is being attempted with supplementary irrigation. Elsewhere dryland cropping dominates, and maize is by far the major food grain crop in all sites outside Mwenezi, where sorghum dominates. Other important crops include cotton, which has taken off dramatically in the new informal settlements in the Chiredzi cluster at Uswaushava, but is important elsewhere too. Gardening is significant in all sites, and irrigated agriculture is important in the A2 sugar cane plots of Hippo valley and the A2 Fair Range farms in Chiredzi cluster. Beyond a small rehabilitated irrigation scheme in Wondedzo Extension A1 scheme in Masvingo cluster there are no further substantial irrigated areas.

With rainfall being so variable across Masvingo province, crop and livestock production must be highly responsive, involving much improvisation and opportunism (Scoones et al., 1996). As people have established new fields, virgin land has come into production. This has been relatively fertile and potentially highly productive, even without fertilisers, but without rainfall little is possible. Thus the pattern of production since settlement, for all farmers outside the irrigated plots, has been highly dependent on the pattern of rainfall, and the droughts in many of the seasons since 2000 had a huge impact on people's ability to establish themselves. By contrast, the good rainfall years resulted in substantial harvests and were vitally important in the pattern of accumulation, allowing for the purchase of new inputs, equipment and livestock.

But rainfall and agroecology were not the only factors affecting the ability of the new farmers to get production going on their new sites. The policy environment was also crucially important.

5.3 The agricultural policy environment

The agricultural policy environment has been highly erratic since 2000. Sudden switches in priorities, levels of support and axes of authority have dramatically affected the availability, affordability and distribution of inputs, notably seeds and fertilisers. The level of extension support in the new resettlements has been highly variable, sometimes even non-existent, and the ability to source agricultural finance has been uncertain and patchy. The economic meltdown had a devastating impact on farmers' abilities to get access to inputs and services of any sort. For most new farmers across our study sites, policy has been highly disruptive and disabling, and most have had to get on with things in the absence of external support.

The story of fertiliser supply is illustrative. A number of factors caused the Zimbabwe fertiliser production to decline from about 500,000 tonnes in 1999 to 330,180 tonnes during the 2006 planting season. Low production has been blamed on lack of foreign currency to import materials, frequent plant and machinery breakdowns and power cuts, and the reduced capacity of the National Railways of Zimbabwe, leading to increased costs of moving raw materials from mines and ports by road. Another factor was the introduction of price controls which, in the face of high levels of inflation, forced fertiliser companies to run at a loss. As a result of these challenges, fertiliser use by farmers declined substantially, as Figure 5.1 indicates.

Figure 5.1 Fertiliser use trends, 1994-95 to 2008-09 season (tonnes)

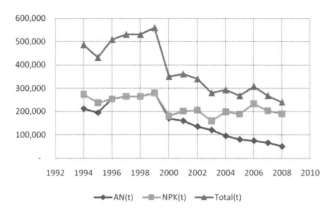

Source: Chemplex Corporation and International Fertiliser Development Corporation, July 2008

Seed supply faced similar challenges. During the three years following the inception of the Fast Track Land Reform, seed production was disrupted on some acquired lands (Sukume, 2009). Seed stock drawdowns and export restrictions helped to stabilise local availability in the period 2001-02 to 2002-03, but low production led to maize seed shortfalls of 18,000 tonnes in 2003-04 and 21,900 tonnes in 2005-06. The 2006-07 season, due to increased production by the new seed-producing farmers under the A2 model, had supplies equivalent to 35,300 tonnes, enough to plant a typical season's crop. However, mounting inflation coupled with inflexible input price controls, later reduced incentives for seed production such that by 2007-08 season supplies were again in deficit. In 2008-09 and 2009-10 a major government and donor effort was launched to boost the supply of inputs through a series of subsidised schemes, although the donor-led scheme was focused on communal areas.[2]

Between 2006 and 2008 the government reverted to top-down price controls, both of inputs (seed, fertiliser) and outputs (notably maize), in a vain attempt to control production, quickly undoing the benefits of the previously liberalised market (Jayne et al., 2002; Jayne and Jones, 1997). Key elements of agricultural policy were transferred from the Ministry of Agriculture to the Reserve Bank of Zimbabwe (RBZ), involving the Joint Operation Command in centralised command planning of the agricultural sector. As the economy collapsed, and the political situation became increasingly fragile, agriculture and food policy became more and more politicised. In this period, this meant that the security forces – and at the local level, youth militia – also became involved. Thus price controls were enforced by the security forces and the army engaged in the distribution of inputs and the implementation of 'command agriculture'.

[2]   See: http://www.fao.org/news/story/en/item/35361/icode/; http://allafrica.com/stories/
200909070005.html; http://allafrica.com/stories/200912160530.html

This had a number of important effects. The combination of low input supplies and low controlled prices led to the flourishing of informal parallel markets. With accelerating inflation, the controlled prices of major commodities such as maize failed to keep pace with input costs, making it difficult for farmers to buy inputs. Input suppliers, distributors and others were unable to make a profit and ceased to operate. The once flourishing agro-dealer networks that existed across Zimbabwe in the past all but disappeared. Under conditions of shortage, subsidised government schemes also crowded out small agro-dealers. Poor availability of fuel, as well as the poor state of roads, further soured the business environment for rural input dealers.

To assist farmers acquire inputs, the government instituted a number of initiatives. The Government Input Scheme, started in 2000, promised to provide inputs, including subsidised fuel, to the farming community for the following six years. However, the Ministry of Agriculture did not get adequate funds and the scheme ended in 2003. Failure to fund agriculture from fiscal resources led to an increasing resort to Reserve Bank of Zimbabwe schemes, the first of which – the Productive Sector Facility (PSF) – was introduced in 2004 to provide financial resources to productive sectors in the face of dwindling private bank finance. Under the PSF for agriculture, the RBZ provided loans at 25% interest for food crop production, a substantial subsidy given that prevailing commercial bank loans were attracting rates of 3-400%. In 2005 a dedicated quasi-fiscal funding mechanism was initiated, the Agricultural Sector Productivity Enhancement Facility (ASPEF), which became the only meaningful source of affordable financing for farmers, particularly those not growing the traditional export crops which attracted alternative funding through contract growing schemes. However, the scheme had two key weaknesses. Its limited funds meant that only a small number of farmers were able to benefit, and it favoured larger-scale farmers. For example, in the 2005-06 season, 80% of ASPEF funds were earmarked for the A2 farmers, with A1 and communal area farmers sharing the alance. PSF and ASPEF loan distributions by Agribank between 2003 and 2006 show that smallholder sector loans covered less than 1% of smallholder farmers (Sukume, 2009).

Operation Maguta, largely funded by the RBZ, was started in 2005 as a way to improve land utilisation. In a statement to Parliament the President introduced the programme as a targeted agriculture project based on 'command agriculture' to boost the country's food security and consolidate the national strategic reserve. In 2005 the programme's objective was to put some 300,000 ha of highly productive, but currently under-utilised, A2 land under grain crops. In the 2006-07 season, the Operation was expanded to support production of food crops in A1 and some dryland communal areas. The focus was on the growing of maize and small grains, especially in the smallholder sector, and winter wheat on the A2 farms. The aim was to ensure that targeted acreages of grains were planted to the key food security crops through provision of land preparation, seeds and fertilisers to selected farmers. Ministry of Agriculure officials were given long lists of, often unachievable, targets and were under severe political pressure to deliver.

A successor programme, the Champion Farmers Programme, was

started in the 2008-09 season. Under this initiative, government undertook to provide inputs to targeted farmers capable of producing high
yields. The idea was to ensure that the inputs available would be put
to the best use by the best farmers to boost food production and food
security. However, both the Maguta and Champion Farmer schemes ran
into similar problems – shortage of inputs, delays in disbursement and
incomplete input packages (e.g. seeds provided but no fertiliser, or basal
but no top-dressing fertiliser). In 2009-10 finance from public, private
and donor sources was increasingly available, but political wrangles
continued to dominate.[3]

Apart from cropping inputs, government has also provided subsidised
tractor and mechanisation services and assets. Through the District
Development Fund (DDF) and the Agricultural and Rural Development
Authority (ARDA), the government rents out agricultural equipment and
machinery, but services have been limited and inadequate (Sukume,
2009). Through the RBZ's Farm Mechanisation Programme, the government distributed machinery and equipment to farmers throughout the
country, including thousands of new tractors, ploughs and harrows.
The second phase included equipment for smallholder farming, such
as ox-drawn ploughs, cultivators, harrows, scotch carts and planters.
However, such equipment was expensive and it benefited a very small
proportion of farmers. For example, nationally, in Phase I of the scheme,
while 44% of tractors went to a vague category called 'top producers',
21% went to government ministers, senators, MPs and government
officials, with only 4% going to 'women and youth'. Over 50% of all
combine harvesters went to government ministers in this phase, according to the RBZ's own data (RBZ, 2007).[4] Across our study sites, only four
farmers benefited from the RBZ agricultural mechanisation scheme; all
were well-connected officials.[5]

The agricultural policy environment until 2009 was characterised
by heavy-handed state intervention funded through quasi-fiscal means
which distorted markets and incentives and undermined the economy.
They benefited some, but they also opened up significant opportunities for patronage, as well as outright theft.[6] The new resettlement areas
were notionally favoured by government policy, in a desperate attempt
to boost production. But the distribution of inputs – whether fertiliser,
seed, equipment or finance – was highly skewed, with very little of it
filtering down to farmers in our study areas. The failure of the top-down
command agriculture and state-directed price control resulted in the

---

[3]   As before, input schemes became embroiled in political disputes, see: http://allafrica.
com/stories/200912140026.html. For details of the World Bank financing, see: http://web.
worldbank.org/external/projects/main?pagePK=64283627&piPK=73230&theSitePK=4094
1&menuPK=228424&Projectid=P117212 and private bank financing: http://allafrica.com/
stories/200911170879.html; http://www.zimtelegraph.com/?p=2382

[4]   Cited in Ministry of Agricultural Engineering, Mechanization and Irrigation Development, Draft Agricultural Engineering, Mechanisation and Irrigation Strategy Framework:
2008-2058, Government of Zimbabwe (February 2008).

[5]   A police officer, a councillor, a provincial local government official and a senior ZANU-
PF official.

[6]   http://www.thezimbabwetimes.com/?p=25504;http://www.zimbabwesituation.com/mar12
a_2009.html#Z4 ; http://www.zimtelegraph.com/news_article.php?cat=23&id=112.

Table 5.1 Trends in draught power strategies (% of households). Households may pursue several strategies in any year

Season	Source of Tillage Draught	A1 self-contained			A1 villagised			A2			Informal		
		SG1	SG2	SG3	SG1	SG2	SG3	SG1	SG2	SG3	SG1	SG2	SG3
2004–05	Own draught	95.7	66.7	64.3	89.1	66.7	56.9	54.5	55.6	45.5	89.5	55.2	24.0
	Rented draught	8.7	33.3	46.4	12.7	37.0	36.2	63.6	44.4	54.5	21.1	34.5	36.0
	Hoes	0.0	4.8	0.0	n.d	3.7	6.9	0.0	0.0	0.0	0.0	6.9	28.0
	Work party	0.0	0.0	0.0	1.8	7.4	17.2	0.0	0.0	0.0	0.0	10.3	20.0
2005–06	Own draught	95.7	57.7	53.3	90.7	50.0	55.2	66.7	66.7	75.0	94.7	75.0	13.0
	Rented draught	17.4	42.3	50.0	7.4	44.4	44.8	44.4	55.6	37.5	5.3	41.7	72.7
	Hoes	0.0	3.8	0.0	0.0	1.9	0.0	0.0	0.0	0.0	0.0	0.0	18.2
	Work party	8.7	0.0	6.7	9.3	14.8	17.2	0.0	0.0	0.0	0.0	0.0	13.6
2006–07	Own draught	91.3	80.8	54.8	88.9	59.3	62.5	60.0	77.8	83.3	100.0	87.5	23.8
	Rented draught	26.1	19.2	45.2	14.8	50.0	42.9	50.0	44.4	16.7	0.0	20.0	81.0
	Hoes	0.0	3.8	0.0	0.0	0.0	0.0	0.0	0.0	16.7	0.0	0.0	0.0
	Work party	4.3	0.0	6.5	1.9	9.3	8.9	0.0	0.0	0.0	0.0	0.0	4.8
2007–08	Own draught	100.0	70.4	48.4	85.2	61.1	55.0	50.0	83.3	100.0	100.0	87.0	55.0
	Rented draught	0.0	33.3	54.8	14.8	40.7	46.7	66.7	33.3	0.0	0.0	17.4	50.0
	Hoes	0.0	0.0	0.0	0.0	0.0	5.0	0.0	0.0	0.0	0.0	4.3	n.d
	Work party	4.3	0.0	0.0	1.9	1.9	1.7	0.0	0.0	0.0	0.0	13.0	5.0
2008–09	Own draught	95.7	70.4	62.1	94.3	65.4	52.1	91.7	61.1	63.6	100.0	86.4	48.1
	Rented draught	4.3	29.6	48.3	5.7	34.6	41.7	8.3	38.9	36.4	0.0	22.7	37.0
	Hoes	4.3	0.0	0.0	0.0	0.0	6.3	0.0	0.0	0.0	0.0	0.0	3.7
	Work party	4.3	0.0	0.0	0.0	1.9	2.1	0.0	0.0	0.0	5.3	0.0	14.8

Source: Annual crop survey (N=400; n.d. = no data)

creation of a strong parallel market, but this was often not sufficient to supply farmers with their needs. Instead, self-reliance and independence from formal state support and markets was required.

Although the policy environment has changed for the better since 2009, how did the new farmers cope during the period from 2000? What were the consequences for production, and how has this shaped the way livelihoods have emerged on the new resettlements? The following sections address these questions, in respect of both crop and livestock production. First, however, we look at the process of establishing productive agriculture, and the importance of key assets and inputs for this.

5.4 Establishing agriculture

As Chapter 4 showed, land clearance across the sites has been extensive, representing a substantial investment of labour. Having access to draught power is critical to arable agriculture across most farms in Zimbabwe. Draught access ensures timely ploughing and planting operations, as well as weeding, without the need for cash for hiring draught spans or tractors.

Table 5.1 tracks changes in tillage strategies in the study areas over the period 2004-05 to 2008-09. This shows the greatest draught access among A1 self-contained households, followed by A1 villagised and informal households, with A2 farmers largely dependent on hiring (mostly tractorised) draught from elsewhere. Over time, though, there has been an increase in access to draught power among all farmers, including those on the A2 schemes. New acquisitions have been particularly important in SG2 and SG3 households which previously did not have draught animals. These changes reflect the broader pattern of accumulation of cattle discussed in Chapter 4. For those without access to draught power, sharing and work parties (*humwe)* are important, especially for SG3 households. But, as herds have grown, the proportion of households dependent on these arrangements has decreased. Over the full period across all sites, the proportion of households renting draught (animals or tractors) has remained high for SG2 and SG3 households in particular. Despite the government schemes discussed above, there has been a shortage of tractors, and most hiring is of local draught teams. However, in the 2009-10 season, there was an increase in private tractor hiring, mostly from people based in towns who had acquired tractors through patronage linkages in the previous year.

Access to inputs and credit was another major challenge faced by the new farmers. As Table 5.2 shows, fertiliser purchase varied significantly, with very little occurring in the drier sites of Mwenezi, and none at all in the A2 ranch site. In the sites with more agricultural potential, there was high variability across years and sites. With inputs increasingly being available only in the major urban centres and on parallel markets, certain sites had locational advantages in accessing inputs.

In addition, new settlers faced problems getting credit to purchase inputs. Apart from schemes in the Masvingo cluster, the proportion

Table 5.2 Percentage of households who purchased fertiliser

Cluster	Scheme type	2002-03	2003-04	2004-05	2005-06	2006-07	2007-08	2008-09
Gutu	A1 self-contained	33.3	45.2	57.1	52.4	38.1	38.1	26.2
	A1 villagised	10.0	26.7	43.3	36.7	56.7	86.7	26.7
	A2	15.4	7.7	46.2	58.3	41.7	n.d.	41.7
Masvingo	A1 self-contained	74.4	84.6	66.7	76.9	92.3	94.9	41.0
	A1 villagised	44.1	55.1	57.6	47.8	49.6	66.1	17.3
	A2	0.0	25.0	25.0	n.d	25.0	75.0	66.7
Chiredzi	A2	3.4	10.3	13.8	40.0	26.7	10.0	65.4
	Informal	0.0	0.0	0.0	0.0	0.0	1.9	2.0
Mwenezi	A1 villagised	3.7	0.0	0.0	0.0	0.0	0.0	0.0
	Informal	0.0	0.0	0.0	0.0	0.0	0.0	0.0

Source: Crop census data (N=400; n.d = no data)

accessing private loans has been very low. Again, the advantage of being near to Masvingo town has been important. Operation Maguta contributed little to input access in 2005-06, but gradually improved coverage up to 2007-08, when many Masvingo cluster farmers benefited; elsewhere coverage was limited.

Crop mixes and production patterns
Despite these travails, how did the new farmers fare? Grains – especially maize – occupy most cropped areas in all sites. With the exception of the informal settlements of Chiredzi, where cotton takes up 28% of the area, grains account for more than 70% of cropped area in all sites. Across sites, A1 and informal settlement farmers grow a greater variety of crops than A2 farmers. The greatest diversity is in the Masvingo A1 village scheme site (Wondedzo Wares), where 13 different crops, including vegetables, were planted in the 2007-08 season. Cotton is important in the Masvingo and Chiredzi clusters, but none was grown by the sampled farmers in Gutu and Mwenezi in 2008. Edible legumes – especially groundnuts and bambara nuts – occupy a significant proportion (16%) of cropped lands in Masvingo and Gutu A1 villagised sites, very often representing fields controlled exclusively by women. Oil seed crops, such as sunflower, take up a limited area, with the highest area being 6.5% in the Masvingo villagised site.

Tables 5.3 and 5.4 compare the 2007-08 and 2008-09 seasons, looking at major crops across sites and success groups.[7] 2007-08 was a very poor cropping season due poor rainfall distribution and input shortages. By contrast, in terms of rainfall amount and distribution 2008-09 was one of the best seasons in recent years. The national maize production in 2007-08 was estimated to have been only 470,000 tonnes, with an average yield of 0.3 t/ha, whereas in 2008-09 it was some 1,242,600 tonnes, from an average yield of 0.8t/ha.[8]

The data thus shows two extremes along a spectrum experienced since 2000. A number of important patterns are evident. First, outputs are concentrated in relatively few sites, especially in a drought year when farmers in the drier areas receive very little. In these sites the variation across years of crop output is very high, ranging from zero to many tonnes, making storage (especially of sorghum) critical for inter-annual food security. Second, the highest outputs per household are seen in A1 self-contained sites, and especially those in the Masvingo cluster. Harvests in 2009 were as high as 32 tonnes of maize in the A1 self-contained site and 64 tonnes in the A2 site, representing a signficant surplus above households consumption needs. In this year, major constraints of storage and marketing were faced. Third, outputs are highly skewed within sites, with relatively few farmers receiving a significant proportion of the output, especially of maize. These are mostly in SG1

---

[7]   Other crops included sugar beans, bambara nuts, sweet potato, rice and wheat, but these were grown by very limited numbers of farmers.
[8]   Second Round Crop and Livestock Assessment Report, Ministry of Agriculture, Mechanisation and Irrigation Development, Government of Zimbabwe, 27 April 2009 (http://www.fanrpan.org/documents/d00706/). Although see: http://www.irinnews.org/Report.aspx?ReportId=85018.

Table 5.3 Crop production from 2008 and 2009 harvests compared by site (average kgs where grown; zero implies not grown)

District	Scheme	Year	Average area used (ha)	Maize	Sorghum	Finger millet	Pearl millet	Cotton	Sunflower	Groundnuts
Gutu	A1 Villagised	2008	2.8	625.0	0.0	750.0	0.0	0.0	40.0	105.6
		2009	3.0	2,869.6	15.0	466.0	0.0	0.0	102.5	196.7
	A1 Self-contained	2008	4.4	1,375.3	0.0	300.0	0.0	0.0	275.0	207.1
		2009	4.6	2,062.8	0.0	214.0	0.0	0.0	40.0	191.8
	A2	2008	8.3	365.0	0.0	0.0	0.0	0.0	0.0	118.8
		2009	9.2	2,822.7	0.0	60.0	413.3	0.0	75.0	312.9
Masvingo	A1 Villagised	2008	4.6	888.5	173.0	46.7	75.0	751.5	178.9	379.1
		2009	4.0	2,776.4	95.0	186.7	0.0	266.7	221.0	442.5
	A1 Self-contained	2008	9.9	2,769.2	200.0	100.0	0.0	1,225.0	200.0	358.3
		2009	10.9	11,039.5	0.0	0.0	0.0	400.0	230.0	643.3
	A2	2008	52.3	52,812.5	350.0	0.0	0.0	700.0	100.0	0.0
		2009	56.3	34,166.7	0.0	1,160.0	0.0	0.0	300.0	0.0

District	Scheme	Year	Average area used (ha)	Maize	Sorghum	Finger millet	Pearl millet	Cotton	Sunflower	Groundnuts
Chiredzi	Informal	2008	14.2	825.0	300.0	0.0	0.0	2,340.0	0.0	100.0
		2009	5.9	2,234.4	1,591.1	413.4	452.3	1,720.0	941.1	887.3
	A2	2008	7.1	650.8	470.9	0.0	50.0	3,014.6	0.0	496.0
		2009	24.2	8,016.7	1,562.5	200.0	0.0	3,100.0	0.0	883.3
Mwenezi	A1 Villagised	2008	6.5	222.7	790.4	0.0	0.0	0.0	0.0	60.0
		2009	6.6	242.6	1,897.6	0.0	0.0	0.0	0.0	332.2
	Informal	2008	10.4	410.0	835.7	0.0	0.0	0.0	0.0	0.0
		2009	7.0	391.6	5,000.0	0.0	0.0	0.0	0.0	553.3

Source: Crop survey, 2008 and 2009 (N=400)

Table 5.4 Crop production from 2008 and 2009 harvests compared by scheme type and success group (average kgs, where zero implies not grown)

District	Scheme	Year	Average area used ha (SD)	Maize	Sorghum	Finger millet	Pearl millet	Cotton	Sunflower	Groundnuts
A1 Villagised and Informal	SG1	2008	6.8	979.7	1,020.8	280.0	75.0	2,865.0	118.0	385.2
		2009	5.0	3,316.7	3,135.7	491.2	479.2	2,350.0	634.1	723.7
	SG2	2008	5.2	482.4	554.3	50.0	50.0	3,625.0	300.0	325.5
		2009	4.7	2,145.6	1,466.7	121.4	602.3	1,263.6	637.7	345.8
	SG3	2008	5.4	449.5	231.6	0.0	0.0	1,492.2	153.3	451.0
		2009	4.5	1,666.5	1,444.7	95.3	180.0	625.0	650.0	285.6
A1 Self-contained	SG1	2008	10.5	3,464.1	300.0	125.0	0.0	1,225.0	200.0	400.0
		2009	12.0	12,070.5	0.0	266.7	0.0	400.0	216.7	667.0
	SG2	2008	5.3	1,668.8	0.0	100.0	0.0	0.0	275.0	130.0
		2009	6.5	4,700.0	0.0	0.0	0.0	0.0	95.0	460.0
	SG3	2008	4.2	655.0	100.0	275.0	0.0	0.0	0.0	275.0
		2009	5.6	3,960.7	0.0	135.0	0.0	0.0	350.0	203.3
A2	All SGs	2008	16.0	13,591.9	325.0	0.0	0.0	1,793.3	100.0	115.0
		2009	23.3	8,943.5	1,562.5	473.3	413.3	3,100.0	187.5	576.2

Source: Crop surveys, 2008 and 2009 (N=400)

and some in SG2, farmers with draught power, more access to inputs and with sufficient equipment and labour.

Yield levels were highest in the A1 farms, supporting the broad argument of the 'inverse relationship' which posits that small-scale farming benefits from the lower supervision costs of family labour. This has been a major argument in favour of 'land-to-the-tiller' reform, focused on smallholder farming (Lipton, 2009; see Chapter 1). However, the relationship is not neat or simple. The slightly larger A1 self-contained farms, for example, seem to fare better than the villagised farms in A1 and informal schemes. This may reflect patterns of asset holding and labour access, as well as skill and commitment. Overall, yields on the larger A2 farms are the lowest of all. But the exceptions are instructive too. For example, average maize yields from the A2 Masvingo cluster farm at Bompst are high, but they rely on substantial infrastructural investment, including irrigation.

5.6 Maize production

Maize is the dominant crop across nearly all study sites and is an important food security crop nationally. The study tracked the pattern of maize production through an annual census of all farmers since 2002. National averages of maize consumption are estimated to be around 165kg per capita, giving an average household requirement (for a family of six individuals) of about 980kg. To assess the food self-sufficiency performance of households in the study sites we used 1,000kg as a yardstick. Table 5.5 presents percentages of study households that managed to attain this level from 2003 to 2009.

The data shows a gradual increase in the percentage of households producing more than a tonne of maize from the 2002-03 season to the 2005-06 season. This represents a process of extensification, as land was cleared until around 2005-06, followed by increasingly intensified production. However, successful intensification has been constrained over this period, due to drought when, despite relatively high levels of inputs, yields were low, and due to input shortages which prevailed particularly from 2005.

A number of qualifications are important when interpreting this data. First, the data from Mwenezi shows a very limited number of people across the years achieving more than a tonne of maize. This is because the major grain crop in these areas is in fact not maize, but sorghum. If the same yardstick is taken, combining maize and sorghum for the A1 villagised and informal sites in the Mwenezi cluster, 57.1% and 72.7% of households exceeded the one tonne threshold in 2009. Secondly, the A2 farm in Mwenezi (Asveld) has remained a ranch, and is more or less exclusively focused on cattle production (with a limited amount of wildlife), and so crop production is correspondingly low or absent. Thirdly, the figures for the A2 sites are affected by the high concentration of cash cropping, notably sugar cane in the Hippo Valley. Finally, as the good rainfall year of 2008-09 showed, significant production was possible despite severe shortages of fertilisers, because of the quality of the relatively virgin soils. However, the opportunity for low input

Table 5.5 Percentage of farmers harvesting greater than a tonne of maize

District	Scheme Type	2002-03	2003-04	2004-05	2005-06	2006-07	2007-08	2008-09
Gutu	A1 self-contained	18.4	50.0	45.5	75.0	63.4	28.6	61.5
	A1 villagised	13.3	39.1	24.0	79.3	63.3	36.7	78.6
	A2	0.0	0.0	44.4	75.0	66.7	n.d	63.6
Masvingo	A1 self-contained	55.3	63.2	56.4	100.0	100.0	51.3	100.0
	A1 villagised	28.0	38.1	45.8	95.7	91.2	15.8	77.9
	A2	0.0	25.0	25.0	n.d	75.0	75.0	100.0
Chiredzi	A2	14.3	38.5	46.2	50.0	66.7	50.0	88.9
	Informal	18.8	10.2	3.9	86.5	51.0	24.5	62.5
Mwenezi	A1 villagised	26.9	8.0	0.0	4.8	0.0	0.0	0.0
	Informal	11.5	11.5	0.0	0.0	26.7	6.7	0.0

Source: Maize census, 2003-09 (N=400; n.d = no data)

Table 5.6 Maize sales, 2006-09

District	Scheme Type	Percentage of farmers selling maize locally				Percentage of farmers selling maize to the GMB			
		2005-6	2006-7	2007-8	2008-09	2005-6	2006-7	2007-8	2008-09
Gutu	A1 self-contained	33.3	31.7	11.9	21.4	52.4	26.8	7.1	2.4
	A1 villagised	27.6	33.3	20.0	56.7	72.4	36.7	23.3	0.0
	A2	8.3	8.3	100.0	8.3	41.7	16.7	n.d.	0.0
Masvingo	A1 self-contained	20.5	10.3	7.7	76.9	97.4	94.9	0.0	13.9
	A1 villagised	14.8	9.6	0.9	55.8	90.4	71.1	0.0	7.7
	A2	100.0	0.0	0.0	66.7	n.d.	50.0	25.0	33.3
Chiredzi	A2	26.7	55.6	40.0	15.4	28.6	11.1	20.0	30.8
	Informal	13.5	16.3	14.3	8.0	19.2	0.0	0.0	0.0
Mwenezi	A1 villagised	9.5	0.0	0.0	0.0	0.0	0.0	0.0	0.0
	Informal	0.0	0.0	0.0	0.0	0.0	0.0	0.0	0.0

Source: Annual crop census, 2006-2009 harvests (N=400; n.d = no data)

Table 5.7 Distribution of crop sales (50kg bags) by success group and scheme type (% of households)

Scheme Type	SG	N	2005-06 0 bags	1-20 bags	21+ bags	2006-07 0 bags	1-20 bags	21+ bags	2007-08 0 bags	1-20 bags	21+ bags	2008-09 0 bags	1-20 bags	21+ bags
A1 self-contained	1	23	0.0	4.3	95.7	13	8.7	78.3	91.3	4.3	4.3	26.1	8.7	65.2
	2	26	29.6	3.7	66.7	50.0	19.2	30.8	96.3	3.7	0.0	51.9	22.2	25.9
	3	31	41.9	9.7	48.4	51.6	22.6	25.8	100.0	0.0	0.0	58.6	24.1	17.2
A1 villagised	1	54	18.5	7.5	74.1	51.9	14.8	33.3	90.7	9.3	0.0	38.9	29.6	31.5
	2	54	25.9	14.8	59.3	38.9	22.2	38.9	98.1	1.9	0.0	52.8	35.8	11.3
	3	56	28.1	19.3	52.6	41.1	25	33.9	98.3	1.7	0.0	67.9	19.7	10.7
A2	1	10	44.4	0.0	55.6	80.0	0.0	20.0	50.0	0.0	50.0	60.0	20.0	20.0
	2	9	66.7	0.0	33.3	66.7	0.0	33.3	100.0	0.0	0.0	70.0	10.0	20.0
	3	10	87.5	0.0	12.5	100.0	0.0	0.0	100.0	0.0	0.0	90.0	0.0	10.0
Informal	1	19	68.4	0.0	31.6	100.0	0.0	0.0	100.0	0.0	0.0	84.2	15.8	0.0
	2	24	91.7	0.0	8.3	100.0	0.0	0.0	100.0	0.0	0.0	96.6	3.4	0.0
	3	21	91.7	0.0	8.3	100.0	0.0	0.0	100.0	0.0	0.0	100.0	0.0	0.0

Source: Annual crop census, 2006-09 (N=400)

production will only be temporary, unless significant investments in soil fertility are made in the future.

Levels of production are very unevenly distributed within schemes, with SG1 households usually, SG2 households mostly and SG3 households rarely achieving the one tonne production level. Patterns of food insecurity are thus highly variable across sites and households and between years. Thus, in 2008-09 only around a quarter of households did not produce enough to feed the household for the year from grain production (including sorghum for the dryland areas). By contrast, in the previous year, with a few exceptions, nearly three-quarters of households were likely to be net purchasers of food during the year. Food insecurity on the new resettlements areas is therefore not universal nor perennial, but it remains a significant challenge.

While some must regularly purchase maize for food, others regularly sell it. To gauge the level of surplus maize production the study examined patterns of selling locally, as well as to the Grain Marketing Board (GMB). This is a rather crude measure, as some farmers who benefited from subsidised inputs from the GMB or other input schemes, were required to sell a portion of their maize crop to the GMB. In addition, maize sales to the GMB were used as a condition for future access to these schemes, or to loans from the Agribank. Despite these qualifications, levels of sales are an indication not only of production capacity, but also market orientation, and are useful in characterising the farming systems across the sites.

Patterns of sales mirror patterns of production across sites and years. With the good harvests of 2006 and 2009, however, we see a very different pattern of marketing. In 2006, the GMB had a formal monopoly on maize marketing. Although farmers could legally move up to 150kg from the farm to urban areas, enforcement officials were sometimes impounding even small amounts. Though sales of maize within the local farming areas were allowed, demand for the grain was lowest during the times when surplus producers wanted to sell. In 2009, restrictions on local sales had been removed and a vibrant local market emerged, though constrained by transport capacity. Prices were significantly higher in the local market compared to those offered by the GMB.

Who have been the surplus producers in the study areas over the period between 2006 and 2009? Table 5.7 summarises the distribution of farmers by quantities of grain sold to the GMB by success groups, showing how SG1 farmers sold the most maize in each scheme type.

Average levels of annual household production on the new resettlements are higher than in comparable communal area settings. Between 1988 and 1990, for example, households in Chivi communal area averaged around 800kg of maize output (Scoones et al., 1996: 16). By contrast, in the old resettlements, significant numbers produced more than a tonne (Kinsey, 2004:1683). However, increases in output were in large part due to expansions of area, as yield levels remained around a tonne per hectare (Kinsey, 2004; Hart-Broekhuis and Huisman, 2001). Our findings echo this pattern. While, on average, output levels have increased significantly, this has been due more to the expansion of cultivated areas than to intensification. Although, as land areas have been cleared, there is some evidence of greater intensification and increases in yields in more recent years, room remains for improvement, as we discuss further in Chapter 11.

As with earlier studies in the communal areas and old resettlements, we see a highly differentiated pattern, with some regularly producing surplus, and others not. This mirrors the pattern observed for the communal areas from the 1980s. Here a 'maize revolution' was sparked by new access to inputs and markets (Rohrbach, 1989; Eicher, 1995), and around 20% of the farming population became regular surplus producers (Stack, 1994; Stanning, 1989; Rohrbach, 1990). As with previous 'green revolutions' elsewhere, it was very unevenly distributed, both geographically and socio-economically. It was also relatively short-lived. The structural adjustment era in particular undermined many of the gains made, and the support infrastructure that fostered the growth in smallholder maize production was removed as a result of liberalisation and reduction in subsidies (Smale and Jayne, 2003). We return at the end of this chapter, and again in Chapter 11, to a discussion of the prospects for production – and a sustained 'green revolution' – on the new resettlements. First, however, we move to other components of the emerging production systems.

5.7 Gardens and irrigation

Gardens – either next to the homestead or along rivers or adjacent to other water sources, such as *vleis* (low-lying valley bottom wetlands) – are a vitally important part of the overall production system (Mharapara, 1995). Very often established and managed by women, they offer the opportunity for high-value, high-input agriculture, contrasting with the relatively low input, extensive dryland crop production discussed above. Supplementary watering characterises these garden sites, and access to water is a critical factor. Irrigation, even on a very small scale, in a chronically water deficit province such as Masvingo, has a significant impact on livelihoods in terms of improving household nutrition, expanding the range of crops grown, lengthening the productive season and providing extra income for the household. Irrigation possibilities in the study areas varied considerably. Sites in Gutu have numerous *vlei* areas which reduces the effort needed to harvest water through manually dug shallow wells. Thus more than 60% of households in all Gutu schemes reported having a garden. In the Masvingo schemes, homestead garden ownership ranges between 25% and 38% of the households. In Chiredzi and Mwenezi typically less than 20% have a homestead garden.

Where easy access to water has been a problem, communal schemes have exploited isolated water sources. An example of such a scheme is the Wondedzo Maguta scheme in the Masvingo cluster, which got assistance from Operation Maguta to rehabilitate a 22ha irrigated plot. A private company – Moving Water Industries – was hired and a new pump was supplied. The area was divided into three blocks and allocated to 95 people (including 19 female-headed households), each getting five lines. To date, maize and sugar beans have been the main crops. A pump minder stays with his family at the pump house. He protects and operates the electric motor and guards crops at the scheme. He is paid US$20 per month and mealie meal. A condition for being allowed into the scheme was the supply of fencing materials, as well as a commitment to contribute towards electricity bills. Despite the small size of the plots, the livelihood benefits are significant. 11 households are not members of the scheme, having been unable to secure fencing wire. They now want to join, and this represents a growing source of tension in the community. The major challenges faced so far include keeping the electric generator going, hiring tractors and accessing wire. There is a similar scheme in Mwenezi, where the former owner of Edenvale farm created a small irrigation plot using river water. It has benefited ten farmers from the Edenvale Village 11 A1 scheme, including several our study sample, each cropping 0.1ha. Again the benefits have been significant, with the opportunities of multiple crops through the year, and off-season sales of green maize and vegetables.

In addition, there have been less organised local initiatives creating micro-irrigation schemes. In Clare A1 self-contained scheme, for example, a former war veteran has settled himself in the middle of a *vlei* and has refused to budge. Nearby, households in the villagised scheme have allocated themselves 70m x 70m gardens, along a stream. Both violate formal natural resource protection guidelines that forbid cropping 30m from a waterway. However, the farmers argue that they are investing in soil conservation efforts, that no risks of erosion exist and that their gardens are highly productive. Without enforcement from government officials, the gardening continues highly successfully in each case. As Chapter 4 showed, the main sources of irrigation water are low technology shallow wells sunk by the settlers. These investments are witness to the significance placed on water access across the sites.

In the A2 schemes outside the sugar estates (see below), there are relatively few large-scale irrigation facilities. In the A2 farms of Fair Range, new farmers inherited some irrigation infrastructure, although this has been extended in a number of cases so that irrigated areas have increased. These farmers have suffered major problems with water supplies because of erratic electricity provision, as well as sabotage of pipes by neighbours. Some have dams on their A2 farms, but lack of resources to bring in electricity and develop irrigation infrastructure is limiting the establishment of irrigated plots. An example of such a farmer is Mr C in Northdale A2 farm in Gutu cluster. He has a dam on the plot and has cleared 20ha for irrigation. He would like to set up an irrigation plot to raise dairy cows, but is unable to replace a vandalised transformer or buy irrigation pipes. The only major new irrigation investment across the study sites is an irrigation plot operated by an A2 farmer at Bompst farm in Masvingo cluster. He uses water piped in from the Mtirikwe dam into the plot through a centre-pivot system which he purchased after being granted the land. On arrival, he grew winter wheat and supplemented his summer crops using the irrigation system, but he has abandoned wheat in favour of horticulture, which has a lucrative market in nearby Masvingo town.

Irrigation, whatever its scale, is a key part of the overall picture of emergent agriculture in Masvingo province. It is, however, very underdeveloped. In such a dry part of the country, investment in irrigation infrastructure, and water resources more generally, will be an essential component of future development (Chapter 11).

5.8 Cotton production

As Table 5.3 showed, cotton production is concentrated in Masvingo and Chiredzi clusters. Chapter 7 explores the cotton value chain in more detail; here we concentrate on production. Cotton is an ideal crop for drier parts of the province, especially those areas with heavy soils. Since cotton production requires the purchase of seed and the marketing of lint, interaction with cotton companies and good transport connections are essential. These conditions are met in Uswausava which, since settlement, has become a major new focus for cotton production and marketing.

Participation in cotton growing, areas planted to cotton and total output have expanded over time (Table 5.8). Cotton production, like maize, is more concentrated among SG1 and SG2 households, but since 2006, when there was a significant expansion in private sector companies operating in the area (see Chapter 7), there has been broad participation.

Table 5.8 Changes in cotton production in Uswhaushava, Chiredzi cluster, 2001-2008 harvests

	2001	2002	2003	2004	2005	2006	2007	2008
% farmers growing cotton	18%	35%	29%	35%	29%	68%	92%	89%
For cotton farmers, average area planted to cotton (ha)	1	1.5	1.6	1.4	1.4	1.7	1.7	2.1
For cotton farmers, average output of cotton (bales = 200kg)	2.3	1.7	0.8	1.6	0.6	5.8	7.5	6.4

Source: Annual crop census, N = 27

Access to inputs is critically dependent on linkages with cotton input supply and marketing companies. These are plentiful in Uswaushava, and there is much competition between them, benefitting the farmers in terms of price, timeliness and the conditions of contracts.

In many respects, despite the lack of tenure security on the informal settlements at Uswaushava, the massive growth in cotton production is a repeat of the success story of the new settlements in the Zambezi valley in the 1980s. Here, new in-migrants from overcrowded communal areas established new settlements and new farm land on a large scale, and cotton production was at the core of the farming system, with positive synergies observed between cotton and food crop production (Govereh and Jayne, 2003). The cotton boom resulted in major knock-on impacts, including the growth of market and service centres such as Gokwe, and a continued in-migration into such areas (Poulton and Hanyani-Mlambo, 2008). While it is too early to tell whether such a dynamic will be repeated in the areas around Uswaushava, the early signs are very positive.

Good yields, high levels of production and a growing skill in cotton production, facilitated by highly competitive market relations, suggest a bright future, if security of tenure is assured. However, this is far from certain. As Chapter 2 noted, these areas on the fringes of the large Nuanetsi ranch are highly contested, and powerful business and political players are eyeing the land for alternative uses. However, in any assessment of the future options, the successes of smallholders, based on a vibrant cotton production system, need to be taken into account.

5.9 Sugar production

In the case of those A2 farmers who received sugar plots, as part of outgrower schemes on the major estates, the irrigation infrastructure was already in place. Farmers were allocated sugar plots primarily across three estates – Triangle, Hippo Valley and Mkwasine (Chapter 7). Many beneficiaries were civil servants, many with a background in agriculture. In contrast to the mixed farming system discussed in previous sections, even when incorporating cotton as a cash crop, cane farming is a very different undertaking. This section offers a brief overview of sugar production in the Hippo valley A2 scheme. Subdivisions of outgrower sugar farms constituted a major portion of A2 schemes in the province. A focused survey was conducted with 35 households in order to examine the dynamics of sugar production following land reform.

New farmers were allocated plots with plot sizes ranging from 9.8ha to 58.1ha. Farmers inherited cane aged between one and 36 months, a relatively young age given the expected production cycle of eight to ten years. Figure 5.2 shows the results for six farming seasons since settlement (mostly 2002-03 to 2007-08). The average yield was highest in the second farming season, at 88 tonnes per hectare, declining to around 56 tonnes per hectare. These yields are low compared to the core estate areas, where inputs are more readily available and management highly focused. However, compared to southern African averages, the productivity of new farmers has been far from disastrous.[9] Nevertheless, a number of challenges have emerged.

The shortage of inputs, especially fertilisers, fuel and other chemicals was a major constraint. Table 5.9 shows the average input use for six farming seasons and the 'industry standard' application rates. Fertiliser application declined at the same time as fuel shortages increased.

Over this period, the relationship between the estate owners and the new settlers became increasingly strained (Chapter 7). As part of sugar contracts, the estate is expected to supply water, fertilisers, agrochemicals and fuel, and sometimes tillage and haulage. Shortages arose,

9 South African industry averages ranged from 60 to 74t/ha between 1995 and 2009. http://www.sasa.org.za/FactsandFigures128.aspx

Figure 5.2 Cane productivity over six farming seasons from settlement

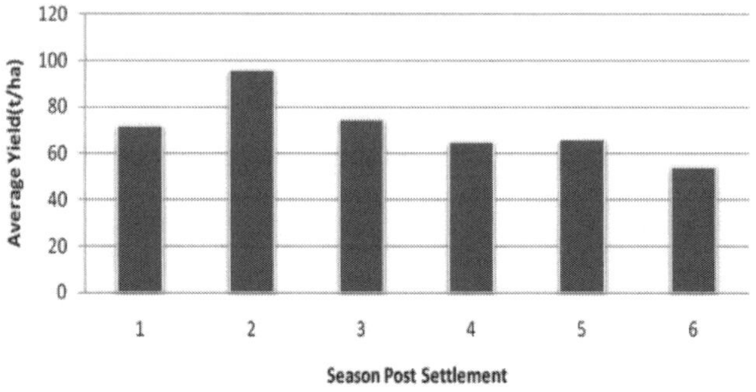

Source: Sugar survey, 2008

Table 5.9 Average amount of fertilisers applied per season in kg per hectare

Input	Standard	2002-03	2003-04	2004-05	2005-06	2006-07	2007-08
Single Super Phosphate	200	185	178	182	132	83	38
Ammonium Nitrate	500	350	319	347	231	170	63
Muriate of Potash	200	172	163	132	86	32	32

Source: Sugar survey, 2008

and accusations of over-charging, late delivery and inefficiency were levelled at the estate. Some new settlers argued that they were being targeted, and that the core estate and remaining outgrowers were not suffering as much. Important determinants of success in cane production include access to transport, irrigation equipment, land preparation equipment and other production assets. No single farmer was fully capitalised in the study area, but there has been some significant acquisition of basic equipment since settlement (Chapter 4). In particular, there was a rise in the ownership of tractors – from 20% in 2003 to 51% in 2008 – and knapsacks, from 29% to 63% over the same period.

In the light of the challenges faced by cane farmers, many settlers have diversified into other crops. This has long been a strategy on the sugar estates, and a diversified portfolio – of wildlife, cattle, citrus and vegetables, as well as cane – has been part of both outgrowers' and estates' strategies. Rather than growing leguminous crops in rotation, as recommended, an increasing number of farmers are removing cane and planting maize and vegetables. Across the sample, an average of 3.7ha was allocated to maize production in 2008, 2.5ha to wheat, 1.6ha to paprika, 1.5ha to beans, 1ha to bananas and 0.4ha to onions. This pattern of diversification accelerated after 2007 when cane production became increasingly difficult. Due to hyperinflationary distortions the payment for outputs was far less than the cost of inputs. This meant that cane was either abandoned, or cane fields converted to other uses.

Unlike the other resettlement sites, on the cane farms there is little room for livestock. Farmers keeping livestock must graze them on peripheral zones of their plots or seek grazing pasture along canals and waterways. For this reason, many A2 cane farmers maintain herds in their communal homes.

5.10 Livestock production

Overall though, livestock populations have been growing on the new resettlements. Cattle, donkeys, goats, poultry and some sheep and pigs are making use of the new fodder resources. Cattle in particular are vital for a range of uses: draught power, transport, milk, manure, meat and sale. And critically, in the period of this study, they are a hedge against inflation. They have wider ritual and cultural importance too, not least as a currency of exchange in bridewealth transactions (Scoones and Wilson, 1988). As discussed in relation to the success rankings, cattle ownership is an important determinant of success and status, and represents a key axis of differentiation.

As Figure 5.3 shows, cattle populations in the province as a whole have fluctuated over time, with major declines during the droughts of 1982-84 and 1991-92. Land reform has resulted in a decline in recorded numbers, but this may be an artefact of poor official reporting. Overall, cattle populations have remained reasonably stable over this period. Most significant of course is the shift in distribution, from large-scale commercial ranches to the new resettlement areas.

At settlement, 39.5% of households across the sites had no cattle. By 2008, this has reduced to 29%. Table 5.10 shows the changes by scheme type and success group. Whereas the proportion of people holding cattle remained constant for SG1 households in A1 villagised schemes, mean cattle holdings increased from 6.3 to 10.4, suggesting a real growth in herd sizes. This reflects a pattern seen in the old resettlements, where average herds increased from three to ten between 1983 and 1995 (Kinsey et al., 1998). In the new resettlements the rate and level of accumulation has been faster and larger, although perhaps more differentiated. The greatest gain since settlement has been experienced by SG2 households in A1 self-contained schemes, where average holdings increased from 1.3 to 10.9. For the A2 households, only the SG1 group experienced a marginal increase from a mean of 18.9 to 20.5, with the other groups experiencing reductions. For the informal schemes, mean holdings for the SG1 households increased from 7.5 to 12.5, with SG2 households experiencing a decline, while SG3 households gained very marginally.

Figure 5.3 Cattle populations in Masvingo province: 1975-2005

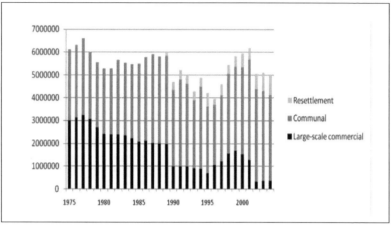

Source: Veterinary Services

Table 5.10 Mean cattle holdings: changes by scheme type and success group

Scheme Type	SG 1		SG 2		SG 3	
	At settlement	2008	At settlement	2008	At settlement	2008
A1	6.3	10.4	4.5	4.5	1.9	2.6
A1 self-contained	11.2	16.2	1.3	10.9	0.9	3.7
A2	18.9	20.5	13.6	14.8	11.1	4.4
Informal	7.5	12.5	4.5	3.8	0.0	0.5

Source: Survey data, 2007-08 (N=177)

The majority of cattle in the new resettlements are female, making up 70% of herds (Figure 5.4). These are largely breeding herds, with the focus being on building up the herd size. Oxen are clearly important for draught power, but many spans are made up of oxen and cows, sometimes combined with donkeys.

People employ many herd-keeping arrangements. Most settlers keep their cattle on their newly acquired plots, some keep a few at their communal homes, while others keep part of their herds on other people's plots. Risk management is central to this strategy. Splitting herds helps in the management of labour and spreads grazing pressure across seasons. Movement between sites over time is a key strategy for herd management (Scoones, 1992a). Insecure tenure may be another factor encouraging herd owners to hedge their bets. The new resettlement

Figure 5.4 Herd composition in Masvingo resettlement herds (Mavedzenge et al., 2006)

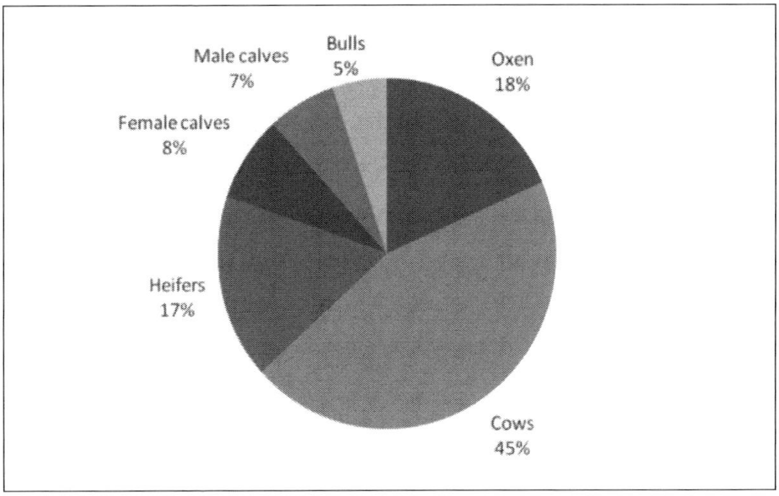

Source: Survey data, 2007-08 (N=177)

areas offer substantial grazing opportunities compared to the communal lands, hence the number of farmers who seek to use other people's plots for their animals.

In addition to cattle, the new farmers have also invested in donkeys, smallstock and poultry. Donkeys are useful for transport and tillage, but there are relatively few given the difficulties in herding them. Table 5.11 looks at patterns of goats and sheep ownership. For all the success groups in A1 villagised schemes, there have been increases in the proportion of people owning goats. A similar trend was observed for the informal schemes. For SG1 and SG3 household in A2 schemes, there were also increases in the proportion of people owning goats, with SG2 households experiencing a decline. The ownership of small livestock is an important source of cash at the household level. Goats and sheep are more readily disposed of than cattle, and so can be sold to cover household needs or emergencies. Goats and sheep are also more easily slaughtered for relish and so the ownership of them can be viewed as an indication of better livelihoods for settlers (Scoones and Wilson, 1988).

Changes in cattle populations are an important indicator of accumulation at the household level, as discussed in Chapter 4. The factors that account for population increases include natural growth, purchases and additions from social networks – bridewealth and other gifts – with by far the largest contribution being from births. Population decreases are explained by sales, deaths, thefts and slaughters. Sales were the largest contributor to herd declines across the sites. A2 schemes have experienced falls in cattle ownership, where losses from thefts and diseases were very common in the period following settlement. In the study sample, 20% of households experienced a net loss in cattle herds, with an average decline of 4.3 animals.

Table 5.11 Changes in the ownership of goats and sheep: from settlement to 2008

Scheme type	Success Group	% households with goats at settlement	% households with goats by 2008	% households with sheep pre-settlement	% households with sheep by 2008
A1 villagised	1	46.2	57.7	8.3	8.3
	2	20.8	45.8	4.3	0.0
	3	55.6	61.1	5.9	0.0
A1 self-contained	1	36.4	54.5	0.0	9.1
	2	11.1	33.3	0.0	0.0
	3	20.0	0.00	0.0	0.0
A2	1	40.0	50.0	10.0	40.0
	2	37.5	31.2	13.3	13.3
	3	42.9	57.1	0.0	14.3
Informal	1	46.2	84.6	0.0	8.33
	2	66.7	100.0	6.7	20.0
	3	25.0	58.3	0.0	0.0

Source: Survey data, 2007-08 (N=177)

In addition to their importance as uses for draught power and transport, local milk and meat consumption, livestock can be an important source of income. For example, 20% of SG1 households in A1 and informal schemes earned money by selling ploughing and transport services in the year before the 2008 survey. The sale of hides and skins (mostly from smallstock) was important for 20% of households in the informal settlements, across success groups, while around a quarter of SG1 and SG2 A2 households engaged in this trade. Milk selling was relatively rare, and involved only a few households in the A2 schemes, while in other areas milk was used for home consumption. Meat sales were similarly rare, and concentrated among a few SG1 households across the schemes. Egg sales were evident in around 30% of SG1 households.

5.11 Accumulating livestock

Many of the new resettlements are thus becoming an important focus for livestock accumulation. While this is highly differentiated, there are wide benefits. The following three cases are illustrative of the emerging patterns:

Case 1
Mrs C of Uswaushava arrived at the scheme with four head of cattle, two cows and two calves. Household proceeds from the sale of cotton and maize were used to finance the acquisition of more. By 2008, the household had 16 cattle, with six cows in milk. On average, about 20 litres of milk was being produced every day. When the household arrived, it had no donkeys, but they had four by 2008, again financed by cotton production. Equally, they had no goats at settlement, but they had 16 by 2008.

Case 2
Mrs M's household, also from Uswaushava, experienced significant herd growth, but then decline. They started with eight cattle, including five cows, which they brought from Makwari. Through births and further acquisitions, the number went up to 28. Several were then sold, with the proceeds being used to purchase a pick-up truck. Some were lost to drought, while others were sold to raise funds for meeting the costs associated with treating the father's illness. The household started with five goats, but they since increased to 18. They had no donkeys but they now have three. Donkeys were particularly useful in ferrying water. Poultry have since been introduced, and the family now have 22 guinea fowl and two turkeys.

Case 3
Mr M at Asveld A2 farm has achieved a rapid increase in cattle numbers since resettlement. He started with 15 in 2000, increasing to 40 by 2008. During this time he sold seven cattle. The proceeds were partly used to finance the purchase of a plough and other farming equipment, such as an ox-cart. They were sold mainly to butcheries, with a few being sold to the Cold Storage Company. He never bought any additional cattle, but his herd was increasing due to natural growth. He attributes the rapid increase to good grazing in the area. At settlement he had ten goats and four donkeys, increasing to 30 and 10

respectively by 2008. The major set-back for the household has been the loss of livestock to traps set by people who hunt wildlife in the area. Since arriving at the plot, he lost ten cattle this way.

Cattle holdings have a direct impact on crop production. Late ploughing and planting, and the inability to be responsive in agricultural production, has a major effect on final outputs. This has been repeatedly shown for communal area production systems (Barrett, 1992), and applies also to the new resettlement areas. Across our sample, cattle holding and maize output and yield are highly correlated.

The total value of cattle on the new resettlements is unquestionably significant. In Chapter 4, we estimated the value of new acquisitions in terms of replacement costs of animals. If we add the value of other livestock populations (donkeys, goats, sheep and pigs), the total value of livestock assets is substantial. Added to this is a range of services and products, especially from cattle, where the value of draught power, transport and manure is substantial (Barrett, 1992; Scoones, 1992b).

Protecting this valuable asset base is essential, but it is under threat. We have already discussed the problem of theft in A2 schemes, but livestock disease is a far greater problem, and affects all livestock populations across the province. With the massive movement of animals between areas because of land reform and exposure to disease-carrying wildlife, there have been some outbreaks, most notably of foot-and-mouth disease (FMD) which broke out in 2003 and spread across the country. While the major outbreaks have subsided, FMD is effectively endemic in cattle populations today, making the prospects of returning to high-value beef exports very challenging (Sibanda, 2008). Since 2000 there has been very little veterinary support in the new resettlement areas. With contracting budgets and a freeze on appointments, government veterinary services were unable to extend their reach to the new resettlement areas, as they were barely coping elsewhere. Imports of dipping chemicals and veterinary drugs were limited.

Data on cattle disease incidence in Masvingo province shows some major increases since the mid-1990s (Figure 5.5). Different diseases have different effects. In indigenous cross-bred cattle, for example, FMD is relatively mild. Diseases which are tick-borne or derived from soil-based organisms caused most mortalities. Blackleg, heartwater, babeosis and anthrax resulted in the largest recorded mortality in this period, and this reflected farmers' ranking of disease impact (Mavedzenge et al., 2006).

Without a network of dip tanks, and with very few veterinary officers visiting the new resettlements, herd owners cope on their own. There was a significant increase in the use of hand sprayers for removing ticks, as well as the purchase of drugs on the informal market (Mavedzenge et al., 2006).

Chapter 7 discusses the marketing of cattle in more depth, and in particular the radical restructuring of the commodity chain. As cattle herds build up, potentials for sale increase. However, most studies estimate that herd sizes must reach at least ten before regular sales are possible (Behnke, 1985). To date, only 39.3% of all cattle owners across the sample have herd sizes this large, so significant sales are not

Figure 5.5: Disease incidence in Masvingo province (reported cases), 1995-2005

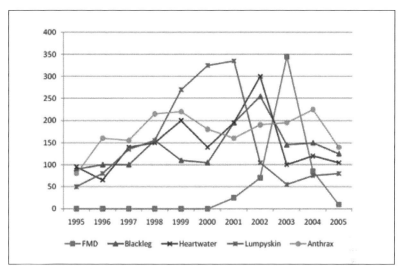

Source: Department of Veterinary Services, Masvingo.

expected. Purchases are also limited due to cash shortages. Across the sites, a total of only 26 cattle were purchased by eight households in the 12 months before the 2008.

While market exchanges are relatively small, the importance of the growing livestock populations – involving a diversity of species – should not be underestimated. This is an important source of wealth and security, and a vital input to agriculture.

5.12 Prospects for production: A new green revolution?

Many argue that land reform is a precondition for a successful green revolution in Africa, so that the scale advantages of smallholder production are taken advantage of (Lipton, 2009). Does the new agriculture in the Masvingo province resettlement areas represent a nascent green revolution?

The signs are mixed. While there has been a substantial increase in production (from a base of effectively zero for crop production), this has been unevenly distributed across time, space and socio-economic group. With their lower establishment costs, the A1 and informal schemes have quickly created fully-functional cropping enterprises. By contrast, a number of A2 farmers are overwhelmed by the scale of their farming operations, and are unable to invest in the necessary equipment and infrastructure. The top 40% of households (SG1 and some of SG2) are producing the majority of outputs and selling the most. This is arguably more evenly distributed than in the communal areas in the 1980s, where a revolution in maize production resulted in massive increases in output. At that time, the highly productive group was a much narrower proportion, around 20% (Stanning, 1989).

While SG1 households generally have the assets and resources for effective farming, others are struggling. However, SG2 households show significant potential, even if it is not yet fully realised. This growth in production has been achieved largely without external support, and with limited external inputs in terms of improved seeds and fertiliser. If a green revolution at all, it is one based on skill, effort and hard labour, and the benefits of new land – primarily a process of agricultural extensification, rather than one of technology-driven intensification, as in the classic green revolution model.

Can this be enhanced through investment and support, transforming extensification into intensification? Clearly there is demand for seeds, fertilisers and other technologies, especially those involving water control. If these are provided, will there be uptake and will this generate a positive cycle of growth? As was clear in Asia in the 1960s and 1970s, the earliest innovators are those who can make use of new technologies in high-risk situations, with poor credit and output markets, although there was substantial spread later on (Lipton and Longhurst, 1989). In the new resettlements a similar dynamic can be envisaged, with SG1 and SG2 farmers in A1 self-contained sites being the most likely to respond to new forms of support, at least initially. Through focused interventions, this could have major impacts, as we discuss in Chapter 11.

The high variability in output due to variations in rainfall (both amount and distribution) is indicative of the fragility of achievements. With climate change expected to affect southern African farming systems dramatically, there is a strong likelihood that such inter- and intra-annual rainfall variability will increase, and average rainfall totals decline (Manatsa and Matarira 2009). Maize production is highly correlated with rainfall (Cane et al., 1994), which implies problems for the future if maize is to be the major source of food security and market sale for new resettlement farmers. Of course, maize is not the only crop grown. Farmers across the study sites have diversified production to cope with such variability and reduce risk. Drought-tolerant crops such as sorghum and millet are vitally important in crop mixes. Cotton too has become important, as have other higher value crops which can give better returns on smaller areas, such as vegetables, paprika and soya beans, especially with improved micro-irrigation systems.

The data presented in this chapter fundamentally challenges the myth that there has been a total collapse in agricultural production, and that the consequence of land reform has been widespread food insecurity in all places in all years. This is simply not the case, at least across the sites in Masvingo. Outside the serious drought years, most households across most schemes have produced enough for their own provisioning, and often substantial amounts for sale. While the newspaper headlines around the world emphasised the collapse of agriculture and the growth in food insecurity in the country, the new farmers were getting on with establishing their new farms and producing, sometimes in very substantial amounts.

This disconnect between perception and reality became most apparent following the 2008-09 season which resulted in very substantial production. At the same time, the aid agencies and those interested in discounting any success in land reform, were proclaiming impending famine and need for massive food imports.[10] In part this mismatch of field reality and broader commentary can be put down to ideological position, but it is also due to the simple lack of data. Formal data collection systems in the country are very weak. The Ministry of Agriculture is unable to undertake in-depth crop assessments, and most figures are simply guesses. While a number of external agencies work with the government as part of the ZimVac and famine early warning systems, their coverage and understanding of the new resettlement areas remains poor, and major inter-agency disputes over figures and their interpretation have often resulted.[11]

But documenting the relative success of agricultural production on the new resettlements does not mean that there are no problems. Far from it. The failure of input supply and delivery has seriously hampered production and, until 2009, the distorting policy environment has undermined deliveries of grain to the formal marketing system – in turn reinforcing the perception that production had collapsed and extreme food insecurity was rife. In terms of cash crops, while cotton appears to be thriving, sugar production has been struggling, although with dollarisation and a return to some sort of sanity in agricultural policy, the prospects look better. The big boom in livestock holdings is very important, but with small herd sizes this is not yet translating into high off-take levels. With veterinary support virtually non-existent in the resettlement areas and dipping all but ceased, protecting animal health is a major challenge.

Success in agriculture is also highly differentiated. Those with assets, labour and capital have made good use of the new land, while others have fared less well. Around 40% of households are producing well and selling regularly. Is this sufficient to generate broad-based growth and feed the nation? As Chapter 11 discusses, support for agriculture will have to be targeted effectively to allow those with the potential to boost production, as well as increase productivity. Others may not be able to achieve high levels of output, but will compose their livelihoods in other ways, sometimes supplying labour to the high producers. These differentiated dynamics in the new resettlement areas are returned to in Chapter 10, as they are key to understanding future agrarian dynamics in the new resettlement areas.

Such patterns of differentiation are important across scheme types too. Agricultural production on A2 farms, A1 self-contained plots and in the villagised areas of A1 and informal schemes has different potentials. There are, however, opportunities for galvanising important synergies on an area basis. These may result in different farmers focus-

[10] See for example: http://www.zimonline.co.za/Article.aspx?ArticleId=5318 from the CFU and http://www.wfp.org/news/news-release/zimbabwe-higher-production-food-insecurity-persists. From WFP, although see: http://www.reliefweb.int/rw/rwb.nsf/db900SID/SODA-7Z2RQ4?OpenDocument&RSS20=02 for a more balanced assessment.

[11] A similar set of policy debates dominated the 1980s and 1990s, and substantial research (e.g. Rukuni and Eicher, 1994) highlighted the structural complexities of food security issues, and what Jayne and Chisvo (1991) identified as Zimbabwe's food insecurity paradox, with hunger existing amid substantial potential (Jayne and Rukuni, 1994).

ing on different elements of a commodity chain (for example, breeding versus fattening stock, or production versus processing of crops), or allow specialisation in products which have strong demand in local markets (for example, horticultural crops). As we discuss in Chapter 11, the opportunities for capitalising on area-based agricultural development, and so fostering economic linkages and multipliers, may be significant, but have barely been addressed.

Small-scale farming, under the right conditions, can generate livelihoods and be a motor of wider growth. But the policy environment for much of the period since settlement has not been supportive. In 2009-10 the situation has improved. With the arrival of the inclusive government and the dollarisation and subsequent stabilisation of the economy, a new agricultural policy regime appears to be slowly emerging, involving a re-liberalisation of markets and the removal of price controls. At the same time, agricultural policy is once again controlled through the Ministry of Agriculture; the RBZ and the security forces have been removed as the main financier and policy maker. However, even with a more benign policy environment, all is not well in the agricultural sector, and a long period of recovery is envisaged.

If the benefits of land reform are to be captured and sustained, a substantial rethink of policy approaches will be required. With diverse, small-scale production systems across A2, A1 self-contained and villagised systems (in communal and resettlement areas), linked to different markets and with different comparative advantages, opportunities for integration not possible under the old dualistic system of the past open up. How the new agrarian structure will perform remains to be seen. But there are many potentials, as well as many challenges. A return to the 1980s or 1990s is not an option. This is a new agrarian system, with new policy priorities. The debate on what this will entail is only just beginning, but hopefully a greater understanding of the potentials and challenges of crop and livestock production contained in this chapter will help in this search for appropriate policy options for the future.

6

Labour ▓ The New
Farm Workers

6.1 Farm labour post-2000

The post-2000 land reform in Zimbabwe has resulted in a significant displacement of farm workers from former large-scale commercial farms.[1] However, the scale and implications of this are much disputed. Triangulating across multiple sources, there seems to be broad agreement that, in the late 1990s, there were around 350,000 farm workers on large-scale farms and estates. Of these, around 150,000 were permanent workers, making up a total population of around one million, including dependents.[2] In the new settlements established after 2000, around 10,000 households were established by those who were formerly permanent farm workers, along with others who were temporary farm workers and joined the land invasions.[3] Perhaps a further 70,000 permanent worker households remained in work on estates, state farms and large-scale farms, including such operations as the sugar estates in Masvingo province.[4] There are also substantial numbers of *in situ* displaced people still on farms but without work, perhaps around 25,000 households according to some estimates. These are predominantly in the Highveld areas where significant farm-worker populations resided on the farms, many without connections elsewhere and originally migrants from other countries in the region.[5] Nationally, this implies

---

[1] See: Magaramombe (2003); Sachikonye (2003a, 2004); Rutherford (2001a, b, 2003); Waeterloos and Rutherford (2004); Hartnack (2005); Chambati and Moyo (2004); Chambati (2007) and Chambati and Magaramombe (2008) for discussion of this issue from different perspectives.
[2] Based on the national census of 1992, and surveys by others including USAID in the late 1990s (Chambati, 2007).
[3] The numbers of FTLRP beneficiaries who were former farm workers is particularly disputed. Our study showed 6.7% of the total sample (Chapter 2), while AIAS studies showed around 10% from the six-district survey (Moyo, 2009). Other estimates have been as high as 15% and as low as 2%. Clearly there is much variability, as well as problems in reporting.
[4] In 2003, the CFU estimated around 85,000 workers were still employed, although this number has undoubtedly declined. Evictions since 2008 have, according to some estimates, resulted in further displacements (JAG/RAU, 2009).
[5] IDMC (2008); Magaramombe (2010).

that around 45,000 permanent worker households were displaced and had to move elsewhere – to other rural areas or towns – while others who were temporary workers had to seek new sources of income, including as labourers on the new farms.

Patterns of displacement and resettlement vary dramatically across the country. In the Highveld areas, where highly capitalised farms required large amounts of labour – for instance for tobacco or horticulture operations – displacements were significant. Outside these areas, the pattern was different. This is the case in Masvingo province, where land reform displaced largely ranch operations which offered limited employment. There are no good estimates of total labour – and dependents – on the case-study sites prior to land reform, but a 'standard' ranching operation would involve one worker per 100 head of cattle. With stocking rates at around ten livestock units per hectare, this would add up to around one worker (plus perhaps five dependents) per 1,000ha of land.[6] The amount of labour would vary depending on the ranching operation and the agroecological conditions. For example, before land reform in the wetter zone of Chatsworth area, the 2,800ha Northdale farm used to stock at one livestock unit per six hectares. There were around 400 beef cattle looked after by four labourers. On the same farm there was in addition a dairy herd of 200, supplemented with irrigated pasture which additionally employed another eight labourers, as well as two herders. In the drier Mwenezi area, the massive 18,000ha Edenvale farm had around 4,000 head of cattle looked after by 40 herders. Today, Northdale is an A2 farm with 11 plots, each employing varying numbers of workers running mixed farming operations, involving both cropping and livestock production. Edenvale farm is now largely an A1 villagised scheme (except for a small portion left with the original owners, an orphanage and an irrigated area), with 18 villages each with 20-30 households, most employing labour. As the rest of this chapter shows, patterns of labour have changed dramatically.

What happened to the former farm workers on the ranches of Masvingo province? Access to resettlement varied from scheme to scheme. This very much depended on the dynamics of the *jambanja* period on a particular farm. Many farm workers did not join the invasions, out of loyalty to their employers or due to the fear of the consequences of doing so. But others did, and this was relatively common in the Masvingo sites, with some farm workers actually leading invasions onto farms that they worked on (Chapter 2). In often very large ranches there was little control over the working population. Farm workers lived in small cottages near the farm houses, but with farm owners often holding multiple farms they were often not resident. Unlike in the tobacco-growing zones of the Highveld, most farm workers in the Masvingo farms were local residents, coming from nearby communal areas and were not from families who originated from Malawi or Mozambique, even if long-settled, second-generation Zimbabwean citizens. This meant they had social connections with nearby communal lands, allowing linkages with the land invasions to be forged.

---

[6] Based on discussions with Provincial Veterinary Department officials, December 2009. See also Clarke (1977).

What happened to those farm workers who did not get land? Our research has not managed to trace all the former farm workers who worked on the study sites, but scattered evidence suggests that most returned to nearby communal lands and sought land from local village headmen. Others already had land and simply returned to their other home where their families lived. Thus, since there were very few farm workers from migrant families, the pattern of 'squatting' on farms where they formerly worked seen in other parts of the country was not evident. Equally, farm workers in Masvingo were not targeted as a group and subjected to intimidation and violence as has been reported in other areas (JAG/RAU, 2008, 2009).

In the past, farm workers have been a highly exploited group (Clarke, 1977; Loewenson, 1992; Amanor-Wilks, 1995; Kanyenze, 2001; Tandon, 2001). While the work by unions, NGOs and government regulation improved their lot, conditions were often very poor.[7] In Masvingo province, monthly wages in the late 1990s ranged from US$10 for a general hand or herd boy, rising to around US$25 for a skilled worker/driver. Wages were supplemented by the provision of housing, and sometimes access to health care and education, but this was rare on the farms in Masvingo because of the low density of farm worker populations and the large distances between farms. This meant that many farm workers' families had no access to support services on the farms, and had to rely on connections in the nearby communal areas, where children were sent to school or where clinics could be found.

Farm labour was not just important in the large-scale commercial sector. The assumption that all smallholder farms in communal and old resettlement areas were simply family farms, with labour exclusively derived from family labour is incorrect. In many areas there is a large floating population of workers, many landless or deeply impoverished (Adams, 1991a, b). Such workers, mostly male, may take up employment as herders or labourers on farms, sometimes in exchange for a cash income, access to milk or maybe occasionally a calf, but very often simply for the provision of accommodation and food. The conditions were often appalling, with no rights or external support. In the 1980s, in southern Zimbabwe, this population was made up of large numbers of Mozambicans who were fleeing the civil war in their own country. With the arrival of peace in Mozambique many returned home, and instead farm labour was made up of Zimbabweans, many of whom had been retrenched as a result of structural adjustment and were too poor to establish homes and farms in their home area. Others were the orphans of parents who had died from AIDS and had not been incorporated into another home, or were too young and poor to establish a home themselves. In addition to labourers, usually unrelated to the farm households, who stayed at the homestead and worked on a semi-permanent basis, there are many other forms of labour arrangement in the

---

[7] The Labour Relations Act (Chapter 28:01) provides the legislative framework for farm workers' wages, and the General Agricultural and Plantation Workers Union of Zimbabwe (GAPWUZ) engages in wage negotiation with employees. While post-Independence compliance with labour laws improved dramatically, minimum conditions were not always adhered to. While the same laws obtain in the new resettlement areas, they are applied in very few places (Chambati, 2008; FCTZ, 2001).

communal and old resettlement areas. These include piecework, where people were paid for the task or by the day or hour in cash or in kind, and collective work, where groups of people are invited to undertake agricultural tasks as part of a communal work party (*humwe*), where either a reciprocal arrangement is understood, or some form of payment, usually in the form of food, beer or *maheu*, is offered.

Advocates of smallholder-focused land reform argue that it should raise farmers' demand for labour, including hired labour, while reducing the supply of labour to the market of land reform beneficiaries. This should in turn increase rural wages, improving the lot of even those who got no land (Lipton, 2009: 23, 53). A number of key questions arise for this study. What has replaced the earlier pattern of farm labour on the large-scale commercial and communal areas or old resettlement farms? Are these beneficial economic dynamics evident? Is there now more or less employment on the farms? Who are the new farm workers, and what are their wages and conditions? And, overall, what does this tell us about emerging patterns of rural differentiation, class dynamics and agrarian change in the new resettlements? These are very difficult questions to answer categorically, but the following sections offer some hints.

What the data from Masvingo adds up to – supported by other surveys – is a challenge to the standard narratives about farm workers in the post-land reform era. Certain farm workers in some places have lost out badly, suffering terrible abuses and deepening impoverishment (Sachikonye, 2003a; JAG/RAU, 2008, 2009), but this has not been universal, and a more differentiated analysis is required. In general, a new configuration of labour has emerged, with substantial numbers of new farm workers of diverse sorts. This has, we argue later, some major consequences for future agrarian change trajectories in the new resettlements.

6.2 Farm labour: changing patterns

Sam Moyo (2009: 14) reports that, following land reform, 'A new pattern of increased farm labour utilisation and (mostly informal, casual and short term) employment has now emerged across a more diverse agrarian structure.' Of course it all rather depends on the definition of a job and what is counted as employment. As discussed above, this ranges from fixed and standardised contracts to the most casual and temporary of arrangements. All are important, but it is very difficult to get to grips with the implications when lumping all types of labour together. First, these are different arrangements, with different implications for people's livelihoods; for some, selling labour is the core of their livelihood strategy, for others farm employment is simply an addition to a range of other activities, often in the off-season for agriculture. Secondly, the relationships between worker and farmer are very different. In some cases, the relationship is that between capitalist farm owner and worker; in others, relatives and friends are engaged as labourers in less formal arrangements.

In the new resettlements the classic division between farm owner and a workforce of labourers is often not so easy to define. Substantial parts of the new labour force may be family labour, sometimes attracted to the new resettlements as part of in-migration (Chapter 3, and below). And hired labour, where wages are paid, may be often on an informal basis, with piecework wages offered. In the period of hyperinflation, especially in 2006-08, cash wages became worthless and payment in kind was essential. Some workers were offered stakes in the farm, with small plots carved out or the opportunity to herd livestock offered. Others took resources in lieu of wages, selling crops, livestock or natural resources from the farm, very often without the knowledge of the farm owner. As with everything in the post-2000 period, the story is more complex than the standard narratives suggest.

The casualisation of labour in informal, temporary arrangements often has a gender dimension. Much of this informal labour is female, reliant on piecework and short-term employment. In the former large-scale farm sector, female labour often had few rights, with access to casual employment afforded through co-residence with a husband with a job (Loewenson, 1992; Goebel, 2005b). Such gendered patterns, as discussed below, are seen on the new resettlements too.

Disaggregating the category 'farm worker' is thus essential. Multiple identities and patterns of belonging exist within the single category (Rutherford, 2001b, 2003). Moyo et al. (2009, Figure 6.2) estimate that 67% of new settlers in six district study sites across the country use hired labour, with an average labour pool of 3.5 persons. Chambati (2007: 32) reports on a detailed study from Zvimba. In A1 farms, a third of households have permanent workers, while around 70% hire part-time workers. By contrast, in the A2 farms, around 60% hire permanent workers and 87% hire part-time workers. A similar pattern exists in our study sites. For the A1 and informal schemes, 60% of households hire in temporary labour, while 19% of households also hire permanent labour. In these sites, on average households hire 1.9 temporary labourers and employ 0.5 permanent workers. In the A2 schemes, all households hire temporary labour and 78% hire permanent labour. In these sites, on average, households hire in 7.3 temporary workers and employ 5.1 permanent workers (Table 6.1)

Permanent labour hiring is most common in the A2 and A1 self-contained schemes, for both cropping and livestock herding. Most permanent labour is male, although this varies across sites. For the A1 villagised and informal sites, seasonal labour is more prevalent, generally women, and especially for cropping tasks. Temporary workers help during land clearing, ploughing, planting, weeding, harvesting and processing and come from a variety of places. Most do not stay at the farm, returning to their homesteads at night. Payment may be in cash, but after 2006 it was mostly in kind, including salt, oil, maize and groundnuts.

The following table looks at how labour hiring patterns for a range of activities are differentiated across success groups in the A1 and informal sites and contrasts these with those found in the A2 farms.

Table 6.1 Patterns of permanent and temporary labour hiring

	A1 and informal					A2				
	Temporary cropping	Temporary livestock	Permanent both	Permanent cropping	Permanent livestock	Temporary cropping	Temporary livestock	Permanent both	Permanent cropping	Permanent livestock
Percentage of households employing workers	20	13	9	11	9.3	67.6	43.5	44.8	71.9	43.3
Percentage of these female	48	31	26	32	25	27	7	23	26	28

Source: Survey, 2007–08 (N=177)

6.3 The new farm workers: case-studies

To get a better idea of the realities of the new farm worker, beyond the generalised statistics presented above, this section offers a series of cases from across our study areas, including all scheme types. These necessarily offer only a partial view, but they do give some insights into the very real hardships of farm labour, and some of the emerging relationships that exist between the new land owners and labour, of different types. The following categories are highlighted: permanent, hired labour with and without the farmer present (men and women, with and without families), temporary piecework labour (mostly female) and collective labour, linked to both kin and church networks.

PERMANENT, HIRED LABOUR AND ABSENT OWNER

My name is IC. I am 21 years old and am a general worker on GT's farm (A2 Northdale, Gutu cluster). I came from Salem farm where my parents own a plot. I am unmarried. I started working for Mr T in September 2008. At present I am paid US$50 per month. In addition to pay I am provided with food and soap. We are accommodated in houses at the farm. GT, a soldier and younger brother of the farm owner, supervises us. There are three workers. We do a variety of jobs that include cattle herding, cultivation, planting, weeding, harvesting, processing and gardening. I get two days off every month. Sometimes he fails to pay us in time but we ultimately get paid. I managed to buy clothes, a radio and a solar converter from my earnings here.

My name is MM. I am 41 years old and work for Mr S on Northdale farm (A2, Gutu cluster). I come from Mazhawidza village in Chief Chitsa's area in Gutu district. I have stayed with my family here at plot 11 Northdale from October 2008. Mr S is a businessman staying in Masvingo. He owns grocery shops. I herd cattle, but I am also involved in other work like erecting cattle kraals, digging manure and crop cultivation. During the cropping period he visits the farm twice per month. I am paid US$70 per month. Mealie meal is provided and he allows us to sell milk and keep the money. We get an average of 15 litres of milk per day. I managed to buy four stools, a radio and clothes for the family since coming here.

My name is NG. I work in Clare farm (A1 self-contained, Gutu cluster). I came from Kunurai village near Morgenster in Masvingo district. I came to this farm where I live with my wife and five children. I earn US$20 per month. In addition to that we are allowed to keep all the crops we cultivate for our own use. We also cultivate a garden and sell vegetables and pocket the proceeds. My main job is cattle herding. The pay is too little. I have no possessions to talk about. At times my wife also works at the plot, although she is not on the payroll.

My name is PZ. I am 30 years old and work for BJ at Clare farm. I came from Chinga village in Serima. I am paid US$80 per month. I am accommodated at the plot together with my wife and two children. We get food and basic grocery items from the owner. Besides that she allows us to go and plough in other

Table 6.2 Labour hiring by activity across success groups

		A1 and informal			A2
		SG1	SG2	SG3	All success groups
Seasonal, temporary labour	% households of those hiring seasonal labour hiring in for clearing and ploughing	28%	22%	23%	44%
	% of these men	77%	58%	75%	61%
	% hiring in for planting/transplanting	13%	20%	8%	42%
	% of these men	18%	56%	67%	57%
	% hiring in for weeding	51%	37%	18%	64%
	% of these men	41%	40%	45%	58%
	% hiring in for harvesting	31%	16%	13%	68%
	% of these men	57%	40%	32%	73%
	% hiring in for herding	22%	13%	3%	43%
	% of these men	68%	75%	n.d.	93%
Permanent labour	% of those hiring permanent labour hiring for cropping	11%	14%	8%	72%
	Average nos hired for cropping	2.0	4.2	2.0	3.8
	% of which men	50%	71%	78%	74%
	% hiring for livestock	14%	14%	0%	43%
	Average nos hired for livestock	1.2	1.2	-	1.9
	% of which men	83%	67%	-	72%

Source: Survey data, 2007-08 (N=177; n.d. – no data)

people's fields using her draught animals and keep the money. I am supplied with overalls and gumboots. I am allowed to go home whenever I request. Since working here, I managed to buy goats which are at my Serima home. We have very good working relations with the employer.

My name is BC. I am 26 years old and I originate from Chikarudzo village near Morgenster Mission. I work for FC at Northdale farm. My father used to work at this farm for the former owner. I grew up here. My father later worked for Mr C after land reform, but has now retired and gone home to Morgenster. I started working at this place under the previous owner in 1997. I stay with my wife in the compound, but she is not part of the workforce. I am paid US$30 per month which is very little. I did not manage to purchase anything substantial with the money. We do not have any protective clothing. There is no supervisor at this plot with four workers. Mr C is fully in charge although he lives in Masvingo town. He visits the plot often. Duties include operating the grinding mill, herding cattle and the cultivation of crops. The job is too much. I think more workers should be employed. We do not have leave days, but we are given time to go and sort out domestic problems back home.

My name is SP. I am 32 years old and I am manager at my uncle's plot in Northdale farm (A2, Gutu cluster). I came to stay with my uncle (my mother's brother) in 2007 after my husband died in 2004 in Birimawe village in Magunje district, Karoi. My children stay in Magunje with my mother-in-law. I am manager at this plot but earning only US$30. The three men I supervise get US$50 each per month! Men do jobs like ploughing, herding cattle, dipping and milking. All workers enjoy good relations with Mr M. Workers normally get off days on Thursdays and Wednesday is half day. If someone has a problem to settle at home one week off can be given. I give mealie meal, soap and meat sometimes to the workers. Mr M has promised to buy overalls and gumboots for us. Since working here I bought clothes and groceries for my kids, some blankets and a cell phone. We stay in pole-and-mud huts which we built ourselves. Mr M's mother lives at the plot too.

Turf ranch, Informal, Mwenezi cluster. Under the former farmer, there were a total of 21 workers – 20 men and 1 woman. Most of these workers still work on nearby farms, mostly the A2 plots. Seven (from a total of 17) settlers on the informal Turf ranch employ permanent workers, totalling 13. Some of these worked on the ranch before. Some former workers are now plot holders at Turf, having joined the invasion. They now pursue both farm labour off the farm, and farming on the farm where they formerly worked. Of the original 21 workers, around half were Shangaans who came from nearby Gezani area; others were Maranda Pfumbi people. The locally-based Shangaans were the ones who predominantly returned to their communal homes following the land invasions, while the others have remained in the area, either as workers or worker-farmers. In addition to new A2 farmers (as in the case of Asveld ranch), a number of farms in the Mateki hills are still occupied by the original owners. Most of these have links with South Africa, and often have second homes there. Over the last few years, few have been resident in Zimbabwe, and only make occasional visits. Surrounding Turf there are six farms of this sort, each with workers managing the plots, and the remaining livestock.

My name is TC. I am 69 years old. I am employed at a plot in Asveld ranch in Mwenezi cluster where I have worked since 2005. I was born in Neshuro and previously worked on the farms in Zvishavane district as a herder. I never went to school, but have skills in carving which I do to supplement my meagre salary. In fact, during 2008, at the peak of the economic crisis, I was not being paid at all. My wife previously stayed with me at the farm, and she was paid for odd jobs. But without pay, she left and returned to our village home where she farms. She sometimes comes to Asveld and collects mopane worms for sale in the villages. All the workers at this and neighbouring farms live in a few houses, part of the original farm dwellings on the ranch. It is very cramped accommodation.

My name is MH. I was born in 1969 and came from Neshuro. I work in Asveld A2 farm. I achieved grade 5 education, but my father was poor and could not afford to educate me further. Later, I was displaced by the building of a dam, and relocated to Nyajena where I married. I worked in various farms during the 1980s and 1990s, and from 1994 worked at Flora farm on the Beitbridge-Harare road. With the farm invasions starting from 2000, the work was disrupted. However I joined the invaders, secretly attending their meetings at night. I got a plot, but the problems of water were many. Me and my wife constructed a well and started a vegetable growing/selling business which has proved successful. I was offered a job at Asveld farm in 2003, with R300 per month as pay. This was very little, and my wife continued with the vegetable business at our resettlement plot. However, the additional cash income was useful and I was able to pursue my carving and shoe repairing businesses from the farm. I am planning to quit: the money is insufficient and the vegetable business on the A1 resettlement is more lucrative.

My name is IS. I work at a plot in Asveld A2 farm. I was born in 1980 in Ngundu area of Chivi communal area. I did grade 7 education, and then worked as a domestic worker. My husband was employed as a worker here, and I later came, getting a job in 2008. The rules are relaxed as the owner only comes once a month, if at all. I get poorly paid, at only R250 per month. I am involved in overseeing the irrigated maize and cotton production on the farm, and also I cook for the other labourers living here. The owners have not employed temporary labour this year, so the pressure of work is high. The men focus on fence repairs, cattle herding and dipping, and receive a higher salary at R300 per month. The job is very tough. The lack of communication is difficult too. If the engine is out of order, messages must be sent 20km to Sheba ranch in order to contact the owners. There are just two huts, made from poles and mud. I share one with my husband and child, while the other is occupied by the three male labourers. We also have a shared kitchen which I manage.

PERMANENT HIRED LABOUR, STAYING AT PLOT WITH OWNER AND FAMILY

My name is GC. I am 36 years old and work at Northdale A2 farm for Mrs GG. I came from Tafirenyika village Mubhada area in Gutu where my wife lives because she cultivates our fields. She stays with our two children back home but visits me once in a while. I began working at this plot for Mrs GG on

16 August 2008. My salary is US$40 per month. In addition to money I am allowed to cultivate one acre each year for myself. The problem is she takes over that land the following season and I move over to another virgin land which I destump and clear again. I am also not given enough time to work my field. I mostly work at night. She provides draught animals for ploughing. My main duties are cattle herding, land clearing and cultivation of crops. There are no stipulated times of duty and the work is mostly very laborious. There is nothing like leave days, but when something has to be settled at my original home she lets me go. I also wish she could provide me with work suits, overalls and gumboots. In spite of everything Mrs G is very free and treats me as her son.

My name is RT. I come from Gutu Runyowa. I am married and stay with my wife at CP's farm (at Clare A1 self-contained). I am CP's nephew: his father is my father's brother. I have accommodation at the homestead. He provides us with all the food and other basic necessities but we buy our own clothes. I am paid US$30 per month. Mr P seldom comes and sometimes I go for two to three months without pay. My job includes herding cattle, crop farming and repairing the plot fence. I so far managed to buy some clothes.

My name is NT. I am 33 years old and work at Mr TM's plot in Clare farm. I am related to TM's wife. I came in August 2009. Before I was working at another plot here, but we had money disputes. I stay with my wife and three children. We are supplied with food. Mr M is a pensioner and stays at the plot. My main jobs are ploughing, weeding, herding cattle and other home chores. I earn US$30 per month and am given old clothes. I have no off days. Since coming I have bought plates, pots and blankets. We have good working relations. He constantly asks me if I have problems so we can settle them.

HOLDING THE PLOT: MANAGING ON BEHALF OF OTHERS

My name is TK. I come from Murehwa in Gusha village and I am looking after Mr KC's plot at Clare farm (A1 self-contained, Gutu cluster). I am married and staying with my family at the plot. I am not a worker, but came to help my relative. Mr C is my aunt's husband. I live here in Mr C's homestead. When he is not here I organise work at the farm, but when he is around he can supervise. Jobs include cropping, mainly maize, groundnuts and beans. There is a garden and when I sell vegetables Mr C gets the money. Cattle herding is another duty. I started residing at the plot in 2005. In return for my labour I get mealie meal, clothes and sometimes money. He just gives me what he wants. I am his relative. Since coming to this place I managed to buy clothes, blankets, rabbits and household utensils.

My name is TC. I am 29 years old and looking after JC's plot at Wondedzo Wares (A1 villagised, Masvingo cluster). I come from Maungwa, Gutu. I am married with two kids. My husband is a trainee teacher at Morgenster College. I came to plot 27 Wondedzo B in December 2009 to help my brother. He is self-employed in Masvingo town and does not stay at the plot. His last employee whom he fired was stealing inputs and other things at the plot. I do not get any pay. Instead I am allowed to grow crops for my own family at this plot. He gives me food and basic necessities.

My name is EM. I own plot 28 in Wondedzo B villagised. I come from Nerupiri Gutu and am married with a wife, two boys and one girl. My brother Nhidza is a cross-border truck driver based in South Africa, but he often comes. I have been managing number 44 Wondedzo B villagised plot on his behalf for a year. The plot used to belong to another relative, CM, who returned to his original home in Nyajena. I supervise workers on jobs such as herding cattle, ploughing, planting, weeding, harvesting and threshing. My children also help in my brother's fields. He gives me US$30 per month and groceries and clothes from South Africa.

My name is EC. I am 19 years old and single. I came here to help Mrs EM at Clare farm as she is a leader at my church. We are both Catholics and I am a member of the Simon Peter group. I do not have a stipulated pay, but she gives me some money. She gives me clothes, blankets and other basics too. I am an orphan so she sometimes supplies my family with maize. I have a sister and brother who stay with our grandmother at home in Serima. My main jobs are crop growing, cattle herding and gardening. I stay at the plot, but she allows me to go home whenever I want to.

PIECEWORK

My name is GZ. I am 28. I come from Zimuto. I am married and live in Zimuto with my three children and husband who is not employed. I move around plots (in Gutu district) seeking for piece jobs like weeding, harvesting and watering vegetable gardens. In most cases I work for food, particularly maize. We did not get a good harvest in Zimuto last season so we are short of food. Most plot holders pay us with maize at a rate of one bucket for weeding ten lines approximately 100 metres long. In some cases I am paid cash at a rate of US$1 per three lines. Some plot holders give me food to eat while working, others do not. Accommodation is provided for the period I will be working. My husband stays at home with the children.

My name is VZ. I am 30 years old. I come from Javangwe village in Serima. I am married with three children. My husband is a farm worker at Driefontein Mission. During the peak growing season every year I go to Clare farm and other surrounding areas to seek for piece jobs, mostly weeding. I do this in order to source money for the grinding mill and for purchasing family basics. Recently I was weeding at Mr C's plot. He paid me one dollar per line, but the lines were too long. On average I manage to work for five dollars per day. Mr M in Lonely farm paid me at a rate of one bucket of maize for 15 lines. I return home every day after work because resettlement plots are near my home area.

My name is JS. I am 46 years old. I was married, but my husband is late. I have a family of five to attend to. I do not have cattle so I must work in other people's fields to get food. I mostly work for maize, clothes and soap. There is no stipulated deal for weeding; you must negotiate with the plot holder. Mr C gave me a bucket of maize for eight lines. Mrs EC of Lonely farm gave me clothes for weeding one acre of groundnuts. Mr V at Lonely farm and Mr C at Clare farm provide food when doing the job. Others do not give anything, and we must work on empty stomachs. I operate from home every day moving around plots with my hoe. At times my children accompany me and help with weeding.

COLLECTIVE WORK

My name is RM. I am a plot holder in Lonely farm (A1 villagised, Gutu cluster). I have a family of seven. I always participate in work parties. Work includes ploughing, weeding, harvesting and threshing. The farmer hosting the party provides food, beer and maheu (a non-alcoholic, maize-based drink). Work parties are fun days since we have an opportunity to group and work together. We will be drinking, singing and dancing after work This year there was a work party at C's plot. There were six spans ploughing. We finished his whole field. We had lots of food and drink. At my plot last season we threshed 82 x 50kg bags of rapoko (finger millet). It took three days. I slaughtered a goat and 30 to 40 people came. They came from surrounding Bath and Salem farms, as well as Serima communal area.

My name is EC. I am a widow and live at the plot in Lonely farm with my two kids. I belong to Paul Mwazha church. In every village Mwazha followers organise themselves into work groups. In Lonely we are seven families. We rotate working days at each household making sure that at the end of the season each member's home was visited. Jobs include weeding, harvesting, manure digging and carrying and any other job a member wants to be done. The host farmer provides food and maheu. The day starts at six o'clock up to 12 midday before it becomes too hot. We also go and work in fields of our members when they are sick. At funerals involving a member we make sure that our contributions are more than other people's.

My name is RM. I am 47 years old and own plot 25 in Wondedzo Wares villagised. I belong to Mwazha church. We team up and help each other in jobs such as weeding, harvesting and threshing. As many as 50 people may come to work. A person needing assistance approaches church leaders who normally accept the request. The host farmer provides meat, maheu and sadza. Members come and work for one day. Any farmer, including non-church members, can request assistance. We do not segregate because we want to convert more followers to our church. We also want to attract community leaders into our church. There are plans to participate in the tradition of Zunde Remambo. We will go and work in Headman M's Zunde field and in sabhuku C's field.

What is clear from these cases is the variety of origins of such labour. Rural labour circulates through a number of relationships and connections. This is a highly complex rural labour market. For example, we have new in-migrants to households, attracted by the opportunities of the new resettlements. These are usually relatives, but this can be a flexible term, and the kin relationship may be quite obscure. Men, women and children are available for farm work, with many new workers being very young. Others arrive as workers, part of the wider circulation of people looking for work; often landless and impoverished people who will accept the offer of food and shelter and may then gradually become incorporated into the households, as quasi-kin, accepted perhaps on a

Table 6.3 Labour dynamics across the study sites

	Gutu			Masvingo			Chiredzi		Mwenezi		
	A1 villagised	A1 self-contained	A2	A1 villagised	A1 self-contained	A2	Informal	A2	A1 villagised	Informal	A2
Average numbers of new arrivals per household available for farm work	2.8	3.3	2.8	2.2	1.7	4.0	2.8	2.3	2.7	3.0	3.0
Average nos arriving as hired workers	0.3	0.4	3.1	0.1	0.6	0.7	0.2	0.7	0.2	0.0	2.5
% new workers female	33%	50%	29%	67%	43%	0%	0%	38%	33%	-	40%
Average age of new worker	22	33	22	37	25	24	31	40	15	-	43
Average education (years) of new workers	9.0	10.2	8.4	1.3	7.7	10.0	3.2	10.6	6.0	-	3.4
% new workers married	67%	50%	46%	67%	57%	50%	0%	17%	33%	-	60%
% new workers relatives of household head	67%	67%	4%	33%	14%	50%	75%	0%	67%	-	0%

Source: Survey data, 2007-08 (N=177)

totem linkage or out of charity. There are also workers who are hired in a more formal way, on the basis of contracts, either as temporary or permanent workers (or variations in between). And, finally, there are those who work on each others' farms as part of reciprocal labour sharing and collective work arrangements, sometimes involving payment of food or drink.

Both permanent and temporary workers on the new farms sometimes come from the same resettlement site, or from nearby ones or communal areas. They are often regarded as members of a broader community, linked through totem affiliation, direct kinship, church membership and so on. The sociological relationship with their employers is very different to that in the old large-scale commercial sector, where the differences between farmer and labourer were defined starkly by race, wealth and culture. In the past, farm workers were always a disadvantaged group, often illiterate and with poor education (Rutherford, 2001b). Today, this is less the case. The new farm workers are often literate, young 'born-frees' (born after 1980) who benefited from the government's compulsory education programme after Independence.

In the following sections, we explore each of these categories, starting with a discussion of the patterns of in-migration into households in the sample between settlement and 2008. We then move to a discussion of patterns of hiring in and out of labour, both seasonal and more permanent, before moving to a discussion of communal labour. The final section highlights the challenges of finding, managing and retaining labour on the new resettlement farms, and the implications this has for agricultural production. The conclusion examines the implications of our emerging understanding of the new farm workers for the class dynamics and patterns of agrarian change unfolding on the new resettlements.

6.4 New labour dynamics

The new resettlements are acting as a magnet for others. As Table 6.3 shows, nearly all households had around three new arrivals since settlement who were available for farm work (i.e. not very young children or aged/infirm people). Of these, some were hired in explicitly as workers, with between a third and two-thirds of hired-in labour being female. Most workers were relatively young (some very young) and with varying periods of schooling. In the A1 areas most new workers were relatives, with the exception of Wondedzo Extension (A1 self-contained) which followed the pattern found in the A2 schemes, where most new hires were not related to the farm owner.

Our data highlights a close relationship between labour dynamics and success group. For A1 and informal scheme households, 11% of SG1 and 13% of SG2 households hire in permanent labour for cropping/herding, while 62% of SG1 and 38% of SG2 households hire temporary or seasonal labour. This contrasts with SG3 households, where only 3% hire permanent labour and 34% hire seasonal labour. Such patterns are indicative of an emerging class-based agrarian dynamic, whereby a limited number of farmers on large plots hire in labour, with labour driving patterns of accumulation for the relatively better off. By contrast, other households sell their labour, often on an informal, casual and temporary basis. As with other studies elsewhere in the country (Moyo, 2009; Chambati, 2007), labour hiring in the Masvingo sites is highly correlated with farm size, asset holdings and other indicators of accumulation.

In labour hiring patterns, relationships exist between different scheme types too. A1 self-contained sites often hire in labour from nearby A1 villagised sites, often with kin networks assisting in the flow of labour between the areas. For example, in the Wondedzo area of the Masvingo cluster, there is a strong labour linkage between Wondedzo Extension (self-contained) and Wares (villagised). Connections are further reinforced through churches, with Zionist and Apostolic Faith congregations often being the basis of labour interactions across sites.

The AIAS studies found that, across their sites, only 8.6% of A1 households regularly hire out labour, and only 3.7% of A2 households do so (Moyo, 2009). This pattern is broadly repeated in the Masvingo sites. Those hiring out their labour tend to be poorer, lower success group households. But this is not universally the case, and the pattern is complex. Since such households are also committing labour to other livelihood activities, the selling of labour is usually a part-time activity limited to a few individuals in the home, and often seasonally defined. Over the whole sample, 45% of households hire out labour (35% on a temporary basis, 13% more permanently, and some both). Hiring out temporary labour is more common in SG3 households, mostly for local agricultural labour. People more frequently leave SG1 than SG3 households on more permanent contracts, including leaving for higher-paid employment. In terms of the supply of agricultural labour, then, the main local source is SG3 households, alongside others from the communal areas and other resettlement sites. The SG1 households are more likely to be involved in salaried, non-agricultural labour away from the site. This confirms the class-based dynamic commented on above, with hiring in and hiring out agricultural labour within sites linked to the emerging class positions associated with different households.

6.5 Communal labour

Communal labour has long been a feature smallholder production systems. A 'work party' (*humwe*) is held, and people join in on a specific task. There is usually no payment, beyond the provision of beer, *maheu* and sometimes food, and there is often a reliance on an extended kin group, as part of a village. Sometimes this is done to help out an elderly or infirm person, or someone with no draught power. On other occasions work parties are held as reciprocal arrangements, with families helping each other out another in sequence over a season depending on labour demands.

As the case-studies highlighted, sometimes churches are the organising focal point. In some instances, church leaders demand payment in labour from their congregations, and church members are called to farms to help out the pastor in the name of the church. This is most common in the new evangelical churches. In the Wondedzo Extension site in Masvingo cluster a highly successful farmer who had nominated himself as head of a church (the so-called Janga Mission) benefited from substantial free labour inputs from his congregations over several years.

Many observers have noted the decline of such labour (and draught) sharing arrangements in the communal areas. They are reliant on close-knit community relations and a differentiation of resource access that allows for the sharing. Is this pattern repeated in the new resettlements? As Chapter 5 showed, over the last six years ploughing was rarely completed as a result of *humwe* arrangements, although draught sharing was very common. Across our sample, labour sharing was more common in some sites, with between 39% and 55% of households benefiting from labour sharing in A1 villagised sites, and between 45% and 91% benefiting in informal sites. By contrast, A2 and A1-self contained sites saw less labour sharing. Most households reciprocated, with exchanges of labour being key to the arrangement. Table 6.4 offers an analysis of labour sharing by success group in the A1 and informal sites, contrasting these patterns with those seen on A2 farms.

Collective work has become an important facet of production in the new resettlements. This is perhaps surprising given the lack of strong social ties binding communities together. However, the experience of the *jambanja* period, combined with the hardships of recent times, have acted to increase the sense of community, and friends, neighbours, church members and kin often work together on a range of activities, even in the apparently individualised plots of the A2 and A1 self-contained schemes (see Chapter 9 for a further discussion of social organisation and the building of communities in the new resettlements).

6.6 Labour as a constraint to production

More hired-in labour is associated with larger farm sizes, representing particularly the A2 and A1 self-contained plots. Thus the average farmed area is 3.7ha for those households with no permanent farm workers, but 7.0ha for those with between three and five workers. However, there is no smooth farm size-productivity relationship, as suggested by the classic inverse relationship. Although total output and yield of grains decreases with increasing farm size (and permanent labour), this pattern does not continue for larger farm sizes. Lipton (2009: 68-84) lists the array of conditions under which an inverse relationship may not hold, including distorted incentives, preferential access to markets and inputs for some and absenteeism of smallholder farmers. Many of these apply in the Zimbabwe case, making it unlikely that such a relationship would hold. However, the data does perhaps indicate a broader pattern, whereby transactions costs per unit of output are lower on smaller farms, primarily because of the ability to manage labour (both family

Table 6.4 Labour-sharing and collective labour arrangements

	A1 and Informal sites			A2
	SG1	SG2	SG3	All success groups
% households benefiting from labour-sharing arrangements	51.0%	43.8%	36.6%	41.2%
Average numbers of person days involved	3.12	3.2	10.4	12.7
Average numbers of people involved	11.8	12.7	8.1	14.9
% households using collective labour for land clearing/ploughing	15.0%	23.5%	11.1%	25.0%
% households using collective labour for planting	7.7%	20.0%	21.4%	26.7%
% households using collective labour for weeding	28.6%	26.1%	18.8%	38.9%
% households using collective labour for harvesting	31.6%	25.0%	20.0%	14.8%
% households using collective labour for herding	57.1%	25.0%	33.3%	28.6%
% households who had members participating in collective labour elsewhere	42.9%	41.3%	52.5%	6.1%

Source: Survey data, 2007-08 (N=177)

and hired), while on larger farms, capital constraints are more critical and override this effect. For this scale of production it is the levels of capitalisation and the relations of production that are more significant, resulting in a direct relationship between farm size and output per unit area, as in much developed-world agriculture (Eastwood et al., 2009).

Certainly, a particular challenge in many farms has been labour management. Many found it difficult to recruit new labour, and even more difficult to retain it. This was in part because of the economic conditions which made wage employment particularly risky in any line of work. Farm worker wages were rendered useless by inflation. Government-stipulated farm wages were very low due to tardy bureaucracy in a fast-changing economic environment. The failure by the plot holder to pay wages regularly resulted in workers resorting to theft of farm equipment and tools. Others went to work for other farmers or sold products from the farm. Many abandoned their jobs and went to live in their home areas in preference to working for a pittance – or some intermittently supplied survival rations – on someone else's farm. Others took to border jumping and joined the flow of migrants to work in the farms of Limpopo Province in South Africa, often returning appalled at the conditions, and sometimes with very little money. On the A2 farms there was a growing demand for skilled labour that could take on a management role, one that would allow owners to be absent for periods of time. Good managers were very hard to find, as all A2 farmers observed, and too often there were complaints of stealing and other malpractices. Overall, supervision and other transactions costs were seen to be too large, and the reliability of labour too low to bother investing in it. Better to rely on relatives attracted to the new resettlements with the promise of accommodation and food, and perhaps grazing and a small plot within the larger farm.

6.7 Conclusions

In the new resettlement areas there are new farm workers of many different types. Much labour is casual, informal, seasonal, underpaid and often female. But there are more, usually partial, livelihoods being created through farm labour now than there were before, even if these are highly vulnerable. In the former large-scale ranches, there was one worker per 250-1,000ha, depending on the agroecological region and the exact nature of the farm's operations (Clarke, 1977).[8] According to our sample data, in a similar area today there may be 1-10 A2 farms, each employing an average of 5.1 permanent and 7.3 temporary workers, or 25-50 small-scale A1 farms, each employing 0.5 and 1.9 respectively (see above). This is not well-paid employment by any calculation, and the conditions are nearly universally poor, but the scale of employment opportunity has certainly increased dramatically.

During the economic crisis, many of the new farm workers had to live through other means in order to supplement their meagre wages. In many cases, farm labour is only one component of 'farm worker' livelihoods. Stealing, illegal activities and moonlighting were essential strategies. The low retention rates of farm labour are also indicative of the poor conditions. The beneficial dynamic of increasing labour opportunities with higher wages has yet to be realised in the Zimbabwe setting. However, this may not be permanent. Certainly in the recent past, for those attempting to accumulate through the hiring of labour – and so firmly to enter a capitalist mode of production – the opportunities have been limited. With changes in the macroeconomic setting, this may change. With a stable currency and low inflation, wage labour becomes an option again, and the positive bidding process seen in other small-scale farming settings may emerge (Lipton, 2009). Livelihoods based on farm labour in the new resettlements may therefore become more attractive.

Improved conditions will not be reliant only on economic conditions. The rights of the new farm workers remain as precarious as before,

---

[8]   This ratio was confirmed in discussions with Masvingo officials who had serviced the farms, and applies to extensive ranching. More were employed on horticultural operations, dairies and as workers in farmers' homes.

perhaps more so. With small numbers of workers on any farm, the possibility of organising labour within or across farms is limited. Those who are unwilling to accept the terms offered were soon dispatched. The reach of labour regulations and the organisation of labour unions and NGOs is limited. Residential rights, and rights to make use of plots, are also uncertain. Since most new farm workers are embedded in the household, and tied through a variety of relationships to the plot holder, labour relations are reliant on informal ties, subject often to the whims of the plot holder. While kinship, friendship or church links may limit some extreme abuses, this is far from guaranteed.

Current policy debates about the implications of the post-2000 reforms on farm labour have focused on how many people have lost their jobs and who has been displaced, with much confusion about the scale and patterns involved. These are important issues, but a sole focus on these questions obscures much complexity. With a fundamental reconfiguration of labour on the farms, new agrarian relations are emerging. As Chapter 10 discusses, some new farmers are accumulating, while others are not, and the role of labour – and particularly its gendered dimensions – is essential in understanding these processes. Labour is a key element of the land reform story in Zimbabwe, and securing the rights of labour on the new farms is going to be an essential but difficult task. Understanding who the new farm workers are, and their social, political and economic position in the new agrarian order, is an important first step towards a 'transformative approach' to the issue of farm labour (Moyo et al., 2000). What is clear is that the old pattern seen in the former large-scale commercial farms has disappeared.

7

Real Markets | The Changing
Political Economy
of Agricultural
Commodities

7.1 An economy in chaos

Between 2000 and 2009, as the formal economy collapsed, the local,
rural economy became increasingly characterised by new markets
and new methods of payment. As Chapter 1 described, the economic
context has fundamentally shaped the experience on the new resettlements in the first decade. Informal trade and smuggling became vital
options for generating foreign exchange at household level. Crossing
international borders became an important strategy for reducing economic hardships, while illegal exports and thefts of livestock for sale
across borders increased. In desperate attempts to boost the economy,
policies focused on centralised production and marketing. As Chapter 5
discussed, this was orchestrated through the RBZ, often with the backing of the security services. Command agriculture aimed at generating
output targets in each province, and, alongside state land and irrigation schemes, the new resettlement areas were targeted as areas where
this might be achieved. Price controls and marketing restrictions were
imposed on what were deemed essential commodities, such as maize
and beef. These policies introduced huge distortions into the agricultural economy, alongside layers of corruption and rent seeking.

This chapter explores these dynamics further by focusing on four
different agricultural commodities – maize, beef, cotton and sugar.
As Table 7.1 shows, the pattern of production at a national level has
changed for different commodities in different ways. Crops associated
with the large-scale sector such as tobacco – along with tea, coffee and
horticulture – have declined significantly from 1990s levels. The same
applies to formally-marketed beef. Grain crops have seen stark changes
too, with wheat production collapsing, and small grain (sorghum and
millets) production booming. Maize production has declined significantly too, and production, now reliant on areas without irrigation, has
increased in variability. Cotton has shown remarkable stability, while
crops such as edible beans, soya beans, groundnuts and sunflower have
increased, in some cases dramatically. Understanding the different
responses – of both production and markets – of different commodities

Table 7.1 National patterns of crop production (2000-01 to 2008-09) and percentage change compared to 1990s averages ('000 tonnes)[1]

Crop	1990s Average	2000-01	2001-02	2002-03	2003-04	2004-05	2005-06	2006-07	2007-08	2008-09
Maize	1,668.6	1,476.2	1,526.3	929.6	1,058.8	1,686.2	915.4	952.6	575.0	1,242.6
% Change	219.3	-11.5%	-8.5%	-44.3%	-36.5%	1.1%	-45.1%	-42.9%	-65.5%	-25.5%
Wheat		250	325	213.0	122.4	135	134	150	75.0	38.0
% Change		14.0%	48.2%	-2.9%	-44.2%	-38.4%	-38.9%	-31.6%	-65.8%	-82.7%
Small grains	50.01	90.7	99.6	35.8	131.2	196.1	128.6	138.6	93.2	270.2
% Change		81.4%	99.2%	-28.4%	162.3%	292.1%	157.1%	177.1%	86.4%	440.4%
Edible dry beans	5.3	7.4	7.2	7.1	10.8	56.8	21.5	30.3	3.8	37.3
% Change	92	39.6%	35.8%	34.0%	103.8%	971.7%	305.7%	471.7%	-28.3%	603.8%
Groundnuts		191	168.7	59	141	135	57.8	83.2	131.5	216.6
% Change	95.51	107.6%	83.4%	-35.9%	53.3%	46.7%	-37.2%	-9.6%	42.9%	135.4%
Soyabeans		175.01	140.82	84.42	41.01	85.82	72.01	70.32	48.3	115.8
% Change	36.41	83.2%	47.4%	-11.6%	-57.1%	-10.1%	-24.6%	-26.4%	-49.4%	21.2%
Sunflower		16.06	30.42	32.06	16.91	20.22	7.42	16.72	5.5	39.0
% Change		-55.9%	-16.5%	-11.9%	-53.6%	-44.5%	-79.6%	-54.1%	-84.9%	7.1%
Tobacco	197.61	236.97	202.57	165.87	81.87	68.97	73.47	55.57	69.815	63.6
% Change	214.11	19.9%	2.5%	-16.1%	-58.6%	-65.1%	-62.8%	-71.9%	-64.7%	-67.8%
Cotton		242.02	280.32	194.22	228.01	198.01	265.03	300.03	226.415	246.8
% Change		13.0%	30.9%	-9.3%	6.5%	-7.5%	23.8%	40.1%	5.7%	15.3%

Source: AIAS from various sources (Moyo, 2009)

[1] Data on crop production is inevitably based only on estimates. These also vary between different sources. Poor data collection systems existed post-2000, resulting in even greater underestimates of production of some crops than existed in the 1990s. For the purposes of our analysis here, however, it is the broad trends and oders-of-magnitude amounts that are important.

is essential, we argue, for exploring the future articulations of different types of agriculture in Zimbabwe.

Understanding these broader patterns has significant implications for future policy. The aim of this chapter is to understand the way markets affected livelihoods between 2000 and 2009. In contrast to more structural and economic analyses of supply, commodity or value chains (e.g. Gereffi and Korzeniewicz, 1994), we focus on market relationships and how these are shaped by social and political processes. The emphasis is on 'real markets' (De Alcántara, 1993; Platteau, 1994), examining how markets work in practice, and the social and political relationships that make them tick. This pushes us to consider issues of social difference in the construction of markets – race, gender, ethnic identity and political affiliation, for example – in addition to the more standard metrics associated with inputs, outputs, returns and rents. The chapter argues that an understanding of social and political embeddedness is central to understanding current – and indeed future – dynamics.

The new agrarian relations created by the land reform have stimulated important interactions across diverse commodity chains, opening opportunities for some and closing options for others. An understanding of how markets and commodity chains function in practice, we argue, is particularly important for economies in chaos, where formal and informal processes run side by side. This allows us to explore how a change from a formalised, linear marketing system, organised around a relatively narrow group of players (Muir-Leresche and Muchopa, 2006), can change to one that has a different, and potentially wider, scope and reach.

7.2 Maize

Maize has always been a political crop, and it became particularly so in the years after 2000. With a series of droughts, economic collapse and a major upheaval in production on the former large-scale commercial farms, ensuring national food supplies became a significant challenge. Aid agencies continued to import food, but its distribution – particularly around election times – became highly politicised, with accusations that areas with significant opposition support were being denied food aid. Production within the country was highly variable (Figure 7.1), and, although a significant proportion of white maize had been produced in communal areas since the 1980s (Mashingaidze, 2006), the decline in large-scale commercial production had major knock-on effects. In the last decade, as resettlement land has expanded, sorghum and millet production has grown (Figure 7.2), but the total amounts produced are small in comparison to maize, and total cereal production broadly follows the pattern shown for maize.

A particularly significant consequence of the appropriation of farms in the Highveld areas was the decline in seed maize production. Seed Co, the major company producing high-quality maize seed, struggled to find seed multiplication sites in the country, and seed supply declined. In part this was due to supply constraints, but equally significant was

Figure 7.1: Maize production trends, 1993-94 to 2008-09

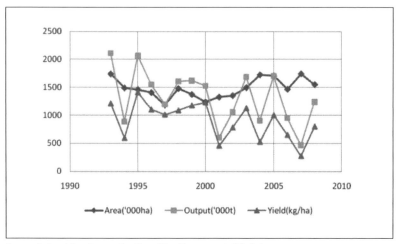

Source: National Crop Forecasting Committee, Government of Zimbabwe

Figure 7.2: Sorghum and millet (pearl and finger) production, 1995-96 to 2008-09

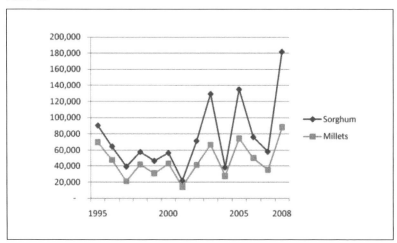

Source: National Crop Forecasting Committee, Government of Zimbabwe

the effect of market interventions of different sorts. Seed Co seed could earn significant returns in Botswana, South Africa or Zambia and so substantial quantities were exported – some illegally, with significant profits being made by well-connected groups of businessmen and politicians. Interventions by the government to try and set prices also meant that seed production became increasingly uneconomic, and most companies wound down production or focused on export markets.

The urgent need to produce enough maize to feed the nation, and to restrict the expenditures on imports, resulted in a series of increasingly rash and desperate policies (Chapter 5), centred on command agriculture.[2] Agricultural officers in each province were supposed to identify suitable areas for production of maize and wheat, and produce sufficient quantities to meet the targets. In some parts of the country, the army was deployed to coordinate the programme, forcing irrigation plot holders to produce for the state. Produce would be purchased by the GMB at a fixed price, and no options for local sales were allowed. Such programmes, not surprisingly, were dramatic failures, often resulting in the squandering of significant resources, and the building of damaging resentment towards the government, and the security services in particular.

As Chapter 5 discussed, Operation Maguta focused on input supply, especially to the new resettlement areas. The state wanted to reward the new settlers and ensure production on the new lands. It was thought that a level of control could be asserted there, and that farmers would commit to supporting the national endeavour and provide grain to the GMB, if inputs were supplied. The RBZ again took charge, allocating significant funds to purchase seed and fertiliser and, in a separate programme, farm equipment. This programme had varied effects, but the late and inadequate supply of inputs resulted in much disgruntlement. Inputs were distributed unevenly, often on the basis of local patronage relations. In addition, the whole programme was open to massive corruption, and has been subject to a number of court cases since, with senior government and army officials, politicians and businesspeople being accused of stealing and reselling inputs.[3] In the 2008 season an attempt was made to target input support more effectively, under the Champion Farmers programme. Extension officials were supposed to identify leading farmers who would make good use of the support. But again the supplies were inadequate, and the programme was subject to manipulation by elites, and further cases of corrupt practice.

The maize market became highly regulated, with price and movement controls defined by the government (Chapter 5). This reversion to the 1980s policies of strict state control after a decade of liberalisation of grain marketing was seriously resented. It was made worse by the effects of hyperinflation. The policies were a major disincentive to production, at least for the formal market. This affected wheat especially dramatically, as marketing and milling were relatively easily controlled compared to maize, and certainly to small grains.

Shortages of bread, flour and mealie meal were common, and hit urban residents especially hard. Illegal movements of maize grain and meal counteracted this to some extent, but they equally allowed opportunities for rent seeking by officials charged with regulating the market. With the growing securitisation of state functions in the build-up to the 2008 elections, regulating maize markets (as well as beef, see below) became a major focus of activity for the youth militia, backed up by the army. Arbitrary fines, confiscations of produce and intimidation of trad-

---

[2] http://www.sarpn.org.za/documents/d0001952/Command_Agric_Zim_Apr2006.pdf.

[3] Police investigate MPs for theft http://www.thezimbabwetimes.com/?p=13277 March 11, 2009.

Figure 7.3 Maize markets connected to Clare Farm, Gutu (highlighted boxes are cross-border linkages)

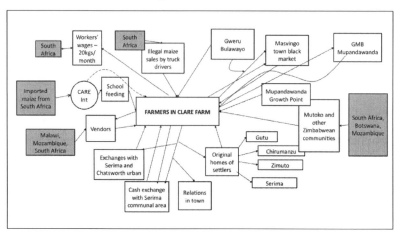

ers were commonplace, highlighting the political tensions surrounding food production and supply during this period. This politicisation – and even militarisation – of markets reached its height in 2008, when major food shortages coincided with the highly contested parliamentary and presidential elections.

The shortage of maize grain (to eat) and seed (to plant) was especially severe in 2008. A discussion in the A1 resettlement in Clare Farm in December 2008 showed how people got access to maize. The diagram drawn by a number of resettlement farmers highlighted a complex web of connections, and a very dynamic informal market – illegal and legal. Exchanges with communal area farmers, and links with their original homes in nearby Gutu and Serima were significant. But most striking was the importance of cross-border connections through remittances in kind, smuggling by truck drivers, and a thriving black market in townships across the province. The traditional suppliers of grain or seed – the GMB, seed dealers or aid-funded projects – are notably absent, or play only a limited role.

As the state tried to regulate the maize market towards its own political ends, farmers had to improvise in order to survive. The massive growth of informal marketing arrangements for grain and seed was driven by the need to survive. Entrepreneurial activity helped offset some of the worst effects of the highly distorting policy regime, making grain and seed available through informal channels. While the international media, donors and international organisations predicted a major disaster, this was, in part, averted by the ingenuity, as well as the sheer desperation, of many informal players. But such a flourishing of activity is not enough; good seeds, cheap fertilisers and reliable sales channels are still needed, and systems for their delivery need to be rebuilt if maize is to thrive in the new resettlements.

Figure 7.4 The beef commodity chain in Masvingo, 2008

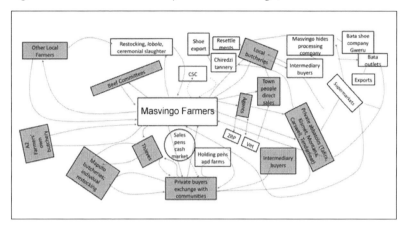

7.3 Beef[4]

In the beef sector, all parts of the commodity chain have radically changed, from production to processing to retailing. In Masvingo province, the transformation of former ranches into mixed farming areas meant that the old beef production system, the core of the former commercial farm economy in the province, was no more. In 2003 there was a serious escalation in foot-and-mouth disease outbreaks, in part triggered by the breakdown in movement control accompanying the farm occupations, which led to a ban on Zimbabwean beef exports. The economic advantages of the beef sector, based as quota allocations to the premium European market, had been wiped out.

Figure 7.4 offers a schematic overview of the beef commodity chain in the province today. The shaded boxes represent actors in the informal sector, complemented by the private sector abbatoirs which emerged in the 1990s. The non-shaded boxes represent the 'old' commodity chain (and associated regulatory agencies). The contrasts could not be more stark. In 2005-06 the so-called commercial herd stood at under 350,000, and deliveries to the Cold Storage Company (CSC) had collapsed almost completely. But this did not mean that nothing was happening. On the contrary, the new scenario involved many more actors and many more connections. As a response to the changes in land use and ownership, and in order to cope with the challenges of a hyperinflationary economy in dramatic decline, all sorts of innovations were becoming necessary.

Since the 1990s especially there has been a dramatic shift of marketing focus from the parastatal CSC to private abattoirs. Total sales, especially since the peak period of the early/mid-1990s, have declined significantly in recent years, returning approximately to those seen in the 1980s. The decline in the commercial herd has occurred over a long period, as export-focused areas became concentrated in the Highveld, and large areas of former ranch land were converted to wildlife-based

---

4   This section is based on Mavedzenge et al. (2008) and Mavedzenge et al. (2006).

operations. Overall, cattle have become increasingly concentrated in the small-scale sector, with communal and resettlement areas now making up around 90% of the total herd.

Since 2000 there has thus been a major transition from a highly concentrated and regulated commodity chain dominated by a few players, to one characterised by huge diversity at all levels. This has been accompanied by a decline in state control and management of the market system and a growth in independent, increasingly informal, economic activity. The result is a massively more diversified and complex – some would say 'haphazard', 'disorganised' and 'chaotic'[5] – marketing system populated by more actors with more relationships. This has allowed better matching of supply with demand, and a diversion of products from a narrow, tightly-controlled market chain from large-scale producers, via a few abbatoirs to supermarket chains and export wholesalers, to a much more diverse web of market relationships, emphasising local sales of lower grade, cheaper meat via small-scale, independent butcheries. This has resulted in a locational shift in the marketing chain too, with meat now being sourced from a much wider range of suppliers, scattered across the small-scale farming areas, both communal and resettlement.

Within Masvingo province a number of abbatoirs operate, linked to intermediary buyers, speculators, transporters and fattening operations. Particularly in the mid-2000s, retailing was no longer concentrated in the supermarkets in town, but among a large number of small butcheries in the urban townships and rural businsess centres. For example, in 2006 there were 31 butcheries in Masvingo town with a weekly throughput of around 90 carcasses; 20 of these butcheries were outside the main business district, in Mucheke township. The number of butcheries also increased in the rural areas: at Ngundu growth point south of Masvingo, for instance, the number increased from two to nine between 2001 and 2006 (Mavedzenge et al., 2008: 626). However, during 2007-08 attempts were made to control beef marketing through price controls, with the police, security forces and youth militias being deployed. This once again disrupted the commodity chain, pushing more activities underground (Mavedzenge et al., 2008).

The dualism of the past was based on the assumption that separation of production systems, and specialisation in different products, was the route to progress. This created an artificial, and ultimately politically untenable, distinction between 'communal' (read African, backward, subsistence, mixed farming) and 'commercial' (read European, modern, forward-looking, export-oriented) systems of production. The separation in production systems – spatially, economically, technically, socially, politically and racially – was replicated through the commodity chain, with separate investment and support for each. For many, both pre- and post-Independence, the beef model, associated with the 'commercial' production system, was seen as necessarily superior, and so worthy of continued, substantial support. The calculations of how much public money has been invested in the commercial beef system since the establishment of the CSC in 1937 have never been done, but any estimate

---

[5] Quotes from participants at the workshop 'Changes in the Livestock Sector Following Land Reform in Zimbabwe: The Case of Masvingo Province' (Mavedzenge et al., 2006).

will show that the level of support (explicit and less so) has been very considerable indeed, undermining claims to the 'economic superiority' of the beef sector.

Today, production and marketing systems are more integrated. Such integration of course has precedents. In the early colonial period, the formal objective of a clear separation of production systems was rarely achieved, as white- and black-owned animals lived alongside each other. More recently, with the heifer exchange systems initiated by white commercial farmers following the 1980s droughts, a much closer linkage between communal and commercial production systems was apparent. Today, speculator buyers, lease grazing systems and fattening sites exist alongside each other, with the main source of animals now being the small-scale communal and resettlement areas.

These new markets are necessarily based on very different social and political relations. The social networks on which the markets of the beef industry operate have changed beyond recognition. The pattern prior to 2000 was based on a tight, often racially-defined, integration of a limited number of players who had strong connections, often based on many years of interaction. The white rancher-speculator-abattoir owner/operator chain was one that had developed over fifty years, based on strong business, friendship and kin relations. This was reinforced in turn by a tight, rather insular social milieu centred on the sports and social clubs of regional towns such as Masvingo. Recent events have shattered this social and economic world, often with traumatic consequences. In the past, white business interacted with African producers and labourers largely on their own terms; this is no longer possible. Both the political and economic conditions have changed so radically that the functioning of the cosy, inward-looking social basis of business and trade is no longer feasible. Instead, new relations have to be brokered, with new entrants coming into these networks, and, indeed, wholly new networks being formed.

There has of course been an emerging black business and political elite involved in the livestock trade for some time, mostly around transport and butchery operations. However, land reform, and the associated political and economic shifts, has changed the landscape radically. New alliances have to be formed, and make political sense, often at a very locally-specific level. Those who formerly dominated the beef trade have responded in different ways. Some have given up; others have retreated into smaller operations with old networks; while others have begun to negotiate relations which accommodate new political and economic realities. Little is known about these new networks and many remain clandestine and informal, but they suggest some important new social, political and racial contours of the business environment for cattle marketing, in Masvingo province and beyond. Given the volatility and uncertainty associated with the economic environment of the past decade, such new business and trading relationships have had to operate under incredibly difficult conditions, at whatever stage in the commodity chain. Time will tell which operations survive and which fail. But, while there will inevitably be a shake-out, the result will not look like the centralised, integrated commodity chain of the past, dominated by a few (mostly white) players.

With more actors and more interactions there are of course both benefits and costs. Today, more people certainly engage in the commodity chain, but increased numbers bring dangers of rising transactions costs, inefficiency and capture by sectional interests. The positive side of the story, however, highlights the dynamic, entrepreneurial activity that has emerged across the commodity chain. The new focus on local production and sale reduces transport costs and adds value locally, but makes oversight and regulation very difficult. With the loss of the major high-value export markets, the total unit value of output has declined, even if the benefits are more evenly distributed than before. In recent years total cattle sales have also fallen, as people build their herds. But questions of future supply are raised. As Chapter 5 shows, with few farmers having enough animals to sell regularly, the market is going to be reliant on a limited but steady flow of relatively low-grade animals sold by farmers who keep them largely for other reasons and dispose of them only when they have to.

Overall, therefore, the existing infrastructure – large abattoirs, fencing, feedlots – and the associated policy frameworks – for disease control, market regulation, credit and financing – do not make sense any more. Some fundamental rethinking of the overall framework for livestock production and marketing is needed (Mavedzenge et al., 2008). This requires, first and foremost, understanding the new relationships and interactions of the 'real' markets on the ground, and finding ways of making them more effective and efficient. Recreating the dualistic patterns of the past certainly does not make economic and political sense following land reform, and probably did not do so before either.

7.4 Sugar

Since 2000, as Chapter 5 has described, sugar production in the lowveld areas has remained under the control of the estates, and new resettlement farmers rely heavily on the long-established and well-connected companies. Such companies suffered many of the consequences of the economic collapse, but export sales shielded them from some of its worst consequences. Their political connections were good too, and this provided extra support. However, as relayed in numerous interviews on the new resettlement farms, the farmers suffered. Until 2009, payments were made in local currency, often some time after harvest, and long after inputs had been purchased. Under hyperinflation, this represented an impossible economic situation. Whilst the marketing of sugar remained under strict state regulation, the crop presented more opportunities for illegal trade in raw and processed sugar, and some new resettlement farmers were able to profit.

The sugar sector is important to Zimbabwe's economy, contributing 1.4% to GDP nationally, and 95% in Masvingo province (Sierevogel et al., 2007). The sector generated US$65 million in foreign exchange earnings in 2005. The two dominant players are Hippo Valley Estates and Triangle Limited, both located in the south-east lowveld of Masvingo province. Mlambo and Pangeti (1996) noted that in 1989, they employed

Table 7.2 Sugar production in the post-2000 period

	2000	2001	2002	2003	2004	2005	2006
Cane (t)	4,385,746	4,231,783	4,634,387	4,065,652	3,415,028	3,530,127	3,681,757
Sugar (t)	540,688	513,732	580,005	502,533	421,999	429,271	446,647
Land (ha)	43,402	44,072	43,983	43,561	43,385	42,862	41,470
Cane tonne/ha	101.0	96.0	105.4	93.3	78.5	82.4	88.8
Sugar tonne/ha	12.5	11.7	13.2	11.5	9.7	10.0	10.8

Source: Sierevogel et al., 2007.

6,000 and 7,500 people respectively. Together with the population of Mkwasine Sugar Estates, the employees' dependants, the private planters and the settler farmers at Chipiwa, the total population supported by the sugar estates amounted to around 120,000. In addition, through its various processing and diversification activities, the industry produces a range of intermediate and finished products for the local market. Among its by-products are ethanol, industrial and potable alcohol, stockfeeds, carbon dioxide and electricity (Mlambo and Pangeti, 1996).

Sugar cane production was a lucrative enterprise, and land reform in the sugar estates became a highly contested issue, presenting new opportunities for politicians and investors with the necessary political connections. Traditionally, Hippo Valley Estates and Triangle Limited produced 70% of the cane from their own farms and Mkwasine Estates, with a capacity to produce 600,000 tonnes of sugar. The balance came from independent commercial growers. Compared with Hippo Valley Estates and Triangle Limited, Mkwasine Estates ceded the most land to land reform. A total of 3,871ha (79.3% of the land available) was redistributed to 217 A2 farmers. Only 442.5ha of the original land was left, eroding the status of Mkwasine Estates as a core estate capable of providing essential support services to the settlers. The core estate of Hippo Valley was not affected by land acquisition, with land acquired coming from the outgrowers. However, damage was done to infrastructure on the estate (Sierevogel et al., 2007). Triangle Limited had the fewest cane fields redistributed, with most of the land taken being previously used for cattle ranching (Sierevogel et al., 2007).

Although resettlement has not affected the total area under cane, there there has been a significant fall in productivity. The contestation over land reform in the sugar estates resulted in protracted legal battles between new farmers and displaced outgrowers, disrupting production and harvesting in the first years following settlement. Combined with the effects of the harsh economic environment, sugar pricing policies and a deteriorating service supply infrastructure (electricity, machinery, spares), the challenges of sugar production were numerous. Table 7.2 tracks sugar production from 2000.

Figure 7.5: The sugar cane value chain

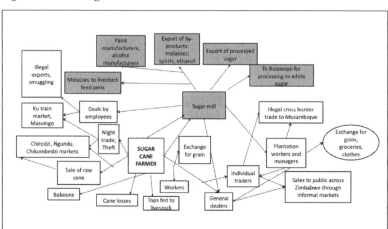

Despite the challenges faced by the industry, sugar exports have continued, to the EU, USA and other markets. As Sierevogel et al. observed (2007: 9): 'During the last six years, the Zimbabwean sugar industry has been able to export sugar to the European Union and, on an annual average ... to comply with the ACP and SPS Quotas respectively of thirty and twenty-five thousand tonnes.' Regional exports have continued to Angola, Botswana, Kenya, Namibia, South Africa and elsewhere. By-products such as molasses and ethanol have helped to improve the viability of sugar cane production, although new settlers argue that they have never benefited from these.

Sugar cane production has been a major challenge for the new A2 settlers. Before dollarisation, farmers were payed in local curency despite the fact that sugar exports continued. The argument by the millers was that the assistance to farmers in the procurement of inputs accounted for the foreign exchange component of exported sugar. Settlers complain strongly about the lack of transparency in the marketing of sugar and the over-charging by millers for the services they provide. Indeed, the subtle politics of sugar production can be seen as a calculated strategy of squeezing the new farmers, creating the basis for tension between settlers and millers.

With the estate owners controlling the production system, outgrowers have few options, and many have diversified their production to include irrigated vegetables and maize to reduce their reliance on sugar. In the 2008 season it did not make sense to invest in cane, and many failed to fertilise, irrigate or harvest. Much cane was simply burnt or left to rot, with some sold in local markets or illegally across the border where reasonable prices could be gained.

In the face of these challenges, there have been significant changes to the sugar cane commodity chain. New transactions have emerged, especially in the marketing of cane. Figure 7.5 depicts the key components. Illegal transactions have increased in importance, and these include individual dealings by employees, thefts of cane, night trade in cane, illegal cross-border trade to Mozambique and the exchange of cane for grain among other things. Sierevogel et al. (2007: 8) observe that 'the sugar industry considers that that up to 60,000 tonnes of sugar was illegally exported into neighbouring countries. This was due to low marketing pricing brought about by pricing controls, in comparison with regional sugar prices, a shortage of foreign currency and the high arbitrage brought about by a controlled exchange rate.'

Thus, although overall sugar production remained relatively stable, and the core estates – with the exception of Mkwasine – remained more or less intact, the uncertainties of the wider economic setting had an impact on the new A2 settlers in particular. Figure 7.5 was drawn by A2 sugar cane farmers in Hippo Valley and illustrates their perception of the value chain. The highlighted sections show the formal interactions with the mill and the range of value-added activities associated. These continue generally as before. However, it is the array of non-highlighted actors and connections that are new, resulting in major new market dynamics. With employees' wages – both on the estates and in the A2 outgrower farms – being eroded by inflation, raw sugar became a vital currency in the lowveld. When not supplied by the company or the outgrower, employees took their own payments in the form of raw cane which saw a massive growth of informal markets, and a burgeoning 'night trade' and barter exchange market. In addition to the formal exports by the estate companies, informal cross-border trade expanded, especially to Mozambique and South Africa, alongside illegal trading within the country.[6] In the disastrous economic conditions of the last decade, the new sugar producers and their employees had little option but to engage in illegal trade, or diversify out of sugar altogether.

With the dollarisation of the economy, cane farmers in the A2 schemes were once again able to contemplate investing in production. But the politics of sugar cane markets on the estates, and the on-going conflicts between outgrowers and estate owners, remains a major issue which is unlikely to be easily resolved. With sugar seen as both strategic and lucrative, the politics of land and markets in the lowveld continues to offer intrigue. As Chapter 1 described, speculation has increased about new investments in sugar and biofuel production in the former Nuanetsi ranch. Reports suggested that significant areas of land had been acquired by a business conglomerate, led by Billy Rautenbach, and backed by senior politicians. Major new investments in dam building, sugar mills and irrigation are being discussed, all involving significant displacement of people – including perhaps up to 6,000 households from Nuanetsi, and the informal Uswaushava settlement area.[7]

The 'real markets' influencing sugar production are deeply bound up with wider political dynamics in the lowveld. Connections between the estates, new investors and powerful politicians fundamentally influence how the commodity chains are constructed. The new settlers

[6]   This illegal market allegedly involved some senior political figures, see: http://www.zimbabwemetro.com/news/vp-mujuru-implicated-in-sugar-scam/.

[7]   'Mugabe to grow sugar cane in Lowveld' http://www.thezimbabwetimes.com/?p=6586, 31 October 31; 'Party big wigs locked in Nuanetsi turf war, http://www.theindependent.co.zw/local/24785-party-bigwigs-locked-in-nuanetsi-ranch-turf-war.html, 17 December 2009; 'Nkomo backs Rautebach project', http://www.thedailynewszw.com/?p=26384, 11 January 2010.

– either A2 outgrowers or other farmers who have invaded land demarcated for sugar plantations – have little voice and almost no influence.

7.5 Cotton

In contrast to the other commodities, cotton has continued to boom since 2000. The cotton industry is of great economic importance to Zimbabwe and the crop has overtaken tobacco as the major agricultural foreign currency earner. In 2004 cotton represented 12.5% of agricultural contribution to GDP. It is an important cash crop for small-scale and communal farmers, particularly in dry years when other crops may fail, but cotton will still provide a return (Mariga, 2006). Cotton has become important for both the sustenance of rural livelihoods and as a source of export revenue. Unlike tobacco, which had been dominated by the large-scale commercial sector, cotton did not see a dramatic decline in overall production nationally in the period following 2000, as Figure 7.6 illustrates.

Figure 7.6 Cotton and tobacco production trends

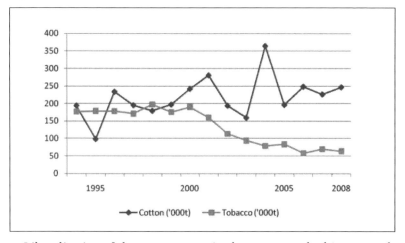

Liberalisation of the cotton sector in the 1990s resulted in a growth of companies and ginning facilitites. This accelerated in the 2000s (Larsen, 2002; Poulton et al., 2006; Poulton and Hanyani-Mlambo, 2008). Government reduced its share in the former state-owned company, Cottco, to 10% in 2000, and the market share of Cottco declined in the following years, from a near monopoly in the 1990s to around 60% by 2004 (Tschirley et al., 2009). Problems with credit repayment plagued Cottco in this period, and the formerly well-regulated system of provision of inputs and a contract to sell with strict grading criteria was challenged by competing companies. A dozen new entrant companies competed in the main cotton areas of the country. Within our study sites the Uswaushava area in the Chiredzi cluster has become a major cotton production zone (Chapter 5). These companies provided inputs on credit and offered effectively a contract farming arrangement. Due to the ability to secure foreign exchange allocations from the Reserve Bank, a number of companies diversified into the cotton market following 2000, including, FSI and, surprisingly, ZESA (the Zimbabwe Electricity Supply Authority). Selective access to foreign exchange for some – especially those with connections – was an important aspect of the highly politicised real economy at this time.

The intense competition between cotton companies nevertheless provided many benefits to farmers, as they were able to pick and choose between different deals. Thus, unlike the experience of other sectors, cotton production was boosted under land reform as a result of opening up of new producing areas by farmers settled under both A1 and A2 resettlement models. Currently it is estimated that there are over 250,000 farmers involved in cotton production (Poulton and Hanyani-Mlambo, 2009). Prior to 2000, large-scale commercial farmers produced around 15% of total cotton production, down from 80% at Independence; after 2000, their production fell to less that 1%. (Hanyani-Mlambo and Poulton, 2004).

Many companies operate in the Ushawushava area. In 2008, Mr LC commented:

> There are many companies operating. Even if Cottco and ZESA supply the seed, there are many who compete for the product. Yes, the contract is there, but we are not going to sell for less. Inputs are supplied on credit. I am a Cottco member. I grow five hectares of cotton and the yield from four is sold to Cottco, the rest is sold to the best payer. FSI, Tarafin, Cargill and Parogate offer good prices. ZESA supplies seeds and chemicals reliably and on time. Cottco is good too: we have known them for a long time. Cottco wants to buy when there are large quantities. The others come quickly even for small amounts; one bale even. Grading quality is between A and D. The quality of seeds is standard across companies. Cottco supplies seed for multiplication. Seed cotton fetches a higher price. Quite a few farmers here do this. It happens in one area to avoid contamination. Sometimes the companies supply chemicals late, so it's good to buy. It all depends on the results of scouting. When we get cash – Zim dollars – we must spend or convert to Rands – or buy scotch carts, livestock, ploughs.

Since the 1980s, and the successful interventions of the Cotton Marketing Board, and especially since liberalisation – first partial, then more complete – cotton has been a great smallholder success story in Zimbabwe. Through most of this period production has increased substantially, input supplies have been provided successfully and lint quality has been maintained, gaining premium prices on the international market (Tschirley et al. 2009; Poulton et al., 2006). While there have been problems with input supplies, particularly fertilisers and pesticides, cotton seed supplies have been maintained, as seed production had long been decentralised and was focused in the small-scale sector. A move from a privatised, but concentrated, local monopoly (with the privatisation of Cottco in 1997), to a more diversified market with more players (although dominated by Cottco and Cargill), has allowed a transition to a liberalised market which, during the 1990s, largely maintained quality, and was supported by a strong public-private research base (Larsen, 2002).

However, in the 2000s procedures for credit provision and lint quality control were undermined as more and more companies entered the market, often with limited knowledge of the sector. This has had potentially negative effects for the industry as a whole, including its international reputation (Poulton and Hanyani-Mlambo, 2009). Nevertheless, liberalisaion has brought substantial advantages. With no attempts to control the sector and centrally manage operations and financing, the distortions observed in other sectors were less apparent. Profitability was maintained in foreign-exchange terms due to the continued devaluation of the local currency over this period, and the ability of companies to retain earnings in foreign exchange was a key factor in assuring viability. Some companies, often using their political connections, were given preferential treatment under export zone deals and so were allowed to retain more foreign exchange than others. Thus, in order to navigate the cotton sector's real markets, various tactics had to be deployed. For example, cotton markets involved extensive side-selling by farmers to 'free-riding' companies, in turn raising the costs of credit and input supply (Poulton and Hanyani-Mlambo, 2009). Different companies operated in different currencies, offering commodities as enticements along with cash. Cargill even offered its own 'bearer cheques' for a while. Overall, the successful 1990s liberalisaton provided a firm basis for the growth of a vibrant cotton sector, with resettlement farmers reaping substantial benefits, although as Poulton and Hanyani-Mlambo (2008) point out, when extreme competition undermines informal coordination within the sector, wider negative consequences can result.

7.6 The political economy of real markets in Zimbabwe

Discussion of the agricultural sector in Zimbabwe is dominated by a narrative of decline and disaster. While the post-land reform transition has indeed been traumatic, with overall agricultural production down, and some commodities seeing serious declines, the story is more complex and subtle than is often portrayed. As the above discussion of commodities has highlighted, the reasons for success or failure are many and complex. Different commodities are associated with different markets, each with their own sociological and political implications. The impacts of land reform on livelihoods is mediated through these 'real markets' – and associated politics and social relations – with highly diverse outcomes.

The economic chaos and political divisions of the past decade have created many opportunities for patronage and corruption. But a longer history must be taken into account too. A series of overlapping phases can be identified, starting with a centralised, technocratic, elite model based on a dualistic system, with heavy state control, that persisted from the colonial era to the 1990s. This was changed, but only marginally, by economic liberalisation and structural adjustment in the 1990s, and only confronted fundamentally by the combined effects of radical land reform and economic collapse from 2000. This released a new form of entrepreneurialism and a radical reconfiguring of commodity chains, involving many new players and relationships. This, in turn, was challenged in 2007-08 by the well-connected political-business-security elite which attempted to re-establish technocratic order and control, but with new masters. In this ongoing struggle, land has been a key weapon, and with it, control over input supplies and markets. In 2007-08, attempts at state control – involving the security services and youth militia – failed dramatically, but had many negative consequences. The various top-down, centrally-directed schemes over the last decade have been highly expensive failures too. They have too often offered opportunities for extracting rent for those in positions of power and influence, thereby undermining development.

There has thus been a changing relationship between the economy and state power and authority in the last decade. The emergence of a second, informal economy blurs the boundaries between the formal and informal, the legal and illegal, changing the social and political relationships of market actors fundamentally. What Janet MacGaffey (1991: 10) argued for Zaire in the 1980s has many echoes for Zimbabwe in recent times:

> Government intervention does not create informal practices but changes the context in which they take place and their legal definition. The margin between the legal and the illegal, the legitimate and illegitimate is often shadowy. Ultimately it is the responsibility of the state to define legitimate economic activity…. The state, however, operates to further the interests of the dominant class. Through the second economy, the citizenry may … also express resistance to the state.

Significant opportunities opened up in Zimbabwe as a result of the emergent second economy. But these changes bring costs and challenges: not everyone has had the opportunity to benefit. While, with new land for many, production and marketing opportunities have widened, this has not been universal. Especially following the politically-motivated clampdowns of 2007-08, access was especially constrained, increasingly being dependent on political patronage relations. However, with dollarisation and the stabilisation of the economy, new economic dynamics open up.

A bigger question is posed, however: have we been seeing a sustained transition, a fundamental reconfiguration of production and markets – a radically new agrarian political economy – or a phase of turbulence and uncertainty, after which a new technocratic and market order will be imposed, controlled by a new set of elite players? Will the forces of neoliberalism and globalisation inevitably result in a reconfigured bifurcation of the agricultural sector, with an export-oriented commercial sector separated from more subsistence-focused 'peasant' production systems (Akram-Lodhi et al., 2009) or have more deep-rooted changes taken place in the agricultural economy? As the chapter has shown, commodity chains have changed radically– from production to processing to retailing. This has fundamentally reshaped the relationship between the state and the market and, despite fairly draconian backlashes, the new dynamic unleashed from 2000 has been difficult to suppress.

The real markets that underpin these new economic arrangements are fuelled by very different relationships, based on new connections and associations. Those who once dominated are adapting fast to new circumstances in order to survive. But this is not easy. Historic costs, inappropriate infrastructure and poor relations – sometimes based on long-term racial hostility or indifference – are making adjustment to the new realities an uphill struggle. What should we make of this emerging scenario? What future challenges arise?

Clearly it is too early to be definitive. The situation remains in flux and, with this, comes uncertainty. However, the rural economy has not collapsed. It is not that there are no markets today – there are just very new markets. Even when uncertainties over land and the economy decline, we believe, these are here to stay. The old dualistic system, the inheritance of the colonial era, sustained more-or-less intact for 20 years following Independence has, almost certainly, gone for good, although new relationships between different forms of agriculture – for example between estates and outgrowers, centralised cotton operations and smallholders and specialised elements of livestock production – will certainly arise.

What broader lessons can be drawn from this assessment? First, as the maize example so starkly illustrates, clumsy, politicised intervention by the state – even with the stated aim of increasing production and marketed output – results in capture, corruption and gross inefficiency. Second, as illustrated by the cotton case, this need not be the case. A competitive, liberalised private sector can deliver effective support to an emerging sector. But this requires coordination and regulation, as well as a stable economic setting, in order to work. Third, as the beef case illustrates, assuming that the past is a model for the future is futile. Fourth, as the sugar case shows, control of land, water and resources associated with valuable cropping operations – especially those with foreign exchange earning potential – will continue to be a source of tension. Tussles between new, smallholder settlers, outgrowers under the A2 schemes, established estates and sugar mills and new investor networks keen on opportunistically grabbing land, will continue. Land reform has reshaped political-economic relations significantly, but only up to a point, as new waves of contestation emerge.

The assessment of the four commodities challenges the myth that there is no dynamism in the agricultural economy. There are problems, for sure, but there has been an unleashing of innovation, diversity and entrepreneurship, with new market connections and governance arrangements being forged. This is occurring especially among new land users, but former landholders are also entering these new markets in new ways; for example by being key to the post-harvest commodity chains as owners of transport businesses, crop processing plants, abbatoirs and wholesale and retail outlets.[8] These opportunities are constrained in the sugar sector by the historic structure of the industry

---

[8]   This was a phenomenon observed following land reform in East Asia (Lipton 2009: 120).

and the power of the major players, and in the beef sector by inappropriate infrastructure and market connections, and the lack of veterinary and other support.

How, then, can a transition to a successful, vibrant agricultural economy be facilitated? Too often the policy discussion reverts to an assumption that all will be saved if there is a return to a large-scale commercial sector, with a revival of a dualistic structure. This, it is argued, provides the economies of scale, efficiencies and skill sets necessary in a competitive global economy. In such a setting, smallholders do not have a chance, as their pre-harvest scale efficiencies are outweighed by post-harvest superiority on a range of counts (Lipton, 2009). This may be the case for some commodities for some markets (say high-value horticulture exported to European supermarkets, high-grade tobacco or top-quality beef cuts for export), but, as we have seen, this is not the sum total of the agricultural economy, nor necessarily the focus for future aspirations given global economic trends. Smallholder production can make major contributions to economic output for some commodities in some markets (Lipton, 2005; Hazell et al., 2007), especially when issues of coordination and intermediation between production and marketing are addressed (Johnson et al., 2003; Kydd et al., 2004; Dorward et al., 2004a).

For the future, a focus on local and regional markets, where barriers to entry are lower, may make more sense, into which the small-scale producer may be able to sell on a highly competitive basis. Under such a vision small and medium-scale producers in the A1 and A2 resettlements can be contributors to a vibrant commercial farm economy, with different products for different markets, and radically revised value chains governed in new ways. Thus the efficiencies of small-scale farming can be captured for production, while linkages to other, larger, more capitalised enterprises may allow post-harvest benefits to be reaped, as with the 'white revolution' in milk production in India (Lipton, 2009: 91). The entrepreneurialism of the informal – often illegal – 'real markets' that have emerged in the last decade is perhaps a good foundation for this longer-term vision. While such informal market networks, cross-border trade and illegal smuggling have emerged in highly uncertain economic conditions, often out of necessity rather than design, they have shown the potential of restructured markets, as in the case of cotton, beef and to some degree maize.

With the establishment of an inclusive government in 2009, the economy stabilised and a tentative recovery can be observed. Notable reforms include the removal of the monopoly on grain trade by the GMB, the elimination of price controls and the introduction of a multi-currency environment. All of these are vital precursors to the emergence of a new agricultural economy, but they are not sufficient. A more searching analysis of the political-economic dynamics of real markets is required if the opportunities that have only been glimpsed are to be siezed, a theme we return to in Chapter 11.

8

Livelihoods | Off-farm Income
Beyond the Farm | & Migration

8.1 Livelihood diversification and deagrarianisation

Livelihoods in rural Africa are highly diversified, and Zimbabwe is no exception. Agriculture may be the mainstay, but it is not the only option; a whole range of off-farm activities are pursued. For the past century, rural Zimbabweans have worked away from their farming areas – in the mines, on the farms and in the cities. Cross-border migration has been an important feature, as people moved to South Africa or elsewhere.

However, the classic circular migration, so typical of southern Africa in the past (Murray, 1980), has changed in recent times. In the past there was a predictable movement of men away from the farm to work following household establishment. Women largely stayed in the rural areas and were responsible for day-to-day farm management, looking after the home and the children. Investments by the male worker – either on a seasonal basis or through longer-term employment – were ploughed back into the farm, building up assets including cattle and equipment, so that by the time of retirement the farm was well capitalised and able to provide support in old age. While this typical pattern was never universal, it was nevertheless very common since the 1930s. However, a number of important changes have happened over the last 30 years. First, investment in farming became only one of a number of routes for remittance income. With the widening availability of education after 1980, people increasingly invested in children's education as a route out of poverty – and possibly out of farming. With the scourge of HIV/AIDS hitting hard from the 1990s (Gregson et al., 2006)[1], the costs of medical care and funerals put an increasing burden on people's finances. Retrenchments following the implementation of structural adjustment policies in the 1990s also had an impact on the flow of remittances and the availability of employment. And, with the collapse of the economy from 1997, the value of off-farm earnings from Zimbabwean sources plummeted.

Resettlement policy since 1980 has emphasised the importance of agriculture-based livelihoods, urging a delinking from off-farm employ-

---

[1] http://www.unaids.org/en/CountryResponses/Countries/zimbabwe.asp.

ment. In the 1980s, permits for resettlement disallowed off-farm work, and insisted on full-time commitment to farming (Potts and Mutambirwa, 1990; Potts, 2000; Chapter 1). Such edicts had limited impact, but they do reflect a recurrent bias in policy thinking in Zimbabwe. The ideal rural livelihood is supposed to be a full-time farmer, working a farm as a business with profitable returns. This is supposed to be a family enterprise with the husband and wife at the helm, although very often with the assumption that the man is in charge. They would use family labour and hire in workers as necessary, and their livelihoods would be sustained through the income earned from farming, based on the notion of a 'viable economic unit', assuming an ideal farm size and enterprise mix, all encapsulated in a business plan (Cousins and Scoones, 2010). This model is of course derived from the large-scale commercial sector which, for many, presents what farming and farmers should be in the ideal world.

Yet, delinking agriculture from wider non-farm economic activity does not make sense. Land redistribution to multiple small holdings, if they generate additional output and income, should in turn result in higher demand for non-farm products through backward production linkages (farm inputs), forward production linkages (processing of farm outputs) and consumption linkages (other goods and services). Estimates of multiplier effects in Africa range from 1.3-1.5, whereby $100 of additional farm output generates an additional $30-50 in the rural non-farm economy (Haggblade et al., 2007, 1991, 1989). In the longer term this can be an important driver of growth more generally (Deininger and Squire, 1998; Lipton, 2009),[2] as we discuss further in Chapter 10.

In any case, given the vagaries of climate, agroecology, prices, markets and policy, spreading risk, smoothing income streams, balancing options and having a diverse portfolio of livelihood options is vital, especially when agriculture is so risky and uncertain. Numerous studies have documented the importance of livelihood diversification in rural Zimbabwe, whether in the communal areas (e.g. Scoones et al., 1996; Campbell et al., 2002; Bird and Shepherd, 2003) or the old resettlement areas (Kinsey, 1999; Chimhowu, 2002). Even in the large-scale commercial sector, the inspiration for the ideal model of full-time farming, most farmers had diversified: real estate, hotels, tourism and wildlife, transport, import-export trading, agricultural processing and marketing were all part of highly diversified portfolios (Selby, 2006). When farming was not so profitable – because of a poor season, a crash in prices or the removal of subsidies – other options were available. Equally, when land reform took place many former commercial farmers (although by no means all) had alternative options to sustain livelihoods, even if the economic loss and personal trauma was high. So too with smallholder farming, where a diversification of livelihoods, involving a range of activities off farm, involving migration or not, are vital in offsetting the impacts of variability or sudden shocks.

Livelihood diversification can occur through different routes (Reardon, 1997; Ellis, 1998; Hussein and Nelson 1998; Barrett et al., 2001). In

---

[2] Although see Hart (1989) on the growth linkages controversy in Asia.

some cases, it is a response to difficult times, and a coping strategy that would otherwise not be pursued. While necessary for livelihood survival, such options do not necessarily improve people's lives, but just avoid destitution or starvation. Diversification may include the collecting and sale of wild foods, gold panning or border jumping; activities that are low return, and some highly risky and illegal. Kinsey (2002, 2009) for example notes how in old resettlement areas the number of off-farm activities increased over time, although the returns from each declined. This he interprets as survival diversification. However, in other cases, diversification may be seen as an opportunity for growth, a chance to expand the range of enterprises and increase the variety of income streams. Opportunity diversification may include establishing a trading business or shop, taking up paid employment or setting up an agro-processing facility. But these require capital investment or educational qualifications which are only available to a few. Later in this chapter, we examine how these types of livelihood diversification are playing out in the new resettlement areas of Masvingo province.

While livelihoods may be diversified at a household level, within households there may be significant specialisation. Different off-farm options are taken up by different genders, age groups and by people with different educational levels. Thus, for example, certain types of trading, craft work, employment and migration patterns may be pursued by women, while men focus on other activities. Younger people may focus on activities requiring harder labour or where the risks are higher, such as gold panning or border jumping. And those with better educational qualifications may be able to gain access to certain types of employment or migration options. In subsequent sections we will explore these contrasts, highlighting the highly differentiated patterns of diversification.

The patterns observed in the new resettlements reflect observations made elsewhere in Africa (Bahiigwa et al., 2005; Ellis and Freeman, 2004). As discussed in Chapter 1, this process of de-agrarianisation or de-peasantisation (Bryceson, 1996, 1999, 2004) is seen by some as indicative of a wider transition away from smallholder, peasant livelihoods (even if diversified) towards a reliance on non-farm income sources. A key question is therefore: is this phenomenon being observed in Zimbabwe, and what implications does it have?

In Chapter 1, four different perspectives on smallholder agriculture, livelihood diversification and redistributive land reform were discussed. All accept that diversification is an essential part of wider livelihoods, but the implications drawn are highly divergent. For some, livelihood diversification is a positive response to new opportunities and a route to offsetting risks presented by agriculturally-based livelihoods, while for others it represents a more fundamental failure of agrarian systems and peasant-based livelihoods, with impoverishment and exploitation the likely outcome for many. In this chapter we will look at the empirical data from Masvingo province and draw some tentative conclusions as to what longer-term dynamics these imply. Are we seeing a decline in agriculture, a de-peasantisation and proletarianisation, with economic forces driving people away from agriculture, or are we seeing increasing investment in peasant-style livelihoods, with smallholder agriculture becoming more central to a locally-driven economy? Of course the particular context of Zimbabwe over the past decade makes any wider generalisations difficult. As the economy collapsed and off-farm farm opportunities declined, investments in rural production became increasingly important. But is this going to be a long-term phenomenon, with new settlers committing to their new farms, or a transitory one, with a reversal occurring when the economy recovers? Despite these imponderables, Zimbabwe remains an interesting test case, where, on a massive scale, redistributive land reform took place, with smallholder agriculture at its centre.

8.2 Off-farm livelihoods

Off-farm sources are important for all household livelihoods in the new resettlements in our study areas. But which activities are important for whom, and how are these patterns differentiated across the sites?

In terms of relative importance of different livelihood options, 70% of households across the study sample ranked cropping as the number one source of income, with the other 30% ranking it second and third. As for non-farming activities, 16.3% ranked employment first, 5.4% ranked remittances first and 8.5% ranked natural resources first (including brick-making, fishing, hunting, sale of firewood, harvesting of mopane worms, thatching grass collection, pottery and basket making and craft work). Table 8.1 offers an overview of off-farm livelihood activities across the study areas. Trading, pottery/basket-making and employment are the most common off-farm activities. Some are more the preserve of men (such as employment), while some are commonly associated with women (such as trading and basket-making). The data also show how off-farm employment is more likely among SG1 households, and those who are better educated than the average, while pottery and basket-making are more common among less educated, younger, SG3 households. Overall, though, Table 8.1 shows how most activities are well distributed across success group, age and educational achievement categories.

The data shows the importance of trading and pottery/basket making in Mwenezi cluster, reflecting both the precariousness of agriculture-based livelihoods in this dryland area, and the proximity to the South African and Mozambican borders which facilitates trading. The Gutu cluster shows the highest participation in off-farm employment, the reasons including a long tradition of mission education in the area, and the easy connections to urban centres. Outside the Mwenezi cluster, households on A2 schemes are more reliant on off-farm employment than other activities, while in the A1 and informal schemes a diversity of options is evident. Trading is significant, as people engaged with restructured markets and commodity chains, as well as cross-border price differences. Overall, the data shows how significant off-farm income is for many households in nearly all sites, across scheme types, success groups, gender, age and educational level. Cross-border trade – legal and illegal – was especially important. Formal employment,

Table 8.1 Non-farm income earning across the study sites

Activity	% Households engaged in activity	% women	Of those engaged, % SG1	Of those engaged, % SG3	Of those engaged, % households with head below average age (45 yrs)	Of those engaged, % households with head above average educational level (8 yrs)
Building and carpentry	3%	0%	50%	33%	33%	33%
Brick-making and thatching	6%	43%	40%	40%	22%	33%
Fishing	3%	56%	17%	50%	33%	33%
Wood carving	1%	0%	50%	0%	100%	0%
Tailoring	3%	29%	60%	20%	40%	60%
Transport business	2%	100%	33%	0%	50%	50%
Grinding mills	1%	33%	50%	50%	100%	0%
Pottery and basket making	16%	62%	28%	34%	57%	21%
Trading	18%	59%	29%	29%	44%	50%
Employment off farm	16%	28%	39%	21%	44%	71%

Source: Survey data, 2007-08 (N=177)

the classic route to livelihood diversification in rural Zimbabwe, is increasingly combined with other activities, including border jumping (for piecework and trade), as well as commodity exchange and natural resource extraction linked to cross-border trade. The consequences of retrenchment from the late 1990s, and the collapse of the value of salaries, especially from the mid-2000s, are major factors in shaping these patterns.

As the eight cases below illustrate, different dynamics of diversification are observable: some for survival and some for accumulation. Understanding livelihood change requires looking at patterns of diversification over time – across a person's life, and across generations. Each of the cases highlights a different dynamic, and a different sense of how access to land through land reform fits into a wider picture of livelihood change:

Case 1: SC, Wondedzo Wares, A1 villagised (SG2)

I came from Gutu communal area where I had three hectares. I am now old, over 80 years. I was a farmer and blacksmith and worked hard to educate my children. Four of my children are teachers, one is a nurse in Masvingo General and one is a soldier. One of my children is now late. He was an extension worker. One of my wives is also now late, but my younger wife helps with the farming. My old field in Gutu has been given to two of my sons. My younger children do not have jobs, but several are border jumpers and go to South Africa, as well as helping out with farming at home. They usually get a job in the farms across the Limpopo and come back after earning some money, bringing goods with them. One son specialises in hunting wild pigs for selling. He travels all over the place: from Zambia to Botswana. Another son attempted to go to the Chiadzwa diamond fields, but he was chased by the heavy security. The sons of my eldest children got really good jobs. One is a cross-border truck driver and lives in South Africa, another works in customs at Beitbridge and two are now in the UK. My sons and daughters, and now even the grandchildren, really help us – sending food and cash. This is how we survive.

Case 2: NA, Bompst A2 (SG2)

I originally came from Gutu, under Chief Makore. My parents influenced me, as they were skilled farmers. I married in Gutu and built good houses in the communal areas. We now have three boys and two girls. In the past I was employed by the Central Intelligence Organisation, but I resigned and now I do my own job. I am an electrician. Since the lake is nearby, I sometimes also fish and sell the produce. In Gutu there was a severe shortage of land. Before resettlement I had a car, four cattle and six goats. All of these were purchased through my jobs. After resettlement, I bought another car, constructed farm houses and have started electrification. Now farming complements my other income. I have been buying cattle too; now I have five. I also employ four workers. Although farming is my main occupation now, my work as an electrician is also important. We live on the farm, and while I am away doing jobs as an electrician my wife runs the farm and manages the labourers. This is a full time job, although she does manage to produce some vegetables for local sales.

Case 3: LC, Uswaushava, informal (SG1)

We originally came from Chivi district under Chief Nemauzhe. The whole family was based in Harare until 1999 when I was retrenched. I was working for a private company making detergents. We then relocated to our communal home and cultivated for one season only. We kept our house in Budiriro township in Harare, which is currently rented out. In 2000, we joined the land occupations in search of a better life. In 2005, two of our boys migrated to South Africa. One of them is employed in a bank, while the other is self-employed as a builder. Two other relatives have since joined the family at Uswaushava. Remittances, mostly in the form of groceries from our two children in South Africa, complement the household's other income. My wife occasionally goes to South Africa as well, selling agricultural produce, especially bambara nuts (nyimo). In September, she went with ten 50kg bags of bambara nuts by bus. The proceeds from the sale have been used to mould bricks, as we want to build another kitchen. Other funds have been reserved to finance the movement of the household belongings (furniture and other assets) from Chivi to the new plot. We have always had other businesses. In Harare, I would buy bales of second-hand clothes from my job and my wife would sell them in the communal areas. I am thinking of starting this business again when people have money. Now we sell groceries and opaque beer at our homestead. There is a roaring trade, especially when the cotton is harvested.

Case 4: Hippo Valley, A2

Due to the low prices being paid for sugar in Zimbabwe, significant quantities are smuggled across the border to Mozambique and South Africa. Workers from Hippo Valley estates, as well as A2 plot holders, are involved in this trade. Illegal crossing points are used to avoid detection by customs officials. In addition to sugar, traders from other parts of the country are transporting tobacco, carvings, doilies and other products. Traders employ people to carry the goods across the border, and they communicate by mobile phone to transporters who pick the goods to transport them overnight to Johannesburg and Pretoria. While resettlement farmers and farm workers gain only a limited share of the profit from this trade, this is still preferable to the low commodity prices from the formal, official market (see Chapter 7).

Case 5: TC, Asveld A2 (farm worker)

I originally came from Neshuro, but started working in the farms long ago. I am now 69. My first job was herding cattle in farms near Zvishavane. I came to work in this area three years ago. My wife was also employed here, but she left and returned to farm at our communal home, as there was no pay. I have not been paid for some months, but I have other ways of earning a living. I carve stools, make cooking sticks and produce hoe handles from the resources on the farm. I sell these to others in the villages nearby. There is also an opportunity to hunt here, but one of the main problems of this place is the poachers who come. They demand food and accommodation, and they set snares which can kill the cattle.

Case 6: GM, Edenvale, A1 villagised (SG3)

I used to be a farm worker, and worked at several farms in the Mateke Hills.

When the land reform happened I left my job. My mother had joined the invasions and got a plot. I have cleared a very small portion of land which my wife farms together with my mother, although she is now old. Most of the time I do other jobs, such as radio and bicycle repairs, as well as well digging, rather than field work.

Case 7: Mrs HB, Edenvale, A1 villagised
I am a cross-border trader, trading baskets and other products in Mozambique. I am a widow, and have no other means of support. This is a good business. I work closely with my friend, Mrs CM. We weave baskets and winnowing trays at home in Edenvale. We buy in ilala palm for the weaving from different places, including Turf ranch. There are many in the new resettlement areas who collect and sell ilala. Different places have different qualities of palm, so we must search out the best. To get the best prices, the products must be well decorated. We need to get hold of dye from the munyii tree, and if not we use carbon paper soaked in boiling water. There is a lot of labour used in making these products, and so the profit is not high. Sometimes we hold work parties and get others to help us, offering some food and maheu drink. The Mozambican bazaars have so many products. We bring soap, flour, rice, cooking oil, baking powder, aluminium pots and second-hand clothes. These are all in high demand in Zimbabwe. Groceries are even cheaper in South Africa, but the border crossing is illegal and more dangerous.

Case 8: IM and TG, Chikombedzi area
We have specialised in cattle driving. The buyers on both sides of the border liase with us, as we know the routes and the officials. This is now the main occupation for both of us [Both have husbands working, but they do not send remittances. Mrs IM's husband is in South Africa, but they do not hear from him; Mrs TG's husband works for National Parks, but they do not get paid]. We charge R300 to drive one beast for sale. From the profits we purchase goods in the Mozambican bazaars, including flour, tea leaves, cooking oil, Vaseline, clothes and other goods. We hire scotch carts in Mozambique to transport the goods up to Malapati bus terminus. Cross-border cattle trading is a lucrative business here. Different markets in Mozambique and South Africa, and currency differentials, make a big difference to our profits. We work closely with Mozambican traders who can arrange sales to buyers on the other side of the border. Getting police and veterinary permits requires paying bribes to the relevant officials. The Mozambican youth militia patrol the area and are always extracting bribes from us Zimbabweans. There is only one person we fear: a Zimbabwean policeman who refuses to take a bribe and confiscates the cattle and sends people to court!

8.3 Natural resources and livelihoods

As the cases above show, off-farm income derived from natural resources is often very important to people's livelihoods. Most study sites were formerly cattle ranches, with relatively little cultivated land and settlement. This meant that fields and homes had to be carved out of the bush.

The new areas offered plentiful natural resources – including wild fruits, grass, palms, reeds, mushrooms and wild animals. Compared to the densely populated communal areas from where many had come, these seemed bountiful places.

Chapter 2 has already discussed the process by which this land was allocated and planned. But this was not just about carving out fields and allocating settlement sites. As people cleared fields and home-stead areas, they were especially careful to retain valuable trees. Other resources, such as hunting areas and reed or grass collection sites, were also highly valued. For example, in the Gutu and Masvingo sites, the *miombo* woodland has a large variety of fruit trees and these now scatter the fields and home sites (Chivaura-Mususa, 2003; Wilson, 1989; Campbell, 1987), including *Parinari curatellifolia* (*muchakata*) and *Uapaca kirkiana* (wild loquat, *mushuku*), for example. In the drought of 2008, *muchakata* became a vital source of food for many. The relatively sour grass of the *miombo* areas is also useful for thatching, and a trade developed in some areas, with women cutting grass in groups and selling it to new settlers establishing their homes. In the Chiredzi and Mwenezi lowveld sites important trees included *Adansonia digitata* (baobab, *mumbuyu*), *Sclerocarya birrea* (*marula, mupfura*), *Strychnos spinosa* (*mutamba*) and other valuable fruit and timber varieties. In the lowveld too the new resettlement areas offered significant resources in the form of mopane worms (*Imbrasia belina*, a valuable food and income source),[3] as well as ilala palm used for basket making (Sola, 2004).

The lowveld areas in particular are also a source of game. Hunting became an important livelihood activity for many, as people culled animals in the process of clearing their land. In the past, people had to steal on to the farms at night, protected by special charms, and were always at the risk of arrest. Following land reform, opportunities for hunting opened up. Reducing wild animal populations was an important precursor to any type of crop agriculture, so snares and traps were set in large numbers. In some areas fish resources became available, often in the dams created in large numbers on the former large-scale farms. These provided new sources of livelihood for many, a few taking up fishing as a full-time occupation. Box 8.1 highlights the diversity of natural resource based activities found in the Mwenezi cluster.

The proportion of households getting income from natural resources is highest in the A1 villagised schemes in the Mwenezi cluster, with 98% of SG3 households, 87% of SG2 and 77% of SG1 households involved. Again, the significance of a particular activity varies by location. For instance, 52% of households in the A1 villagised schemes (Edenvale farm) are involved in basket weaving, while 63% are involved in the harvesting of mopane worms.

Natural resources also have benefits for livelihoods beyond generating cash income. Studies have shown how wild resources amount to a significant resource value when all values – direct and indirect – are accounted for (Campbell et al., 1997b). In terms of livelihoods, they may be critical for nutrition, for example, for certain people at certain times of the year (Gomez, 1988). Wild fruits in particular are often unrecogn-

[3] http://www.mopane.org/.

Box 8.1 Natural resource based livelihood diversification, Mwenezi cluster

The rich natural resources of the new resettlement areas provide plenty of opportunity for cross-border trade. Trade in ilala products is the most common. Hundreds of traders come to the markets at Chikwalakwala in Mozambique. As Mrs CM from Edenvale complained, 'There are too many people these days. The result is that prices are often not good.' More lucrative, is the trade in hides. As RT explained, 'Those that are much in demand include pythons, civet cats and leopards. There are buyers of these hides who come from Mozambique and South Africa and operate across the farms.' Biltong is also big business. Both Edenvale and Turf ranches are important sources. Those from the farms who hunt small game complain that they are now competing with National Parks officials who, because they are poorly paid, are hunting and producing biltong in large quantities. Meat from kudu, impala and buffalo is cured and dried, and the wives of the Parks officials sell it locally and across the border. 'We cannot compete with these guys,' RV complained. 'They flood the market.' Mopani worms are another important resource, often collected by women and traded in South Africa where, particularly in Venda areas, they are an important relish. Traders come from Beitbridge to Turf ranch, for example, and buy from local collectors. A number of illegal crossing points are used to transport mopane worms in large quantities. Indians in South Africa buy them and pack them in small bags for sale.

---

ised as a vital resource, but are essential to strategies of diversification, offering food or income at times of the year when agricultural production is limited.

Natural resources are used by different groups of people. Firewood, thatch grass and reed collection (and sometimes sale) is carried out mostly by women, while hunting and fishing are dominated by men. Wild fruits are particularly important for children, such as when herding or en route to and from school. An analysis of natural resource use in relation to success group showed the importance of income derived from natural resources for SG3 and SG2 households, especially those in the Mwenezi and Chiredzi clusters.

Mineral resources – notably through gold panning – have been an important source of income, especially for younger people in poorer households. Across the study sites there are no major gold panning areas inside the resettlements, but there are significant places near the Wondedzo schemes in Masvingo cluster and the Uswaushava informal scheme in the Chiredzi cluster. The major rivers and tributaries of the region have seen massive numbers of people congregate for gold panning, particularly in the dry season. This alluvial panning is illegal, as the authorities fear major degradation of riverine resources. The sale of gold through black market channels is also prohibited, so such activities carry risks. But with livelihoods insecure, and the possibility of earn-ing extra money, this source of livelihood has become very common, especially since the devastating droughts of the early 1990s.

From 2006-07, with the discovery of high-quality surface diamonds in the Chiadzwa area of Manicaland, there has been another attrac-tion: the prospect of great riches from diamond prospecting. Groups of youths – and some older people too – made the journey along the Mutare road to Chiadzwa in search of their fortunes. A number made significant sums of money, and the area became a magnet for diamond diggers, traders, currency dealers and those providing food and sup-plies for the prospectors. As the numbers swelled and the scale of the deposits became evident, the Chiadzwa area attracted the attention of politicians, the police and the security services. In 2008 a major clamp-down occurred, and the illegal mining was stopped. The army was deployed and many people were arrested. Helicopters circled the area, and people were beaten and money was confiscated. Rumours circula-ted that senior politicians and security officials had an interest in the diamonds, and the free-for-all was ordered to be stopped.[4] Those who had gone to Chiadzwa to seek their fortune fled, and those who had left the resettlement study sites returned empty-handed.

Valuable minerals are key to Zimbabwe's economy, and in the past a blind eye has been turned towards prospecting and mining at the very small scale. But when significant resources are at stake, a different politics evolves, as in the case of the Chiadzwa diamonds. Regulating gold panning, by contrast, is more difficult. Spread out across numer-ous rivers and streams, panners have become adept at evading the authorities. In the more organised areas, officials are paid off, or become involved themselves in the trade.

Across the resettlement sites, natural resources are thus a vital source of livelihood, especially for poorer people and those living in more marginal areas. While the standard narrative that land reform has resulted in massive environmental destruction can be challenged, how to ensure sustainable use remains an issue. As new communities have been formed on new land, resource management rules have had to be established. In the past, traditional approaches to resource manage-ment – such as the protection of sacred groves or wetlands – have been important, but with local authority over land and resources remaining highly contested on the new resettlements, effective common property resource management has often not yet emerged. This, as Chapter 9 dis-cusses, remains a major challenge for the future.

8.4 Migration

Chapter 3 has shown how movement into and out of the settlement sites is a continuous process; this section focuses particularly on migration away from the resettlement site in search of off-farm employment.

---

[4]   http://www.hrw.org/sites/default/files/reports/zimbabwe0609web.pdf; http://www.kuba tana.net/html/archive/archspecialentry_index.asp?spec_code=090816diamondex&sector =ECON.

There have been significant changes in migration patterns in recent decades, and the classic pattern of demographically defined circular migration discussed above, while still existing, is only one among an increasing number of pathways that people follow (Andersson 2001; Potts and Mutambirwa, 1990, 1997). Others include long-term overseas migration, either within southern African or further afield. In the last decade this has accelerated, as those who were able sought employment or refuge outside Zimbabwe, where economic conditions and employment opportunities were more conducive.[5] This included movements to Europe, where many highly skilled Zimbabweans took jobs as care workers in the UK ('Harare North') and elsewhere (Mbiba, 2005). This movement to 'join the BBC' (care workers were dubbed the 'British Bottom Cleaners') (McGregor, 2007) or other professions, or simply to join relatives, involved substantial numbers of people and resulted in the establishment of new migrant networks (McGregor, 2009; Bloch, 2008; Bracking and Sachikonye, 2008). Others moved to South Africa, Botswana, Namibia or elsewhere in SADC, often taking up professional, civil service and teaching posts. Cross-border migration took on other forms. Border jumping became strategy for many, particularly the youth, and involved the illegal crossing of the border to South Africa to take up employment in the farms of Limpopo province or do menial work further afield. The risks included crossing through barbed wire fences, and sometimes areas containing dangerous wildlife.[6] There was a constant threat of arrest and deportation, and employment conditions were sometimes appalling (Rutherford and Addison, 2007). However, it was seen by many as a preferable alternative to the situation in Zimbabwe, and, despite the risks, was an important option for a significant number of people. Some border jumpers stayed years in their jobs in South African and Botswana, while others were deported or aimed only to stay for a short period before returning home with groceries, equipment and foreign exchange cash.[7]

Other forms of migration are more temporary. We have mentioned the massive growth in informal trading. Much of this was relatively local, but some involved significant movement. With the Zimbabwe dollar collapsing, and the value of cash increasingly worthless, the need for foreign exchange meant that cross-border trade was an essential part of many people's livelihoods. This was particularly so in the Mwenezi cluster where cross-border trade in grain, live animals, biltong, baskets and other local products boomed (Chapter 7). Products were exchanged either for cash or for other goods (including groceries, household commodities, clothes and farm inputs), and the informal trading networks expanded significantly. Very often women took charge of this trade, although there was specialisation, with men being more dominant in livestock trading, while women focused on crafts and exchanges for household goods. These market transactions often took

---

[5]   Estimates vary, but possibly up to three million people left the country during this period (see http://iom.org.za/site/index.php?option=com_content&task=view&id=63&Itemid=68).
[6]   http://www.irinnews.org/Report.aspx?ReportId=84186; http://www.migration.org.za/ report/zimbabwean-migration-southern-africa-new-trends-and-responses.
[7]   http://www.irinnews.org/report.aspx?Reportid=85468; http://www.irinnews.org/pdf/ Zimbabwe_IOM.pdf.

people away from their homes for days, if not weeks, on end. Groups of traders often worked together, and support networks evolved. Dodging customs officials and border controls became a fine art, and knowledge, skill and connections were necessary. A secondary market in such services developed, with specialists offering safe passage across borders at night, overseeing bribe transactions or supplying transport, accommodation or food. With the borders at Beitbridge, Francistown and Chikwalakwala often become clogged with huge numbers of people moving, extra opportunities for extracting bribes emerged, and more transactions were required. It was often a very slow, difficult process, but one that allowed commodities and cash to flow back to Zimbabwe on a significant scale.

There have also been cases of opportunistic mass migration. For example, movement to Chimanimani and the forest estates in the eastern highlands occurred on a large scale after 2000 as areas opened up for gold panning; people from across the country camped out by rivers and streams, often living at the sites for months. The destruction of forests and riverine areas was extensive (Marongwe, 2007), but many people generated a livelihood, even if precarious, illegal and environmentally destructive.

Finally, there has been displacement, and thus forced migration, as a result of political violence. This was not a feature of our study sites, but it was significant in other parts of the province, particularly in those areas which voted against the ruling party in the first round of elections in 2008. A report from CADEC Masvingo, observed that, 'As ZANU-PF, with the assistance of the military junta intensified its campaign, many victims fled their homes to settle in towns and other open spaces like bus terminuses. The rest in rural areas sought hiding in mountains. While the victims fled, their homes were burnt and assets were looted.' Although temporary, such movements involved much hardship and a disruption of livelihoods, and the few months in mid-2008 when violence exploded will be remembered for a long time.

Data from the questionnaire survey showed that most migration from the study sites was by men, with urban areas and South Africa being the dominant destinations. Of the 107 male migrants in the survey sample (N=177 households), linked to 28% of households, a third had migrated illegally. On average 2.14 males were providing remittances to each of these sample households. In addition, there were 21 female migrants who were providing remittances, linked to 8% households. Of these, under a quarter had migrated illegally.

The following cases, together with Table 8.2, offer some insights into the different patterns of migration, and their implications for livelihoods.

MALE MIGRATION TO OFF-FARM WORK, NOW WITH FIRMER LINKS TO RURAL PRODUCTION

VC, Wondedzo Wares (SG1)

I used to work at Renco mine as an engineer, but retired a few years back. My sons are all employed, working in Zimbabwe. One is a fitter and turner, another is a bank manager and two are truck drivers. One stays at home here, running his truck driving business. We came from Nyajena area, and look for-

ward to productive farming here. The soils are good, and markets are nearby. My wife and I run the farm, hiring in labour (although our children help out). My wife sells vegetables too. The funds and groceries sent from my sons are important, but because of the economic situation it is often us who help them out with food.

SK, Edenvale (SG1

My husband works in South Africa. He sends remittances nearly every month. Groceries like flour, sugar and soap are sent. He also sends plastic buckets. I use these as payment for people to work in our fields. Through his work we have bought cattle and so have enough draught power. I have young children and need funds to hire labour to make farming a success. My husband's work is essential to get our new farm going, but he is planning to return to farm soon.

SM, Turf (SG2)

My husband works for the National Railways of Zimbabwe in Bulawayo. He has had this job for many years and it has kept us going. Our sons were well educated – up to O level. They now work in South Africa, mostly doing piece jobs on the farms. They do send us remittances from time to time. Since my husband is absent, I manage the farm. His salary is poor so he does not send much, but in the past we have bought many things for our farming from his salary. I also make some baskets and other craft work for local sale, but farming is my main job.

ABSENTEE LANDOWNERS, EMPLOYED/LIVING ELSEWHERE, WITH MORE TENUOUS LINKS TO RURAL PRODUCTION, OFTEN VIA WORKERS

Hippo Valley A2

The least successful plot holders (SG3) in Hippo Valley are those who are work-ing elsewhere, and rarely visit the farm. In our sample, CT works in Harare, rarely comes to the farm and in mid-2008 his workers had not been paid for months. Similarly, RD is absent, living in Chiredzi, while her sister operates the plot. Again in this case, the workers are poorly paid, and investment and production is low. By contrast, although five of the eight SG2 households in the sample had jobs elsewhere, they were visiting the plots regularly, man-aging workers effectively and investing in the plot. Mr MM is a teacher at a nearby primary school, and in addition to his job he manages his own and his brother's plots. JM works in Triangle estate as a manager, but visits almost daily. Although he has insufficient equipment, his yields are good. CM is a teacher in Harare, but she manages to visit regularly. She is a widow, and her son helps her with farm management. TM is a retired headmaster and stays in Chiredzi with his family. He travels regularly to the Hippo Valley plot and he and his wife can often be seen in the fields. ZM works in Masvingo, but has invested in the plot, and owns a tractor, periloader and a car which allows him to travel to the area.

LONG-DISTANCE MIGRATION TO THE INTERNATIONAL DIASPORA

MS, Wondedzo Wares (SG2)

I came from Charumbira area originally, and joined the land invasions. I came with my son. I am now 75 years old and currently occupy the plot and manage it, hiring in labour for farm work. My son migrated to the UK with his family.

He managed to get a job through a recruiting agency doing care work. His wife too has got a job, and there are other relatives where they live. They send funds home, but not much. The farm is only coming up slowly. The main thing my son invests in is livestock. There are over 40 cattle on the farm and now quite a number of pigs. The cattle provide plenty of milk which we sell.

SHORT TERM AND ILLEGAL MIGRATION – BORDER JUMPING AND CROSS-BORDER TRADE

Chikombedzi area

I was in an abusive relationship, and my husband tried to beat me. I ran from the place and joined other women moving across the border to Bende Mtale township in South Africa. On my first trip I had no orders, but I just wanted to learn the system from others. The other traders brought biltong, milk, chickens and baskets. It was month end and the trade was successful. I now have joined the group. When the South Africans get the grants and pensions at month end, there is plenty of business. The difficult thing is crossing the border. There are so many South African police patrolling. We call boys in the locations [townships] and they help transfer the goods. We go in groups of 10-20, mixing up with the border jumpers. The border jumpers are mostly young men who go on to the farms or even as far as Jo'burg to look for jobs. Some of the women have boyfriends in South Africa who provide accommodation and also funds to support families at home. There is a big danger when the Limpopo is in flood, so we cannot cross. There are also crocodiles. Also the South African farmers get angry and chase us because they say we kill their cattle. The route is infested with thugs who steal cash and goods. This is why we go in groups. In the months towards Christmas when trade is good and the border jumpers are returning home, many thugs come, sometimes armed with knives. The Zimbabwean soldiers also demand cash or food from the traders too. They can conduct strip searches and take everything. Other soldiers help out and provide transport when there is no bus, as long as we pay.

MIGRATION FROM URBAN EMPLOYMENT TO RURAL AREAS THROUGH RESETTLEMENT

SC, Wondedzo Wares (SG2)

I came from Masvingo town. Before I did not have any land. I tried to seek some in Bikita, but failed. My family is now growing – we have five children and we stay here on the new plot. My eldest son has got a job as a teacher. I was an administrator for the National Youth Service from 1980 up to 1998. I built a good house, purchased a car and had a good life in town. But with no job, town is not the place to be. I used my connections to get a plot here. I have now invested in farming assets – I have seven cattle, a scotch cart and other farm equipment. I don't have any other jobs these days – my whole focus is on farming. However, my wife is a dressmaker and she can make money from sewing.

EM, Wondedzo Wares (SG2)

I came from Masvingise, but the place was no good for farming. We had very little land. We have three young children and needed more land. We sought land under the fast-track programme and got a plot here. Until last year, I was a teacher, but I resigned because the pay was poor. I am now concentrating on farming. My wife however is still a teacher, and stays with the children. I move

*between my plot here and her place of work. My brother stays full-time on
the plot and manages it. I am now doing a business management course, and
hoping to improve my job prospects.*

Periods of absence varied across the clusters, with migrants from Gutu
being away on average the longest, at around six years, and those from
Mwenezi the shortest, at around two years. There were large ranges in
all cases, with a maximum absence of nearly 30 years in one case. A
large number of migrants were away for periods of a year or under. This
reflects the different patterns of migration discussed above, with households in the Gutu cluster being linked into longer-term migrations,
particularly to the urban centres of Zimbabwe, and proximity to the
border, leading to short-term migration to South Africa, being common
in the Mwenezi cluster.

These patterns are also reflected in the skill levels of migrants. Those
with skills included teachers, nurses, plumbers, mechanics, security
personnel (police and army), carpenters and builders. They numbered
56 in the survey sample, coming from 25% of mostly SG1 households.
These migrants tended to move to higher-paid jobs, often with longer-
term contracts, in Zimbabwe or abroad. Another group (28 individuals
coming from 12% of households), without formal training, included
drivers, farm workers and general labourers tended to be from SG2 and
SG3 households; they migrated for a shorter period and had lower paid
jobs, and so lower remittance levels.

8.5 Remittance flows

Remittances have long been important in Zimbabwe. Studies from the
communal areas (Jackson and Collier, 1988; Scoones, 1990) and old
resettlement areas (Kinsey, 1999; Hoddinott, 2006) all showed that
remittances make up a significant proportion of total income, ranging
between 50% and 70%. They remain vital today (Maphosa, 2007; Tevera
and Chikanda, 2009). Remittances are thus an essential contribution to
total income (both in cash and kind); and particularly because they can
offset the risks of agriculture-based production and the vagaries of local
economic conditions.

Following Independence, investment in children's education paid
off. Educated people from the rural areas (mostly men, but increasingly
women too) were able to get relatively well-paid jobs as teachers or civil
servants, as well as in private industry. Racial bars on employment were
removed, and the economy grew in parallel with a substantial investment in government services. A remarkable number of older households
in our sample had sons and daughters who were qualified teachers, for
example. For much of the 1980s and 1990s, this was a standard route out
of the rural areas. While connections were retained, and even homes
and farms established, the remittance connections to parents and other
relatives was the major economic tie. For less skilled people there were
also jobs in town, on the farms and in the mines. While paying less, they
nevertheless allowed remittances to be sent back to the rural family.

All this changed from the late 1990s; as the economy collapsed,

Table 8.2 Migration patterns by success group and A2 households

		A1 and Informal sites			A2
		SG1	SG2	SG3	
Numbers absent	% of households with members currently absent	47%	48%	47%	50%
	Average numbers currently absent	1.55	1.58	1.78	1.06
Who	Males: %	97%	87%	87%	94%
	Females: %	3%	13%	13%	6%
Top three destinations	1	Zimbabwe urban area – 48%	South Africa (illegal) – 53%	South Africa (illegal) – 44%	Zimbabwe urban area – 76%
	2	South Africa (illegal) – 32%	Zimbabwe urban area – 40%	Urban area – 34%	South Africa (illegal) – 12%
	3	South Africa (legal) – 10%	Rural area (resettlement, communal area or commercial farm) – 3%	Rural area (resettlement, communal area or commercial farm) – 6%	Rural area (resettlement, communal area or commercial farm) – 12%

		A1 and Informal sites		A2
	SG1	SG2	SG3	
Top three occupations 1	Unskilled labourer/piece-worker – 34%	Skilled manual worker (builder/carpenter etc.) – 38%	Skilled manual worker (builder/carpenter etc.) – 27%	Unskilled labourer/piece-worker – 50%
2	16%: Skilled manual worker (builder/carpenter/etc.)/soldier/police/security/driver/mechanic	Unskilled labourer or piece-worker – 14%	Unskilled labourer or piece-worker – 23%	Skilled manual worker (builder/carpenter/etc.) – 19%
3	Skilled (factory) worker – 6%	Driver/mechanic – 10%	Teacher, health worker, government worker (clerical/admin), builder/carpenter, skilled factory worker, aid farm worker – 10%	Skilled (factory) worker – 13%
Years away: average (SD) Average (SD)	4.6 (5.9)	8.9 (18.1)	5.5 (4.6)	8.1 (5.9)
Returns % households with member who returned in last year	14%	15%	18%	9%

Source: Survey data, 2007–08

Table 8.3 Percentage of households receiving remittances (and percentages receiving different forms)

Cluster	Scheme type	Receiving remittances 2007-08	Cash	Food	Farm inputs
Gutu	A1 villagised	53%	33.3	33.3	5.5
	A1 self-contained	50%	29.4	29.4	5.8
	A2	30%	60.0	40.0	10.0
Masvingo	A1 villagised	77%	29.4	26.4	2.9
	A1 self-contained	68%	7.7	46.0	7.6
	A2	100%	100.0	0.0	0.0
Chiredzi	A2	39%	38.5	27.8	5.5
	Informal	40%	10.0	13.3	3.3
Mwenezi	A1 villagised	45%	45.0	45.0	10.0
	A2	36%	50.0	50.0	50.0
	Informal	50%	54.5	54.5	9.0

Source: Survey data, 2007-08 (N=177)

retrenchments occurred on a massive scale. For much of the 2000s, even those still formally in a job were not paid a living wage, and remittances to the rural areas became impossible; indeed, as we discuss below, reverse flows of support emerged – from rural to urban areas. This made remittances from outside Zimbabwe all the more important. Thus, more important than the proportion of households receiving any remittances, is the amount, and whether it is in foreign exchange. Data on cash income and transfers was impossible to collect during this period because of the distortions of hyperinflation and the dominance of an exchange system in commodities rather than cash. However, it is clear that there has been an increasingly skewed distribution of remittances, with only those older households with educated children working overseas in relatively stable and well-paid jobs receiving cash remittances of any significant amount. Remittances received were in the form of cash, food or farm inputs, in different combinations. As Table 8.3 shows, in 2007-08 cash and food were the most common type of remittance, with many households receiving both. Farm inputs were relatively unimportant, and most cases represented one-off gifts rather than a regular remittance source. During this period, cash remittances were almost always in foreign exchange.

The flow of support was not all one-way, however. With the collapse of the economy, the livelihoods of migrants in urban areas became increasingly difficult. Those on the resettlement areas began to support their kin, providing remittances from the rural to the urban areas: 8% of households supported urban migrants with cash, while 13% supported them with food. Food provisioning to urban migrants was most common in the Masvingo cluster A1 study sites. Given their proximity to Masvingo town, a regular supply of food from the new farms provided an important boost to relatives living in town. 3% of households also supported migrants in starting up businesses in town.

8.6 Changing relationships between the urban and rural economies

This discussion of the off-farm economy and migration has highlighted a number of important points about the evolving livelihood strategies on the new resettlements.

First, in the past decade we have observed a shifting geographical relationship between the rural spaces of the new resettlements and the wider national, regional, even global, economy. Links between the rural and urban economies remain vitally important, but differ from the classic rural-urban dynamic of the past. In the context of the declining economy of Zimbabwe in the past decade, movement across borders in search of a stable currency as a source of remittance has been critical. This has meant the establishment of new migration pathways and support networks. Very often such new livelihood opportunities have been illegal and involve high levels of personal risk.

Second, as the classic pattern of rural-urban migration has changed, and new migration pathways have emerged, there has been an increasingly stark differentiation in opportunity and return. As the Zimbabwean economy contracted, those in low-paid jobs were the first to lose them. Educated, well-trained civil servants suffered too, as wages were transformed into a pittance due to hyperinflation. It was only those with access to foreign remittances sources who were able to weather the storm. And even for this group it was not easy, given the low pay, poor conditions and often serious abuses and xenophobic attacks that were the context of low-paid, unskilled work in South Africa in particular.[8] Only those with relatively stable, higher-paid jobs abroad were really able to contribute to the remittance flows in any regular and substantial way.

Third, there has been a substantial shift in economic relationships between town and countryside. Flows of food from the new resettlement farms to support urban migrants are a new phenomenon. While in the past few decades, food from the rural areas was sent to urban-dwellers as luxury goods (some bambara nuts, some green mealies or

---

[8] http://news.bbc.co.uk/1/hi/world/africa/7414214.stm.

a special delivery of millet flour), the sending of food for survival has not been common, at least since the 1920s and 1930s when the former reserves kept the new mineworkers in food.

Fourth, the new settlers are definitely not full-time farmers. All livelihoods are made up of a portfolio of on- and off-farm activity. This helps confront risk, smooth income and diversify options. Since rainfall-dependent agriculture is an inherently risky enterprise, especially in the dry zones of the country, expecting a full-time farming commitment of new settlers is clearly foolish. However, many strategies have involved survival diversification – wild fruit collection or gold panning, for example – and illegal, risky migration, such as border-jumping. Notably absent has been policy thinking supporting opportunity and growth-oriented livelihood diversification, both in the past and today.

Fifth, while household livelihood portfolios show substantial diversification, individuals may be quite specialised. This is often highly gender and age dependent, as different people develop particular business, trading, craft or trade skills and markets. These specialised occupations require the building up of customers and market connections to make them viable enterprises; again, such efforts suffer from a severe lack of support.

In sum, the past decade has seen a fundamental change in the relationships between town and countryside, between the farm and other employment and between the rural areas of Zimbabwe and the wider world, within and beyond the southern African region. While off-farm income sources and remittances remain vital, and the new settlers are not full-time farmers in the sense constructed in some policy discourses, the opportunities in the new resettlements are very real. The new resettlements have proved highly attractive to a wide range of people, as we have shown. In the past, the rural areas – and certainly the communal lands – were seen as places to retire, somewhere where family rituals took places and where people should be buried. This remains the case, and indeed most new settlers in the new resettlements regard their communal homes as 'home' (*kumusha*). The new resettlements are regarded, instead, as places of economic opportunity, much in the same way as the urban areas and off-farm employment once were.

As previous chapters have shown, opportunities are very real, but to be realised they require hard work, ingenuity and persistence. Livelihoods have to be constructed anew, and diversification is essential – everyone produces some maize and vegetables on a plot somewhere, as well as often having different businesses; and for some all of this is carried on at the same time as attending a job, even if the pay is paltry. The period of economic collapse has changed people's outlook. Diversification, entrepreneurialism, hedging bets and building portfolios have become a necessary part of survival – for everyone, not just the poor. Survival means resourcefulness, and a reliance on the state, NGOs or development projects has been futile.

How then should we interpret this data on livelihood diversification? Are we seeing a crisis of employment (Bernstein, 2004), where livelihoods are squeezed through people's inability to reproduce themselves through agriculture, and with this a process of de-agrarianisation and increasing rural impoverishment (Bryceson et al., 2000)? Or are we seeing a new livelihood dynamic, where new, productive diversified livelihoods, rooted in agriculture, are possible because of the new opportunities for growth and enterprise on the resettlements (Lipton, 2009)? With land reform there have been more people shifting to land-based livelihoods, the opposite of de-agrarianisation. But will this be sustained? As the economy recovers, there may be a rebalancing of people's livelihood portfolios, and some may yet leave the land in search of better returns elsewhere. Certainly some people's livelihoods are highly precarious and survival diversification is widely evident. But, in parallel, as new farmers continue to 'accumulate from below' through successful agriculture, links to off-farm enterprises, providing services and consumption goods, are increasing, in a potentially positive spiral. Thus, as we argue further in Chapter 11, broader economic growth, rooted in smallholder production, but involving significant livelihood diversification, must be fostered as part of new policy thinking.

9
Territory, Authority & Social Dynamics

9.1 People in places

As new territory has been opened up through land reform, new forms of authority have emerged. This has resulted in very different outcomes in different places, and often intense contestation over legitimacy and control. Patterns of authority shifted over time – from the period of *jambanja* during the land invasions to the reassertion of state and other forms of traditional authority. Again, the simplistic stories of chaotic, disorganised and unplanned land reform do not stand up. As this chapter shows, understanding the highly differentiated social dynamics of land reform, and the underlying political dimensions of conflict, is critical if effective forms of land governance are to emerge.

As discussed in Chapter 2, the pattern of land invasions – who was involved, where they came from, the links between invaders and party authorities, as well as the individual characters of base commanders and war veteran leaders – had a huge impact on who got land where. It is this complex combination of individual charismatic characters, underlying social dynamics, wider political forces and long-existing forms of local, traditional authority that resulted in particular patterns in particular places. As discussed in Chapter 1, there is much dispute about the political interpretation of this critical period in Zimbabwe's recent history. No simple story will suffice. As this chapter shows, in some places land invasions and subsequent authority structures were led and directed by people closely linked to party structures, and were in turn supported by the state and its security apparatus. In other areas this was definitely not the case, even though war veterans and others with links to the ruling party and the state were present. In yet others, the contests were substantially about ethnic identities and rights to land – issues of land restitution, not just redistribution. And in still other places, contests over chiefly authority in the new lands quickly overshadowed any party political dimensions.

In this complex mix, there were often intense contests between men and women, older and younger settlers, traditional and modern institutions, ruling party officials and others, and even between different church followings. The character of the state was always ambiguous: sometimes very present, sometimes completely absent; sometimes violent, sometimes benign. No clear lines of authority existed, and negotiation within local contexts was all. Many commentators have argued that innovations in the practices of governance often take place at the margins of the state, frequently in the context of major social upheaval, and in settings of conflict and sometimes violence (Das and Poole, 2004). In these spaces, citizenships and identities are refashioned, and processes of exclusion and inclusion are played out which may have long-term consequences (Peters, 2004).

How relevant are these perspectives, largely taken from other conflict-ridden settings, for Zimbabwe? Many commentators have depicted the recent period solely in negative terms. Bond and Manyama (2002), for example, talk of Zimbabwe's 'plunge', and the loss of economic and political norms and freedoms. Eric Worby (2003) talks of the 'end of modernity' and the abandonment of 'development' in favour of violence and exclusionary sovereignty. All of these commentaries have validity and reflect on important dimensions of recent history. Our intention is not to dismiss them, but to add nuance and complexity; and, through a more fine-grained empirical analysis, offer another dimension to the story which presents more hope for the future.

As Zimbabweans look forward to the rebuilding of public authority, administrative capacity and technical and basic service support in the resettlement areas, forms of authority and legitimacy in particular contexts will be crucial. Rebuilding the state, and rural governance that work for development, is clearly not just a matter of refinancing old institutions, investing in service delivery, flooding areas with aid and NGO projects, and then assuming that things will work smoothly. Reconstruction must take account of what has gone before: the disruptions, forms of violence, as well as the innovations in institutions and processes. Future development must therefore sensitively, carefully and strategically intervene in ways that allow a functional, responsive and accountable state to emerge. As the subsequent sections show, this will not be easy – and each area will require a different, often finely tuned, approach.

One of the major planks of the future agenda for any Zimbabwean government – and its donor partners – will of course be dealing with 'the land question', and particularly issues of tenure and authority. However, land policy must go beyond the admittedly crucial and politically essential elements such as multiple farm ownership and fair compensation. In particular, it must address issues of land tenure, boundary definition, ownership and use rights and the structure and functioning of rural institutions, both 'traditional' and 'modern'.

Zimbabwe's new resettlement areas are highly contested and extremely variable. But this is the context in which new policy must work. Neat, formulaic solutions of course will fail, but what might work? This chapter documents the realities of land struggles, contests and disputes, and the emerging challenges for land governance across the Masvingo study sites. This is being played out around blurred boundaries, overlapping authorities and unclear rights; all in the context of very weak capacity and even weaker data on land, its use and ownership arrangements.

9.2 *Jambanja*

The period of *jambanja* has come to define the land reform process in Zimbabwe. This was the time when chaos appeared to reign. For some this was seen as a spontaneous uprising; a land movement that was to catalyse the 'third chimurenga'. For others it was a ruthless intervention by a failing state in order to hold on to power. The picture on the ground was much more complex.

After 2000, the term *jambanja* quickly became a popular way of describing this chaotic time, where danger, disorder and violence were always just around the corner. Marko Sibanda popularised the term in his chart-topping song *Jambanja Pahotera*, which depicted a fight over extra-marital affairs between two couples. *Jambanja* literally means violence or angry argument, but the term has been used in many different ways to refer to the farm invasions, the invaders and political violence more broadly. A popular catch-phrase of the time was *jambanja ndizvo* (violence is the answer). Tagwirei Bango put it succinctly in 2001:

> For new words to get accepted into a language, they must reflect the mood of the time, fill in a vacuum in the standard lexicon and be accepted as an appropriate form of expression. Thus, the word *jambanja* which became part of our vocabulary in the past two years, helped people to accept their confusion with an executive order directing the police to ignore crimes classified as political. *Jambanja* means state-sponsored lawlessness. The police are not expected to intervene or arrest anyone in a *jambanja* scene because those taking part will have prior state blessing and approval. But, only one interest group, war veterans and ZANU(PF) supporters, is allowed to engage in a *jambanja* (*Daily News*, 21 November 2001, quoted by Chaumba et al., 2003a: 540).

An early phase of this study focused on Fair Range ranch in Chiredzi district and documented the process of land invasion during 2000. Joseph Chaumba and colleagues (2003a: 533-4; 541-3) describe the scene:

> A visitor ... in early 2000 would have encountered a scene familiar to newspaper readers at the time around the world. What had once been a heavily forested cattle and game ranch was 'scarred' by the randomly scattered rudimentary huts of 'farm invaders'. Fences had been pulled down, trees chopped, cart-tracks and footpaths established, pasture ploughed up, and wildlife and cattle slaughtered. This ostensibly chaotic space was peopled by an anarchic bunch of self-proclaimed liberation war veterans, disaffected jobless and landless youths, and spirit mediums who appeared to be beyond the restraint of the police, and were even encouraged in their lawlessness by members of the governing ZANU-PF party ....

> ... *Jambanja* came to refer to all the illicit activities on these farms that rapidly became normalised. On Fair Range this included closing farm roads; cutting down trees; poaching; cattle theft and mutilation; starting fires; attacking game guards; demanding meat and

mealie meal from white farmers; looting property and sugar cane; ordering farmers, farm workers and neighbouring villagers to attend political rallies; defying police orders; and, at one stage, appropriating a police vehicle. The *jambanja* landscape was characterised by a proliferation of signposts proclaiming 'No go area – war veterans inside'. This was a visibly politicised landscape where Zimbabwean flags were planted on anthills or hung from trees and ZANU-PF posters proclaiming that 'Land is the economy, the economy is land' and 'Zimbabwe will never be a colony again' plastered on trees and gate posts. This was countered by the message 'Vote MDC' spray painted on every available surface from rocks to road signs, to the road itself. The presence of the farm invaders thus served a dual role. As well as appropriating land they were part of the ongoing ZANU-PF political campaign for the parliamentary and presidential elections of 2000 and 2002. The invaded farms were often literally a no-go area for outsiders (even the police sometimes) – somewhere for those instigating political violence to hide securely and from which to base intimidatory attacks on opposition supporters in neighbouring communal areas (Human Rights Watch, 2002). They were also cast by some, particularly evangelical Christians, as spaces of immorality, inhabited by 'degenerates' and 'drunkards' who otherwise would 'roam around shopping centres'.

But at this time no one really knew whether the land invasions would be permanent. People referred to the occupations as 'demonstrations'. For many, the occupations were symbolic, aimed at drawing attention to the land issue generally, and certain land claims specifically. Land invaders fluctuated in numbers as people moved between their homes in the communal areas and the base camps. The expectation from informants at Fair Range was that at some later stage the government would allocate land formally and new settlements would be 'properly planned'. But despite the apparent disorder there was actually much organisation and a rapid emergence of structures, plans and forms of authority. As Joseph Chaumba and colleagues (2003a: 534) explain from the fieldwork in 2000:

> A closer inspection of the former ranch would have revealed that all was not quite as disordered and chaotic as first appeared. The rudiments of a self-imposed technical land-use plan were evident in the siting and layout of the new homesteads and arable plots. These had been carefully pegged at regular intervals – in some cases measured out with tape measures – and the apparently motley collection of invaders were carefully organised into cells run by base commanders.

The Fair Range ranch base commander explained:

> People were allocated 50 ha as part of the demonstrations. We pegged ourselves, when giving plots we used a tape measure. We could not give land in the waterways although some did it. Some cleared, few farmed, although a woman got some bales of cotton …. We were doing the occupations in order to make the government see us. The pegging of lands helped them see us. (Chaumba et al., 2003a: 543)

Given the resistance to planned development, and particularly conservation measures, such a resort to pegging, implementing streambank cultivation bans and encouraging soil conservation, would seem out of place amongst the revolutionary rhetoric of the war veterans and their followers. But of course the deployment of technical practices and tools, alongside the imagery of the linear spatial ordering of colonial land-use planning, was a way in which the occupations could be made 'visible' and so gain recognition by the state. Thus the land invaders needed to be 'seen by the state', and so had to act like the state (cf. Scott, 1998). The most visible and, critically, symbolic way of doing so was to plan and peg the land. This was what the state had done since the Rhodesian era, and was a tangible and legible expression of power over land and its use. The land invasions were thus not a rejection of modernity. Indeed, the deployment of technocratic routines, symbols and images reinforced the idea that what people wanted was indeed development, and in order to fulfil their dreams they needed the state to recognise them, and help them.

The base camps were highly ordered places. With war veterans and war collaborators leading, military-style discipline was imposed. This was not the chaotic setting of many popular accounts. However, they were certainly not democratic, liberal spaces; a strong hierarchical authority structure was insisted upon. In this period the main organisational structure was the Committee of Seven, involving a base commander (chair), treasurer, women's and youth representatives alongside ordinary members.

One of the base commanders in Fair Range ranch explained (Chaumba et al., 2003a: 540-1):

> It was a hard time for us as the pioneers of *jambanja*. We must all be frank, it was a tough time. Imagine [having] to sleep in the bush not knowing where your next meal will be coming from. We just survived on handouts from different people including farmers and relatives. I was one of the first people to come here. Before that we had held several meetings at cell, ward, branch and district levels to plan and mobilise people to go into the farms. It was a difficult time trying to convince people that we mean it ... On 16th February more than 1000 people, mainly from Sangwe communal area and Chiredzi, came. We thought it wise to elect leaders from different places. Youths were also chosen and elected to maintain vigilance. During this time food came from rural areas. There was a register that was marked every day and a roll call done twice a day during the morning and evening. This was all for security reasons. If someone wanted to go to his rural area he would tell the seven member committee his reasons for going, how many days for and when he was likely to come back.

In all our sites similar processes unfolded (Chapter 2). Individuals had to negotiate this complex array of fast-changing authority in order to resolve disputes and make claims. Sometimes different groups of land invaders had to compete in this process – sometimes coming to accommodation, sometimes coming to blows. In some instances the former landowners accepted the land invaders and provided support in exchange for some deal about a portion of the land and very often continued use of the farmhouse; in other cases, major conflict arose. How these patterns of conflict and accommodation unfolded had a huge impact on what happened subsequently. In places where the invasion was straightforward and where a clear authority structure emerged, usually centred around a war veteran base commander and the Committee of Seven, the emergence of new institutions and authority structures was usually smooth. However, if conflicts over authority were a central part of the *jambanja* phase, these often spilled over into the subsequent period; and in many places, as we document below, conflicts have plagued the establishment of the resettlements now for many years.

9.3 Contested control

Despite the prominence of the *jambanja* period in popular imaginations, it was actually quite short. The FTLRP was launched in mid-2000 and very soon officials from the Ministry of Lands and extension agents were sent out to peg formally the designated areas. Permits to occupy, and offer letters, were then issued to those with pegged plots. At the same time the programme for allocating A2 plots was initiated. With some invasions having occurred on land allocated to A2 farms, this resulted in conflicts between land occupiers and state officials. Substantial areas in Masvingo remained as informal settlements, without state recognition (including our sites at Uswaushava and Turf, for example). Thus, from this period, a clear administrative division existed between A1 and A2 resettlements, with 'informal' sites not being recognised at all. However, the distinctions between the FTLRP's neat divisions and the practice on the ground were not so clear.

In all cases the original land invaders wanted large, self-contained plots. During the informal planning phase of the *jambanja* period often large areas were demarcated. These were effectively A2-style plots, and the invaders (or at least their leaders) imagined a future of small-scale commercial farming. As MH from Wondedzo Extension commented: 'We are no longer called peasant farmers, but commercial farmers!' However, informal agrarian planning by war veterans during the *jambanja* phase and formal replanning of the same areas by AREX and the Lands Department subsequently had to contend with the intractable challenge of 'inclusion' versus 'viable' farm units. FTLRP blueprints of viable land units were compromised or abandoned altogether in favour of equity considerations in order to cater for the large numbers of people coming onto the land. For example, in the Gutu cluster, war veterans at first pegged 100ha self-contained plots per household. Comrade M, the base commander, allocated himself double this. But, when numbers of land-hungry people grew, plot sizes were reduced by half, and more and more villagised schemes were created to accommodate the still swelling numbers.

In addition to size, there were important differences in the way land was pegged by the original invaders and the subsequent technocrats. Sanangwe A1 site provides an illustrative example. As part of the initial occupation, the invaders pegged plots on richer soils along the banks of the Mtirikwe river. They argued that positioning their fields along the river would allow them to irrigate the land and get water for their homes. Measures were taken to avoid erosion, including bush fencing along the river bank. They identified several spots where cattle could be watered, arguing that this would mean that cattle did not trample along the whole length of the river. However, the settlers were soon shifted from this area when repegging occurred, and the land-use planning criteria in use since the 1930s were invoked, moving the settlement and fields to the crest of the hill and leaving the low-lying areas for grazing. This, people argued, has negatively affected the success of their resettlement area. They are now far from water sources and insufficient boreholes have been sunk. With the exception of a few gardens along the river bank, the rich alluvial soils are under-used and they must farm on the dry and sandy toplands. Only one borehole, which keeps breaking down, was drilled to serve 64 house-holds. Sanangwe residents must now travel a long distance back to the river to fetch water when the borehole is not working. As if that was not enough, the area they were removed from was later allocated by district officials to people who had to be moved from a farm designated for A2 farmers. Because of the richer riverine soils, these new settlers are getting higher yields than those who originally occupied the land, generating much resentment.

The advent of A2 schemes resulted in much disgruntlement too. War veterans and other leaders of the land occupations argued that it was they who should be getting the largest areas of prime land, and not 'chefs' (top officials) from town, or those who could fill in the forms. These people, they argued, did not join the struggle for the land. Some well-connected war veterans did manage to shift to the A2 plots, but many failed. As described in Chapter 2, very often the way land was divided up depended on deals made with the Ministry of Lands officials at the time of official planning and pegging. Thus leaders of the origi-nal land invasions gained access to the A1 self-contained plots, while others were shifted to villagised schemes where more people could be accommodated. In some cases plot sizes on the A1 self-contained plots were comparable to the smaller A2 plots, and so the administrative dis-tinctions laid out in the FTLRP planning documents had less traction on the ground.

As people settled into their new areas, the *jambanja* period institu-tions of the base commander and Committee of Seven still had important roles to play. In addition to negotiating with the state authorities of the state over land-use planning, they increasingly had to articulate with other forms of 'traditional' authority – notably chiefs and their headmen, as well as spirit mediums, rain messengers and church lead-ers. The relatively confined and well-ordered lines of authority were increasingly contested, and new negotiations unfolded.

Across our sites, contests over chiefly authority have been especially significant. With new areas of land opening up, chiefs and headmen tried to exert control over these new territories, often claiming that past ancestors had occupied the areas. Land reform, they argued, had been a process of restitution, and they, through evidence of burial sites and past settlement, along with religious sites where spirits resided, had new authority. For example, in the Gutu cluster, Chief Chiriga reasserted authority in Clare and Lonely farms. His argument is that the area belonged to the Madyira clan dominant in the area. His territorial control is enforced through village heads (*sabhukus*) and two chief's aides. The chief also works together with coordinators (former war veterans) and the Committees of Seven. However, chiefly authority is not without dispute. People complain that the chief orders them to stop work for seven days if a top Madyira clan member dies. Authority is further entrenched by spiritually-based claims about sacred sites. 'Barurwe Mountain is sacred and was the meeting place of our forefathers,' said Chiriga's son. 'Mysterious fires burn at night but there will be no trace of burning the next day. The former white farmer fenced off a perennial pool at the top of the mountain to prevent his cattle from falling into it. The next morning poles and fences were scattered all over the place without any sign of human interference.' The chief has issued orders preventing people from ploughing around and cutting trees on the sacred mountain where special clan rites are conducted. As in the past, the state has also made use of chiefly authorities, and ZANU-PF was often at pains to enlist particular chiefs as agents of state and party control. As time progressed, development projects such as Operation Maguta were used by the state as levers to capture allegiance of particular chiefs.

The following two cases illustrate the tensions involved in these new conflicts over authority:

Case 1: Masvingo cluster

A bitter dispute emerged between Chief Chikwanda and Chief Makore. Chikwanda in particular has been asserting authority over large areas, stretching into Gutu, Makore's traditional area (Mujere, 2010). Violence broke out between the factions and during 2009 Chief Makore sought police protection.[1] In the Masvingo cluster, local people believe there is a perennial pool on top of Sanangwe mountain in which rice grows. When the rice reaches maturity and starts to wilt the first rains start to fall. 'The spirits in Sanangwe Mountain belong to Chief Makore,' said Mrs. AM. 'This is a sacred mountain, my son, you do not go picnicking on it, otherwise snakes will chase you out.' Chikwanda's people contest this. The headman appointed by Chief Chikwanda argued: 'This place contains burial grounds of my ancestors. The cultural burial grounds of Ambuya vaZarira of the Chikwanda clan are in the same area.' Chikwanda's people insist that the area is his because Chief Makore rules in Gutu administrative district, while he rules in Masvingo district. However, since most people came to the area during the land invasions from Gutu, their original allegiances were to Makore. This meant there was a long period of uncertainty in all of the Masvingo cluster study sites. In the end, Chikwanda won and celebrations were held. He installed his headman, Musara, a plot holder in Thorn Grove farm, along with sabhukus across the area. In Wondedzo Wares, one of Makore's headmen was expelled and sent back to Gutu as Chikwanda's people asserted their authority. As people explained, Musara generally ignores the Committee of Seven and rules through sabhukus and selected clan members, appointed as headmen. The chief's messenger transmits his messages to villagers.

---

[1] 'Boundary Dispute – Gutu Chief Formally Seeks Police Protection', *The Herald*, Masvingo Bureau, 9 July 2008, http://allafrica.com/stories/200807090355.html.

Case 2: Mwenezi cluster

Two headmen are contesting Turf Ranch. Both have appointed different sab-hukus *which confuses the settlers. Chief Chinana's headman argues that long ago, before people were forced out to make way for white commercial farms, the area belonged to his ancestor Gezani wa Mateke, after whom the Mateke Hills of Turf ranch were named. Chief Chinana has a sacred place in the area. SM, a new settler, was fined a cow when she accidentally caused a fire which destroyed structures at the shrine. Some Chinana elders think the sentence was too lenient. Chief Chitanga's headman claims that the area was given to him by local government officials from Mwenezi. The stalemate continues. Further north, in Edenvale ranch, Chief Chitanga, again claiming authority from Mwenezi district council, is battling it out with Chief Mpapa. Like Chinana, Mpapa argues that his forefathers were evicted from Edenvale to create room for white commercial farms. A local leader, appointed by Mpapa as a village* sabhuku *and holder of traditional sacred sites in Edenvale ranch, explains:*

> *I was born in 1941 and knew this place belonged to Mpapa. I was grown up when Chitanga was still a small boy working at Mwenezi Office as a messenger at the court. He came from nowhere. Chitanga has no respect for the traditions of this area. His place is to the north, near Lundi river. He knows nothing of the sacred places here. Yet he is trying to put a* sabhuku *in each village. These farms are where the ruins of the Mpapa people are. Mpapa's people came to invade the land to take it back again.*

This competition between 'traditional' authorities in Edenvale has been exacerbated by confusion over district boundaries. The land invasions were led by SM, a war veteran and Shangaan follower of Mpapa. Until 2007 he had the upper hand as no one knew which district Edenvale fell into. Most assumed that it was Chiredzi, as that was the number on most people's identity card, and the local MP was for Chiredzi South constituency. However, from 2007, the people who came from government – extension workers and others – as well as NGOs were all from Mwenezi. This was the moment when Chitanga's people took charge. Food aid in particular became an important weapon. Only those showing strong allegiance to Chitanga were allocated food rations via an NGO programme. Chitanga's faction also benefited from the government's mechanisation programme, and ploughs, harrows and cultivators were handed out to followers. Chitanga was also allegedly claiming a beast from each person who wished to be given the sabhuku *post. All households were also supposed to pay a tax to Chitanga's* sabhukus *– ten rands each, or one full mug of mopane worms. The war veterans allied to Mpapa complained they got nothing, although one who was well connected apparently got a plough via Chiredzi district. The now late MP for Chiredzi South did not intervene, despite the fact that he had supported the Mpapa group at the time of the invasions. With changes in district boundaries, different forms of political and administrative authority were being exerted, and old alliances based on ethnic Shangaan affiliations were no longer so relevant.*

At a meeting at the nearby Ironwood ranch on 18 May 2007, tensions rose. Chitanga had come to install his sabhukus. *He was accompanied by an official from the Ministry of Lands from Mwenezi, a uniformed army officer and a delegation composed of people the locals did not know. When Mpapa's people objected to the installation of Chitanga's people, saying that this was their land where their ancestors came from, the other group started singing political songs, and accusing them of belonging to the opposition. The Mpapa group said this was absurd. They led the land invasions, and Chiredzi South, their constituency, had always been a solid ZANU-PF area. Some in the Mpapa group then began to attack the Ministry of Lands official, accusing him of usurping the local authority structures. He knelt down and pleaded with the angry crowd, saying he was simply escorting Chitanga. The meeting soon broke up. B, the local leader coordinating Chitanga's campaign, took Chitanga and his delegation to his homestead where a goat was slaughtered and a party was held before the officials returned to Mwenezi.*

The disputes continued through the election period of 2008, with sporadic eruptions of violence as the two camps competed – not so much around party affiliation as in other areas, but around forms of local authority, which mattered more to people. By 2009, some were more sanguine. GM, for example, explained his perspective: 'In Edenvale, it is Mpapa's sabhukus who are responsible for local traditional functions such as circumcision parties and traditional activities. They are the keepers of the sacred places. Chitanga's sabhukus are responsible for development. They deal with food distribution, for instance, and are connected to Mwenezi district, the centre for the delivery of services.' Given the tensions and animosities, whether this division of responsibility is sustainable only time will tell. The division between 'tradition' and 'development' is a theme which is repeated in other areas too, and is an important feature of contemporary governance arrangements, as will be discussed further below.

As these cases highlight, politics, often exerted through party structures within local government, was always present. As LC, a settler in Edenvale commented: 'ZANU-PF was the backbone of *jambanja*. The ruling party encouraged people to stand firm and never to give the enemy a chance to recolonise this place like before. Land is what we fought for and our relatives died for this land.' Land became the main source of political patronage and, as the economy declined, perhaps the last remaining asset the political elite had at their disposal. During the elections in 2005, and especially in 2008, party control in the resettlements was tightened. Enlistment of chiefs, war veterans and others was vital. Food aid, input supplies and mechanisation programmes were used as political weapons to buy allegiance. But it was never straightforward, as the cases above highlight. Many had split loyalties and, as the voting patterns showed, solid support for ZANU-PF, despite the enticements and the threats, was far from guaranteed, no matter what people said in public.

In addition to technocratic, political and chiefly authorities, the new land users had to contend with spiritual authority too. In the past, spirit mediums have been central to struggles over land (Lan, 1985; Spierenberg, 2004). In southern Zimbabwe land guardianship and spirit control differs from other areas, but is nonetheless of vital importance (Bourdillon, 1982; Ranger, 1999; Fontein, 2006a, b). War veterans and land invaders had to take account of the spirit world. As part of an early phase of fieldwork, we described a case from Chiredzi district where the Chitsa people had invaded a portion of Gonarezhou national park and had established a series of villages:

Not long after the ten villages had been established ... five of the villages started to be regularly 'attacked' by an elephant ... destroying over 30 huts, and chasing people from their fields. As the district War Veterans Association leader admitted, this was a deeply worrying development and it 'has prompted us to ask questions why this is happening – only one elephant is destroying, yet there are many elephants in Gonarezhou'. The conclusion drawn was that the ancestral spirits of the area must be very angry because there was something about the occupation that was not done correctly – causing offence. (Chaumba et al., 2003b: 601)

While traditional religion played a critical role during the liberation struggle of the 1970s, it was perhaps not such an important consideration during the 2000s. Ambuya VaZarira, a spirit medium (*svikiro*), living close to Wondedzo and Sanangwe study farms in Masvingo district, complained about being side-lined: 'I played a pivotal role in the Second Chimurenga protecting children [guerilla fighters]. Zarira means protection and we won. But now we are not considered. We are not like *n'angas* [traditional healers] who demand money, we only expect tokens of appreciation. We are there to provide a service, as demanded by our ancestors.' Ambuya VaZarira offers rainmaking ceremonies in the area. However, as discussed above, her authority, and that of Chief Chikwanda, is contested, and alternative sacred sites are identified by those who claim that Chief Makore is in control. Although allied to Chief Chikwanda – they share the same totem – Ambuya VaZarira's influence is not encouraged by Chikwanda's increasing control of the area, as he is a member of the Johanne Masowe Apostolic Church which does not recognise spirit mediums.

Thus, as Joost Fontein (2006a, b, 2009) has argued, the shared war legacy of war veterans, spirit mediums and some chiefs offers similar languages and symbols, hence the emergence of a hybrid vision, mixing 'tradition' with party politics, 'new religions' and technocracy in complex ways.

9.4 Continued land conflicts

Contests over the new lands continue. While nearly everyone regards the land reform as irreversible, outstanding legal challenges and policy dilemmas remain. A group of dispossessed white farmers took the Zimbabwe government to the SADC tribunal, arguing that the expropriation of land under the FTLRP was illegal.[2] The tribunal agreed on technical grounds, but the wider political consensus suggests that such claims are unlikely to go far. The issue of compensation is still alive, however, and extensively debated.[3]

---

[2] http://www.newzimbabwe.com/pages/farm75.19086.html; http://www.zimbabwede mocracynow.com/2009/09/04/legal-opinion-re-zimbabwe-and-the-juristiction-of-the-sadc-tribunal/.
[3] http://www.thestandard.co.zw/local/22497-west-urges-govt-to-implement-gpa-fully-to-unlock-donor-aid.html.

As discussed in Chapter 2, 2008 and 2009 saw a new round of land invasions and major disputes over some areas. The heightened political tensions around the 2008 elections, and the prospect of an inclusive government that might end land-based patronage, resulted in a range of speculative land claims by politically-connected elites. While there remains debate about the origins and motivations of the land occupations in 2000, there was little doubt about the politically-motivated origins of this new 'land grab'.

As ever, it is important to understand the particular contexts. In some instances, these new land expropriations were the result of disputes between ZANU-PF factions, with certain individuals getting the upper hand due to the continuously shifting allegiances within the party; in others, business interests, allied to political elites, took advantage of the political and economic uncertainty to enter into land speculation deals; and in other instances, there was a spillover from the earlier land occupations, with people moving to new areas having missed out earlier on. Within our study areas, opportunistic land grabbing by elites occurred during 2008 and 2009, resulting in the eviction of several white farmers whose land had, supposedly, been secure. In each of these cases the evictions were precipitated by the claims of top officials who had previously not been rewarded with land. Several other invasions occurred, including of farms in the Masvingo cluster, again where the presumption had been that the white owner had been allocated the land.

Conflicts between new settlers and the state have emerged in other areas too, particularly those that were not recognised by the FTLRP. The Uswaushava site has remained highly contested. No one in the area has been granted offer letters, and it remains an informal and thereby illegal, settlement, of perhaps 6,000 households. The area is formally under the Nuanetsi ranch, owned by the Development Trust of Zimbabwe (DTZ). Some part of the area had been designated as A2 plots, but the area had been invaded, under the leadership of the charismatic war veteran, Comrade KM. Having been ignored by government for several years, KM and others from across Uswaushava blockaded the highway using logs and brushwood for a full day, demanding that government stop trying to evict them, and issue offer letters to the settlers. Comrade KM passed away in 2007, and the leadership of the area was significantly weakened. Despite assurances at election times, including at a rally from President Mugabe himself, nothing has been forthcoming, and settlers are worried about the future. This concern accelerated during 2008, when evidence of new investments in the area emerged, as discussed in Chapter 2. In addition, rumours exist of plans by Chinese investors to set up a substantial irrigated sugar cane plantation in the area, as well as suggestions that there are others eyeing up the land for wildlife enterprises. Villagers in Uswaushava complain of regular harassment by DTZ staff who, they claim, purposely drive cattle into their crop lands. The stand-off between settlers, the state and business interests continues, and technical officials are reluctant to engage in any replanning of the area.

The other study area which remains unrecognised is the Turf ranch site in the Mateke hills of Mwenezi district, which has a mix of untouched farms managed by (often absent) white farmers, new A2 plots and some informal village settlements. In the past, the area was divided up as hunting blocks, and a mix of wildlife hunting and livestock ranching occurred. Many of the blocks were owned by South Africans; most had other properties south of the Limpopo and few lived full-time in the Mateke hills. This is an extremely remote area, where state control is fragmentary at best. However, in part because of this lack of control, there have been many conflicts over land. Officials do not have a firm grip on who has been allocated what, and there have been several occasions where two people have been allocated the same block by different officials (in some cases from different districts). The land invaders claimed one area because of its fine soils, but the area is contested by several others. A neighbouring white farmer allegedly gave a sheep to a Mwenezi district official as a bribe to remove the land invaders. The government official reportedly came in person with an audit team. In the process he apparently fell in love with the rich Turf ranch soil and openly voiced his desire to take over the place. Standing in front of the large pole-and-mud church built by settlers, he scornfully remarked: 'To build such a huge building in an unauthorised place – we will turn it into our garage!' The settlers were despondent, and expected to be evicted. They later held a meeting and sent a delegation to Rutenga to enquire about their fate from the local MP. Each villager contributed to the bus fares, and the group met the MP who advised them to stay put, assuring them that if the official continued disturbing them he would lose his job. This meeting reduced their anxiety, but they remain without offer letters.

As these examples demonstrate, even a decade after the land occupations, in some places uncertainty often reigns over land allocations, boundaries and control. This has some major implications for production and livelihoods, as the next section discusses.

9.5 Towards tenure security

All discussions of land in Zimbabwe make the argument that security of tenure is essential (Rukuni, 1994a). However, there are almost as many interpretations of what land tenure security means as there are documents and commentators. This is reflected in the international debate, with some arguing that titling is a requirement for growth (de Soto 2001), while others show how communal systems are as productive, if not more so, than areas with other forms of tenure (Feder and Noronha, 1987; Bruce and Mighot-Adholla, 1994). There has been a wide recognition across Africa that communal tenure systems offer many advantages (Roth and Haase, 1998; Cotula et al., 2004), and that titling of communal land often results in capture by elites (Sahn and Arulpragasam, 1991 for Malawi; Barrows and Roth, 1990, for Kenya). The contrary, evolutionary, argument, is that, as the value of output increases, there are greater incentives to privatise and invest in titling systems (Platteau, 2008), and thus different tenure systems can be expected depending on the type and value of agriculture found.

This debate remains far from resolved, but it is particularly distorted in Zimbabwe, given the privilege that large-scale, freehold commercial farming has enjoyed since the colonial era. Some argue that tenure security – and with it, 'modern', 'efficient' production systems – can only emerge through freehold title, which provides collateral for credit finance. In the past, large-scale commercial farm land was held under freehold, and this has become the 'gold standard' of property rights for many, especially those who argue that freehold title property rights are the precondition for successful commericial agriculture. Others hold that leasehold arrangements are sufficient, especially if of long duration, and that legally-binding leases should be adequate as collateral. This is the proposed basis for A2 schemes, including all remaining large-scale commercial farm areas. However, the clauses that allow the state to intervene if lease conditions are not fulfilled, may undermine the value of such arrangements, as this increases the risk for private lenders. Still others point to the tenure security in the communal lands, and the substantial investment that has occurred in resettlement areas, as evidence that either communal tenure arrangements, overseen by traditional and district administrative authorities, or permits-to-occupy (or offer letters) are sufficient, especially if combined with state guarantees for credit and lending (Moyo, 2009). Such systems are relatively cheap to operate, in contrast to the significant costs of cadastral survey and land administration that other systems can entail (Deininger and Jin, 2006; Deininger et al., 2008 for Ethiopia).

Land and property are intimately linked with social and governance arrangements at a local level (Berry, 1989, 1993, 2002; Peters, 2002, 2004) and are embedded in the social and cultural fabric (Lund, 2006; Cousins, 2009). Tenure is not just about the legal and administrative definition of property rights, but also the social and political underpinnings of land use, and so is often highly context dependent, with a great deal of blurring between the formal and informal (Lavigne-Delville, 2003; Benjaminsen and Lund, 2003). Tenure security emerges from effective land governance, and an acceptance of particular norms and practices. Effective land governance, in turn, derives not only from accepted principles about land use rights and regularised routines of administrative practice, but also from perceptions of different actors. Uncertainty over land and its use persists among settlers themselves, technical agencies of the state, credit agencies and banks, as well as external investors and donor agencies. This has had a debilitating effect on development, and must remain one of the top priorities for policy attention, as we discuss in Chapter 11.

Perceptions of tenure security have shifted dramatically over the past decade. In the *jambanja* period, everything was up for grabs, and security was assured only once former owners had been evicted and the invasion recognised by the state as part of the FTLRP. Pegging by Lands Department and agricultural extension officers, even if very perfunctory, was an important indicator that the invasion was being recognised. The issuing of offer letters by the Lands Department has been a haphazard process, with much confusion. Those in receipt of them have indicated that they feel secure, but there have been cases where they have been overturned through local political manoeuvring. For A2 plots, 99-year

leases had been promised, but delays in the land audit process and subsequent surveying has meant that no one in our sample sites had yet
received a formal lease, and all were relying on offer letters. These have
been insufficient to gain bank finance, and political connections and
patronage linkages, along with personal financing, have been the main
routes to supporting new A2 enterprises. On the sugar estates, cane
farmers with offer letters have been able to engage with the mill and
estate management, but only on very poor terms. For those in the informal settlements, there has been no security of tenure. Multiple promises
from politicians and administrators have been made, from the President
downwards, but no offer letters have been forthcoming. As state administrative control reasserts itself in these areas, it is unclear whether the
under-the-radar activities of continued *jambanja* will be allowed, especially if other politically powerful players want the land.

The standard ways of thinking about land tenure policy in Zimbabwe's rural areas therefore do not easily apply to the new resettlements.
A significant rethink is required. In the past, there was a neat division
between freehold private tenure on large-scale commercial farms and
communal tenure in the communal areas, and a version of this linked
to a permit system in the old resettlement areas. Today, a more diverse
form of tenure is emerging. The A2 areas are notionally privately held,
but have elements of communal arrangements within them, given the
lack of fences and the permeability of boundaries. The A1 schemes are
more communal in character, although self-contained areas more clearly resemble the A2 sites. Within all areas there is a mix of private and
communal, with flexible and overlapping boundaries. Land is allocated
through a variety of routes, some formally through the District Land
Committee, councillors and scheme committees; other allocations are
through informal arrangements, inheritance and, on occasions, sales
and leasing. While commercial land transactions are illegal, these
'vernacular markets' (Chimhowu and Woodhouse, 2006) are important, even if it involves simply the paying of a small bribe, especially
as access to the new resettlement areas is closing down following the
land occupations.

A key question for the future is whether the emerging system is able
to respond to changing demand for land over time. Ideally there will
emerge a flexible allocation system that will allow some people to get
out of farming and leave the resettlement areas, while allowing others
to acquire land. In the long term, the land occupations cannot dictate forever who has land and who does not; needs and demands will
change. Equally, the danger of continuing to add more and more people
to the land, in response to political pressure, is a real one, requiring
new solutions. For this reason, a continuous process of land reform is
required, governed effectively through a land commission (Chapter 11).
Land renting and sales, as well as forms of tenancy system, if regulated
effectively to avoid consolidation and capture, can be important parts of
this dynamic (cf. Deininger and Jin, 2006 for Ethiopia).

9.6 Local land governance

What type of land governance arrangements are emerging in the new resettlements? If a new system is to be built that articulates with more formal legal arrangements governing property rights, it must emerge from existing practice if it is to command wider authority. This section explores some of the practices of local land governance as seen in the new resettlements of Masvingo province. The new leaders of the resettlement areas – whether war veterans, village headmen, councillors or hybrid combinations – must continuously deal with boundary disputes, the allocation of land following inheritance, and accommodating new people. These are almost daily issues. The following cases illustrate the diversity of challenges faced.

Sanangwe farm has become increasingly crowded with the designated grazing area of the original settlers being taken over by a new group who had been transferred from another farm (see above). Grazing has become very short, and cattle from the villagised areas of Sanangwe often stray into the neighbouring, unfenced A1 self-contained plots of Elandskop farm. This has led to serious disputes between the two groups. The Sanangwe people argue that 'all the land is ours – how can they chase us and the cattle? These people just behave like whites. In fact worse, as the whites had so much land that they turned a blind eye.' The *sabhukus* of the two areas have negotiated a truce, but it is an uneasy one, and new conflicts are inevitable, particularly in times of drought. As the Elandskop farmers gain resources and invest in fencing this may escalate, as fences are cut to allow cattle into what the Sanangwe people regard as underutilised areas. This case illustrates tensions between crowded villagised settlements and A1 self-contained and A2 plots, particularly as fences are erected. The conflicts are reminiscent of those between white farmers and communal area people, but, as Sanangwe people point out, they are heightened as more and more people compete for the area. While large-scale commercial ranchers could very often 'turn a blind eye', new settlers are less likely to.

Conflicts have also emerged within settlement communities. HC is an absentee farmer who acquired land in Clare farm through political connections after the land invasions. He has not integrated himself with the emerging community, and remains aloof. One plot holder commented: 'He is proud. He thinks he is above us. He did not join the invasion, but has a large plot.' His plot is fenced with brand-new barbed wire. It is managed by workers and contains a growing number of cattle. However, during the dry season of 2007 it became increasingly clear that the resources in his 25ha plot were insufficient to sustain the growing herd, so he ordered his workers to cut the wire and drive the cattle into the unfenced plots of his neighbours. Most other people operate a communal system of herding across the plots, and so this action was deeply resented. Some of his cattle destroyed a neighbour's dry season garden in a nearby *vlei*, and they were not herded in ways that others expected. Being often absent, and also well connected, the local leaders felt unable to reprimand him, although the workers were talked to. This case illustrates the dilemmas of communal management when 'free riders' operate outside collective control. This is especially a problem in the A1 self-contained and A2 sites where unfenced individual plot ownership combines with a lack of community cohesion.

Disputes can also arise over land-use plans and formal pegging. A situation arose in Lonely A farm where one farmer settled, together with his five wives and a large family, in an area designated for grazing. He had high-level connections through his son, and initially the other settlers were afraid to evict him. Later, a letter was sent from the Councillor to seek an eviction order. Formal planning regulations were given as the reason. The man had settled on an unallocated plot designated as grazing and the area was said to be 'above carrying capacity' of 90 households. In addition, the farmer was argued to be contravening environmental regulations by farming in a wetland, too close to a stream bank. The letter was supported by the Seven Member Committee, and the former base commander, now a councillor. It had no effect whatsoever and the person remains there to this day. This case highlights the conflicts over land use planning that have arisen across the sites. The formal rules for land use planning, rooted in colonial legislation and practices, are often disputed, and may be particularly so by powerful individuals or groups wishing to make use of prime land near water sources. While base commanders, councillors and other officials may repeat the rules, these may not be adhered to.

The informal borrowing of land is common in the Mwenezi cluster sites. In this area some people acquired substantial tracts of land on behalf of their sons. These were often senior patriarchs, the heads of large polygamous families. For example, in Turf ranch, the base commander and local pastor, HM, has a large plot of land reserved for his sons, and when new people come they can borrow it. JJ came in 2008, and made use of HM's land because he did not have time to clear his own. HM explained: 'Payments for using land are expected only after the first season. If the land is borrowed just for a season it is usually because someone had a problem. However, the owner might be happy to see a bag of grain as a gift.' Although informants denied that there was a land market and that it was possible to purchase land, this case illustrates how informal borrowing and sharing arrangements can combine with an emergent land hiring system, especially when there are large disparities in land holding.

The allocation of land following the death of a settler poses a particular problem in the context of unclear forms of land governance and administration. Procedures vary across the sites. In the informal sites of Uswaushava and Turf ranch, inheritance follows the pattern found in the nearby communal areas, whereby if a husband dies his wife holds the plot until an elder son takes it over. This is administered by the local *sabhuku* with no recourse to other officials. In other areas similar forms of family inheritance operate, but there is a requirement to inform the Ministry of Lands, so the new ownership is registered. However, registration is often not clear, especially when the holder of the original offer letter is absent and other caretakers have been using the plot. In some cases, it is unclear who actually is the *bona fide* plot holder, and sometimes this is disputed. In Clare farm, the local councillor – also a member of the Gutu District Lands Committee – explained that they had an informal arrangement with the committee whereby half of all vacated plots could be allocated by the scheme committee (the former Committee of Seven) and the other half could respond to the growing list of applications that were being received at district level. However, in practice most reallocations have occurred within the scheme, either through family inheritance or allocations to other scheme members' relatives. This example highlights the hybrid nature of land governance arrangements, and the negotiated nature of rules particular to different places.

In a number of instances there are two people claiming the same land, both arguing that they have the right to reside and farm there. For example, in village 6 in Edenvale ranch A1 site Mrs RC came during the land invasions and claimed a plot that was allocated by the war veterans. Several years later, Mr MC came and claimed the same plot. He said he had been allocated it by the government, and showed a letter (although this was not a formal offer letter). A violent dispute arose, and the police had to be called. This dispute reflected the division in the area between two factions, each allied to a different chief. The issue was reported to the *sabhuku* (Chitanga faction) and the plot was divided.

By contrast, in Clare farm two people occupied the same plot, but this arose from a genuine misunderstanding and lack of knowledge of plot boundaries. Both families had constructed houses, and the local committee and Ministry of Lands officials decided that the boundaries had to be redrawn to accommodate them. Each of these cases illustrates, in different ways, how a combination of local power and uncertainty about land allocation and boundaries can result in serious conflict, with often no easy resolution.

Land governance thus relies on a complex mix of actors and institutions. No standard rules apply, and negotiated solutions at the local level are always required. Imposing a top-down, even if well designed, system will not be possible in this environment; an approach is needed within which rights, regulations and responses are clear and consistent, and are rooted at the local level, as we discuss in Chapter 11.[4] As more disputes occur, new forms of land governance will have to be invented that match local realities, and take account of the inequalities and social divisions (Peters, 2004).

9.7 Gendered rights

A critical feature of any new system of land governance in Zimbabwe will be the guaranteeing of women's rights to land.[5]

---

[4] Important parallels exist with South Africa, especially around the contests over the Communal Land Rights Act (Claasens and Cousins, 2008).

[5] Calls for changes in the law have been made by a range of advocacy groups, see: http://www.irinnews.org/Report.aspx?ReportId=51928 (see also Pankhurst and Jacobs, 1988; Chimedza, 1988; Goebel, 1999, 2005a, b). For a wider discussion across Africa, see Whitehead and Tsikata (2003), Walker (2003), Englert and Daley (2008), O'Laughlin (2009) and Jacobs (2009) among others.

While we have argued that the new resettlements provided an opportunity for the emancipation and empowerment of women, with an escape from the patriarchal strictures of the communal lands – in particular for widows, divorcees and women ostracised from communities through accusations of witchcraft – this was often only temporary. Long-standing 'traditions', that act to exclude women, and deny their rights, have often been reimposed, as chiefs, headmen and *sabhuku* have reasserted control, often in alliance with (usually male) base commanders, war veterans and other leaders.

In Chapter 2 we noted that 12% of women got land in the new resettlements, with their own names on the relevant offer letters. In some cases, especially in the Mwenezi cluster, they were the wives of polygamous men, and were being used as a part of a land speculation strategy to secure land for male heirs. However, those with offer letters were only a minority; most women make use of the new land in the context of marriage, as the wives of male landholders. In discussions, many women argued that this was not a problem. They had good working relationships with their husbands, and as part of differentiated production and livelihood systems focused on different activities. When the question was raised about whether women should have their names on the offer letters, most agreed it was a good idea, and a few argued that it was an urgent priority. Such a picture of harmonious family relationships is not universal; those whose rights had been undermined by abusive husbands or highly unequal sharing of resources within the marriage were unlikely to speak up in such discussions. For such women, securing rights to land in a more formal way would allow a firmer protection from institutions and practices with extreme and entrenched gender biases in Zimbabwe's rural areas – including the 'liberated' spaces of the new resettlements.[6]

Women's roles in local administrative structures are similarly variable. They usually had prominent positions in the Committees of Seven, although rarely as base commanders or chairpersons. The committees were generally required to have representatives of war veterans, women and youth, and in most cases in our study sites this was adhered to. However, committee structures have often given way to a more traditional form of leadership, focused on the chief and the *sabhukus*.

Some women, such as healers, spirit mediums and rain messengers, have exceptional powers, and much respect is accorded them. A few, through arguments about spirit guardianship, gained land, as a result of close alliances with war veteran leaders. But, as Ambuya VaZarira complained (see above), the appreciation of such spirit-based leadership was limited, and some quite powerful *svikiros*, such as herself, were marginalised by new forms of authority. In any case, even if articulated by a female *svikiro*, the restitution claims over land, graves and ancestral sites remained around male lineages and traditional leaders, who are exclusively male.

The emancipatory potentials of resettlement were short-lived, frag-

[6] See the gender analysis of laws in Zimbabwe prepared for the Women in Land in Zimbabwe group (http://www.kubatana.net/docs/women/wlz_gen_analysis_agrilaws_zim_0207.pdf). For the wider debate on the pros and cons of formalisation, see Jackson (2003) and Agarwal (2003).

mentary and often illusory. Just as with the earlier resettlement schemes, where similar hopes were raised (Jacobs, 2000; Goebel, 2005a, b), the pattern of land access and authority remains skewed against women, even if there are fewer complaints against the *status quo* than is sometimes assumed. This may not necessarily require the liberal solution of individualised land title for women and men, but instead securing a broader set of collectively-based rights, within family, kin and community relationships and jointly-owned land (O'Laughlin, 2009).

9.8 Emerging communities

Over 160,000 new households – around a million people – have settled on new land since 2000 across Zimbabwe. Central to the social dynamics of this process has been the establishment of new communities. While the process of invasion proved important for cementing ties and bonding people, this was no guarantee that a successful, coherent, functioning community would emerge.

Social networks, replicating those found in communal areas, have emerged in various forms in the new resettlement schemes. These include work parties, funeral assistance and religious-based interactions. For example, in mid-2008 there was a funeral at Nyengera homestead in Lonely farm. The husband of the deceased woman was not present. People contributed money and bought a coffin and food for the funeral. In the same farm, there was a work party at M's home, a poor widow who did not own cattle. A total of 14 spans of cattle came to assist from Lonely, Clare and Salem farms. The whole field was ploughed in one day.

Other forms of networking and interaction are also significant. In discussions on this topic, farmers in Wondedzo and Sanangwe mentioned interactions at village, school and political meetings as important, as well as relationships at church gatherings and agricultural training events. Some formal groups have been established. For example, in the A1 villagised Wondedzo Wares scheme a committee of four men and three women organise the sourcing and transport of farming inputs. Inputs are sourced from Masvingo and the committee hires transport normally from the government transport pool or a private operator. A women's group known as Fushai has also been established. The group is a savings group where members pool their resources together and loan to one another, with the loan repayable in two weeks.

Across the schemes, however, only 13% of all household heads identified themselves as members of a formal association, such as a registered club or union. Most of these memberships were in the A1 schemes, with very limited formal associational activity seen in the A2 and informal schemes. More informal arrangements – as well as membership of churches – are much more dominant. However, where there is a need to organise more formally this has emerged. As Box 9.1 shows, this has been an important aspect of the A2 sugar estate site at Hippo Valley, although the emerging association has not had an easy time.

Most forms of organisation on the new resettlements are, however,

---

Box 9.1 The Commercial Sugar Cane Farmers' Association

In 2002, a committee was elected to represent the new farmers on the sugar estates, with Mr. G as chairperson. Once the settlers successfully moved onto their plots, new challenges emerged. These included shortage of finance to start farming and lack of farming knowledge in sugar cane growing, as well as lack of equipment and transport. The committee managed to source loan funds from the CBZ, which paid for the training of new settlers and enabled farmers to buy inputs and pay wages. The committee also managed to acquire a fleet of tractors on hire-purchase from the CBZ, but it failed to service this loan, and the tractors were repossessed and auctioned. In 2003, an administration office was established, and Mr. T was employed as the head, with a few supporting staff. An immediate need was to raise funds for paying the new employees and meeting other expenses. This was to be raised from member subscriptions. There was a review of the membership structure, culminating in automatic membership for all the new cane outgrowers. A system was put in place whereby millers would levy each farmer and remit the money to the organisation. A 2% levy is deducted from the total payment due to each farmer. Notable during this time was that there was no constitution governing the running of the newly formed institution. As such, there were complaints relating to its governance. Towards the end of 2004, a general meeting was called and new committee members were elected. Besides playing an intermediary role between the farmers and the various stakeholders in the sugar cane industry, the committee was the main route for bargaining over sugar prices. From 2006, prices paid by the millers barely covered the expenses incurred in production. Bargaining for a high sugar price remained an illusion and farmers remained underpaid. In 2008, farmers were finding it difficult to pay workers and support themselves, and disgruntlement over the performance of the committee escalated among the now 600 members.

---

more informal. One of the most significant sources of organisation is the churches. In a number of areas religious affiliation and land invasions were tightly linked. For instance, Comrade B, Wondedzo's base commander and current *sabhuku*, settled at *jambanja* together with around a dozen households from his Johanne Marange Apostolic sect. PC, a former farm worker and war veteran collaborator, and leader of an invasion in another part of Wondedzo farm, established his own church, the Janga Mission, and regularly used the labour of church followers on his farm after settlement. In nearby Sanangwe, a large group of Johanne Marange followers are allied with one of the competing *sabhukus* and were part of the land invasion. This *sabhuku* has, in turn, allocated land to a number of church followers since then. A similarly strong link between church membership and scheme leadership exists in Turf Ranch, where Pastor HM, formerly the base commander, leads a strong following who were the core of the land invasion. Settlers on Clare and Lonely farm live very close to the long-established Rufaro Apostolic Faith Mission. Members of the mission were strong supporters of the land invasions in the area, and many followers are part of the new population of setters.

Beyond being important as a social basis for gaining access to land, the churches also provide an important context for collective work, service support and welfare. As one settler commented: 'During *jambanja* the churches were not so prominent, as it was a hot political climate. But with the problems people face today, they are really important.' At Turf Ranch, churches are important for collective labour, with the dominant churches in the area - Zion, Seventh Day Adventist and the Apostlic Faith Mission – all organising work parties with their congregations. Together the congregations have built a pole-and-mud church which they share, and join in multi-denominational services. As Pastor HM explains, this has really brought the community together, even if they have come from very different places.

As Abigail Barr (2004) has shown for old resettlement areas, the development of social relations – in the form of what she terms 'social capital' – is essential in the movement from establishment to production. While investments in infrastructure and tangible assets of all sorts are critical (Chapter 4), this less obvious, but equally important, aspect of building communities is essential. It is vital for individual production (e.g. through the sharing of labour and draught power), mobilising support and services (e.g. through organising input supplies), creating social solidarity (e.g. to confront enemies such as those trying to take over the land) and exerting voice (e.g. articulating demands to the state).

The processes of creating communities, forming social solidarities and cementing social relationships are a vital part of the emergence of the new resettlements. However, there are severe limits to local organisation – whether through formal associations, churches, traditional leadership or new committees – in the face of an unresponsive and unaccountable state. The exercise of voice without organisational and political clout is, as the experience of the sugar producers' association shows, very limited. More structured forms of organisation – such as a nationally federated farmers' union – are all but absent in the new resettlements. Only a handful of people identified membership of the Zimbabwe Farmers' Union, supposedly the national representative body for small-scale farmers, as one of their associational activities. The Union has limited capacity, and in many people's view is in any case too close to the state to provide an effective source of countervailing power in the way that the Commercial Farmers' Union did for large-scale commercial farmers in the past (Herbst, 1990).

In Chapter 11 we will return to the question of the importance of farmer organisations, and the role these must have in pushing agendas in favour of new resettlement farmers. But, as previous sections have highlighted, 'resettlement farmers', like 'small-scale farmers' more broadly, are not in any way a homogenous group. A huge array of livelihood strategies and class positions exists. Can a single organisation represent peasants, worker-peasants and an emergent rural bourgeoisie, at the same time as accommodating differences related to ethnicity, gender and religious affiliation, let alone dealing with the highly fractured party political allegiances that have so divided people in the recent past? The new resettlement areas are a highly differentiated, highly fractured social space, with seemingly limited potential to forge a strong, coherent and influential political voice.

To return to the questions posed at the beginning of this chapter, how can this highly dynamic, yet extremely differentiated and diverse, setting provide the basis for the re-establishment of accountable, responsive institutions which can drive development? In the past decade people have largely gone it alone. But, as we have discussed, there are severe limits to voluntarism and localism; if future development pathways are to be realised, a wider transformation must take place. The concluding section of this chapter reflects on these challenges.

9.9 From *jambanja* to development: reconstructing the state from below?

In the period from 2000, both the capacity and legitimacy of the state collapsed. Local government in particular became intensely politicised, as key committees and operations were taken over by war veterans and party cadres (McGregor, 2002; Hammar, 2003, 2005). Much of the election violence during 2008 was organised through state structures, including the local administration and the security services. Given this recent experience, what is the potential of reconstructing the state from below?

As previous sections have discussed, this is already happening. It is somewhat haphazard and often conflictive, and there are no clear lines of authority, responsibility and accountability, as axes of power and control overlap, and demarcations are often blurred. But, in some important senses, there are emergent forms of public authority, dealing with the day-to-day challenges of boundary conflicts, land inheritance, plot allocation, service provision and wider development. A recurrent feature, repeated across all sites, is the flexibility of posts and people. Numerous transitions have occurred – from war veteran base commander to *sabhuku*; from land invader to local councillor; or from district party official to representative of the chieftaincy. Identities and identifications are hugely variable, and have changed dramatically over time. The overall trend has been a move from authority structures centred on war veterans and the Committee of Seven to the extension of traditional authority structures, centred on chiefs, headmen and *sabhukus* – even if the same individuals are involved.

Development has been happening, even if not at the pace that most settlers desired. In most instances this has been development without the state, and with no external aid in the form of donor-funded projects. Just as government intervention (mostly focused on input programmes) became intensely politicised, so too has donor aid, with the so-called 'humanitarian-plus' programmes run through NGOs avoiding the new resettlement areas almost completely. In 2009 a massive programme of agricultural input support was announced through a consortium of donors to be implemented by NGOs, but this was to be directed to the communal areas, and not the 'contested areas' of the new resettlements; although some did filter through, either by active diversion or simple mistake. But despite this highly distorted, deeply politicised external environment, there is actually much going on. Efforts towards development – beyond the individual investments discussed in Chapter 4 and the commercial enterprises discussed later in Chapter 10 – have been substantial. Churches have been built, schools and clinics constructed, roads cut and collective water points dug.

Such efforts, however, impressive though they are, are not sustainable without external support. The state has often shown an uneasy ambivalence towards the new resettlements, not quite knowing what to do, and often without the resources to do much anyway. And donors and NGOs have largely remained sitting on the fence and avoided committing themselves. Episodes such as Operation Murambatsvina have highlighted the ambiguous character of the state – at one time backing the land invasions and the new resettlements and at the next moment invoking draconian planning laws to undermine development efforts on the ground. Across the sites there was huge disappointment expressed at the failure of the government to come in and support the new settlers. Operation Maguta and the mechanisation programme were seen to be inadequate and often poorly targeted, while the absence of extension workers, veterinarians, dip tanks, road maintenance, borehole drillers, irrigation engineers and all the other support services that might have improved the potential of the resettlement areas was highlighted in all group discussions across the schemes.

Central to considerations about the future governance of the land are questions of what the land reform was for. Jospeh Mujere (2010: 19) sums it up succinctly: 'Whilst for the technocrats the land redistribution programme is about taking land from the minority white farmers and giving it to the landless black majority, the traditional authorities did not quite see the programme in the same way. Instead, they view it as an opportunity to reclaim lost ancestral lands, graves, mountains, and sacred places and also to re-establish their *nyika* boundaries which had been greatly altered during the colonial period.'

Over the last decade, there has been a simultaneous reassertion of technocracy and tradition, and the creation of new forms of hybrid governance. As authority and power in the rural areas is reimagined, so too is the nature of the state and its interactions with citizens. The creative solutions generated by the necessity of solidarity, organisation and building a sense of community have emerged on the margins of state action and practice, but are in turn shaping the way it is being reconstructed. Highly essentialised, narrow and exclusionary versions of citizenship have been imposed in the name of nationalist politics (Rutherford, 2003), Yet, as Joost Fontein (2006a, b) argues, such narrow forms of nationalism and extreme forms of exclusion may have actually opened up new opportunities for the assertion of new languages, imaginations, aspirations, practices and forms of authority, as well as new sites of conflict. Diverse aspirations and complex imaginaries have been unleashed that combine striving for modernity, as witnessed by the incredible efforts invested in gaining access to inputs, improving agricultural production, defining land use plans and reappropriating tradition and the role of chiefly and spiritual authority. As Fontein (2009) argues, false contradictions between 'modernity' and 'tradition' and 'sovereignty' and 'development' have been presented in the literature, while the practice on the ground represents a more nuanced mix.

The future must accommodate these hybrid visions and complex forms of governance, but, as Pauline Peters (2004: 304) cautions, we must accept not only that 'relations around land are socially "embedded" but that they are embedded in unequal social relationships'. Thus, with our focus on the hybrid, negotiated nature of emerging social relations around land, we should not forget that these reveal major conflicts between classes, genders and generations. Power and authority are channelled in particular ways: by the technocratic state, by political elites, by chiefs and lineages and by gendered relations. The evolving institutional terrain in the new resettlement areas is therefore characterised by diverse forms of organisation and diffuse, disconnected and often arbitrary forms of authority. But this is not infinitely variable: certain structural factors shape what is unfolding on the ground and, due to unequal relations of power, there are clear winners and losers. These new negotiations over land are often highly specific, dependent on particular and very recent histories of invasion and settlement, and the composition of people on the new land, their social relations, motivations and aspirations. Once again, no simple story can be told.

Thus, as elsewhere in Africa, the institutions governing land are deeply rooted in negotiated, often fuzzy and ambiguous, social relations and networks (Berry, 1989, 2002, 2009) that are usually riven with power, conflict and division (Peters, 2004, 2009). In Zimbabwe, this is a critical moment of experimentation and innovation in land governance, but this is being carried out on highly uneven social and political terrain. In the concluding chapter, we argue that standardised, imposed solutions, or those resurrected from the past, will not work; account must be taken of the complex, hybrid character of emerging institutional and governance arrangements. But at the same time the uneven power relations which construct new types of public authority and institutional forms must equally be taken on board if new, accountable and equitable forms of governance are to emerge in the Zimbabwean countryside.

10

Livelihood Pathways & Economic Linkages | Emerging Impacts of Land Reform

10.1. Livelihoods and agrarian change

This book set out to ask how people have fared since they got new land. As the previous chapters have shown, a wide range of activities contribute to highly differentiated livelihoods in the new resettlements. There has been substantial investment in farm assets and infrastructure (Chapter 4), and agricultural production and marketing has been growing, even if variably (Chapters 5 and 7). A wide array of livelihood activities is seen. At one time people may be more reliant on land-based livelihoods, including farm labour (Chapter 6), and at another on non-farm activities, either locally or through migration (Chapter 8). In important respects, the simplistic generalisations about Zimbabwe's land reform are not borne out.

But what do these findings imply for patterns of agrarian change, and the unfolding class and political dynamics in the countryside? Has land reform produced such a radically altered agrarian structure that a new economic dynamic is emerging? What forms of production, investment and accumulation are ongoing, and how is this affecting patterns of social and economic differentiation? Is there a potential for substantial and sustained 'accumulation from below' (Neocosmos, 1993; Cousins, 2010), rooted in new forms of rural petty commodity production, based on small-scale agriculture? These are important questions for the future, as these processes of agrarian change will shape political and economic trajectories for many years to come. In particular, we need to ask: what are the longer-term implications of the replacement of a large-scale commercial farming sector owned and controlled by a small group with a more diverse set of farming enterprises of different scales? Can the new farmers generate not only subsistence livelihoods, but also surpluses to feed the nation and create broader wealth?

As Ben Cousins (2010: 15) argues: 'land reform and accumulation from below are necessary to reconfigure a dualistic and unequal agrarian structure which is itself a structural cause of poverty'. This requires the creation of a new group of farmers and entrepreneurs to fill the 'missing middle' between very small-scale survival farming and large-scale commercial operations (Hall, 2009; Cousins, 2007). Accumulation from below implies that 'the inherited agrarian structure is radically reconfigured so that much larger numbers of people begin to participate in the agricultural sector and benefit substantially from such participation. However, it also suggests that these new producers must be able to produce as least as much (if not more) than large-scale commercial farmers, replacing them in supplying local, national and international markets' (Cousins, 2010: 16).

A number of studies have attempted to assess the pattern of rural differentiation and its broad class characteristics in Zimbabwe (Bush and Cliffe, 1984; Cousins et al., 1992; Moyo, 1995). Based on an extensive review of the 1980s literature on rural differentiation in Zimbabwe's communal areas, for example, Ben Cousins and colleagues (1992: 12-13) identified four types of rural household, distinguishing petty commodity producers from worker-peasants, the semi-peasantry and the rural petit bourgeoisie. In the former settler wage labour economies of southern Africa, hybrid class identities exist, given the close interactions between rural and urban spaces, agriculture and wage labour. In their categorisation, petty commodity producers combine capital (owning the means of production) and labour (providing primarily family labour) in the farm enterprise. They can meet a significant proportion of their simple reproduction needs from direct production.[1] While they have the potential to engage in expanded reproduction, their capacity to sustain capital accumulation is still constrained. Worker-peasants are a hybrid group, combining elements of the proletarian and the (partially commoditised) petty commodity producer. The semi-peasantry are the most marginalised and impoverished group, and include significant numbers of women. They are insecure with respect to both rural production and wage labour. Finally, the rural petit bourgeoisie have, according to this classification, moved beyond simple reproduction and into (relatively) sustained capitalist accumulation, employing and extracting surplus from wage labour. They often have diversified livelihoods, drawing on rural and urban sources of income. However, according to Cousins and colleagues 'they are only petty capitalists and clearly not an "agrarian bourgeoisie" in the classical sense'.

These agrarian class dynamics necessarily take on a particular character in southern Africa, given the historical distortions of a colonial migrant labour economy. The relationships between the core economy and the rural 'labour reserves' thus had huge impacts on patterns of class and social differentiation in the countryside (Arrighi, 1973). However, in contrast to some assessments that view rural people as a relatively homogenous 'semi-proletariat', there are – as we have seen throughout this book – important patterns of differentiation. These are not necessarily along classical lines, as parallel processes of proletarianisation and the emergence of successful petty commodity production take place, creating important hybrid class categories such as worker-peasants (Cousins, 2010). As Bernstein (2009: 73) explains, many must seek their livelihoods:

---

[1] Including daily reproduction (maintaining the means of production and levels of consumption) and generational reproduction (raising the next generation of family labour) (Bernstein, 2010).

... through insecure, oppressive and increasingly 'informalised' wage employment and/or a range of likewise precarious small-scale and insecure 'informal sector' ('survival') activity, including farming; in effect, various and complex *combinations* of employment and self-employment. Many of the labouring poor do this across different sites of the social division of labour: urban and rural, agricultural and non-agricultural, as well as wage employment and self-employment. This defies inherited assumptions of fixed, let alone uniform, notions (and 'identities') of 'worker', 'trader', 'urban', 'rural', 'employed' and 'self-employed'.

Given this diversity of hybrid livelihood strategies and class identities, how does accumulation take place? As Cousins (2010:17) argues for South Africa: 'Successful accumulation from below would necessarily involve a class of productive small-scale capitalist farmers emerging from within a larger population of petty commodity producers, worker-peasants, allotment-holding wage workers and supplementary food producers'. In Zimbabwe, the potential for this is highly dependent on wider political and economic relations, and most especially on those elites who, despite their political rhetoric, are not fully committed to a more radical reconfiguration of land, livelihoods and agrarian relations.

This chapter therefore asks whether in the new resettlements we are seeing a process of accumulation from below - where new 'middle farmers' are contributing to economic development, urban food supplies and employment – or whether relationships are dominated by processes of accumulation from above – where accumulation derives from from oppressive, exploitative and extractive political and market relations, de-linked from local-level commodity production. Or whether indeed there is some combination of these dynamics, and so tensions and conflicts between groups. In order to answer these central issues, we must delineate the patterns of economic activity and their political dimensions, identifying the contours of social differentiation and class formation. This allows us in turn to evaluate not only the longer-term livelihood trajectories being pursued, but also what political and economic alliances are being forged between different groups structuring the wider agrarian political economy. While necessarily speculative, such insights allow us to make some assessments about likely future changes, and the longer-term impacts of Zimbabwe's land reform.

10.2 Wider economic linkages

One of the critiques of Zimbabwe's land reform has concerned its impact on the wider economy. The disruption of large-scale commercial agriculture has certainly had negative consequences. Declines in production, restructuring of value chains and reductions in investor confidence, credit flows and input supplies have all resulted. Over time, and with the right support, can a reconfigured agriculture revitalise the sector, and indeed overcome the inequalities, inefficiencies and distortions that have affected the large-scale sector over decades? And can this be built on the back of successful local-level production and accumulation from below?

One of the central claims made of redistributive land reform is that it provides the basis for broad-based economic growth. Opening up the opportunities for smallholder farming by giving people access to land should, it is argued, provide a motor for growth that is both efficient and equitable (see Chapter 1). Processes of accumulation from below on small farms should in turn generate wider economic benefits. Whether linked to local or wider national or even global markets, there are potentials for various linkage and multiplier effects (Delgado et al., 1998; Haggblade et al., 2007). In much of Africa, consumption growth linkages have been found to be especially important (although for an alternative view, see Hart, 1989). The extent to which such linkages are realised is, of course, a function of many other factors, including market organisation, social relations, education, infrastructure and institutional coordination (Kydd et al., 2004; Dorward et al., 2004b).

With new people on the land, and with at least a significant proportion generating regular surpluses (Chapter 5), we should expect new demands for a range of products and services, resulting in turn in a growth in overall economic activity. This should have ripple effects into the wider economy, generating employment and economic growth. Did this happen in Zimbabwe, or did the wider economic and political turmoil derail it?

Chapter 7 offered some evidence from the perspective of agricultural commodity chains. Cotton was clearly booming, via a growing and increasingly competitive formal sector, and so generating jobs, income and investment. The former beef industry, based on commercial ranching, had, by contrast, collapsed, with negative impacts on the CSC, the supermarkets and the ranches themselves. But instead, an informal market had exploded, with new market chains, retail outlets and intermediaries being established, and much potential for new, better distributed economic activity. For maize the picture was much more negative. Input supply systems had collapsed as their economic viability had previously been assured by the large-scale commercial sector and, instead, inputs, sometimes of dubious quality, were being sourced through informal markets. At the same time formal maize marketing had – at least in 2008 - more or less ceased, being replaced by a variety of trading and exchange arrangements. While the situation was much more positive in 2009-10, following a good harvest and dollarisation, the re-establishment of a thriving input supply and maize market remains still some way off.

Thus, a mixed picture emerges from an assessment of different agricultural commodity chains, but what of more general economic activity? Prior to resettlement, many of the large-scale farmers ran small businesses that supported their farm-worker populations. These included farm shops, butcheries and grinding mills; all of these closed with the departure of the white owners. Following land reform, the population swelled, creating new demand, and many new enterprises were established to serve a new, and much expanded, customer base. While we did not attempt a full quantitative assessment of economic linkages and multipliers, nor an evaluation of changes in the regional economy, we carried out a simple enterprise audit across the study sites. New enterprises were evident in all of them. These included tuck shops, drinking places, mobile stores and a range of other services, ranging from well digging to tractor hiring to fencing. Much local consumption demand is satisfied by the cross-border movement of settlers, mostly women, who bring back goods for local exchange. This is complemented by mobile shops – traders moving around the area selling items such as sugar, soap, paraffin and salt in exchange for agricultural commodities. According to our surveys, there has been an explosion of such businesses in recent years.

In addition, there has been a growth of enterprises aimed at adding value to agriculture. For example, capitalising on their agricultural successes, Wondedzo resettlement farmers have started a number of agricultural processing activities, in particular focused on soya beans, an increasingly popular crop. Soya beans can be roasted, ground and mixed with wheat to produce 'bread'. 'Powdered milk' can also be produced from soya, as well as cooking oil. The residues can be used as chicken feed, while soya 'chunks' are substitutes for meat and mince. In the context of a scarcity of other commodities, there is a roaring trade, both locally and in nearby markets. Farmers are also producing cooking oil from sunflowers. One has purchased a hand-driven oil expresser, retaining a portion of the oil as payment, while residues are used to feed chickens. A number of farmers also produce peanut butter for sale in local markets.

On a larger scale, in the nearby A1 self-contained plots, Mr M, a businessman based in Masvingo, has fenced his farm and established a cattle-fattening business with profits from his transport business. He has between 80 and 100 cattle on the 85ha plot at any one time. He buys them from the local areas and takes 10-15 at a time to the CSC abbatoir in Masvingo for service slaughter. The meat is then sold on to butcheries in Harare. He has recently been buying Brahman animals from nearby commercial farmers, as they have good feed-meat conversion ratios. The animals are all fed on the plot. He buys molasses, cotton seed cake and GMB crush, which is mixed with grass cut by women from the nearby resettlement areas. In late 2008, he had seven workers, five of whom are resident on the plot, while the other two live in the villagised portion of Wondedzo Wares resettlement area.

These new enterprises have resulted in a rapid growth of markets, particularly around Masvingo town. The most famous of these is the 'Ku Train' market which is a hive of activity on the days the train comes to town. The market stretches along the tracks and urban customers flock there. Traders come from far and wide, bringing a huge range of agricultural produce, fresh and processed, legal and illicit. Those from our Gutu study sites were able to connect to this key market, despite the relative long distance, since the train tickets were cheap. They brought agricultural produce (especially bambara nuts and groundnuts), along with vegetables and maize, often in large quantities. Some sold processed goods: peanut butter, roasted green mealies or cooked meals. They would stay at the market, either sleeping outdoors or with friends and relatives in the township, until the train returned.

Overall, however, all new entrepreneurs have struggled given the economic conditions of the past decade. New enterprises are generally oriented towards providing consumption goods and services for farm production, and trade operates at a small scale. The level of capitalisation is low and turnover and returns often small. However, before dismissing these efforts completely, we must again recall the extreme and uncertain circumstances under which they have emerged. Hyperinflation in particular made cash transaction impossible, and the lack of any credit for small businesses meant that borrowing for up-grading was off the cards. In addition, arbitrary, politically-motivated interventions by the state, such as Operation Murambatsvina ('clean up'),[2] and the continued insistence on compliance with very strict and wildly out-dated planning regulations has undermined the capacity of new enterprises to operate in the open, with full market advantage.

A prime example of the struggles against outside authority can be found in the Uswaushava informal resettlement. Situated along the Ngundu-Chiredzi road, the location is ideal for business, attracting not only local residents but also passing trade. With no nearby business centre and a large number of new settlers in the area, there was a captive market. Soon after settlement, around ten businesses were established, including tuck shops and beer drinking establishments. They were basic structures, but began to create a small market centre where trade of all sorts took place. This all changed when Operation Murambatsvina removed all non-registered trading sites. In many urban areas, this campaign was directed against opposition supporters, and became highly politicised, displacing many people. But in the new resettlements, this was not the case, with ZANU-PF supporters and war veterans suffering as much as others. In Uswaushava, despite protests and petitions led by the now late Base Commander, the government removed nine businesses. By 2008 there remained only one tuck shop, run by a teacher, and a beer drinking place, run by Mr LC. The previously vibrant informal business centre was no more. As a local resident explained: 'There are no formal township plans, so we are not allowed to build. A township on the other side of the road was pegged by Lands. We keep going to them and they say, just wait.' The lack of formal recognition of this site, and the draconian planning regulations used to justify Operation Murambatsvina, have conspired against the blossoming of local enterprises. Mr LC had initially invested in several tuck shops for selling groceries, but these were torn down in 2005. They then moved to selling opaque beer from a shelter at their homestead, which was fortunately next to the road. However, for other products, the consequences of Murambatsvina have been that Uswaushava residents have had to make the trip to Chiredzi to shop. This is both expensive and time consuming.

The extent and persistence of these enterprises – many reviving and taking off following dollarisation in 2009 – is witness to the potential economic benefits of land reform. Given the low population densities on the former farms in our study areas, and the narrow supply chains that linked to farm-level activities, the scale and scope of economic activity following land reform has certainly increased, despite the challenging conditions. Moreover, what has changed in particular is the nature of

---

[2]   Tibaijuka (2005); Potts (2006a, 2008); Batton and Masunungure (2007); Vambe (2008).

economic relations. No longer are trading enterprises, for example, controlled by a few, larger companies or individuals, but because of the informal, sometimes illegal, nature of new 'real markets', other entrepreneurs are able to fill the gap. Trading in low volumes and through social networks people were able to dodge the consequences of price control, Operation Murambatsvina and cross-border import restrictions. Others have established businesses that needed no circumvention of the formal rules, but responded to a new demand for services, whether tractor ploughing, threshing, well digging or tailoring.

The result has thus been a new social and geographical configuration of the rural economy. Commerce no longer happens in the old market centres, created to serve the white commercial farming areas, or the downtown commercial districts of urban centres like Masvingo. Instead, business is booming in the townships on the peripheries of the formerly white towns or in more dispersed ways through mobile trade across the new resettlement areas. The interconnections and complementarities between resettlement sites become important too in this reconfiguration of economic activity. Entrepreneurs in A2 or A1 self-contained schemes, with more land and resources, are able to generate economic linkages with other A1 and communal areas.

But the big question remains: will such a nascent local economic dynamic persist in the context of economic recovery? Will the big players return and swamp these new entrepreneurs with lower prices, better supply chains and more effective responses to changing demand? In terms of of agricultural commodities, Chapter 7 has already noted a move beyond the old, narrow commodity chain in favour of a more diverse value chain, involving more players, with more equitably distributed benefits. This has been happening for beef, cotton and, to some extent, maize. However, for other entrepreneurs the future looks more uncertain. Following the stabilisation of economy in 2009 and the removal of price controls, the formerly dominant retailers and rural-focused businesses (e.g. equipment and input supplies, borehole drilling etc.) have returned; sometimes under new ownership structures, but very often not. This was remarkably quick, and the resilience of capitalist enterprises was once again demonstrated. In a matter of days, the supermarket shelves were full, and suppliers had new equipment and inputs for sale. While this was initially all imported goods, local supply has gradually returned, with businesses along supply chains reopening.

Even if such enterprises out-compete many of the more informal businesses established over the last decade, they must be responsive to new demand and supply patterns. Here the potential for new supply chains from the new resettlements opens up, requiring new skills in business and marketing strategy for the new farmers. In the future, as we argue further in the concluding chapter, interventions must start with an understanding of the new configurations of the rural economy, and seek ways to catalyse entrepreneurship and local economic activity in order to foster the forward and backward linkages that the post-2000 land reform offers. This requires a positive recognition of the potentials, as well as the limitations, of new patterns of accumulation and surplus generation on the new farms.

10.3 Patterns of accumulation

At an aggregate level, the new resettlement schemes are doing well, and in many respects remarkably well, given the economic and political turmoil that has enveloped Zimbabwe over much of the last decade. Any rough calculation of aggregate economic output which includes crop and livestock production, together with local off-farm economic activity, shows substantial returns per hectare across all sites, with the A1 and informal sites clearly performing substantially better than the A2 sites. Add into the equation the very substantial investment in rural infrastructure (notably housing, but also wells, fencing and gardens), returns per unit area, as well as investment levels, are unquestionably substantial.

Small-scale capitalist farmers, successful petty commodity producers and worker-peasants of different sorts, most notably in the A1 self-contained sites, are generating significant surpluses for sale, and providing the basis for continued investment in productive agriculture, as well as other enterprises. This, we argue, demonstrates a pattern of accumulation from below, based on a significant group of new 'middle farmers' with new land. While, as discussed below, such patterns are highly variable across schemes, sites and social groups, a significant group of settlers in the new resettlements are on an upward livelihood trajectory, driven by agricultural production.

A question often posed is whether the resettlements are an improvement on what was there before. Is this new pattern of accumulation replacing large-scale capitalist enterprises with overall net benefits in terms of livelihoods and economy? This is an impossible question to answer easily. It all depends on what is valued (say local livelihoods versus export earnings), what the opportunity costs are (loss in jobs, foreign exchange etc.) and what the scarce, limiting factor is (land, labour or capital) in order to calculate returns of what in relation to what. These are, in the end, social and political choices, and so are not amenable to simple economic analysis. However, in the most stark terms, the returns (measured across economic activities) per unit of land from the new resettlements (despite all the problems and limitations) are certainly higher than the low intensity, low employment, extensive ranch production systems that they replaced in Masvingo province, even allowing for some portion of irrigated agriculture.

Calculations, and so figures, vary, but estimates of net revenue for cattle ranching of US$9-12 per hectare per annum have been recorded for extensive ranching systems in the drier parts of Zimbabwe during the 1980s and 1990s (Child, 1988; Jansen et al., 1992; Kreuter and Workman, 1992). Revenue streams from extensive wildlife were around half this level, although returns were boosted by trophy hunting in particular. With changing price levels and subsidy patterns, the economics of beef production has not been stable since these studies, so large margins of error can be applied. But in terms of simple orders of magnitude, the new mixed farming systems of the A1 and informal resettlements are clearly out-performing extensive cattle or wildlife ranching on a per area basis by a substantial margin.

Questions are, however, raised about the A2 farms. Outside the irrigated areas, where different problems apply, the dryland A2 sites have largely performed poorly. We have discussed the reasons for this: lack of commitment of the owners, absenteeism, poor labour management, limited capital investment, lack of infrastructure, poor connections to markets, conflicts with neighbours and so on. Clearly, with vanishingly few exceptions, the new A2 farms are not yet performing anywhere near their capacity, and are not able to replace the large-scale commercial sector in terms of either investment or production. A number of A2 farmers relied on patronage connections to gain access to land. Given the limits of the state's largesse, such strategies of accumulation from above have been highly constrained. As a result, land has remained idle and investment has been small. This of course has strategic implications, and raises again the question, pursued in more depth in the concluding chapter, of whether, and if so how, a 'commercial' agricultural sector might re-emerge in Zimbabwe – albeit with a different scale, orientation and type of commodity and market specialisation. This was certainly envisaged in the overall policy for A2 resettlement, and encapsulated in the approved business plans, but, as yet, has not been implemented in practice.

A focus on the administrative models (A1 versus A2 etc.) is of course both misleading and inappropriate. Overall, a more flexible approach is required that allows the dynamics of accumulation and entrepreneurship to be rewarded. Expecting some farms to perform as commercial enterprises because they are 'A2', while constraining others because they are 'A1' simply does not make sense. While, as we have discussed elsewhere, land markets must remain regulated to avoid rapid consolidation and resulting landlessness, flexibility in land sizes through leasing, land transfer and transition is undoubtedly required (Chapter 9). This is already happening, but often under the radar, involving deals for example between new A2 farmers, former commercial farmers and new investors. But when such arrangements are exposed, officialdom cries foul, arguing that they upset formal policies and plans.[3] Yet flexibility in land holdings – a type of continuous land reform (cf. Rukuni et al., 2009) – will allow the process of accumulation from below to flourish. Quite clearly, a strategy based on centralised support, patronage and accumulation from above, is not going to realise the benefits of land reform. A simple reshuffling of racial patterns of ownership is insufficient and, instead, a more dynamic, entrepreneurial vision is required and needs to be facilitated and supported.

10.4 Patterns of differentiation

Across the million or more people who have gained land through land reform in the last decade, there is a vast diversity of experience. Not everyone is on an upward trajectory propelled by accumulation from below. And, at the same time, not everyone has benefited from patronage support and accumulation from above. Thus to locate our wider

---

3   'Chiefs in land scam', *The Herald*, 7 March, http://www.herald.co.zw/.

Table 10.1 Socio-economic differentiation by study site and success group

	A1 villagised			A1 self-contained			A1 informal			A2		
	SG1	SG2	SG3	SG1	SG2	SG3	SG1	SG2	SG3	SG1	SG2	SG3
Age of household head	41	39	38	38	38	36	42	36	30	44	44	47
Educational level of household head	Grade 7	Form 2	Form 2	Form 2	Form 2	Form 2	Grade 7	Grade 7	Grade 7	Form 3 or better	Form 3 or better	Form 3 or better
Land holding (ha)	4.8	4.3	4.5	37.1	33.3	32.5	7.0	6.7	6.7	182.5	126.8	153.1
Area cropped (ha)	3.8	3.3	3.2	9.9	6.0	5.7	5.9	4.9	2.8	11.3	12.4	8.1
Cattle owned (nos)	6.8	4.3	2.7	15.4	6.9	6.2	12.2	3.3	0.8	48.5	24.5	8.9
Maize output in 2006 kg	3,466	2,593	2,105	9,900	3,480	2,695	2,626	1,863	1,006	25,150	2,914	6,100
Sales (GMB and local) in kg in 2006	1,968	1,319	1,076	7,302	1,950	1,305	632	142	196	19,550	1,477	4,375
% owning a scotch cart	65%	50%	55%	79%	46%	33%	53%	50%	21%	29%	48%	27%
House type (% with tin/ asbestos roof)	51%	48%	54%	35%	48%	48%	53%	54%	67%	71%	78%	58%
% receiving remittance	41%	33%	21%	43%	46%	43%	26%	29%	35%	29%	27%	31%

Source: Survey data, 2007-08

discussion, we must ask about emerging patterns of differentiation, and the implications for emerging class dynamics in the new resettlements. How important are the different dynamics of agrarian change identified above in different places, and what are the implications for wider processes of social and economic change?

As previous chapters have amply shown, patterns of investment, production and accumulation are far from uniform. Social and economic differentiation exists between sites, and across and within households. Axes of differentiation include social class, gender, age, ethnicity and location. These patterns of differentiation thus influence the way the new social and economic relations – on and off farms – are being played out, and so define the emerging class characteristics in the new resettlements. As Chapter 3 has discussed, the composition of the post-2000 resettlements is very different from either the communal lands or the old resettlement areas. On the A1 sites – at least on average – people are more educated, younger and with more assets, particularly cattle. Alongside people who have relocated from the communal areas are others – business people, civil servants and those with political connections. Households are growing, as more people come to the new lands; and migration to and from the new resettlement areas is an important dynamic. It is therefore inadequate to treat the new resettlements as either extensions of the communal lands (for A1 sites) or scaled-down versions of commercial farming (for the A2 sites). Nor will simple ascriptions of 'subsistence' or 'commercial' farming work either. These are new areas, with new people and different livelihood and production systems, and so deserve an analysis which does not carry assumptions from elsewhere.

Table 10.1 presents some basic data on key socio-economic indicators across all the sites, first introduced in Chapter 2, and here relating these to 'success groups'. In all sites, success groups, as defined by local ranking exercises, are directly correlated with indicators of wealth, including land area, cattle holdings, equipment owned, type of house and engagement with the market. Some significant contrasts exist, indicative, as we discuss below, of emerging class dynamics. For example, in A1 self-contained sites, SG1 households' maize production in 2006 was nearly three times that of SG2 households in the same sites, while sales were nearly four times as large, despite land holdings and cropped areas being comparable. The SG1 households, however, own more than double the number of cattle and significantly more own scotch carts than their SG2 counterparts, demonstrating the differentiated nature of asset accumulation across households.

Across the data presented in this book, a number of recurring patterns emerge. First, and most obviously, there is marked differentiation across settlers – different assets, different livelihood activities and different livelihood opportunities are evident. This applies across all of the sites. There is a strong correlation between a range of socio-economic indicators and local perceptions of 'success'; although with high levels of variation. Yet the factors that differentiate households are specific to particular sites. For the schemes in the higher agroecological potential areas, crop production and sales to the GMB are seen as particular indicators of success. In the drier areas of Chiredzi and Mwenezi, livestock feature more prominently, although irrigated agriculture is important for the A2 sites.

Second, there are some marked differences between scheme types – as well as much blurring. For the A1 and informal schemes, having sufficient assets for farming – and particularly draught power and farm equipment – is seen as essential to success. For the A2 schemes, a wider array of capital equipment is required, but also essential is the ability to pay, manage and supervise workers. For the A2 farmers, access to external resources is vital. Those without were seriously struggling, as access to credit or other sources of finance was absent in this period. Transport businesses, for example, provided an important source of investment resources for the new farms in several cases. A2 farmers were also often reliant on patronage support from the state through the farm mechanisation and other schemes. Being 'well connected' was a vital element of the accumulation from above strategies of some A2 farmers, not only to get the farm in the first place, but keeping it going.

Third, the presence of key adult members of the household is essential. This was emphasised again and again in the ranking workshops, highlighting how success is not just about material wealth and asset ownerships, but relates to the supervision of labour, and also to overall management, planning and investment efforts. Absenteeism – especially of both the senior male and female household members – results in caretaker arrangements with relatives or workers, and this limits success. In the communal areas, absence of the male household head due to patterns of circular migration has long been a feature of the split-location livelihood strategies pursued. However, the sort of investment required in the start-up phase of the new resettlement farms (clearing land, building up assets, farming under very difficult conditions, managing new labour) requires, many argued, that everyone be present. On the A2 farms, most farmers have homes elsewhere, but it is the frequency of visits and the style of management of workers that are particularly important.

Fourth, illnesses and deaths in the household are a key influence on lack of success. HIV/AIDS prevalence is high, and leads to high levels of morbidity and mortality. Many of the SG3 households had suffered deaths or prolonged illnesses in the family. This resulted in exits from the schemes (Chapter 3), or falls in production that led others to come in to make use of the land. It is this type of misfortune that can shift a livelihood pathway dramatically from an upward course to one that is suddenly downwards. The absence of a key household member may cause the disappearance of remittance income, labour and more general advice, skills and support. The death of both parents results in radical reconfigurations of households, with orphans taking on new responsibilities and other relatives entering the households as carers. Such events have material, but also emotional and psychological impacts. It is not surprising that, facing such traumatic upheavals, some decided to return to more familiar and supportive settings in the communal areas.

Fifth, external sources of funds through remittances are important across the sites. Links to South Africa are particularly prominent in the Mwenezi sites. Having access to remittance income is vital, and particularly if paid in rand. Before the dollarisation of the economy, local salaries were effectively worthless, so the influence of remittances from teachers or other civil servants, for example, was less than it had been in the past. However, many of these individuals had built up resources before, and were profiting from these past investments in cattle or equipment. Multiple forms of off-farm income earning were evident – from local piecework to relatively large commercial enterprises in towns (shops, restaurants, transport businesses). Some had begun to engage in 'value added' activities linked to agriculture on the new farms, including beer brewing, meat and milk sales and irrigated horticulture. The use of natural resources on or near the new farms was also important, including the hunting of wildlife, production of biltong, harvesting of wild fruits and insects, and gold panning. Some off-farm activities were illegal, including unlicensed gold panning, cannabis growing and, perhaps the most important and popular activity among younger males, jumping the border to South Africa.

Sixth, across the success groups a demographic pattern is observed. Those in SG1 tend to be older, having accumulated assets in the relatively good times of the 1980s and 1990s. They may have worked in this period, and had returned home to the communal areas before joining the land invasions. Those in SG2 are overall younger, sometimes the sons of those in SG1. They are often better educated, having benefited from post-Independence investment in education, unlike their older parents who often missed out, particularly during the liberation war. SG3 are a more mixed group, including younger households trying to establish themselves and struggling under the harsh conditions, and older households who had suffered deaths and illnesses, sometimes due to old age, but more often through HIV/AIDS. Household sizes are however larger in SG1 groups, making the per capita distribution of outputs and resources comparable to those in SG2. The attraction of new household members (as extended visitors, hired or family labour and orphans) to the relatively successful SG1 households is an important dynamic with both positive and negative impacts on livelihoods, as discussed in Chapter 3.

Seventh, as discussed in Chapter 5 regarding draught power and Chapter 6 regarding labour, relationships between households across success groups are a key dynamic in the A1 sites, but are less important in the A2 schemes. In the A1 sites, sharing of draught, labour and food occurs between households on the same scheme – and indeed links are common with the former home sites in the communal areas. These networks are vital for both agricultural production and provide broader forms of social protection. They are especially important for the more vulnerable households in SG3. However, because people did not necessarily settle as kin or lineage groups, the dynamics differ from those in the communal areas, and the process of establishing linkages between household – through kin, church or other affiliations – is only gradually developing, as it did in the 1980s resettlements.

How then do we make sense of this enormous diversity? What broader patterns emerge which allow us to examine relationships between groups and processes of change over time? In essence, what does the data tell us about the relationship between land reform, livelihoods and agrarian change?

10.5 A livelihood typology

Previous work on livelihoods in rural Zimbabwe has offered various typologies of livelihood strategies. For example, Chimhowu (2002) and Chimhowu and Hulme (2006) offer five broad categories based on work in the frontier lands of northern Zimbabwe, both on formal and spontaneous resettlement sites. These include back-foot strategies, pursued by chronically poor households, without productive assets and no external support who are often candidates for exit; crisis strategies, involving households with a semi-subsistence farming strategy and who are often casualties of retrenchment or HIV/AIDS; survivalist strategies followed by vulnerable, non-poor households of average wealth who have secure livelihoods in good seasons, but are vulnerable during bad ones; and two types of accumulation strategy, the first being Master farmers/*hurudza* with assets and savings, focusing on agriculture, a high risk strategy which works as long as rains fall and markets function, and the second being village entrepreneurs who base their livelihoods on the buying and selling of agricultural commodities, and local business activity.

Echoing this classification, a more generic livelihood typology has also been proposed by Dorward (2009a) and Dorward et al., (2009). This emphasises the dynamic changes and wider aspirations of households, contrasting those that are 'hanging in' (surviving, but poor – including crisis and survival strategies), 'stepping out' (diversifying away from agriculture, both locally and through migration) and 'stepping up' (accumulating locally, largely through agriculture). Mushongah (2009) has added a fourth strategy, 'dropping out', focusing on those essentially destitute households reliant on different forms of social protection, and often in the process of exiting.

Each of these typologies relates (often rather implicitly) to a class-based analysis. Thus, those 'hanging in' or 'dropping out' may constitute the semi-peasantry and failing petty commodity producers in Cousins and colleagues' 1992 classification, while those 'stepping out' could largely be seen as worker-peasants. Finally, those 'stepping up' – through whichever accumulation strategy – include the emergent rural petit bourgeoisie, as well as the more successful petty commodity producers and worker-peasants.

In relation to our discussion of 'success groups', SG1 households clearly include an emergent rural petit bourgeoisie (accumulating assets, hiring in labour, selling surplus produce etc.); although many in this group are more easily categorised as petty commodity producers, some more successful than others, as, for many, the core focus of livelihood strategies is on reproduction, not accumulation. Worker-peasant households, able to link off-farm income with successful agricultural production, are also evident in our SG1 category. By contrast, SG3 households include many so-called semi-peasants and worker-peasants who often are selling their labour to SG1 households, at least on a seasonal, temporary basis and are failing to accumulate, and many are barely able to reproduce themselves and so must either leave the area, or survive through often desperate means. SG2 households are a mixed group, and so present an interesting challenge in relating the success ranking to class-based analytical categories. Here we see multiple class identifications, ranging from those who are on the upward track, and rapidly accumulating (and so moving from petty commodity production towards being part of a rural petit bourgeois) to those who are surviving, while not doing badly, but through a variety of means (petty commodity production, off-farm diversification, employment etc.). Thus, in sum, class dynamics in the new resettlements are complex, often highly contingent and not easy to categorise neatly. Of course, as we have discussed earlier, cutting across all groups there are age, gender and ethnic-based dimensions of differentiation, as well as patterns defined by education, urban connections, religion and church membership and political affiliation.

In the table below, we identify 15 different livelihood pathways based on a detailed analysis of the transcripts of the success ranking workshops in all sites. In these workshops, all known households were described, allowing an identification of the core livelihood strategy for 360 cases. In addition, more detailed information on 120 households was available in the individual and household biographies which were collected. In identifying different livelihood strategies, we have linked these to the categories of dropping out, hanging in, stepping out and stepping up. However, as is clear from the table, within these broad categories there are different strategies evident, often associated with identifiable classes. So, for example, within the 'hanging in' category, we have identified asset-poor farmers and those pursuing straddling livelihoods (petty commodity producers), along with survival diversification (peasant-workers) and keeping the plot (not really a rural livelihood strategy at all, but an insurance for the future). In the stepping up category, we have *hurudza* (successful farmers) and semi-commercial farmers (many of whom could be defined as an emerging rural petit bourgeoisie), alongside rural entrepreneurs (successful worker-peasants) and those who are accumulating 'from above' through patronage connections.

The table presents the percentage distribution of different livelihood types by scheme type. A2 farmers are well represented, for example, in the new (semi-) commercial farmer group, as are part-time and cell phone farmers. A smaller group is identified as 'farming from patronage', deriving substantial benefits from external linkages. Those in the informal settlements have the highest percentage in the 'asset poor farming' and 'chronically poor and destitute' groups, while self-contained A1 farmers have the highest percentage in the stepping up '*hurudza*' group.

Overall, the distribution of households across the broad livelihood categories shows 35% 'stepping up' – on an upward accumulation trajectory. Most of these households are, in the terms described above, accumulating from below, while a small minority (1.4%) are accumulating from above, through patronage relationships. A further 21.4% of households have livelihood strategies centred on diversification ('stepping out'). These include diverse worker-peasants, around 70% of whom are also accumulating from below, linking on-farm production with off-farm income earning in dfferent ways. Others include those who are struggling ('survival diversification', 2.8% of all households)

Table 10.2 A livelihood typology for new resettlement households

Category	Strategy	A2	A1 self-contained	A1 villagised	Informal	Total	Description
		54	72	159	75	360	N
Dropping out (10.0%)	Exits	3.7%	2.8%	4.4%	6.7%	4.4%	Those who have abandoned their plot due to deaths in the family, other commitments, or having been removed through administrative (land audit) or political means. No-one living there currently.
	Chronically poor, destitute	0.0%	1.4%	4.4%	5.3%	3.3%	No assets, reliant on help from others, limited farming.
	Ill health	0.0%	1.4%	3.8%	1.3%	2.2%	As above, but suffering severe consequences of death or ill-health of one or more family members.
Hanging in (33.6%)	Asset poor farming	1.9%	16.7%	16.4%	33.3%	17.8%	Limited assets (of cattle, labour etc.), relying on others to help out with draught power, etc.
	Keeping the plot	11.1%	15.3%	8.8%	8.0%	10.3%	The plot is being kept for the future – either for inheritance purposes or for later investments when conditions improve. A few relatives and/or workers occupy the plot.
	Straddling	0.0%	1.4%	10.1%	4.0%	5.6%	Maintaining multiple homes/farms/herds, both in the resettlement area and the communal land, but not producing much on new plot.
Stepping out (21.4%)	Survival diversification	0.0%	2.8%	1.9%	6.7%	2.8%	Border jumping, gold panning, *makorokozo* (dealing), sex work. Limited farm assets and low production, sufficient for household food security in only some years.
	Local off-farm activities	5.6%	1.4%	7.5%	4.0%	5.3%	Building, trading, craft activities etc., complement farming, and offset production deficits in some years.

Category	Type						Description
Stepping out (21.4%)	Reliance on remittances from within Zimbabwe	0.0%	2.8%	9.4%	1.3%	5.0%	Teachers, civil servants and others, with a farming base and some remittance income, allowing investment and some accumulation on farm (although limited).
	Reliance on stable remittances from outside Zimbabwe	0.0%	0.0%	5.0%	10.7%	4.4%	Those with children in South Africa (or beyond, including UK) sending regular remittances in foreign exchange, allowing more substantial investment in the resettlement home and a buffer against low agricultural production.
	Cell phone farmers	16.7%	6.9%	0.0%	0.0%	3.9%	Those with other business interests/sources of income who fail to visit the farm regularly and are not really investing significantly. Workers and farm managers run the operation, the plot holder lives and works elsewhere.
Stepping up (35.0%)	*Hurudza*	0.0%	26.4%	22.0%	16.0%	18.3%	The 'real farmers', accumulating through agriculture, as some in the communal areas did before. They sell regularly to a diversity of markets. Sufficient farm resources – cattle/draught, equipment, etc. Often hire in significant labour.
	Part-time farmers	33.3%	11.1%	6.3%	2.7%	10.6%	Farming not the sole enterprise, but a core livelihood activity supported by off farm work. Accumulation on farm significant, and assets sufficient for farming. May hire in labour through remittance income sources.
	New (semi-)commercial farmers	22.2%	6.9%	0.0%	0.0%	4.7%	Those with skills and resources who have a large plot (A2 or A1 self-contained). Investment in farm through off-farm businesses or employment paying in foreign exchange. They have started to farm productively, reinvesting in the plot.
	Farming from patronage	5.6%	2.8%	0.0%	0.0%	1.4%	Those who have received support from the state through various forms of patronage and been able to invest in the farm. Mostly A2 farmers. Production may be significant.

and those 3.9% households who are 'cell phone farmers' who are not investing significantly in their farms.

Nearly half of all households, according to this classification, are accumulating from below, with a very small group reliant on processes of accumulation from above. In addition, it is important not to forget others whose livelihood trajectories are less positive, and where accumulation is minimal or negative. Of all the households in the sample, there are 34% who are only 'hanging in' and an additional 10% who are 'dropping out', including some who have already left ('exits'). It is an extremely mixed picture.

Of course, no typology is ever definitive and watertight, and is inevitably a subjective interpretation of complex data. There are always variations and blurring of categories, and people move between categories over time, sometimes quite suddenly. However, a typology of this sort does highlight the significant variation in conditions and potentials of new resettlement farmers. This has some major implications for the forms of support required. For those in the 'dropping out', and perhaps for some in the 'hanging in' category, exit to alternative forms of livelihood may well be a good option. But transitions to new, non-agrarian livelihoods must also be supported, through the provision of alternatives within the resettlement areas or elsewhere, and the dangers of exit followed by extreme destitution must prevented by forms of social protection that support the most vulnerable, as we discuss in the final chapter.

For those following a 'stepping out' strategy, support needs to focus on developing off-farm opportunities that are sufficiently productive, and not low return, risky or illegal options, to allow a link to investments in the new resettlements and in farming. This is not always the case, as risky, sometimes illegal, survivalist livelihood strategies do not allow much investment and accumulation. For those who are 'stepping up', further support is required – especially in relation to credit and infrastructure – that will allow patterns of accumulation from below to continue (see Chapter 11). Where such accumulation is based on patronage relations (from above), clearly, this is not sustainable and a different trajectory must be sought, based on a sustained, legitimate and transparent form of support.

People are of course not stuck in one livelihood strategy forever. As the biographies throughout the book show, there is immense dynamism, as people move from phases of 'stepping out', accumulating assets through off-farm activities, to periods of 'stepping up', where accumulation through farming is possible. Others suffer downward trajectories, precipitated by misfortune or ill health. The loss of a job may mean that an individual or household may shift from a 'stepping out' strategy to one that is just 'hanging in'. A poor harvest or an illness may then push them further towards 'dropping out'. All these categories are highly gendered, with men and women often pursuing different livelihood strategies. While this analysis has focused on the household, a more in-depth assessment of intra-household dynamics is also required in order to understand how individuals' fortunes change.

A clear message emerging from this analysis is the need for supporting such flexibility and dynamism and avoiding the dangers of locking people in to particular livelihood options by virtue of their status, location or through unnecessary and restrictive planning or administrative frameworks. If the changes unleashed by land reform are to generate wider, longer-term benefits, processes of accumulation from below must be supported – both those 'stepping up' into more productive agriculture and those 'stepping out', generating surpluses through linking on- and off-farm enterprises. While the wider benefits of land reform should not be ignored, those who are unable to benefit from new land should be allowed to seek alternatives. As rural economies grow, this may involve farm-based employment (Chapter 6), or it may involve engaging in non-farm enterprises (Chapter 8). For some, exit through migration elsewhere may be a better option, releasing land for others who can make use of it.

10.6 Conclusion

Such patterns of differentiation, represented in diverse livelihood strategies and pathways, are an inevitable consequence of a dynamic political and economic process, and cannot be ignored. A populist pretence that all new farmers are somehow members of a uniform semi-subsistence peasantry or, by contrast, have the potential to be new commercial farmers is foolhardy and misleading. A more targeted – and thereby more effective – engagement with emerging livelihood and agrarian change dynamics is required if the wider benefits of land reform are to be realised.

What then are the emerging patterns of agrarian change, and how do they relate to changing class formations in the Zimbabwean countryside? In the 1990s, Ben Cousins and colleagues (1992: 21-22) argued that, despite the successes of smallholder production in the 1980s, the prospects for agricultural petty commodity producers were likely to be constrained during the 1990s by the just-emerging impacts of structural adjustment and economic reform, although a few in some areas were likely to thrive. The expansion of a rural petit bourgeoisie, in the absence of significant agrarian reform, was unlikely. Structural adjustment was likely to hit worker-peasants hardest, with remittance flows and employment opportunities constrained. The semi-peasantry was similarly likely to be hard hit, and a growing 'feminisation of poverty' in the rural areas was predicted. Alliances between worker-peasants and the semi-peasantry, with a rallying call around land reform and job creation, was, they suggested, the most likely political outcome of the class dynamics of that period.

In important respects, these predictions were very accurate. After 1997 in particular, alliances were struck across these and other groupings not yet identified in this earlier analysis, and land reform was indeed the rallying point, as Moyo and Yeros (2005) have argued. What a new agrarian class structure implies for the future of agrarian politics remains less clear. Alliances are often highly fragile, contradictory and always shifting. With such a diverse group of people on the new land, with complex and hybrid identities – in class, ethnic, political and other terms – simple formulae for understanding the relations emerging in the new resettlements do not exist.

Returning to the questions posed in Chapter 1, has land reform resulted in a 're-peasantisation' of the countryside, or are we seeing the emergence of new capitalist forms of farming for a few, with others providing labour and service support? Has land reform resulted in an explosion of productive activity, based on dynamic accumulation from below, with the potential to drive economic growth more broadly? Has land reform undermined the capacity for successful capitalist production by the division of land into plots insufficient for a successful livelihood, resulting ever-increasing cycles of poverty and destitution? Or, indeed, is there some combination of all these dynamics in play?

A decade after the land reform, and in a period of substantial political and economic upheaval, it is too early to tell what agrarian economic and political dynamics will emerge in the longer term. But hints are evident. As this book has repeatedly shown, the new resettlements are not replicas of what has gone before. A new process of agrarian change has been unleashed, although its directions and consequences remain highly uncertain. The political and economic alliances that will be struck in the coming years will define whether an emerging group of 'middle' farmers and entrepreneurs – representing perhaps around half of all households – will be able to help transform the rural economy, or whether older patterns of dualism, with new elites in the driving seat, will be reimposed.

What about the other households? While numerically small, the elites, reliant in recent years on accumulation from above, exert disproportional influence, and may yet act to upset or frustrate the energetic entrepreneurialism of others. Where do the remaining 44% of households – those in the 'hanging in' and 'dropping out' categories – fit into this picture? Will they be able, with the right support and incentives, to accumulate in the future? Will they supply the labour for emergent capitalist farmers, transforming into a new rural proletariat? Will they move into non-farm work, adding value to local production? Or will they, as some assume, become destitute and require external support and protection?

At this point, we cannot answer these questions. What we have observed on the ground does not represent the political and media stereotypes of abject failure; but nor indeed are we observing universal, roaring success. Inevitably, as with most rigorous and sober analysis, the story is somewhere in between, and requires some detailed unravelling. In a balanced, empirically informed assessment of land reform impacts and consequences, the diverse dimensions of success and failure must be taken on board. This requires a fundamental rethinking of the future for rural Zimbabwe, which is the subject of the final, concluding chapter.

11

Lessons from Zimbabwe's Land Reform

11.1 Introduction

Land reform has unleashed a process of radical agrarian change. This was not just a modest process of transfer to black beneficiaries as in past attempts at resettlement, and has been the case in other land reform efforts elsewhere in the region (Aliber et al., 2010; Werner and Odendaal, 2010). Because of its scale, it fundamentally changed agrarian structure, livelihoods and the rural economy. There are now new people on the land, engaged in new forms of economic activity, connected to new markets and carving out a variety of livelihoods. New socio-economic processes are unfolding, creating new patterns of class, gender and generational differentiation. New social, political and institutional processes are evolving, generating new identities and identifications linked to new senses of citizenship, territory and belonging. As control was imposed in the new lands following the invasions, contests over legitimacy and authority have erupted, with major implications for land governance and the role of the state. This was not a replication of the past, but a radically new scenario, one that remains highly variegated and dynamic across space and time.

In important respects, this does not represent a 'classic' land reform, where predatory, pre-capitalist landed property was taken over or where large-scale capitalist farms were nationalised. In Zimbabwe, large-scale, privately-owned commerical units – some highly successful – were taken over and replaced with (largely) small-scale farming. In this sense, Zimbabwe is 'exceptional' (Bernstein, 2004). However, with over seven million hectares taken, and a million or more new people settled, it represents a significant turning-point in the post-colonial trajectory of the former settler economies. The 'death of land reform' was clearly over-exaggerated (Lehmann, 1978; Lipton, 1993).

With land being removed from commercial production, the benchmark for the performance of the new agrarian configuration is high – even accounting for the underutilisation of land and inefficiencies of large-scale farming. Our data identifies an emerging process of 'accumulation from below', rooted in petty commodity production and small-scale capitalist farming. This is not a naïve, populist argument for peasant agriculture or a romantic vision of yeoman farming. Such producers are linked into circuits of capital and are actively engaging with markets. But if the new resettlements are to contribute not only to local livelihoods, but also national food security and economic development, they require investment and support – just as was done from the 1950s for white agriculture. This means infrastructure (dams, roads), financing (credit systems), input supply (fertiliser, seed), technology (intermediate and appropriate) and coordination mechanisms (institutions and policy) that allow agriculture to grow and be sustained. This must be unlike in the 1980s when an emergent green revolution was extinguished by structural adjustment. If the right steps are taken, the prospects for significant developmental gains are good, far exceeding those of the low return-low employment beef ranching systems that most new farms replaced in Masvingo province.

Contemporary Zimbabwe, as we have shown, is a highly complex and dynamic setting, with many policy challenges to engage with. This book has hopefully provided some insights into this, and in doing so has confronted some recurrent myths about Zimbabwe's land reform. This final chapter offers a brief overview of some of the key findings, and outlines a ten-point agenda for the way forward, before a final reflection on the lessons from Zimbabwe for the southern Africa region as a whole.

11.2 Land and livelihoods: new directions in Zimbabwe

In Chapter 1 we introduced a number of perspectives on land and livelihoods debates, each with different implications for our understanding of agrarian change and the role of redistributive land reform. Given the data presented across the chapters of this book, which perspectives have the most traction in the Zimbabwe setting – and particularly in Masvingo province?

Are we, for example, seeing the emergence of a new form of productive agriculture centred on small-scale production, a new green revolution forged by petty commodity producers or the middle peasantry, transformed from marginalised worker-peasants or semi-proletarians through land reform? This is certainly the hope of many, with the new resettlements being seen as the potential driver of economic growth more broadly. The potentials of such a dynamic are evident, with significant numbers of households, especially across A1 and informal sites, producing regular surpluses, selling to the market and accumulating from below.

Is this a process built on locally-controlled production and economies, representing the idealised vision of the 'peasant way' of the Via Campesina movement? There have indeed been many aspects of the post-2000 experience which echo this vision, but this has been out of necessity rather than choice, as links to markets and wider commodity circulation have been limited by the economic crisis. Farmers in the new resettlements are not averse to engaging in cash cropping or adopting new technologies. Indeed, one of the great success stories from our study sites is the cotton production from Ushwaushava, where farmers readily sell into a highly competitive capitalist market.

What are the limits of the small-scale farming model? Can only large-scale, highly capitalised and specialised farming meet the challenges of a globalised economy? Is the resurrection of the large-scale commercial sector, and a recreation of a dualistic agrarian structure, a must for Zimbabwe's reconstruction? Here we have to disaggregate. For some commodities and for some markets, the critique of the smallholder path probably stands up. But there are other issues to consider. Scale may be important for some production systems, but there are certainly ways of linking relatively smaller producers into a wider system of specialised commercial production. The A2 outgrower plot arrangements on the sugar estates show potential, for example. The same has been argued for tobacco, although there have been many teething problems.[1] For high-value beef production systems, scale may be significant as herd sizes must be large in order to gain sufficient off-take to make the enterprise economic, although in practice many of the challenges around gaining access to high-value markets are less about production and more about disease control and product safety (Scoones et al., 2010). As the transition from maize and other field crops to horticulture or floriculture by large-scale commercial farmers during the 1990s showed, large land areas are not the basic requirement of high-value agriculture; more important are market connections, regulation compliance and quality control, all of which require skill, networks and significant capitalisation (Kydd et al., 2004; Lipton, 2005).

So, depending on the broader vision for the agricultural sector and the appropriate balance between food crops for self-provisioning, crops for local sale and high-value export crops, the new agrarian structure must respond. Today, there are few incentives, no direction and a vacuum in policy thinking. But a more searching assessment reveals how, given the availability of resources, the distribution of farm sizes and the location of different farm types, a more articulated and integrated agricultural sector might emerge. This may require incentives for specialisation among some A2 or A1 self-contained farms for instance, while others pursue broader-based mixed farm strategies. In sum, while the argument in favour of large-scale commercial agriculture in the context of globalisation has its merits, as a generalisation it is flawed. Global processes of commodification may act to (re)create 'bifurcated agrarian structures' (Akram-Lodhi et al., 2009), with separate commercial export and subsistence farming sectors, but extreme divergences, as existed in Zimbabwe before 2000, need not be the result. Indeed, for sound economic and social policy reasons, they should be avoided.

What about the argument that an expansion of smallholder production through populist 'land-to-the-tiller' reform leads inevitably to intensified differentiation, across a range of class, gender and generational axes? This, so the argument goes, results in the creation of an impoverished underclass, with people unable to reproduce themselves through agricultural livelihoods and, as a result, becoming increasingly reliant on poorly-paid, informal employment or, worse, illegal activities and complete destitution (Bernstein, 2002, 2003). These would typically

[1] http://allafrica.com/stories/200911270899.html.

be households in the lowest success group, those just 'hanging in', or indeed in the process of 'dropping out'. However, as we have argued, such people need not end up as destitute or part of an underclass of 'foot-loose' labour, if a wider process of growth and accumulation from below is occurring. New opportunities for farm employment, off-farm enterprises and other economic activity will emerge, potentially helping to transform the fortunes of those presently unable to make it as successful small-scale farmers.

There are also those who are clearly not struggling, but nor are they engaging in much production. Such people make up what David Moore (2004: 406) has termed a 'conspicuously consuming "élite" (wealthier than a "middle class", but with little interest in the production, signifying a 'proper' bourgeoisie) with its base in "trade" and rent-seeking at best, speculation and crime at worst'. What prospects are there for this group – small, but nevertheless significant because of the power they wield – transforming into productive users of the land? This is an open question, and one that could hold the key to the future of agrarian change in Zimbabwe (Moyo, 2009; Raftopoulos, 2009). For, if this group dodges the land audit, clings on to the land and fails to invest in it, with land continuing to be a source of patronage, then the political pressures to support a successful agrarian reform will not arise. Of course, elite pacts are often essential for truly transformatory processes of poverty reduction and development (Hossain and Moore, 2002), and so compromises will inevitably be required, but these must not undermine the potentials of agrarian reform in the way that corrupt 'land grabs' are doing. A more solid, coherent political consensus is needed which sees the potentials, as well as the limitations, of the new agrarian structure, and manages the competing visions, interests and positions in ways that result in a wider developmental outcome. While in recent years there have been steps in the right direction, a more effective, longer-term political settlement is clearly required, rooted in more widely accepted forms of public authority.

Thus the social, economic and political dynamics which will drive policy and so agrarian futures in the longer term remain unclear and contested. Simple explanations which homogenise and aggregate are obviously insufficient. The configuration of interests is complex and contradictory, with multiple class, gender and racial-ethnic divisions. Zimbabwe's land reform has been neither a populist revolution by the peasantry nor a corrupt take-over by elites and political 'cronies'. Visions for the future remain disputed, as are the policy narratives which underpin them. For this reason, in the advocacy, negotiation and positioning that will unfold in the coming years, it is essential to be clear about goals and visions, myths and realities and the implications of the policy narratives which derive from them.

11.3 Zimbabwe's land reform: myths and realities

As this book has repeatedly shown, the reality on the ground often does not match the myths perpetuated in many quarters. Myths and realities do not match. An appreciation of ground realites requires radical new thinking in policy circles, and the creation of alternative narratives about the future. Old models and assumptions must be abandoned in the search for new ideas and thinking, and new strategies must build on what has happened in the past decade. Where positive experiments have occurred, these must not be overlooked and undermined in the rush to impose new interventions. Support for resettlement must be attuned to local circumstances. In a global review of resettlement programmes, Bill Kinsey and Hans Binswanger, for example, argue that: 'Settlement programs are too often designed with the assumption that all settlers will succeed. This has led to centralised administration and rigid designs, rather than decentralised approaches, flexibility in implementation, support for spontaneous settlement, and reliance on settlers' own investment capacity' (1993:1477).

For the most part, the post-2000 resettlement did not suffer from top-down technocratic intervention; indeed the absence of almost any external support was a feature of it. The outcome resulted from a complex trade-off between local conditions, particular histories and contingent circumstances and the structuring forces of nationalist politics, technoractic planning models and local institutional arrangements, mediated by diverse forms of 'traditional' and 'modern' political authority, gender dynamics and social relations. With the state and other actors now re-engaging, we must ask what else should be done?

There has been a flurry of 'reconstruction plans' developed, offering blueprints for the future.[2] Too often these have been produced with very little reference to empirical data, and they resort to standard ways of thinking, repeating myths and reconstructing standard narratives. Thus, for example, many of the myths we have challenged in this book are alive and well and appear in consultancy terms of reference and reports presented as advice to government and donors. Overall, as Bracking and Cliffe (2009) point out, 'reconstruction' is often seen as an extension of a neoliberal economic reform project, without a broader questioning of assumptions and priorities.

What then should be the priorities for rural livelihood development in the new setting be? Below we offer some suggestions based on our analysis. But how generalisable is our assessment? Is it just a particular case, one that can be dismissed as an outlier? As we have argued before, we believe not. While the Masvingo case-studies each show striking particularlities, there are important trends and patterns, and these echo findings from elsewhere in the country (Moyo et al., 2009; Matondi, 2010). No one site is the same, so extrapolations and generalisations are risky, but, as we argued earlier, the findings from Masvingo do offer insights into large parts of Zimbabwe, especially those areas outside the highly capitalised farming areas of the Highveld.

In Chapter 1 we introduced five myths that have plagued rational debate about Zimbabwe's land reform. As with all myths, they are not

---

[2] http://www.iol.co.za/index.php?set_id=1&click_id=84&art_id=nw20090330143756499 C334121; http://www.cato.org/zimbabwe; Moyo and Ashurst (2007); UNDP (2008); and see commentaries in Moss and Patrick (2006); Samson (2009); Chimhowu (2009). Eppel et al. (2009), among others.

grounded in solid empirical findings, but are linked to broader narratives, informed by social and political values and positions that,
through stating and restating, become accepted as part of wider discourse. They are often very difficult to dislodge, even in the face of
substantial counter-evidence. Such alternative views are in turn reject-
ed as not generalisable; not compatible with institutional norms and
assumptions (cf. Leach and Mearns, 1996).

However, the aim of challenging myths with data on complex realities
is not to create new myths. Our aim, instead, is a more dispassionate,
evidence-based assessment rooted in careful sampling and analysis.
While there is no single story of land reform in Zimbabwe, on the basis
of the evidence presented in this book, we reject each of the five myths.

Myth 1: Zimbabwean land reform has been a total failure
Across the country over 145,000 small-scale farms (A1) and over 16,000
commercial units (A2) have been established (Table 1.3). In Masvingo
province, 1.6m ha have been redistributed to over 33,000 households
(Table 2.2), and further land has been taken by perhaps 8,000 households in informal settlements. As we have shown, across these sites
there is much variation. Smallholder A1 and informal farmers have
fared best, where there is low capital investment and a reliance on local
labour. Some have done very well, while others are struggling. On the
new commercial A2 farms, by contrast, the economic meltdown prevented substantial capital investment, and new enterprises have been
slow to take off. Yet, in interviews with new settlers, despite the problems, there is widespread acclaim for the resettlement programme: 'Life
has changed remarkably for me because I have more land and can produce more than I used to', said one. As Chapter 10 discussed, around
half of the households in our sample are on an upward livelihood trajectory. Through a combination of agricultural production and off-farm
activities, there is a strong dynamic of 'accumulation from below'. A
new agrarian structure is fast emerging, and centre-stage is an important 'middle farmer' group, cutting across A2, A1 and informal scheme
types and rooted in successful petty commodity production. Zimbabwe's land reform has created challenges and opportunities, winners and
losers, but cannot be characterised as an abject failure.

*Myth 2: The beneficiaries of Zimbabwean land reform have been largely
political 'cronies'*
While no one denies the operation of political patronage in the allocation of land since 2000, the overall pattern is again mixed. As Chapter
2 shows, across the sites surveyed 68.2% of new settlers were classified
as a diverse 'ordinary' group, with about half of all new settlers coming
from nearby communal areas (with higher proportions in the A1 villagised and informal sites). The new settlements are not dominated
by a rich, politically-connected elite. However, such a group certainly exists, especially in the A2 schemes, and is influential beyond its
numbers. Benefiting from patronage relations and 'accumulation from
above', such people are a stark contrast to the majority who are relatively poor people in need of land and keen finally to gain the fruits
of Independence. A new social and economic order is fast emerging in

the Zimbabwean countryside, one that will require carefully-attuned policy support to foster the undeniable, but as yet unrealised, potentials. Processes of differentiation are revealing contrasting patterns of accumulation and class division. While significant numbers are doing well and accumulating from below, there are others who are either struggling or profiting from patronage support. These divisions – structured around class, gender and generation – are already a source of conflict. The way these conflicts play out, and so structure processes of agrarian and livelihood change, will determine the future of the new political and economic landscape of rural Zimbabwe.

Myth 3: There is no investment in the new resettlements
International media images of destruction and chaos have dominated the headlines about Zimbabwe's land reform. While there has certainly been substantial damage done to the basic infrastructure of commercial agriculture, there has also been significant new investment, almost all of it private, individual efforts generated through local accumulation from below. As Chapter 4 showed, new settlers have cleared land, built homes, purchased farm equipment and invested in livestock. We estimated that on average across sites over US$2,000 had been invested per household in a range of assets and improvements. However, patterns of investment are highly differentiated between households and across sites. Those able to accumulate through local production and income earning have hooked into an upward livelihood trajectory (SG1 and many SG2 households), yet there are others who remain struggling ('hanging in') and others have 'dropped out'. Differences exist across sites too. For example, the investment picture on the new A2 farms is less encouraging. However, a few A2 farmers – with access to alternative, external sources of income – have managed to develop new enterprises. Local investment is clearly insufficient though. The key policy challenge for the future is how to support the existing processes of accumulation from below – through a combination of livelihood strategies, and involving a diverse mix of small-scale capitalist farmers, petty commodity producers and worker-peasants.

Myth 4: Agriculture is in complete ruins creating chronic food insecurity
Agriculture in Zimbabwe has been through difficult times over the past decade. Yet, as discussed in Chapters 5 and 7, the picture is highly differentiated. The commercial agriculture sector went through a massive restructuring during the 1990s to focus on specialised production of high-value commodities, and generally diversifying away from mainstay food produciton. The output of exports has crashed, but the picture for other commodities is more complex. While operating well below potential, due to drought and the poor supply of seeds and fertilisers, production of cereals and cotton, for example, has been maintained, while some crops, such as edible beans, have boomed. In the relatively wet seasons of 2005-06 and 2008-09, 77% and 69% of households in the A1 schemes of the Gutu cluster produced more than a tonne of maize, sufficient for household provision and some sales. In the Masvingo cluster 98% and 91% of A1 households were in this category in these years (Chapter 5). This was not replicated in the drier areas where the food

security situation has been very precarious, although the substantial storage of sorghum produced in 2009 will certainly provide an important food security cushion for coming years. Cotton has proved a highly resilient crop, and by 2007-08 in the dryland Chiredzi informal site, around 90% of farmers were growing it, producing on average 1.4 tonnes of cotton for sale amounting to over US$500 income per annum.

Thus, across our sites, we see a very positive dynamic of productive agriculture by 40-50% of households. These 'middle farmers' are successfully accumulating from below in mixed farming systems. This is a larger group than we saw in the maize revolution of the 1980s, but it is certainly not everyone. Where we have seen less success is on the small-scale commercial plots in the A2 schemes. Here a complementary specialised, capitalised agriculture has yet to emerge, and the area-based synergies with the A1 farmers are as yet mostly only potentials. A key policy challenge must be to facilitate a process whereby more capitalised commercial agriculture takes off. This, as we discuss below, must not recreate an unhelpful dualism – between A2 and A1 schemes – but must involve flexible land holdings and diverse pathways of entrepreneurialism.

Myth 5: The rural economy has collapsed
The informal rural economy has been adapting fast, even while the formal economy has been in dire straits for most of the past decade. As Chapter 7 showed, the beef sector is a good example. In the past there was a reliance on a few suppliers from large-scale ranchers, going through a few abattoirs. Today, newly-emerging supply chains are linking the new resettlement areas with feedlots and butcheries in very different patterns of ownership and management. Unlike the old dualisms of the past, where large numbers of people were excluded from active participation in the agricultural economy, the processes of accumulation from below mean that new players are involved, benefits are being more widely distributed and economic linkages are more embedded in the local economy. As we argue further below, a focus is required on area-based economic development, to capitalise on new linkages and multipliers generated by the land reform. Such new support must be careful not to undermine the entrepreneurialism that has emerged in recent years, and a broad-based approach to growth must be fostered which avoids capture by elite interests and powerful players.

Thus a more positive picture emerges of Zimbabwe's land reform than those so often put forward. But debunking myths is one thing, what alternatives are there? What new narratives should guide policy, and how can the complexity described throughout this book be accommodated? The next section identifies ten key priorities for the way forward.

11.4 Ten priorities for policy

The emerging styles of production and economy on the new resettlements require a particular type of support, attuned to diverse people and contexts, along with an acknowledgement of a complex interrelatedness in livelihood and economic systems that spread from farm to town, from resettlement area to communal area and from livestock to crops to off-farm production. This is not classic subsistence agriculture and a classic 'peasant' economy. These are dynamic, market-driven systems, linked across enterprises and spaces, creating a particular pattern of investment and accumulation. Such processes of accumulation from below are certainly firm foundations for growth, but will need support if they are really to take off (Kinsey, 2009; Chitiga and Mabugu, 2008). A very different policy response will be required if the existing dynamism of the new resettlements is to be supported in order to sustain livelihoods for the future.

The task of rebuilding Zimbabwe's rural economy is a huge one. A major restructuring of land use and ownership, combined with economic collapse and a lack of systematic government investment, has created huge challenges of transition.[3] What do the findings of this research suggest for the way forward?

Land administration

A land audit is identified as a major priority by nearly all policy stakeholders.[4] The rules of single farm ownership and appropriate use must be adhered to if the land reform as a whole is to be credible. However, there is a danger that an audit can revert to a technocratic exercise, an attempt to reimpose order on an assumed chaotic land reform process. As we have seen throughout this book, the land reform very often had its own order and rationale. There needs to be a flexibility in farm sizes and production systems; strict adherence to planning models makes little sense. It is not surprising that few A2 farmers have followed the business plans submitted to the Ministry of Lands, given the economic situation in the past few years, and so these should not be used as a benchmark. Indeed, new support to develop appropriate business plans – not ones plucked from textbooks, as in the case of most of the applications – is needed so that the A2 farms can thrive.

A land audit should instead be seen as largely a political-legal exercise focused on reducing the worst excesses of patronage and land grabbing, in particular parts of the country, and on helping to release underutilised land for new users committed to accumulation from below. The main culprits are well known, and an audit will have to have substantial political clout and credibility for it to function effectively. If some significant reversals in land occupancy occur, removing land acquired through corrupt practice and accumulation from above, this will have a major impact on the wider land reform programme's legitimacy. For the future, enforceable legislation must provide regulations against capture by elites or speculative investors to avoid inefficient and inequitable consolidation of land holdings and land disenfranchisement, especially of the poor and women. For example, such regulations should be able

---

[3] The Global Political Agreement, for example, spells out priorities only in the vaguest of terms. http://www.kubatana.net/html/archive/demgg/080915agreement.asp?sector=OPIN.
[4] http://allafrica.com/stories/201001080803.html; http://allafrica.com/stories/20091229 0014.html; http://allafrica.com/stories/200905070903.html.

to prevent the mass sales and rapid speculative land accumulation by local or foreign elites and companies that could result in the reversal of redistributive gains.

The establishment of an independent land commission will be required, perhaps decentralised in order to devise approaches suited to different districts and provinces. It must oversee a continuous, transparent and fully accountable process of land reform, allowing for ongoing transfers according to agreed criteria. This must allow those who are successfully accumulating to continue to do so, while equally allowing others to exit agriculture, and new allocations to be made to those with the potential to invest and engage in small-scale agriculture – including those disenfranchised by the post-2000 land reform, such as women and farmworkers, as well as new entrants, especially youth. As land is reallocated, a just and equitable approach to compensation must be enacted, whereby reasonable costs are paid for land improvements and legitimate land acquisitions, shared across tax payers, rural and urban, and timed in a way that does not undermine the capacity to continue to redistribute (FAO, 2008; Lipton, 2009).

Land security and tenure
As discussed in Chapter 9, security of land holdings is an essential prerequisite for successful production and investment. But tenure security arises through a variety of means. Existing legislation allows for a wide range of potential tenure types, including freehold title, regulated leases, permits and communal tenure under 'traditional' systems. All have their pros and cons; there is no 'gold standard' or assumed 'evolution' towards an ideal, as is sometimes suggested. Instead, appropriate tenure regimes must derive from an analysis of the trade-offs between options. For example, policymakers must ask, given the available resources and capacity for land administration, can the appropriate level of tenure security be achieved through low-cost means? Or, given the dangers of rapid land appropriation, what minimal safeguards need to be deployed which do not undermine the capacity of credit and land markets to function? Or, what other legal or financial assurances and coordination mechanisms must be added to ensure that private credit markets function effectively under leasehold or permit systems?

These are very real dilemmas and are encountered the world over, especially in relatively resource-poor settings where capacity is underdeveloped (Bruce and Mighot-Adholla, 1994; Toulmin and Quan, 2000; Cotula et al., 2004). A debate that is constructed around the false promise of an assumed ideal of freehold tenure may actually undermine opportunities and stall agricultural growth. The big question for Zimbabwe today, is what makes sense given the current situation, and given available administrative resources and capacity constraints? What tenure regime will help get agriculture moving and investment flowing, and support the new agrarian structure? With the appropriate regulatory conditions and a streamlined land administration system (neither of which exists to date), the leasehold and permit systems offer considerable promise. They have the potential to allow flexible, but regulated, land markets to flourish and rural finance systems to operate. This reflects international thinking on the issue, where low-cost land registration and administration based on leases and permits have been shown to be highly effective, including offering women rights to land as individual or joint registered holders (World Bank, 2003; Deininger and Jin, 2006; Deininger et al., 2008).

This does not mean that freehold tenure is not an option for the future, nor does it preclude a reform of communal tenure, perhaps extending versions of the approach developed for the A1 areas to the communal lands. As the 1994 Land Tenure Commission argued so effectively, hybrid approaches that offer the best of customary, communal tenure arrangements, but with new forms of security offered through legally-binding arrangements, may be of great importance in such areas (Rukuni, 1994a). For now, though, the priority must be the new resettlement areas, including providing some assurances to those living in informal settlements. This represents a substantial area of land, and a considerable number of people and land units. Achieving tenure security in these areas must be a policy priority, and this must be driven by a discussion based on clear principles[5], and an eye to rapid, effective implementation, rather than an ideological positioning and 'gold standard' ideals.

This will mean investing in land governance, building the effectiveness of local institutions to manage resources, resolve disputes and negotiate land access in clear and accountable ways. Without attention to these issues, conflicts will escalate as uncertainties over authority and control persist. This will have damaging consequences for both livelihoods and environmental sustainability. Support for rebuilding public authority from below must therefore be at the top of the agenda, and linked to a revitalisation of local government and state capacity for service delivery.

Input supply: fertiliser, seeds and subsidies

The success of new farmers on the resettlements has been severely hampered by the lack of inputs, notably fertiliser and seeds (Chapter 5). While farmers have benefited from the use of virgin soils, as soil fertility declines alternative forms of fertilisation, including inorganic fertiliser, will be required. In the past Zimbabwe stood out in the region as the place where improved seeds and fertiliser were commonplace, even in the smallholder areas. Adoption of hybrid maize had reached over 90% by the 1990s and fertiliser use was high in the wetter areas by regional standards (Rusike and Sukume, 2006). This situation has dramatically changed in the last decade. Fertiliser use has collapsed and the use of improved seed has declined substantially. Even if farmers wanted to buy hybrid or open-pollinated seed it has often been unavailable. Attempts to provide subsidised input support have been woefully inadequate, and subject to highly corrupt practices. With the economic chaos of recent years, the once well-regarded seed and ferti-

---

[5] In a recent note on tenure policy dilemmas, seven principles were outlined: democratic accountability to allow state oversight, a flexible but regulated market to allow increases and decreases in land holdings, facilitation of credit and investment, regulation against capture by elites and land speculators, guarantees of women's access, a low administrative burden and the generation of revenues and incentives to encourage effective land administration and utilisation (see http://www.ids.ac.uk/go/idspublication/land-tenure-dilemmas-next-steps-for-zimbabwe).

liser industries in Zimbabwe have had a very difficult time. Capacity has been undermined, and many skilled workers having left the companies. Those with international operations have diverted their attention to other countries in the region.

However, a revitalisation of the inputs sector is not simply a matter of reinstating what was there before. These industries were developed on the back of a large-scale commercial agricultural sector with a particular pattern of demand. The new agricultural sector has different needs – different seeds, different fertiliser mixes, different pack sizes – and will likely respond to very different market signals. Providing the support for a new green revolution in Zimbabwe's resettlement areas must take account of this changed context. Some companies – notably Seedco, Cottco, and South African firms such as Pannar – have long sold into the smallholder market, making use the extensive networks of rural dealers, with much success (Kelly et al., 2003), and will no doubt do so again. However, the overall business model will have to change, and new risks will have to be taken on board as the stable supply of guaranteed quantities in large volumes to large-scale operations effectively ceases.

Thus, state support to the private companies in the agricultural input sector will be vital. Purchase guarantees for a subsidised programme of input support (through direct provision of seeds and fertilisers or through vouchers) is one option, as has been tried during 2010. Input subsidy schemes are notoriously inefficient, however, and open to substantial abuse. They also may act to undermine local seed systems which need support. But under particular conditions, focused subsidies can help the regeneration of an agricultural economy, creating an upward spiral, where increased production results in increased employment and investment. The well-documented experience from Malawi (Dorward and Chirwa, 2009) is instructive and may provide the basis for a model for Zimbabwe. Certainly, a plan for kick-starting the agricultural economy is required, but this must recognise the new agrarian structure and not assume old patterns and priorities. Subsidised input support for smallholders should be at the centre of this, but such a programme needs careful design, and safeguards against corrupt practices. Phasing out will of course be the difficult part, as Malawi has been finding. As input support becomes an expected part of the political contract with the government of the day, inputs become an electoral issue, with each party trying to outbid each other in the scale and scope of subsidies being offered. This puts a massive pressure on the exchequer and few donors are willing to bankroll such schemes for long.

Most such subsidy programmes focus on improved maize, but there can be other models for other crops. Cotton provides a good example in Zimbabwe, where outgrower arrangements allow input supply to be linked with a credit package and contract sales, and issues of coordination and intermediation which so often limit smallholder participation in wider markets are (largely) dealt with (Chapter 5). Similar approaches have been used with paprika and some horticultural crops (Masakure and Henson, 2005). Tobacco is equally a candidate for such arrangements. The relationship between outgrowers and sugar estates also provides the basis for guaranteed input supply. However, such contract farming and outgrower arrangements need to be carefully regulated in conditions where effective monopoly power is exerted (as we saw for the sugar estates) so that farmers get a fair deal. This will require state monitoring, but also the building of strong farmer organisations and unions to facilitate bargaining (see below).

Water, wells and irrigation
Land reform is certainly an important precondition for a new phase of successful agricultural growth based on smallholder production, but land without water is useless (Derman and Hellum, 2007; Makhado et al., 2006). Many of the new resettlement sites in Masvingo province are in dry, semi-arid areas where rainfall is low and variable. With the prospects of climate change adding to the variability of seasonal rainfall, ensuring reliable supplies of water is critical. Most new resettlements have limited water supplies for domestic use, cattle or irrigation. The scale of the former ranches was so large that water points were very scattered, and any irrigation infrastructure tended to be only close to the original homestead.

A basic well building/borehole drilling programme for domestic use will have to be a priority. As Chapter 4 has shown, many new settlers have invested in new wells. But these are often unprotected and relatively shallow, and upgrading is probably beyond the means of most. Investment in village sites is relatively easy, but providing water infrastructure to the self-contained and A2 farms is a different question. Here, private investments will have to be the main route to increasing water availability. As for irrigation, this again must be a major priority for new external investments (Chimhowu, 2009). The main irrigated sites in our study areas were in Chiredzi district, including the sugar estates and the Fair Range farms. These were all A2 sites which had inherited functioning irrigation infrastructure. As Chapter 5 described there have been major problems with irrigation supply due to erratic electricity, the breaking down of pumps and the stealing of water from pipelines. With a more stable economic and political situation, such conditions will hopefully improve. Investment in irrigation on the A2 farms will again have to rely on private investment, and will require cooperative arrangements across farms for investments such as pumping stations and pipelines.

As Chapter 5 discussed, the level of organisation of irrigation farmers is growing, and with good support for business and investment planning, this type of infrastructural development will be possible. Across the A1 sites there are some small-scale irrigation areas already existing, and some have been refurbished by government programmes in recent years. But these are vanishingly few and there remains substantial demand for irrigation. Much of the success of white-owned commercial agriculture was built on substantial state and private investment in irrigation, dams and other forms of water control. Again the question arises: what is the appropriate infrastructure for small-scale irrigation in the new resettlement schemes, and who will pay?

The state has invested in irrigation schemes in the communal lands, distributing 0.1ha plots to applicants, but these were heavily controlled by agricultural extension officials and without government or

NGO project funds they often folded (Manzungu and van der Zaag, 1996). Micro-irrigation has been more successful, with gardens being the source of year-round vegetables and maize. These have already sprung up in the new resettlements, largely illegally along river banks and in *vleis*, and are an important basis for livelihood strategies. These need to be capitalised upon and supported, with appropriate environmental measures applied to ensure that erosion is minimised. Simple technologies such as drip irrigation or rope-and-washer pumps offer opportunities for supplemental irrigation (Belder et al., 2007; Faulkner and Lambert, 1990). Even simpler technologies such as the famed Phiri infiltration pits, familiar to many new settlers from Chivi and beyond, are also highly effective, allowing slow seepage of water from sudden rainfall into the field, boosting the water holding capacity of the soil dramatically (Murwira et al., 2001).

All of these efforts will require finance and support. While some initiatives are low cost and can be undertaken through private initiative – indeed already are being so – others will require more substantial investment. Much of this is of a one-off sort, or at least with low level maintenance. A similar effort is required to that invested in the large-scale commercial farms in the 1950s – when thousands of small dams and irrigation plots were built with government support – or the communal areas in the 1980s when boreholes were dug to improve water supplies across the country. This sort of basic infrastructural investment has not occurred in the new resettlements. With the government broke and the donors and NGOs avoiding the new resettlements, people have been left to get on with it. This has resulted remarkable gains, as we have shown, but this is not enough.

Credit and rural finance
A frequent complaint heard on the new farms, and particularly in the A2 schemes, is the lack of finance or credit. In large part this has been a consequence of the economic conditions. With hyperinflation, loans meant nothing and credit systems could not work. Those who have got access to finance have generated it either themselves, usually through employment paid in foreign exchange, or through corrupt deals with finance institutions. A number of Reserve Bank schemes were intended to supply funds to new farmers, processed through Agribank and other state-controlled agencies, but these very rarely found their way to ordinary farmers; most were siphoned off and used by elites with good connections, fuelling patterns of accumulation from above.

But beyond the question of economic contexts and corruption, there is also the issue of the design of financial services schemes. Many commercial banks argue that without land as collateral (i.e. freehold tenure), lending to smallholder farmers is too risky. However, past experiences with agricultural loan schemes in Zimbabwe shows that default rates are relatively low and, if well administered, a commercial lending operation is perfectly feasible (Chimedza, 2006; Zumbika, 2006). And, in any case, as discussed before, titled land need not be the only form of collateral. In other settings leasehold property is regarded as a secure basis against which to loan, and there are of course other assets such as livestock, vehicles and buildings which can serve the same purpose.

In discussion with the private sector banks, the government needs to design a set of rural finance schemes, based on realistic expectations of collateral provision, perhaps together with some state-based guarantees. This could potentially release substantial resources from the private financial institutions into the rural economy.[6]

For smallholders with low turnovers and a diverse portfolio of enterprises, standard loan arrangements make little sense. Most of the existing (and indeed past) schemes for agricultural finance or loans for cattle purchase were wholly inappropriate for such smallholders. Yet, micro-finance, savings and credit is an area where there has been much positive experimentation, including in Zimbabwe.[7] Equally, financing deals and joint ventures between new farmers, big and small, may offer potential, forming new alliances for production and marketing. If the new farming areas are to be a focus for significant agricultural growth in the coming years a fundamental rethink of rural financing is required. The government will need to use both sticks and carrots with the finance industry, but once appropriate models have been found, and this will require innovation and experimentation, their importance should not be underestimated.

Local economic development
Land reform has reconfigured rural areas dramatically. No longer are there vast swathes of commercial land separated off from the densely-packed communal areas. The rural landscape is now virtually all populated and farmed – or at least this is a possibility in the future. A1 villagised and informal sites abut A1 self-contained farms and A2 farms. Links to communal and former resettlement areas are important too, with exchanges of labour, draught animals, finance, skills and expertise flowing in all directions. As a result, economic linkages between agriculture and wider markets have changed dramatically. This has resulted in the growth of new businesses to provide services and consumption goods, although many of these have suffered badly in the period of economic crisis; many, too, operate in the informal economy, sometimes illegally. The potentials for economic diversification – in small-scale mining, hunting, cross-border trade and a host of other enterprises – are currently constrained by legal and regulatory restrictions. A regulatory framework will always be required, but it must not be excessively and inappropriately restrictive. Businesses must be encouraged to flourish in support of rural livelihoods, capturing synergies with local agricultural production.

To make the most of this mosaic of land uses and economic activities, an approach focused on area-based, local economic development is required. This would facilitate investment to encourage linkages and multipliers, across activities, adding value to production in the local area (Quan et al., 2006). Such approaches provide the basis for planning in new ways which recognise not just the farm, or artificially precise land administration types, but the wider area and social and economic interactions. An area-based approach means that linkages (of labour, capital, services, markets) are fostered, and that this results in multi-

---

6 http://allafrica.com/stories/200805060781.html.
7 Raftopolous and Lacoste (2001) ftp://ftp.fao.org/docrep/nonfao/AD706E/AD706E00.pdf.

pliers (of production, consumption etc.) that boost the wider economy. As Zimbabwe's economy recovers from deep crisis, fostering alternative economic configurations, linked to agricultural production on the new resettlements, must be central. Accumulation from below has been hampered by political and economic impediments since 2000, but with economic stabilisation and growth, potentials open up. As in the 1980s, a growth in urban wage-earning, together with support for small-scale agriculture, would enhance the prospects for accumulation from below by successful petty commodity producers and small-scale capitalist farmers, but now in the context of a radical land redistribution, and so with much broader impacts.

There are good reasons to expect land reform to increase economic growth through smallholder production and so foster such diverse economic linkages (Haggblade et al., 2007; Lipton, 2009). However, although reducing inequality has been widely been shown to be good for growth (Ravallion, 2001), this is not guaranteed. For this to work there has to be a set of interlinked motors of growth, with demand and supply for different goods and services being matched across the area. Investments in coordination are therefore critical (Kydd et al., 2004), allowing markets to function and finance to flow effectively. There is no point in seeing area-based development simply as an administrative arrangement. This was the problem of the Rural District Councils Act in Zimbabwe, which attempted to integrate administration across communal area and large-scale commercial farms. Councils saw the farms as a source of tax revenue and there was a failure to capitalise on the potential of integrated economic growth.

In the past, the historical inheritance of extreme dualism, cultural and racial difference and on-going antagonism between groups meant that integration did not happen on any meaningful scale. Today, with a new set of players engaged in local economic activity and accumulating from below in a new spatial configuration, the possibilities open up. This should be a key role for revived local government authorities. Again, as with all parts of government, district councils are moribund – without funds or capacity, and certainly with no ability for economic planning. An area-based approach needs to draw in the private sector, farmer groups and government agencies, but with strong leadership from a revived local government, with new mandates and capacities. Investment in infrastructure must be an early priority, allowing roads, water, markets and other service infrastructure, such as schools and clinics, to match the new geographic configuration of economic activity. This is not going to happen quickly, but as a longer-term strategic objective, perhaps piloted in a few areas, an area-based approach to local economic development may provide the foundation for a rural economic revivial, rooted in the dynamics of successful accumulation from below.

Agricultural research and extension
The public research and development system for agriculture in Zimbabwe has nearly collapsed. Once the pride of southern Africa, research capacity has shrunk as people have left and infrastructure has been neglected (Tawonezvi and Hikwa, 2006). Important research efforts, some established over decades, have ceased. Agricultural extension

has suffered major losses of qualified staff too, and mobility has been severely restricted by lack of funds and fuel. Most new resettlements do not have dipping infrastructure to allow tick populations to be controlled. The result has been a massive explosion of tick-borne disease, with major implications for cattle production. There is a severe lack of veterinary staff, and very few drugs or vaccines. In most resettlement areas, there is no resident extension worker or veterinary assistant, and those who visit do so only rarely.

How have people managed? Within the resettlement areas there are many with training, including Master Farmer certificates, and not a few former extension workers and officials of the Ministry of Agriculture. Such individuals are often the centre of informal advice networks. Others rely on connections with private sector suppliers, for example of seeds, veterinary drugs or tick sprayers. This has provided a solid basis for service support in many sites, in the absence of state provision. But new farmers – struggling with new production and marketing settings, and managing often highly vulnerable natural resources, without any investment in conservation works – do require skilled support. What should this consist of?

It will certainly be different from that provided for decades in the communal areas, and from the standard advice supplied to the large-scale sector. Our livelihood typology suggests that there are 15 different livelihood groups in the new farms (Chapter 10). Responding to them will require a major rethink of the agricultural research and development system. Alongside the standard agronomic, veterinary or soil conservation advice, farmers require support for market development, infrastructure investment, financing systems, business planning and so on. These were never a major priority of agricultural research and extension in the past. For example, support for building new value chains, linking formal and informal markets and providing support for quality assurance are areas where a major gap exists. Equally, new types of technology will be required, intermediate between those suitable for the communal areas and large-scale farms. Technologies which offer opportunities for post-harvest processing and value addition are in particular demand. A demand-led, participatory approach will therefore be required for new clients with new needs (cf. Hagmann et al., 1999). Approaches to delivery must change too. With a more educated, better-connected farming group, greater use can be made of of mobile phones, the Internet and other communication tools. Farmer-to-farmer innovation and extension approaches also have great potential, making use of the existing skill base and experience of the new settlers. And within all this, the researchers and extension officers, and the institutions that house them, will require retooling, reorganising and revamping, based on continuous needs assessment and priority-setting.

Clearly a return to the past where the state provided extension support and backed substantial research efforts is unlikely to return soon, if ever. Cost-recovery and cost-sharing approaches are required, along with public-private partnerships for the delivery of services (e.g. through para-veterinarians, agro-dealers etc.). New models are required, but there is an urgent need to rebuild some form of support structure for the new resettlements. If the aim is for the resettlements to become the focus for renewed economic growth, letting people get by on their own is an inadequate strategy.

Safety nets and social protection

Not everyone on the new resettlements is going to succeed. Our success rankings show there is very variable success, and some are really struggling – just hanging in. Others, as our exit survey showed, have dropped out, abandoning their land and returning to their original homes. Resettlement is always going to be dynamic, with people coming and going; some succeeding, some failing, often as a result of a series of unexpected, highly contingent events. While the above policy challenges have been focused on those who are on upward trajectories, accumulating from below, there are always others. In some cases, in some years, this may be the majority of people. For these settlers, the new land is an invaluable form of social security. But agriculture in dry areas, with limited support and few assets, is tough, as we have seen. An unexpected dry spell may ruin a cropping season. A death or illness in the family may reduce critical labour or increase demands on expenditure. The loss of a job may mean that critical remittance income dries up. All of these happen regularly across our sample, sometimes in combination and with devastating consequences.

What should social protection involve? Classic safety net systems involve handing out welfare, usually food. This is important for those in real trouble, but may not be appropriate for others, as it increases dependency. So-called productive safety nets, or transformative social protection (Ellis et al., 2009; Hulme and Shepherd, 2003) provide alternatives, and are more appropriate for those who at least have aspirations for 'stepping up'. These might include input support (vouchers for seed and fertiliser, for instance), restocking through smallstock loans, support for school fees or the provision of tools and basic farm equipment. All of these provide the basis for improving agricultural production, and a way out of extreme poverty. Targeting, financing and monitoring all are important policy considerations, but there is much experience of such approaches internationally to draw on (Devereux, 2001).

For some, there should be less focus on improving existing livelihoods, and more on facilitating diversification, 'stepping out'. Those who cannot make a go of it on the new resettlements need support to provide alternative livelihoods, through skill or business development, for example. The poor and vulnerable, reliant on risky and illegal sources of livelihood, suffer most from inappropriate legislation and excessive control, and so will benefit most from the removal of restrictions and an effective promotion of alternative livelihood options.

Social protection in the resettlement areas has had to rely on informal networks of support. These have been weak or absent, as 'communities' in the resettlements are only beginning to form. Reliance has been on immediate kin, and links with former homes and church networks. Informal support through the local 'moral economy' will remain important, but it is no substitute for more systematic state provision. This must be tailored to the new setting, supporting exit as well as diversification, and focusing on investments that support wider economic activity, rather than creating dependency traps for the poor.

Farmers' voice and representation

Representation and voice are critical if new government – and indeed non-government and private – initiatives are to unfold, responding to the challenges highlighted above. But, as we have seen, the new residents of the resettlement areas are not a uniform group. Reflecting a wide range of interests, the 'new farmers' are highly diverse in class, gender and generational terms. Such diversity is a weakness, and is reflected in the lack of influence small-scale farmers have had in political and policy processes over the years. By contrast, the large-scale commercial sector has long been powerful, with a well-organised and relatively well-resourced union, with access to politicians, donors, international agencies and others with power and influence (Herbst, 1990). Even today, with the sector largely disappeared, the large-scale commercial farming groups, either through the Commerical Farmers' Union or the breakaway lobby group, Justice for Agriculture (JAG), have a surprising amount of influence, particularly through their continued international connections. The Zimbabwe Farmers' Union (ZFU), notionally the representative body for smallholder farmers, is weak, and has limited capacity. It always represented the relatively elite groups in this sector, and continues to do so today (Bratton, 1994b; Moyo, 2001). Other groups focus on particular commodities, such as tobacco or sugar, and have greater potential.

Formal organisation in the new resettlements is thus weak. As Chapter 9 described, the structures that formed the basis of the land invasions – the base commanders, the Committees of Seven, etc. – have often given way to other hybrid arrangements, and there is little collective solidarity across groups and between schemes. At a more micro level, there are emergent organisational forms focused on particular activities – a garden, an irrigation scheme, a marketing effort – but these are unlikely to become the basis of representation and voice. Politics has been so fraught in recent years that many shy away from seeing political parties and local party structures as the basis for lobbying for change. Indeed, and certainly since the electoral violence and intimidation of 2008, identifying with a political party, especially the opposition MDC, has become an invitation to retribution and trouble. In other words, the prospects for organised representation and voice among resettlement farmers look weak.

Building a new set of rooted farming organisations, linked to an influential apex body, will be a long-term task, and will be highly dependent on the unfolding political alliances in rural areas. In earlier sections we have identified a 'middle farmer' group, generating surpluses through accumulation from below represented by a diverse range of small-scale capitalist farmers, petty commodity producers and worker-peasants. There is also a large group of less successful farmers, worker-peasants and others with different needs and interests. And there are those elites reliant on political patronage who are accumulating from above. Developing a common cause across such divisions is unlikely, and alliances will have to be struck. The organisational politics of building such a representative and influential farmers' movement will be challenging.

However, unlike in the past when smallholders could easily be marginalised, and were courted only at elections for their votes, small-holders now control one of the most important economic sectors in the country, and must be relied upon for urban food supply. Even if the elite urban middle classes dismiss the rural areas as backward and remote, the politics of the countryside cannot be ignored. As the war veterans showed after 1997, and especially during the land invasions, Zimbabwe's rural politics has taken on a new form, and organised groups may exert substantial pressure in ways that, in the past, seemed unimaginable. How the new configuration of political forces will pan out in the future is a subject of hot debate (Eppel et al., 2009), but the role of agrarian interests, including small-scale farmers, will undoubtedly be important.

Beyond patronage: rights and redistribution
Since Cecil Rhodes and the pioneer column, and indeed long before then, land has been synonymous with politics in Zimbabwe (Palmer, 1977). In the post-Independence period, calls for land reform coincided on a regular basis with elections. Populist and nationalist rhetoric, however, covered up elite manoeuvres that allowed the capture of land and resources for personal gain (Alexander, 2006). This has certainly been part of the post-2000 story, as political and security elites have grabbed land, making use of patronage connections. This continued even after the establishment of the inclusive government in 2009. While there are few in this category in our study sites, they exert considerable influence. As the state's resources declined, land became one of the main sources of political patronage in the last decade. Disgruntled security officers were paid off, wayward politicians were pulled into line and solid supporters were rewarded with the only resource the state had access to – land. Violence and intimidation, and an abuse of the rule of law, were often used to effect this. Such a strategy of accumulation from above, we have argued, runs counter to the dominant process of accumulation from below. This has undermined the land reform programme's credibility and legitimacy both nationally and internationally.

Even if such abuses occurred only in certain parts of the country and on relatively few farms, the fact that it was possible at all – and was in turn advertised globally across the media – has meant that the myths about Zimbabwe's land reform have been perpetuated. This dismal narrative, however, hides the wider story which this book has tried to tell. For the future, as we have argued, a successful land audit and the revival of a transparent and efficient land administration system are important precursors for reversing the patterns of patronage and corruption. Offering land to those with the potential for accumulation from below will allow the growth and equity goals of redistributive land reform to be met.

In order to balance the goals of redistribution, and the need for equity and redress – and rights – and thus assure legitimacy and justice, more accountable administrative and regulatory procedures are therefore required, and they must be upheld and enforced consistently and pro-cactively. This is a difficult balancing act, and requires leadership and confidence in the political process, features which remain absent in

Zimbabwe today. The extreme positions that have characterised recent political discourse need not remain as a divisive 'rupture' (Raftopoulos, 2003). A reframed discourse must encompass both redistribution/redress and rights/responsibilities, avoiding seeing these as polar opposites. A focus on rights need not emphasise only (neo)liberal notions of individual freedom and property rights, and an advocacy of redistribution must also accept compensation for those who lose out. The current impasse cannot be resolved by technocratic measures alone; only with the required political debate can land be viewed once again as a source of livelihood and economic wealth, not simply as a source of political patronage.

11.5 Beyond Zimbabwe: implications for southern Africa

These ten challenges are huge, but if they are met, Zimbabwe's land reform may yet realise some of the promised potentials, with a new economic dynamic in the rural areas, fuelled by accumulation from below and founded on small-scale agriculture. The first decade has been difficult, and many important lessons have been learned. The next decade, given the right support and policy environment, combined with political and economic stability, must be the moment when the real benefits of redistributive land reform and a reconfigured agricultural economy can be shown. Reflecting on the experience of resettlement in the 1980s and 1990s and contrasting this with the 2000s, Bill Kinsey notes how inevitably there is a transition from establishment, where production inevitably dips, to investment and growth (Kinsey, 2009). In the 1980s, this transition took a number of years, a period that was prolonged in the 2000s by the worsening economic and political situation. However, as Kinsey notes, there is an important sense of déjà vu. Resettlement in the 1980s was initially written off as a disaster, but, in the end, proved an unexpected success. Given the right support, the same could be the case for the new resettlements, but on a much larger scale, benefiting many more people.

Elsewhere in the southern Africa region, it is often asked: 'could it happen here?' A mixture of fear and alarm often combines with a deep lack of knowledge of the situation on the ground. Scare stories are repeated across academic debate, media commentary and public discourse.[8] On the face of it, Zimbabwe had many similarities with South Africa and Namibia in particular. Like Zimbabwe, both inherited a dualistic agrarian system, the result of dispossession through colonialism and apartheid. Agricultural industry and all GDP indicators in the formal economy are dominated by large-scale commercial concerns, often owned and controlled by whites. The racial politics of land-ownership, with a deep divide between poor, overcrowded former homelands or communal areas and the commercial farming zones, present many similarities. And alternative urban wage employment is increasingly limited due to structural unemployment and jobless growth.

---

[8] *Business Day.* "It could happen here", quoted by Lahiff and Cousins (2001: 654). See also http://news.bbc.co.uk/1/hi/programmes/crossing_continents/7493060.stm.

Such similarities have to be put into context, however (Goebel, 2005c; Lahiff and Cousins, 2001). The structure of the wider economy, political interests and priorities and agroecologies are hugely different. For example, in South Africa smallholder agriculture has remained marginal, while options for employment have existed in towns (Hall, 2009; Lahiff and Cousins, 2005). In Namibia, extreme aridity means that the potential for small-scale agriculture based on cropping is non-existent in most of the country and large-scale ranching or wildlife-based enterprises are the most likely option. Both are well-established and profitable industries where extensive land with little other use represents an important comparative advantage. And politically, despite the ritual nods towards reform, neither the ANC nor SWAPO have shown much inclination to commit to radical land reform, beyond the range of a few ill-conceived and susequently failing projects (Aliber et al., 2010; Werner and Odendaal, 2010). The political centre of gravity in South Africa has been in the urban areas; in organised labour and increasingly elite capital and international investment (Seekings and Natrass, 2002). As a major player in the globally important emerging economies, small-scale agriculture and redistributive land reform have not been a major focus, and the 'two economies' have persisted (Cousins, 2007). While the rural vote is important, jobs are a more important electoral issue than land (Lodge, 2003). In Namibia, perhaps more surprisingly, the northern communal areas, despite being the base of support for the ruling party, remain marginal in national economic decision-making (Melber, 2008). The failure of land movements to take off in either country, despite attempts such as the Landless People's Movement in South Africa (Greenberg, 2004), is perhaps indicative of the low purchase that land issues have in political processes.

But who knows what the future holds. In the mid-1990s no one thought that a radical land reform might unfold in Zimbabwe. Many argued for the necessity of land reform as the basis for long-term economic growth, of course, just at many do in South Africa and Namibia (Lipton and Ellis, 1996). For example, in 1996 some of the authors of this book concluded:

> ... urgent solutions to the problems of land scarcity will have to be sought in the coming decades. It may now be time to explore a wider range of land redistribution opportunities abandoning the strict adherence to a standardised, packaged settlement model and testing other options. If they are to address the fundamental problems of the communal areas, such options must offer new land of reasonably high potential and in sufficient quantities to begin to satisfy land needs ... If these conditions are satisfied, evidence suggests that a vibrant small-scale sector can offer Zimbabwe a bright future, both satisfying food needs and entering cash crop production for export ... However, if the challenges of land redistribution are not met, then communal area livelihoods will continue to be undermined with the associated costs of food aid, social disquiet and spontaneous migration. (Scoones et al., 1996: 230)

Sam Moyo and others have made well-argued appeals for land reform in Zimbabwe over a much longer period (Moyo, 1986, 1995, 2000), but the political-economic configuration meant that substantial, radical change remained unlikely. This all changed after 1997, and very rapidly indeed; and without anyone predicting either the scale or rapidity of the transformation which followed. Within a few years the agrarian structure of the country had been radically changed – almost certainly forever – and the country had been plunged into a deep political and economic crisis that lasted over a decade. Of course these were highly particular, contingent political circumstances, peculiar to the time and place. The circumstances were described in Chapter 1 at greater length, but included the economic crisis precipitated by structural adjustment, the increasing effectiveness of an opposition movement backed by organised labour and white capital, a divided ruling party with a crisis of legitimacy, a large organised group of disgruntled and disenfranchised war veterans and few other options for patronage and political favour beyond land. Although these conditions are unlikely to be repeated elsewhere, elements of them do exist in other countries in southern Africa, and tensions over land and resources, some overt, some less so, are never far away.

But perhaps the 'dread' question, 'could it happen here?' is the wrong one. A more appropriate question is: Are there any of the more positive lessons learned about the opportunities for livelihoods following land reform that are relevant elsewhere? Here we can be more concrete. The answer is an unquestionable, yes – although, as ever, with important caveats. Given the right support (still absent in Zimbabwe), land reform involving small-scale agricultural production can generate production and livelihoods in a sustained way through processes of accumulation from below. For South Africa and Namibia, in different ways, this may be an important lesson (Cousins, 2010). Deep scepticism remains in both countries about the potentials of a smallholder model. Debates about farm 'viability' are stuck in discussions about business models representing scaled down versions of large-scale commercial farms, and so the projects that are foisted on land reform 'beneficiaries' rarely, if ever, work (Cousins and Scoones, 2010; Lahiff and Cousins, 2005). Where postitive stories do emerge, people have broken free from the shackles of standardised planning imposed by government agencies, and innovated on their own. Informal settlement, linking production to markets in new ways, has shown opportunties for success. But these have been on the margins, and have received limited attention (although see Aliber et al., 2010; Lahiff et al., 2008).

Surely, some argue, in South Africa and Namibia there is no demand for land reform: look at the failure of land reform projects and the results of surveys which show that land and agriculture is not people's top priority (CDE, 2005, 2008); and anyway large-scale commercial agriculture is far more 'economic'. This was of course an argument used in Zimbabwe for many years. A number of responses are required. First, the failure of projects rarely tells us more than the fact that such projects were badly designed and implemented. Too many land reform projects across southern Africa are almost designed to fail, so absurd are the assumptions embedded in them. Hooked into a market-led reform programme, the prospects for agrarian transformation remain limited (Lahiff et al., 2007; Borras, 2003). Second, if people have diversified their livelihoods, it is not surprising that they prioritise jobs over agriculture. People do not have a single livleihood option, they want diversity; and if land and agriculture are not at the top of the list they may be second or third. And different people prioritise differently – men and women, richer and poorer, older and younger; so simplistic generalisations usually hide greater complexity.

Finally, of course, large-scale commercial agriculture must remain part of the picture. As discussed above, how this happens remains a subject of much (often confused) debate in Zimbabwe. Simply stating that large-scale production is always more economically viable is deeply unhelpful. Yet again, the debate hinges on the notion of viability. With a narrow definition, focused on returns to some factors of production, and in relation to certain markets, one result will emerge; while with a more holistic livelihoods focus, a different version of viability is relevant (Cousins and Scoones, 2010). As we have said before, the interpretation is not a matter of science, but a matter of politics – and so there is a choice; one that has not been widely deliberated upon. A mix of farm types of different sizes, focused on different markets and with different kinds of producers, but interacting in productive ways to add value and create economic synergies, appears to us the most effective way forward. This must capitalise on the very real potentials of small-holder producers to accumulate from below and contribute to economic growth and wider welfare, while at the same time acknowledging the scale advantages for some operations. Such a vision would require a flexible approach to land holdings, abandoning a dualistic agrarian economy, and allowing scaling up and down depending on comparative advantage, investment opportunities and farmers' commitment.

A failure to deliberate on these issues and imagine alternative futures only leads to bottling up trouble for the future, as Zimbabwe found to its cost. As Edward Lahiff and Ben Cousins commented in respect of South Africa: 'As long as land reform is seen narrowly as a means of advancing the political needs of the ANC, at home and abroad, rather than as a means of creating sustainable livelihoods for the mass of the rural population, Zimbabwe-style rural unrest remains more than a possibility' (2001:665). Whether the deeper lessons of Zimbabwe's land reform are learnt – for Zimbabwe itself or for the wider region – will depend on whether empirical data and analysis of the sort presented in this book are taken on board in the discussions of what happens next. There are important lessons to be learned, and they suggest that radical revisions of policy and practice are required following land reform. If the myths continue to trump the realities, however, misguided policy and inappropriate support will be the result. If the reverse is true, there are real prospects for a bright future for rural livelihoods in the new resettlements in Zimbabwe.

REFERENCES

Abel, N. and Blaike, P. (1989) 'Land degradation, stocking rates and conservation policies in the communal rangelands of Botswana and Zimbabwe', *Land Degradation and Development*, vol. 1, no. 2: 101-23.

Adams, J. M. (1991a) 'Female wage labour in rural Zimbabwe', *World Development*, vol. 19, no. 2-3: 163-77.

— (1991b) 'The rural labour market in Zimbabwe', *Development and Change*, vol. 22, no. 2: 297-320.

Agarwal, B. (2003) 'Gender and land rights revisited: exploring new prospects via the state, family and the market', in S. Razavi (ed.) *Agrarian Change, Gender and Land Rights*, Blackwell Publishing, Oxford.

Akram-Lodhi, A. H., Borras, S. M. and Kay, C. (eds) (2007) *Land, Poverty and Livelihoods in an Era of Globalization*, Routledge, London.

Akram-Lodhi, A. H. and Kay, C. (2009) 'The agrarian question: peasants and rural change', in A. H. Akram-Lodhi and C. Kay (eds) *Peasants and Globalization: Political Economy, Rural Transformation and the Agrarian Question*, Routledge, London.

Alexander, J. (2006) *The Unsettled Land: State-making and the Politics of Land in Zimbabwe, 1893–2003*, James Currey, Oxford.

— (2003) '"Squatters", veterans and the state in Zimbabwe', in A. Hammar, B. Raftopoulos and S. Jensen (eds) *Zimbabwe's Unfinished Business: Rethinking Land, State and Nation in the Context of Crisis*, Weaver Press, Harare.

— (1994) 'State, peasantry and resettlement in Zimbabwe', *Review of African Political Economy*, vol. 21, no. 61: 325-45.

Aliber, M, Maluleke, T., Manenzhe, T., Paradza, G. and Cousins, B. (2010) *Livelihoods after Land Reform: South Africa Country Report*. Livelihoods after Land Reform Project, Institute for Poverty, Land and Agrarian Studies (PLAAS), University of the Western Cape, Cape Town.

Amanor-Wilks, D. (1995) *In Search of Hope for Zimbabwe's Farm Workers*, Dateline Southern Africa and the Panos Institute, Harare.

Andersson, J. (2007) 'How much did property rights matter? Understanding food insecurity in Zimbabwe: A critique of Richardson', *African Affairs*, vol. 106, no. 425: 681-90.

— (2001) 'Reinterpreting the rural-urban connection: migration practices and socio-cultural dispositions of Buhera workers in Harare', *Africa*, vol. 71, no. 1: 82-112.

Arrighi, G. (1973) 'Labour supplies in historical perspective: a study of the proletarianisation of the African peasantry in Rhodesia', in G. Arrighi and J. Saul (eds) *Essays on the Political Economy of Africa*, Monthly Review Press, New York, NY.

Ashley, C. and Maxwell, S. (2001) 'Rethinking rural development', *Development Policy Review*, vol. 19, no. 4: 395-425.

Bahiigwa, G., Mdoe, N. and Ellis, F. (2005) 'Livelihoods research findings and agriculture-led growth', *IDS Bulletin*, vol. 36, no. 2: 115-20.

Barr, A. (2004) 'Forging effective new communities: the evolution of civil society in Zimbabwean resettlement villages', *World Development*, vol. 32, no. 10: 1753-66.

Barrett, C., Reardon, T. and Webb, P. (2001) 'Non-farm income diversification and household livelihood strategies in rural Africa: concepts, dynamics, and policy implications', *Food Policy*, vol. 26, no. 4: 315-31.

Barrett, J. (1992) 'The economic role of cattle in communal farming systems in Zimbabwe', *Pastoral Development Network Paper*, no. 32. Overseas Development Institute, London.

Barrows, R. and Roth, M. (1990) 'Land tenure and investment in African agriculture: theory and evidence', *Journal of Modern African Studies,* vol. 28, no. 2: 265-97.

Behnke, R. (1985) 'Measuring the benefits of subsistence versus commercial livestock production in Africa', *Agricultural Systems*, vol. 16, no. 2: 109-35.

Belder, P., Rohrbach, D., Twomlow, S. and Senzanje, A. (2007) *Can Drip Irrigation Improve the Livelihoods of Smallholders? Lessons Learned from Zimbabwe*, Global Theme on Agroecosystems, Report no. 33, ICRISAT, Bulawayo, Zimbabwe.

Benjaminsen, T. A. and Lund, C. (eds) (2003) *Securing Land Rights in Africa*, Frank Cass, London.

Bernstein, H. (2010) *Class Dynamics of Agrarian Change*, Fernwood, Halifax NS.

— (2009) 'V.I. Lenin and A.V. Chayanov: looking back, looking forward'. *Journal of Peasant Studies, vol.* 36, no. 1: 55-81.

— (2005) 'Rural land and land conflicts in sub-Saharan Africa', in S. Moyo and P. Yeros (eds) *Reclaiming the Land: the Resurgence of Rural Movements in Africa, Asia and Latin America*, Zed Books, London.

— (2004) '"Changing before our very eyes": agrarian questions and the politics of land in capitalism today', *Journal of Agrarian Change*, vol. 4, no. 1-2: 190-225.

— (2003) 'Land reform in southern Africa in world-historical perspective', *Review of African Political Economy*, vol. 30, no. 96: 203-26.

— (2002) 'Land reform: taking a long(er) view', *Journal of Agrarian Change,* vol. 2, no. 4: 433-63.

Berry, R. A. and Cline, W. R. (1979) *Agrarian Structure and Productivity in Developing Countries*, Johns Hopkins University Press, Baltimore, MD.

Berry, S. (2009) 'Property, authority and citizenship: land claims, politics and the dynamics of social division in West Africa', *Development and Change,* vol. 40, no. 1: 23-45.

— (2002) 'Debating the land question in Africa', *Comparative Studies in Society and History,* vol. 44, no. 4: 638-68.

— (1993) *No Condition is Permanent: The Social Dynamics of Agrarian Change in Sub-Saharan Africa*, University of Wisconsin Press, Madison, WI.

— (1989) 'Social institutions and access to resources', *Journal of the International African Institute*, vol. 59, no. 1: 41-55.

Binswanger, H. P. and Deininger, K. (1993) 'South African land policy: the legacy of history and current options', *World Development,* vol. 21, no. 9: 1451-75.

Binswanger, H. P., Deininger, K. and Gershon, F. (1995) 'Power, distortions, revolt and reform in agricultural land relations', in J. Behrman and T. N. Srinivasan (eds) *Handbook of Development Economics,* vol. 3, no. 4.

Bird, K. and Shepherd, A. (2003) *Chronic Poverty in Zimbabwe's Semi-Arid Areas,* Chronic Poverty Research Centre Working Paper, no. 18, University of Manchester, Manchester.

Bishop, J. (1995) *The Economics of Soil Degradation: An Illustration of the Change in Productivity Approach to Valuation in Mali and Malawi,* LEEC Paper DP 95–02, IIED, London.

Blair, D. (2002) *Degrees in Violence: Robert Mugabe and the Struggle for Power in Zimbabwe,* Continuum Books, London.

Bloch, A. (2008) 'Zimbabweans in Britain: transnational activities and capabilities', *Journal of Ethnic and Migration Studies,* vol. 34, no. 2: 287-305.

Bond, P. (2007) 'Competing explanations of Zimbabwe's long economic crisis', *Safundi,* vol. 8, no. 2: 149-81.

— (2000) *Elite Transition: From Apartheid to Neoliberalism in South Africa,* Pluto Press and University of Natal Press, London and Pietermaritzburg, SA.

Bond, P. and Manyama, M. (2002) *Zimbabwe's Plunge: Exhausted Nationalism, Neoliberalism and the Search for Social Justice,* University of Natal Press, Pietermaritzburg, SA.

Borras, S. M. (2003) 'Questioning market-led agrarian reform: experiences from Brazil, Colombia and South Africa', *Journal of Agrarian Change,* vol. 3, no. 3: 367-94.

Borras, S. M. and Franco, J. C. (2010) 'Contemporary discourses and contestations around pro-poor land policies and land governance', *Journal of Agrarian Studies,* vol. 10, no. 1: 1-32.

Borras, S. M., Edelman, M. and Kay, C. (2008) 'Transnational agrarian movements: origins and politics, campaigns and impact', *Journal of Agrarian Change,* vol. 8, no. 2-3: 169-204.

Borras, S. M., Kay, C. and Akram-Lodhi, A. H. (2007) 'Agrarian reform and rural development: historical overview and current issues', in A. H. Akram-Lodhi, S. M. Borras and C. Kay (eds) *Land, Poverty and Livelihoods in an Era of Globalization,* Routledge, London.

Bourdillon, M. (1982) *The Shona Peoples: An Ethnography of the Contemporary Shona,* Mambo Press, Gweru, Zimbabwe.

Bracking, S. and Cliffe, L. (2009) 'Plans for a Zimbabwe aid package: blueprint for recovery or shock therapy prescription for liberalisation?' *Review of African Political Economy,* vol. 36, no. 119: 103-113.

Bracking, S. and Sachikonye, L. (2008) *Remittances, Poverty Reduction and Informalisation in Zimbabwe, 2005-6: A Political Economy of Dispossession?* Brookes World Poverty Institute (BWPI) Working Paper no. 28, BWPI, Manchester.

Brand, C. M. (1994) 'The Communal Lands Reorganisation Programme in Zimbabwe', *Review of Rural and Urban Planning in Southern and Eastern Africa,* vol. 1: 53-74.

Bratton, M. (1994a) 'Land redistribution, 1980-1990', in M. Rukuni and C. Eicher (eds) *Zimbabwe's Agricultural Revolution,* University of Zimbabwe Publications, Harare.

— (1994b) 'Micro-democracy? The merger of farmer unions in Zimbabwe', *African Studies Review,* vol. 37, no. 1: 9-37.

Bratton, M. and Masunungure, E. (2007) 'Popular reactions to state repression: Operation Murambatsvina in Zimbabwe', *African Affairs*, vol. 106, no. 422: 21-45.

Brett, E. A. (2005) *From Corporatism to Liberalisation in Zimbabwe: Economic Policy Regimes and Political Crisis (1980–1997)*, Crisis States Programme Working Papers Series no. 58, London School of Economics, London.

Bruce, J. and Migot-Adholla, S. E. (1994) *Searching for Land Tenure Security in Africa*, Kendall Hunt Publishing, Dubuque, IA.

Bryceson, D. (2004) 'Agrarian vista or cortex: African rural livelihood policies', *Review of African Political Economy*, vol. 37, no. 102: 617-29.

— (1999) 'African rural labour, income diversification and livelihood approaches: a long-term development perspective', *Review of African Political Economy*, vol. 26, no. 80: 171-89.

— (1996) 'De-agrarianisation and rural employment in sub-Saharan Africa: a sectoral perspective', *World Development*, vol. 24, no. 1: 97-111.

Bryceson, D. and Jamal, V. (1997) *Farewell to Farms: De-Agrarianisation and Employment in Africa*, Ashgate Publishing, Aldershot, UK.

Bryceson, D., Kay, C. and Mooij, J. (eds) (2000) *Disappearing Peasantries? Rural Labour in Africa, Asia and Latin America*', Intermediate Technology Publications, London.

Buckle, C. (2001) *African Tears: The Zimbabwe Land Invasions*, Covos Day Books, London.

Bush, R. and Cliffe, R. (1984) 'Agrarian policy in migrant labour societies: reform or transformation in Zimbabwe?', *Review of African Political Economy*, vol. 11, no. 29: 77-94.

Byres, T. (2004) 'Neo-classical neo-populism 25 years on: déjà vu and déjà passe. towards a critique', *Journal of Agrarian Change,* vol. 4, no. 1-2: 17-44.

Campbell, B. (1987) 'The use of wild fruits in Zimbabwe', *Economic Botany*, vol. 41, no. 3: 375-85.

Campbell, B. M., Bradley, P. and Carter, S. E. (1997a) 'Sustainability and peasant farming systems: observations from Zimbabwe', *Agriculture and Human Values*, vol. 14, no. 2: 159-68.

Campbell, B. M., Luckert, M. and Scoones, I. (1997b) 'Local-level valuation of savanna resources: a case study from Zimbabwe', *Economic Botany*, vol. 51, no. 1: 59-77.

Campbell, B. M., Jeffrey, S., Kozanayi, W., Luckert, M., Mutamba, M. and Zindi, C. (2002) *Household Livelihoods in Semi-Arid Regions: Options and Constraints*, Center for International Forestry Research (CIFOR), Bogor, Indonesia .

Cane, M. A., Eshel, G. and Buckland, R. W. (1994) 'Forecasting Zimbabwean maize yield using eastern equatorial Pacific sea surface temperatures', *Nature*, vol. 370: 204-5.

Carter, M. R. (1985) 'Identification of the inverse relationship between farm size and productivity: an empirical analysis of peasant agricultural production', *Oxford Economic Papers,* vol. 36, issue November: 131-45.

Cavendish, W. (2000) 'Empirical regularities in the poverty-environment relationship of rural households: evidence from Zimbabwe', *World Development*, vol. 28, no. 11: 1979-2003.

Centre for Development and Enterprise (CDE) (2008) *Land Reform in South Africa: Getting Back on Track*, Research Report, no. 16, Centre for Development and Enterprise, Johannesburg.

— (2005) *Land Reform in South Africa: a 21st Century Perspective*, Research Report, no. 14, Centre for Development and Enterprise, Johannesburg.

Chambati, W. (2007) *Emergent Agrarian Labour Relations in New Resettle-*

ment Areas, African Institute for Agrarian Studies (AIAS) Mimeograph Series, AIAS, Harare.

Chambati, W. and Magaramombe, G. (2008) 'An abandoned question: farm workers', in S. Moyo, K. Helliker and T. Murisa (eds) *Contested Terrain: Civil Society and Land Reform in Contemporary Zimbabwe*, S & S Publishing, Johannesburg.

Chambati, W. and Moyo, S. (2004) *Impact of Land Reform on Farm Workers and Farm Labour Processes*, African Institute for Agrarian Studies (AIAS) Mimeograph Series, AIAS, Harare.

Chaumba, J., Scoones, I. and Wolmer, W. (2003a) 'New politics, new livelihoods: changes in the Zimbabwean lowveld since the farm invasions of 2000', *Review of African Political Economy*, vol. 30, no. 98: 379-403.

— (2003b) 'From jambanja to planning: the reassertion of technocracy in land reform in south-eastern Zimbabwe?', *Journal of Modern African Studies*, vol. 41, no. 4: 533-54.

Cheater, A.P. (1982) 'Formal and informal rights to land in Zimbabwe's black freehold areas: a case-study from Msengezi Africa', *Africa*, vol. 52, no. 3: 77-91.

Child, B. (1988) *'The Role of Wildlife Utilization in the Sustainable Economic Development of Semi-arid Rangelands in Zimbabwe'*, DPhil thesis, Oxford University.

Chimedza, R. (2006) 'Rural financial markets, 1924-1991', in M. Rukuni, P. Tawonezvi, and C. Eicher, with M. Munyuki-Hungwe and P. Matondi (eds) *Zimbabwe's Agricultural Revolution Revisited*, University of Zimbabwe Publications, Harare.

— (1988) *Women's Access to and Control over Land: the Case of Zimbabwe*, Department of Agricultural Economics Working Paper ABE 10/88, University of Zimbabwe, Harare.

Chimhowu, A. (2009) *Moving Forward in Zimbabwe: Reducing Poverty and Promoting Growth*, Brooks World Poverty Institute, University of Manchester, Manchester, UK.

— (2002) 'Extending the grain basket to the margins: spontaneous land resettlement and changing livelihoods in Hurungwe district, Zimbabwe', *Journal of Southern African Studies*, vol. 28, no. 3: 551-73.

Chimhowu, A. and Hulme, D. (2006) 'Livelihood dynamics in planned and spontaneous resettlement in Zimbabwe: converging and vulnerable', *World Development*, vol. 34, no. 4: 728-50.

Chimhowu, A. and Woodhouse, P. (2006) 'Customary vs. private property rights? Dynamics and trajectories of vernacular land markets in sub-Saharan Africa', *Journal of Agrarian Change*, vol. 6, no. 3: pp 346-71.

Chitiga, M. and Mabugu, R. (2008) 'Evaluating the impact of land redistribution: a CGE microsimulation application to Zimbabwe', *Journal of African Economies*, vol. 17, no. 4: 527-49.

Chivaura-Mususa, C., Campbell, B. and Kenyon, W. (2003) 'Land use options in dry tropical woodland ecosystems in Zimbabwe: the value of mature trees in arable fields in the smallholder sector, Zimbabwe', *Ecological Economics*, vol. 33, no. 33: 395-400.

Claasens, A. and Cousins, B. (eds) (2008) *Land, Power and Custom: Controversies Generated by South Africa's Communal Land Rights Act*, University of Cape Town Press, Cape Town.

Clarke, D. (1977) *Agricultural and Plantation Workers in Rhodesia: A Report on Conditions of Labour and Subsistence*, Mambo Press, Gwelo, Zimbabwe.

Cliffe, L. (1986) *Policy Options for Agrarian Reform in Zimbabwe: A Technical Appraisal*, Food and Agriculture Organization of the United Nations (FAO), Rome.

Collier, P. (2008) 'Politics of hunger: how illusion and greed fan the food crisis', *Foreign Affairs*, November/December.

Coltart, D. (2008) *A Decade of Suffering in Zimbabwe Economic Collapse and Political Repression under Robert Mugabe*, Development Policy Analysis, no. 5, The Cato Institute, Washington, DC.

Cotula, L., Toulmin, C. and Hesse, C. (2004) *Land Tenure and Administration in Africa: Lessons of Experience and Emerging Issues*, International Institute for Environment and Development (IIED), London.

Cousins, B. (2010) *What is a 'Smallholder'? Class Analytical Perspectives on Small-Scale Farming and Agrarian Reform in South Africa*, Working Paper 16, January 2010. PLAAS, University of the Western Cape.

— (2009) 'More than socially embedded: the distinctive character of 'communal tenure' regimes in South Africa and its implications for land policy', in B. B. Mukamuri, J. M. Manjengwa and S. Anstey (eds) *Beyond Proprietorship: Murphree's Laws on Community-based Natural Resouce Management in Southern Africa*, Weaver Press, Harare.

— (2007) 'Agrarian reform and the 'two economies': transforming South Africa's countryside', in L. Ntsebeza and R. Hall (eds) *The Land Question in South Africa: The Challenge of Transformation and Redistribution*, HSRC Press, Cape Town.

— (2003) 'Zimbabwe's crisis and the politics of land, democracy and development in Southern Africa', in A. Hammar, B. Raftopoulos and S. Jensen (eds) *Zimbabwe's Unfinished Business: Rethinking Land, State and Nation in the Context of Crisis*, Weaver Press, Harare.

Cousins, B. and Scoones, I. (2010) 'Contested paradigms of 'viability' in redistributive land reform: perspectives from southern Africa', *Journal of Peasant Studies*, vol. 37, no. 1: 31- 66.

Cousins, B., Weiner, D. and Amin, N. (1992) 'Social differentiation in the communal lands of Zimbabwe', *Review of African Political Economy*, vol. 19, no. 53: 5-24.

Cusworth, J. (2000) 'A review of the UK ODA evaluation of the land resettlement programme in 1988 and the land appraisal mission of 1996', in T. Bowyer-Bower and C. Stoneman (eds) *Land Reform in Zimbabwe: Constraints and Prospects,* Ashgate, Aldershot, UK.

Cusworth, J. and Walker, J. (1988) *Land Resettlement in Zimbabwe: A Preliminary Evaluation*, Evaluation Report no. EV 434, Overseas Development Administration (ODA), London.

Das, V. and Poole, D. (eds) (2004) *Anthropology in the Margins of the State: Comparative Ethnographies*, James Currey, Oxford.

Davies, R. (2005) 'Memories of underdevelopment: a personal interpretation of Zimbabwe's economic decline', in B. Raftopoulos and T. Savage (eds) *Zimbabwe: Injustice and Political Reconciliation*, Institute for Justice and Reconciliation and Weaver Press, Cape Town and Harare.

De Alcántara, C. H. (ed.) (1993) *Real Markets: Social and Political Issues of Food Policy Reform*, Frank Cass, London.

De Soto, H. (2001) *The Mystery of Capital: Why Capitalism Triumphs in the West and Fails Everywhere Else*, Black Swan: London.

Deininger, K. (1999) 'Making negotiated land reform work: initial experience from Colombia, Brazil and South Africa', *World Development*, vol. 27, no. 4: 651-72.

Deininger, K. and Binswanger, H. (1999) 'The evolution of the World Bank's land policy: principles, experience and future challenges', *The World Bank Research Observer*, no. 14: 247-76.

Deininger, K. and Jin, S. (2006) 'Tenure security and land-related investment: evidence from Ethiopia', *European Economic Review*, vol. 50, no. 5: 1245-77.

Deininger, K. and Squire, L. (1998) 'New ways of looking at old issues: inequality and growth', *Journal of Development Economics*, vol. 57, no.2: 259-87.

Deininger, K., Hoogeveen, H. and Kinsey, B. (2004) 'Economic benefits and costs of land redistribution in Zimbabwe in the early 1980s', *World Development*, vol. 32, no. 10: 1697-709.

Deininger, K., Ali, D. A., Holden, S. and Zevenbergen, J. (2008) 'Rural land certification in Ethiopia: process, initial Impact, and implications for other African countries', *World Development*, vol. 36, no. 10: 1786-812.

Delgado, C., Hopkins, J. and Kelly, V. A. (1998) *Agricultural Growth Linkages in Sub-Saharan Africa*, International Food Policy Research Institute (IFPRI) Research Report, no. 107, IFPRI, Washington, DC.

Derman, B. and Hellum, A. (2007) 'Livelihood rights perspective on water reform: reflections on rural Zimbabwe', *Land Use Policy*, vol. 24, no. 4: 664-73.

Devereux, S. (2001) 'Livelihood insecurity and social protection: a re-emerging issue in rural development', *Development Policy Review*, vol. 19, no. 4: 509-17.

Dorward, A. (2009) 'Integrating contested aspirations, processes and policy: development as hanging in, stepping up and stepping out', *Development Policy Review*, vol. 27, no. 2: 131-46.

Dorward, A. and Chirwa, E. (2009) *Fertiliser Subsidies: Lessons from Malawi for Kenya*, Future Agricultures Consortium Briefing Paper, February, Brighton.

Dorward, A., Anderson, S., Nava Bernal, Y., Sanchez Vera, E., Rushton, J., Pattison, J. and Paz, R. (2009) 'Hanging in, stepping up and stepping out: livelihood aspirations and strategies of the poor', *Development in Practice*, vol. 19, no. 2: 240-47.

Dorward, A., Fan, S., Kydd, J., Lofgren, H., Morrison, J., Poulton, C., Rao, N., Smith, L., Tchale, H., Thorat, S., Urey, I., and Wobst, P. (2004) 'Institutions and policies for pro-poor agricultural growth', *Development Policy Review*, vol. 22, no. 6: 611-22.

Drinkwater, M. (1991) *The State and Agrarian Change in Zimbabwe's Communal Areas*, St Martin's Press, New York, NY.

Eastwood, R., Lipton, M. and Newell, A. (2009) 'Farm size' in R. Evenson and P. Pingali (eds) *Handbook of Agricultural Economics*, vol. 4, North Holland, Amsterdam.

Eicher, C. (1995) 'Zimbabwe's maize-based green revolution: preconditions for replication', *World Development*, vol. 23, no. 5: 805-18.

Elliott, J., Burnside, N. G., Broomhead, T., Kinsey, B. and Kwesha, D. (2006) 'The nature and extent of landscape change under land resettlement programmes in Zimbabwe', *Land Degradation and Development*, vol. 17, no. 5: 495-508.

Ellis, F. (2000) *Rural Livelihoods and Diversity in Developing Countries*, Oxford University Press, UK.

— (1998) 'Household strategies and rural livelihood diversification', *Journal of Development Studies*, vol. 35, no. 1: 1-38.

Ellis, F. and Freeman, H. (2004) 'Rural livelihoods and poverty reduction strategies in four African countries', *Journal of Development Studies*, vol. 40, no. 4: 1-30.

Ellis, F., Devereux, S. and White, P. (2009) *Social Protection in Africa*, Edward Elgar Publishing Ltd., Cheltenham, UK.

Englert, B. and Daley, E. (eds) (2008) *Women's Land Rights and Privatization in Eastern Africa*, James Currey, Oxford.

Eppel, S., Ndlela, D., Raftopoulos, B. and Rupiya, M. (eds) (2009) *Developing a Transformation Agenda for Zimbabwe*, Idasa, Cape Town.

Fan, S., Hazell, P. and Haque, T. (2000) 'Targeting public investments by agro-ecological zone to achieve growth and and poverty alleviation goals in rural India', *Food Policy*, vol. 25, no. 4: 411-28.

Farm Community Trust of Zimbabwe (FCTZ) (2001) *The Impact of Land Reform on Commercial Farm Workers' Livelihoods*, FCTZ, Harare.

Faulkner, R. and Lambert, R. (1990) 'The use of the rope-washer pump in micro-scale irrigation, *Proceedings of the Institution of Civil Engineers*, Part 1, vol. 88, no.1: 81-90.

Feder, G. and Noronha, R. (1987) 'Land rights systems and agricultural development in sub-Saharan Africa', *World Bank Research Observer*, vol. 2, no. 2: 143-69.

Fontein, J. (2009) '"We want to belong to our roots and we want to be modern people": new farmers, old claims around Lake Mutirikwi, southern Zimbabwe', *African Studies Quarterly*, vol. 10, no. 4.

— (2006a) 'Languages of land, water and 'tradition' around Lake Mutirikwi in southern Zimbabwe', *Journal of Modern African Studies*, vol. 44, no. 2: 223-49.

— (2006b) 'Shared legacies of the war: spirit mediums and war veterans in southern Zimbabwe', *Journal of Religion in Africa*, vol. 36, no. 2: 167-99.

Food and Agriculture Organization of the United Nations (FAO) (2008) *Compulsory Acquisition of Land and Compensation*, FAO, Rome.

— (1979) *World Conference on Agrarian Reform and Rural Development: Report*, FAO, Rome.

Foster, G., Makufa, C., Drew, R. and Kralovec, E. (1997) 'Factors leading to the establishment of child-headed households: the case of Zimbabwe', *Health Transition Review*, supplement 2 to vol. 7: 155-68.

Fox, R. C., Rowntree, K. M. and Chigumira, E. C. (2006) 'On the fast track to land degradation? A case study of the impact of the Fast Track Land Reform Programme in Kadoma district, Zimbabwe', in Highland 2006 Symposium, 19-25 September 2006, Mekelle, Ethiopia.

Frost, P., Campbell, B., Luckert, M. and Mutamba, M. (2007) 'In search of improved rural livelihoods in semi-arid regions through local management of natural resources: lessons from case-studies in Zimbabwe', *World Development*, vol. 35, no. 11: 1961-74.

Gereffi, G. and Korzeniewicz, M. (eds) (1994) *Commodity Chains and Global Capitalism*, Greenwood Press, Westport, CT.

Goebel, A. (2005a) *Gender and Land Reform: The Zimbabwe Experience*, McGill–Queen's University Press, Montreal, Canada

— (2005b) 'Zimbabwe's 'fast track' land reform: what about women?', *Gender, Place and Culture*, vol. 12, no. 2: 145-72.

— (2005c) 'Is Zimbabwe the future for South Africa? The implications for land reform in southern Africa', *Journal of Contemporary African Studies* Vol. 23, no. 3: 345-70.

— (1999) '"Here it is our land, the two of us": women, men and land in a Zimbabwean resettlement area', *Journal of Contemporary African Studies*, vol. 17, no. 1: pp 75-96.

Gomez, M. (1988) 'A resource inventory of indigenous and traditional foods in Zimbabwe', *Zambezia* XV: 53-73.

Govereh, J. and Jayne, T. (2003) 'Cash cropping and food crop productivity: synergies or trade-offs?', *Agricultural Economics*, vol. 28, no. 1: 39-50.

Grandin, B. (1988) *Wealth Ranking in Smallholder Communities: A Field Manual*, Intermediate Technology Publications, London.

Greenberg, S. (2004) *The Landless People's Movement and the Failure of Post-apartheid Land Reform*, School of Development Studies, University of KwaZulu-Natal, Durban.

Gregson, S., Garnett, G., Nyamakapa, C., Hallett, T., Lewis, J., Mason, P., Chandiwana, S. and Anderson, R. (2006) 'HIV decline associated with behaviour change in eastern Zimbabwe', *Science*, vol. 311, no. 5761: 664-66.

Griffin, K., Khan, A. R. and Ickowitz, A. (2004) 'In defence of neo-classical neo-populism', *Journal of Agrarian Change*, vol. 4, no. 3: 361-86.

— (2002) 'Poverty and distribution of land', *Journal of Agrarian Change*, vol. 2, no. 3: 279-330.

Gunning, J., Hoddinott, J., Kinsey, B. and Owen, T. (2000) 'Revisiting forever gained: income dynamics in resettlement areas of Zimbabwe, 1983-1996', *Journal of Development Studies*, vol. 36, no. 6: 131-54.

Guyer, J. and Peters, P. (1987) 'Conceptualising the household: issues of theory and policy in Africa', *Development and Change*, vol. 18, no. 2: 197-214.

Haggblade, S., Hammer, J. and Hazell, P. (1991) 'Modeling agricultural growth multipliers', *American Journal of Agricultural Economics*, vol. 73, no. 2: 361-374.

Haggblade, S., Hazell, P. and Brown, J. (1989) 'Farm-non-farm linkages in rural sub-Saharan Africa', *World Development*, vol. 17, no. 8: 1173-1201.

Haggblade, S., Hazell, P. and Reardon, T. (eds) (2007) *Transforming the Rural Nonfarm Economy: Opportunities and Threats in the Developing World*, Johns Hopkins University Press, Baltimore, MD.

Hagmann, J. with Chuma, E., Murwira, K. and Connolly, M. (1999) *Putting Process into Practice: Operationalising Participatory Extension*, AgREN Network Paper no. 94, Overseas Development Institute (ODI), London.

Hall, R. (ed.) (2009) *Another Countryside?: Policy Options for Land and Agrarian Reform in South Africa*, PLAAS, Cape Town.

Hall, R. (2004) 'A political economy of land reform in South Africa', *Review of African Political Economy*, vol. 31, no. 100: 213-27.

Hammar, A. (2005) *Disrupting Democracy? Altering Landscapes of Local Government in Post-2000 Zimbabwe*, Crisis States Research Centre, Discussion Paper no. 9, London School of Economics, London.

— (2003) 'The making and unma(s)king of local government in Zimbabwe', in A. Hammar, B. Raftopoulos and S. Jensen (eds) *Zimbabwe's Unfinished Business: Rethinking Land, State and Nation in the Context of Crisis*, Weaver Press, Harare.

Hammar, A., Raftopoulos, B. and Jensen, S. (eds) (2003) *Zimbabwe's Unfinished Business: Rethinking Land, State, and Nation in the Context of Crisis*, Weaver Press, Harare.

Hanyani-Mlambo, B. and Poulton, C. (2004) *Zimbabwe Country Report, 2003*, report produced for the project "Competition and Coordination in Cotton Market Systems of Southern and Eastern Africa", Imperial College London, Wye, UK.

Harrison, E. (2006) *Jambanja*, Maioio Publishers, Harare.

Hart, G. (2002) 'Linking land, labour and livelihood struggles', *South African Labour Bulletin*, vol. 26, no. 6: 26-9.

— (1989) 'The growth linkages controversy: some lessons from the Muda case', *Journal of Development Studies*, vol. 25, no. 4: 571-5.

Hartnack, A. (2005) '"My life got lost": farm workers and displacement in Zimbabwe', *Journal of Contemporary African Studies*, vol. 23, no. 2: 173-92.

Harts-Broekhuis, A. and Huisman, H. (2001) 'Resettlement revisited: land reform results in resource-poor regions in Zimbabwe', *Geoforum*, vol. 32, no.3: 285-98.

Hasluck, D. (2003) 'Leasing and sharecropping contracts for increasing beneficiary access to land' in M. Roth and F. Gonese (eds) *Delivering Land and Securing Rural Livelihoods: Post-independence Land Reform and Resettlement in Zimbabwe*, University of Zimbabwe and University of Wisconsin-Madison, Harare and Madison, WI.

— (1998). *An Analysis and Some Proposals on the Zimbabwe Government Land Acquisition and Land Reform Programe.* Commercial Farmers Union, Harare.

Hazell, P., Dorward, A., Poulton, C. and Wiggins, S. (2007) *The Future of Small Farms for Poverty Reduction and Growth*, 2020 Discussion Paper, no. 42, IFPRI, Washington, DC.

Herbst, J. (1990) *State Politics in Zimbabwe*, University of Zimbabwe Publications, Harare.

Hill, K.A. (1994) 'Politicians, farmers, and ecologists: commercial wildlife ranching and the politics of land in Zimbabwe', *Journal of Asian and African Studies*, vol. 29, no. 3-4: 226-47.

Hoddinott, J. (2006) 'Shocks and their consequences across and within households in rural Zimbabwe', *Journal of Development Studies*, vol. 42, no. 2: 301-21.

Hoogeveen, J.G.M. and Kinsey, B. (2001) 'Land reform, growth and equity: emerging evidence from Zimbabwe's resettlement programme – a sequel', *Journal of Southern African Studies*, vol. 27, no. 1: 127-36.

Hossain, N. and Moore, M. (2002) *Arguing for the Poor: Elites and Poverty in Developing Countries*, Institute of Development Studies (IDS) Working Paper, no. 148, IDS, Brighton, UK.

Hughes, D. M. (2003) 'Rezoned for business: how eco-tourism unlocked black farmland in eastern Zimbabwe', *Journal of Agrarian Change*, vol. 1, no. 4: 576-99.

Hulme, D. and Shepherd, A. (2003) 'Conceptualizing chronic poverty', *World Development* vol. 31, no. 3: 403-23.

Hussein, K. and Nelson, J. (1998) 'Sustainable livelihoods and livelihood diversification', IDS Working Paper, 69, IDS: Brighton.

Human Rights Watch (2002) 'Fast track land reform in Zimbabwe', *Human Rights Watch* 14, 1: 1-44.

Indigenous Commercial Farmers Union (ICFU) (1998). *Land Redistribution, Use and Mangement in Zimbabwe: A Concept Paper.* ICFU, Harare.

International Assessment for Agricultural Knowledge, Science and Technology for Development (IAASTD) (2008) *Agriculture at a Crossroads*, Island Press, Washington, DC.

International Fund for Agricultural Development (IFAD) (2001) *The Challenge of Ending Rural Poverty*, Oxford University Press.

Jackson, C. (2003) 'Gender analysis of land: beyond land rights for women?', *Journal of Agrarian Change*, vol. 3, no. 4: 453-80.

Jackson, J.C. and Collier, P. (1988) *Incomes, Poverty and Food Security in Communal Lands of Zimbabwe*, Department of Rural and Urban Planning, Occasional Paper No. 11, University of Zimbabwe, Harare.

Jacobs, S. (2009) *Gender and Agrarian Reforms*, Routledge, London.

— (2000) 'Zimbabwe: why land reform is a gender issue', *Sociological Research Online*, vol. 5, no. 2, http://www.socresonline.org.uk/5/2/jacobs.html.

JAG/RAU (2008) *Reckless Tragedy: Irreversible? A Survey of Human Rights Violations and Losses Suffered by Commercial Farmers and Farm Workers from 2000 to 2008*, report prepared by the Research and Advocacy Unit

(RAU) and Justice for Agriculture (JAG) Trust, Harare.

— (2009) *If Something is Wrong … The Invisible Suffering of Commercial Farm Workers and their Families Due to 'Land Reform'*, report prepared by the Research and Advocacy Unit (RAU) and Justice for Agriculture (JAG) Trust, Harare.

Jansen, D., Bond, I. and Child, B. (1992) *Cattle, Wildlife, Both or Neither: Results of a Financial and Economic Survey of Commercial Ranches in Southern Zimbabwe*, Multispecies Animal Production Systems Project Project Paper 27, Worldwide Fund for Nature (WWF), Harare.

Jasanoff, S. and Wynne, B. (1998) 'Science and decision-making', in E. Malone and S. Rayner (eds) *Human Choice and Climate Change, Vol. 1: The Societal Framework*, Battelle Press, Columbus, OH.

Jayne, T. and Chisvo, M. (1991) 'Unravelling Zimbabwe's food insecurity paradox', *Food Policy*, vol. 16, no. 4: 319-29.

Jayne, T. and Jones, S. (1997) 'Food marketing and pricing policy in Eastern and Southern Africa: A survey', *World Development*, vol. 25, no. 9: 1505-27.

Jayne, T. and Rukuni, M. (1994) 'Managing the food economy in the 1990s', in M. Rukuni and C. Eicher (eds) *Zimbabwe's Agricultural Revolution*, University of Zimbabwe Publications, Harare.

Jayne, T., Govereh, J., Mwanaumo, A., Nyoro, J. K. and Chapoto, A. (2002) 'False promise or false premise? The experience of food and input market reform in east and southern Africa', *World Development*, vol. 30, no. 11: 1967-85.

Johnson, M., Hazell, P. and Gulati, A. (2003) 'Role of intermediate factor markets in Asia's Green Revolution: lessons for Africa?', *American Journal of Agricultural Economics*, vol. 85, no. 5: 1211-16.

Kanyenze, G. (2001) 'Zimbabwe's labour relations policies and the implications for farm workers', in D. Amanor-Wilks (ed.) *Zimbabwe's Farm Workers: Policy Dimensions*, Panos Southern Africa, Lusaka, Zambia.

Keeley, J. and Scoones, I. (2003) *Understanding Environmental Policy Processes: Cases from Africa*, Earthscan, London.

Kelly, V., Adesina, A. and Gordon, A. (2003) 'Expanding access to agricultural inputs in Africa: a review of market development experience', *Food Policy*, vol. 28, no. 4: 379-404.

Kinsey, B. (2009) *Survival or Growth? An Assessment of the Impact of a Generation of Land Redistribution on Food Security and Livelihoods in Zimbabwe,* paper originally for the 8th North Eastern Workshop on Southern Africa (NEWSA), 17-19 October 2008, Burlington, VT.

— (2003) 'Comparative economic performance of Zimbabwe's resettlement models', in M. Roth and F. Gonese (eds) *Delivering Land and Securing Rural Livelihoods: Post-Independence Land Reform and Resettlement in Zimbabwe*, University of Zimbabwe and University of Wisconsin-Madison, Harare, Zimbabwe and Madison, WI.

— (2002) 'Survival or growth? Temporal dimensions of rural livelihoods in risky environments', *Journal of Southern African Studies*, vol. 28, no. 3: 615-29.

— (1999) 'Land reform, growth and equity: emerging evidence from Zimbabwe's resettlement programme', *Journal of Southern African Studies,* vol. 25, no. 2: 173-96.

— (1983) 'Emerging policy issues in Zimbabwe's land resettlement programs', *Development Policy Review*, vol. 1, no. 2: 163-96.

Kinsey, B. and Binswanger, H. (1993) 'Characteristics and performance of resettlement programs: a review', *World Development*, vol. 21, no. 9: 1477-

94.
Kinsey, B., Burger, K. and Gunning, J. (1998) 'Coping with drought in Zimbabwe: survey evidence on responses of rural households to risk', *World Development*, vol. 26, no. 1: 89-110.

Kreuter, U. P. and Workman, J. (1992) *The Comparative Economics of Cattle and Wildlife Production in the Midlands of Zimbabwe*, World Wide Fund for Nature, Project Paper No. 31, WWF, Harare.

Kriger, N. (2006) 'From patriotic memories to 'patriotic history' in Zimbabwe, 1990–2005', *Third World Quarterly*, vol. 27, no. 6, pp 1151 - 1169

— (2003) *Guerrilla Veterans in Post-War Zimbabwe: Symbolic and Violent Politics, 1980-1987*, Cambridge University Press, Cambridge, UK.

Kydd, J., Dorward, A., Morrison, J. and Cadisch, G. (2004) 'Agricultural development and pro-poor economic growth in sub-Saharan Africa: potential and policy', *Oxford Development Studies*, vol. 32, no. 1: 37-57.

Lahiff, E. and Cousins, B. (2005) 'Smallholder agriculture and land reform in South Africa', *IDS Bulletin*, vol. 36, no. 2: 127-31.

— (2001) 'The land crisis in Zimbabwe viewed from south of the Limpopo', *Journal of Agrarian Change*, vol. 1, no. 4: 652-66.

Lahiff, E. and Scoones, I. (2000) *Land Theme Paper*, Sustainable Livelihoods in Southern Africa Working Paper 2, Institute of Development Studies, Brighton, UK.

Lahiff, E., Borras, S. and Kay, C. (2007) 'Market-led agrarian reform: policies, performance and prospects', *Third World Quarterly*, vol. 28, no. 8: 1417-36.

Lahiff, E., Maluleke, T., Manenzhe, T. and Wegerif, M. (2008) *Land Redistribution and Poverty Reduction in South Africa: The Livelihood Impacts of Smallholder Agriculture under Land Reform*, Research Report, no. 36, PLAAS, Cape Town.

Lan, D. (1985) *Guns and Rain: Guerrillas and Spirit Mediums in Zimbabwe*, James Currey, London.

Larsen, M. (2002) 'Is oligopoly a condition of successful privatization? The case of cotton in Zimbabwe', *Journal of Agrarian Change*, vol. 2, no. 2: 185-205

Lavigne-Delville, P. (2003) 'When farmers use 'pieces of paper' to record their land transactions in francophone rural Africa: insights into the dynamics of institutional innovation', *European Journal of Development Research* vol. 14, no.2: 89-109.

Leach. M and Mearns, R. (eds) (1996) *The Lie of the Land: Challenging Received Wisdom on the African Environment*, James Currey, Oxford.

Lehmann, D. (1978) 'The death of land reform: a polemic', *World Development*, vol. 6, no.3: 339-45.

Lipton, M. (2009) *Land Reform in Developing Countries: Property Rights and Property Wrongs*, Routledge, London.

— (2005) *The Family Farm in a Globalizing World: The Role of Crop Science in Alleviating Poverty*, International Food Policy Research Institute (IFPRI) 2020 Paper, no. 40, IFPRI, Washington, DC.

— (1993) 'Land reform as commenced business: the evidence against stopping', *World Development*, vol. 21, no. 4: 641-57.

Lipton, M. and Ellis, F. (eds) (1996) *Land, Labour and Livelihoods in Rural South Africa. Volume Two: Kwazulu-Natal and Northern Province*, Indicator Press, Durban, South Africa.

Lipton, M. and Longhurst, R. (1989) *New Seeds and Poor People*, Unwin Hyman, London.

Lodge, T. (2003) *Politics in South Africa: From Mandela to Mbeki*, Indiana

University Press, Bloomington, IN.
Loewenson, R. (1992) *Modern Plantation Agriculture: Corporate Wealth and Labour Squalor*, Zed Books, London.
Luckert, M. and Campbell, B. (2002) *Uncovering the Hidden Harvest: Valuation Methods for Woodland and Forest Resources*, Earthscan, London.
Lund, C. (2006) 'Twilight institutions: public authority and local politics in Africa', *Development and Change*, vol. 37, no. 4: 685-705.
MacGaffey, J. (1991) *The Real Economy of Zaire: The Contribution of Smuggling and Other Unofficial Activities to National Wealth*, James Currey, Oxford.
Magaramombe, G. (2003) 'Farmworkers: The missing class in Zimbabwe's Fast Track Resettlement', in M. Roth and F. Gonese (eds) *Delivering land and securing rural livelihoods: Post-independence land reform and resettlement in Zimbabwe*, University of Zimbabwe and University of Wisconsin-Madison, Harare and Madison, WI.
— (2010) 'Agrarian displacements, replacements and resettlement: 'displaced in place' farm workers in Mazowe district', *Journal of Southern African Studies*, vol. 36, no. 2: 361-75.
Makhado, J., Matondi, P. and Munyiki-Hungwe, P. (2006) 'Irrigation development and water resources management', in M. Rukuni, P. Tawonezvi, and C. Eicher, with M. Munyuki-Hungwe and P. Matondi (eds) *Zimbabwe's Agricultural Revolution Revisited*, University of Zimbabwe Publications, Harare.
Mamdani, M. (2008) 'Lessons of Zimbabwe', *London Review of Books,* vol. 30, no. 23: 17-21.
Manatsa, D. and Matarira, C. (2009) 'Changing dependence of Zimbabwean rainfall variability on ENSO and the Indian Ocean dipole/zonal mode', *Theoretical and Applied Climatology*, vol. 98, nos 3-4, 375-96.
Manzungu, E. and Van der Zaag, P. (eds) (1996) *The Practice of Smallholder Irrigation: Case-studies from Zimbabwe*, University of Zimbabwe Publications, Harare.
Maphosa, F. (2007) 'Remittances and development: the impact of migration to South Africa on rural livelihoods in southern Zimbabwe', *Development Southern Africa*, vol. 24, no. 1: 123-36.
Maponga, O. and Ngorima, C. (2003) 'Overcoming environmental problems in the gold panning sector through legislation and education: the Zimbabwean experience', *Journal of Cleaner Production* 11 (2), 147-57.
Mariga, I. (2006) 'Cotton research and development, 1920-2004', in M. Rukuni, P. Tawonezvi, and C. Eicher, with M. Munyuki-Hungwe and P. Matondi (eds) *Zimbabwe's Agricultural Revolution Revisited*, University of Zimbabwe Publications, Harare.
Marongwe, N. (2009) 'Interrogating Zimbabwe's Fast Track Land Reform and Resettlement Programme: A Focus on Beneficiary Selection', PhD thesis, University of the Western Cape, Cape Town.
— (2007). *Redistributive Land Reform and Poverty Reduction in Zimbabwe*, Livelihoods after Land Reform Project Paper, PLAAS, Cape Town.
— (2003) 'Farm occupations and occupiers in the new politics of land in Zimbabwe', in A. Hammar, B. Raftopoulos and S. Jensen (eds) *Zimbabwe's Unfinished Business: Rethinking Land, State and Nation in the Context of Crisis*, Weaver Press, Harare.
— (2002) *Conflicts Over Land and Other Natural Resources in Zimbabwe*, Regional Environment Organisation (ZERO), Harare.
Masakure, O. and Henson, S. (2005) 'Why do small-scale producers choose to produce under contract? Lessons from non-traditional vegetable exports

from Zimbabwe', *World Development,* vol. 33, no. 10: 1721-33.

Mashingaidze, K. (2006) 'Maize research and development' in Rukuni, M., Tawonezvi, P. and Eicher, C. with Munyuki-Hungwe, M. and Matondi, P. (eds) *Zimbabwe's Agricultural Revolution Revisited,* University of Zimbabwe Press, Harare, 363-78.

Masiiwa, M. (ed.) (2004) *Post Independence Land Reform in Zimbabwe: Controversies and Impact on the Economy,* Friedrich Ebert Stiftung, Harare.

Mate, R. (2001) `Land, women and sugar in Chipiwa', in P. Hebinck and M. Bourdillon (eds) *Women, Men and Work: Rural Livelihoods in South-eastern Zimbabwe,* Weaver Press, Harare.

Matondi, P. (ed.) (2010) *Inside the Political Economy of Redistributive Land and Agrarian Reforms in Mazowe, Shamva and Mangwe Districts in Zimbabwe,* Ruzivo Trust, Harare.

Mavedzenge, B. Z., Mahenehene, J., Murimbarimba, F., Scoones, I. and Wolmer, W. (2008) 'The dynamics of real markets: cattle in southern Zimbabwe following land reform,' *Development and Change,* vol. 39, no. 4: 613-39.

— (2006) *Changes in the Livestock Sector in Zimbabwe following Land Reform: The Case of Masvingo Province,* Institute of Development Studies, Brighton, UK.

Mbiba, B. (2005) 'Zimbabwe's global citizens in 'Harare North' United Kingdom: some preliminary observations', in M. Palmberg and R. Primorac (eds) *Skinning A Skunk: Facing Zimbabwean Futures,* Nordic Africa Institute, Uppsala, Sweden.

McGregor, J. (2009) 'Associational links with home among Zimbabweans in the UK: reflections on long- distance nationalisms', *Global Networks,* vol. 9, no. 2: 185-208.

— (2007) '"Joining the BBC (British Bottom Cleaners)": Zimbabwe migrants and the UK care industry', *Journal of Ethnic and Migration Studies,* vol. 33, no. 5: 801-24.

— (2002) 'The politics of disruption: war veterans and the local state in Zimbabwe', *African Affairs,* vol. 101, no. 402: 9-37.

Melber, H. (ed.) (2008) *Transitions in Namibia: Which Changes for Whom?,* Nordic Africa Institute, Uppsala, Sweden.

Mharapara, I. (1995) 'A fundamental approach to dambo utilization', in R. Owen, K. Verbeck, J. Jackson and S. Steenhuis (eds) *Dambo Farming in Zimbabwe,* University of Zimbabwe Publications, Harare.

Mlambo, A. and Pangeti, E. (1996) *The Political Economy of the Sugar Industry in Zimbabwe 1920–1990,* University of Zimbabwe Publications, Harare.

Mombeshora, S. and Le Bel, S. (2009) 'Parks-people conflicts: the case of Gonarezhou National Park and the Chitsa community in south-east Zimbabwe', *Biodiversity and Conservation,* vol. 18, no. 10: 2601-23.

Moore, D. (2004) 'Marxism and Marxist intellectuals in schizophrenic Zimbabwe: how many rights for Zimbabwe's left? A comment', *Historical Materialism,* vol. 21, no. 4: 405-25.

— (2003) 'Zimbabwe's triple crisis: primitive accumulation, nation-state formation and democratisation in the age of neo-liberal globalisation', *African Studies Quarterly,* vol. 7, no. 2–3: 35-47.

— (2001) 'Is the land the economy and the economy the land? Primitive accumulation in Zimbabwe', *Journal of Contemporary African Studies,* vol. 19, no. 2: 253-66.

Moss, T. and Patrick, S. (2006) 'After Mugabe: applying post-conflict recovery lessons to Zimbabwe', *Africa Policy Journal,* vol. 1, no. 1: 21-36.

Moyo, G. and Ashurst, M. (eds) (2007) *The Day after Mugabe: Prospects for*

Change in Zimbabwe, Africa Research Institute, London.

Moyo, S. (2009) *Agrarian Reform and Prospects for Recovery,* African Institute for Agrarian Studies, Harare.

— (2007) *Emerging Land Tenure Issues in Zimbabwe,* African Institute for Agrarian Studies, Harare.

— (2001) 'The land cccupation movement in Zimbabwe: contradictions of neoliberalism', *Millennium: Journal of International Studies,* vol. 30, no. 2: 311-30.

— (2000a) *Land Reform under Structural Adjustment in Zimbabwe,* Nordic Africa Institute, Uppsala, Sweden.

— (2000b) 'The political economy of land acquisition and redistribution in Zimbabwe, 1990-1999', *Journal of Southern African Studies,* vol. 26, no. 1: 5-28.

— (1998) *The Land Acquisition Process in Zimbabwe (1997/8),* United Nations Development Programme, Harare.

— (1995) *The Land Question in Zimbabwe,* SAPES Books, Harare.

— (1986) 'The land question' in I. Mandaza (ed.) *Zimbabwe: The Political Economy of Transition 1980–1986,* Centre for Development of Economic and Social Research in Africa (CODESRIA), Dakar, Senegal.

Moyo, S., Chambati, W. and Murisa, T. (2009) *Fast Track Land Reform: Trends and Tendencies,* Report of the baseline district studies, African Institute for Agrarian Studies, Harare.

Moyo, S. and Yeros, P. (2007) 'The Zimbabwe question and the two lefts', *Historical Materialism,* vol. 15, no. 3: 171-204.

— (2005) 'Land occupations and land reform in Zimbabwe: towards the national democratic revolution', in S. Moyo and P. Yeros (eds) *Reclaiming the Land: The Resurgence of Rural Movements in Africa, Asia and Latin America,* Zed Books, London.

Moyo, S., Rutherford, B. and Amanor-Wilks, D. (2000) 'Land reform and changing social relations for farm workers in Zimbabwe', *Review of African Political Economy,* vol. 27, no. 84: 181-202.

Muir-Leresche, K. and Muchopa, C. (2006) 'Agricultural marketing', in M. Rukuni, P. Tawonezvi and C. Eicher with M. Munyuki-Hungwe and P. Matondi (eds) *Zimbabwe's Agricultural Revolution Revisited,* University of Zimbabwe Publications, Harare.

Mujere, J. (2010) 'Land, graves and belonging: Land reform and the politics of belonging in newly resettled farms in Gutu, 2000-2009', Livelihoods after Land Reform in Zimbabwe Working Paper 9, Livelihoods after Land Reform Project, PLAAS, South Africa.

Mukamuri, B., Manjengwa, J. M. and Anstey, S. (2009) *Beyond Proprietorship: Murphree's Laws on Community-based Natural Resource Management,* Weaver Press, Harare.

Murray, C. (1980) 'Migrant labour and changing family structure in the rural periphery of southern Africa', *Journal of Southern African Studies,* vol. 6, no. 2: 139-57.

Murwira, K., Hagmann, J. and Chuma, E. (2001) 'Mainstreaming participatory approaches to SWC in Zimbabwe', in C. Reij and A. Waters-Bayer (eds) *Farmer Innovation in Africa,* Earthscan, London.

Mushongah, J. (2009). 'Rethinking Vulnerability: Livelihood Change in Southern Zimbabwe, 1986-2006', DPhil thesis, University of Sussex.

Mutizwa-Mangiza, N. and Helmsing, A. (eds) (1991) *Rural Development and Planning in Zimbabwe,* Avebury, Aldershot, UK.

Nel, E. and Rogerson, C. (2009) 'Re-thinking spatial inequalities in South Africa: lessons from international experience', *Urban Forum,* vol. 20, no.

2: 141-55.

Neocosmos, M. (1993) 'The Agrarian Question in Southern Africa and "Accumulation from Below": Economics and Politics in the Struggle for Democracy', Scandinavian Institute of African Studies, Research Report no. 93, Uppsala, Sweden.

Nyambara, P. (2001a) 'Immigrants, "traditional" leaders and the Rhodesian state: the power of "communal" land tenure and the politics of land acquisition in Gokwe, Zimbabwe, 1963-1979', Journal of Southern African Studies, vol. 27, no. 4: 771-91.

— (2001b) 'The closing frontier: agrarian change, immigrants and the "squatter menace" in Gokwe, 1980–1990s', Journal of Agrarian Change, vol. 1, no. 4: 534-49.

O'Laughlin, B. (2009) 'Gender justice, land and the agrarian question in southern Africa' in A. Akram-Lodhi and C. Kay (eds) Peasants and Globalisation: Political Economy, Rural Transformation and the Agrarian Question, Routledge, London.

— (1998) 'Missing men? The debate over rural poverty and women-headed households in southern Africa', Journal of Peasant Studies, vol. 25, no. 2: 1-48.

Owens, T., Hoddinott, J. and Kinsey, B. (2003) 'The impact of agricultural extension on farm production in resettlement areas of Zimbabwe', Economic Development and Cultural Change, vol. 51, no. 2: 337-57.

Palmer, R. (1990) 'Land reform in Zimbabwe, 1980–1990', African Affairs, vol. 89, no. 335: 163-81.

— (1977) Land and Racial Domination in Rhodesia, Heinemann, London.

Pankhurst, D. and Jacobs, S. (1988) 'Land tenure, gender relations and agricultural production: The case of Zimbabwe's peasantry' in J. Davison (ed.) Women, Agriculture and Land, Westview, Boulder, CO.

Peters, P. (2009) 'Challenges in land tenure and land reform in Africa: anthropological contributions', World Development, vol. 37, no. 8: 1317-25.

—(2004) 'Inequality and social conflict over land in Africa', Journal of Agrarian Change, vol. 4, no. 3: 269-314.

— (2002) 'The limits of negotiability: Security, equity and class formation in Africa's land systems', in K. Juul and C. Lund (eds) Negotiating Property in Africa, Heinemann, Portsmouth, NH.

Platteau, J.P. (2008) 'The evolutionary theory of land rights as applied to sub-Saharan Africa: a critical assessment', Development and Change, vol. 27, no. 1: 29-86.

— (1994) 'Behind the market stage: where real societies exist', Journal of Development Studies, vol. 30 (Part 1): 533 - 77, vol. 30 (Part 2): 753-817.

Potts, D. (2008) 'Displacement and livelihoods: the longer term impacts of Operation Murambatsvina' in M. Vambe (ed.) The Hidden Dimensions of Operation Murambatsvina in Zimbabwe, Weaver Press, Harare.

— (2006a) '"Restoring order"? Operation Murambatsvina and the urban crisis in Zimbabwe', Journal of Southern African Studies, vol. 32, no. 2: 273-91.

— (2006b) '"All my hopes and dreams are shattered": urbanization and migrancy in an imploding African economy – the case of Zimbabwe', Geoforum, vol. 37, no. 4: 536-51.

— (2000) 'Worker-peasants and farmer-housewives in Africa: the debate about "committed" farmers, access to land and agricultural production', Journal of Southern African Studies, vol. 26, no. 4: 807-32.

Potts, D. and Mutambirwa, C. (1997) '"The government must not dictate ...": Rural urban migrants' perceptions of Zimbabwe's land resettlement pro-

gramme', *Review of African Political Economy*, vol. 74: 549-66.
— (1990) 'Rural-urban linkages in contemporary Harare: why migrants need their land', *Journal of Southern African Studies*, vol. 16, no. 4: 671-98.
Poulton, C. and Hanyani-Mlambo, B. (2009) *The Cotton Sector of Zimbabwe*, Africa Region Working Paper Series no. 122, World Bank, Washington, DC.
Poulton, C., Kydd, J. and Dorward, A. (2006) 'Overcoming market constraints on pro-poor agricultural growth in sub-Saharan Africa', *Development Policy Review*, vol. 24, no. 3: 243-77.
Poulton, C., Davies, R., Matshe, I. and Urey, I. (2002) *A Review of Zimbabwe's Agricultural Economic Policies: 1980-2000)*, ADU Working Paper 02/01, Imperial College, Wye, UK.
Quan, J., Davis, J. and Proctor, F. (2006) *Rural Development from a Territorial Perspective: Lessons and Potential in sub-Saharan Africa*, University of Greenwich, London.
Raftopoulos, B. (2009) 'The crisis in Zimbabwe, 1998-2008', in B. Raftopoulos and A. Mlambo (eds) *Becoming Zimbabwe: A History from the Pre-Colonial Period to 2008*, Weaver Press, Harare.
— (2006a) 'Reflections on opposition politics in Zimbabwe: The politics of the Movement for Democratic Change (MDC)', in B. Raftopoulos and K. Alexander (eds) *Reflections on Democratic Politics in Zimbabwe*, Institute for Justice and Reconciliation, Cape Town.
— (2006b) 'The Zimbabwean crisis and the challenges for the left', *Journal of Southern African Studies*, vol. 32, no. 2: 203-19.
— (2003) 'The state in crisis: authoritarian nationalism, selective citizenship and distortions of democracy in Zimbabwe', in A. Hammar, B. Raftopoulos and S. Jensen (eds) *Zimbabwe's Unfinished Business: Rethinking Land, State and Nation in the Context of Crisis*, Weaver Press, Harare.
Raftopoulos, B. and Mlambo, A. (eds) (2009) *Becoming Zimbabwe: A History from the Pre-Colonial Period to 2008*, Weaver Press, Harare.
Ranger, T. (1999) *Voices from the Rocks: Nature, Culture and History in the Matopos Hills of Zimbabwe*, James Currey, Oxford.
Ravallion, M. (2001) 'Growth, inequality and poverty: looking beyond averages', *World Development*, vol. 29, no. 11: 1803-15.
Reardon, T. (1997) 'Using evidence of household income diversification to inform the study of rural non-farm labour markets in Africa', *World Development*, vol. 25, no. 5: 735-47.
Richardson, C. (2007) 'How much did drought matter? Linking rainfall and Gross Domestic Product growth in Zimbabwe', *African Affairs*, vol. 106, no. 424: 463-78.
— (2005) 'The loss of property rights and the collapse of Zimbabwe', *Cato Journal*, vol. 25, no. 3: 541-64.
Robilliard, A-S., Sukume, C., Yanoma, Y. and Löfgren, H. (2001) *Land Reform and Poverty Alleviation in Zimbabwe: Farm-Level Effects and Cost-Benefit Analysis*, TMD Discussion Paper, no. 84, International Food Policy Research Instittue (IFPRI), Washington, DC.
Roe, E. (1991) 'Development narratives', *World Development*, vol. 19, no. 4: 287-300.
Rohrbach, D. (1989) *The Economics of Smallholder Maize Production in Zimbabwe: Implications for Food Security,* International Development Papers, no. 11, Michigan State University, East Lansing, MI.
Rosset, P., Patel, R. and Courville, M. (eds) (2006) *Promised Land: Competing Visions of Agrarian Reform*, Food First Books, Oakland, CA.
Roth, M. and Gonese, F. (2003) *Delivering Land and Securing Rural Liveli-*

hoods: *Post-Independence Land Reform and Resettlement in Zimbabwe*, University of Zimbabwe and University of Wisconsin-Madison, Harare and Madison, WI.

Roth, M. and Haase, D. (1998) *Land Tenure Security and Agricultural Performance in Southern Africa*, University of Wisconsin-Madison, Madison, WI.

Rukuni, M. (1994a) *Report on the Inquiry into Appropriate Agricultural Land Tenure Systems. Volume 1: Main Report; Volume 2: Technical Reports*, Government Printers, Harare.

— (1994b) 'The evolution of agricultural policy: 1890-1990', in M. Rukuni and C. Eicher (eds) *Zimbabwe's Agricultural Revolution*, University of Zimbabwe Publications, Harare.

Rukuni, M. and Eicher, C. (eds) (1994) *Zimbabwe's Agricultural Revolution*, University of Zimbabwe Publications, Harare.

Rukuni, M., Nyoni, J. and Matondi, P. (2009). *Policy Options for Optimisiation of the Use of Land for Agricultural Productivity and Production in Zimbabwe*, World Bank, Harare.

Rukuni, M., Tawonezvi, P. and Eicher, C. with Munyuki-Hungwe, M. and Matondi, P. (eds) (2006) *Zimbabwe's Agricultural Revolution Revisited*, University of Zimbabwe Publications, Harare.

Rusike, J. and Sukume, C. (2006) 'Agricultural input supply', in M. Rukuni, P. Tawonezvi, and C. Eicher, with M. Munyuki-Hungwe and P. Matondi (eds) *Zimbabwe's Agricultural Revolution Revisited*, University of Zimbabwe Publications, Harare.

Rutherford, B. (2008) 'Conditional belonging: farm workers and the cultural politics of recognition in Zimbabwe', *Development and Change*, vol 39, no. 1: 73-99.

— (2003) 'Belonging to the farm(er): Farm workers, farmers, and the shifting politics of citizenship', in A. Hammar, B. Raftopoulos and S. Jensen (eds) *Zimbabwe's Unfinished Business: Rethinking Land, State and Nation in the Context of Crisis*, Weaver Press, Harare.

— (2001a) 'Commercial farm workers and the politics of (dis)placement in Zimbabwe: colonialism, liberation and democracy', *Journal of Agrarian Change*, vol. 1, no. 4: 626-51.

— (2001b) *Working on the Margins: Black Workers, White Farmers in Postcolonial Zimbabwe*, Weaver Press, Harare

Rutherford, B. and Addison, L. (2007) 'Zimbabwean farm workers in northern South Africa', *Review of African Political Economy*, vol. 34, no. 111: 619-35.

Sachikonye, L. (2003a) 'From "growth with equity" to "fast-track" reform: Zimbabwe's land question', *Review of African Political Economy*, vol. 30, no. 96: 227-40.

— (2003b) *The Situation of Commercial Farm Workers after Land Reform in Zimbabwe*, Catholic Institute for International Relations and Farm Community Trust of Zimbabwe (FCTZ), London and Harare.

Sadomba, W. Z. (2008) 'War Veterans in Zimbabwe's Land Occupations: Complexities of a Liberation Movement in an African Post-Colonial Settler Society', PhD Dissertation, Wageningen University, The Netherlands.

Sahn, D. and Arulpragasm, J. (1991) 'Development through Dualism? Land Tenure, Policy and Poverty in Malawi', Working Paper, no. 9, Cornell Food and Nutrition Programme, Cornell University, Ithaca, NY.

Scoones, I. (2009) 'Livelihoods perspectives and rural development', *Journal of Peasant Studies*, vol. 36, no. 1: 171-96.

— (1998) *Sustainable Rural Livelihoods: A Framework for Analysis*, IDS Working Paper, no. 72, Institute for Development Studies, Brighton, UK.

— (1995) 'Investigating difference: applications of wealth ranking and household survey approaches among farming households in southern Africa', *Development and Change*, vol. 26, no.1: 67-88.

— (1992a) 'Coping with drought: responses of herders and livestock in contrasting savanna environments in southern Africa', *Human Ecology*, vol. 20, no. 3: 293-313.

— (1992b) 'The economic value of livestock in the communal areas of southern Zimbabwe', *Agricultural Systems*, vol. 39, no. 4: 339-59.

— (1990) 'Livestock Population and the Household Economy: A Case Study from Southern Zimbabwe', PhD Thesis, Imperial College, University of London, London.

Scoones, I., Bishi, A., Mapitse, N., Moerane, R., Penrith, M-L, Sibanda, R., Thomson, G. and Wolmer, W. (2010) 'Foot-and-mouth disease and market access: challenges for the beef industry in southern Africa', *Pastoralism*, vol. 1, no. 2: 135-61.

Scoones, I. and Wilson, K. (1988) 'Households, lineage groups and ecological dynamics: issues for livestock research and development in Zimbabwe's communal areas', in B. Cousins (ed.) *People, Land and Livestock: The Socio-economic Determinants of Livestock Production in Zimbabwe's Communal Areas*, CASS, University of Zimbabwe, Harare.

Scoones, I. and Wolmer, W. (2003) 'Livelihoods in crisis: challenges for rural development in southern Africa', *IDS Bulletin*, vol. 34, no. 3: 1-14.

— (2002) *Pathways of Change in Africa: Crops, Livestock and Livelihoods in Mali, Ethiopia and Zimbabwe*, James Currey, Oxford.

Scoones, I., Devereux, S. and Haddad, L. (2005) 'Introduction: new directions for African agriculture', *IDS Bulletin*, vol. 36, no. 2: 1-12.

Scoones, I. with Chibudu, C., Chikura, S., Jeranyama, P., Machanja, W., Mavedzenge, B., Mombeshora, B., Mudhara, M., Mudziwo, C., Murimbarimba, F., Zirereza, B. (1996) *Hazards and Opportunities. Farming Livelihoods in Dryland Africa: Lessons from Zimbabwe*, Zed Books, London.

Scott, J. (1998) *Seeing like a State: How Certain Schemes to Improve the Human Condition have Failed*, Yale University Press, New Haven, CT.

Seekings, J. and Nattrass, N. (2002) 'Class, distribution and redistribution in post-apartheid South Africa', *Transformation*, vol. 50, no. 1: 1-30.

Selby, A. (2006) 'Commercial Farmers and the State: Interest Group Politics and Land Reform in Zimbabwe', DPhil Thesis, Oxford University, UK.

Sender, J. and Johnston, D. (2003) 'Searching for a weapon of mass production in rural Africa: unconvincing arguments for land reform', *Journal of Agrarian Change*, vol. 4, no. 1 and 2: 142-64.

Shivji, I., Gunby, D., Moyo, S. and Ncube, W. (1998) *National Land Policy Framework*, Government of Zimbabwe, Harare.

Shutt, A.K. (1997) 'Purchase area farmers and the middle class of Southern Rhodesia, c. 1931-1952', *International Journal of African Historical Studies*, vol. 30, no. 3: 555-81.

Sibanda, R. (2008) 'Market access policy options for FMD-challenged Zimbabwe: a rethink'. Transboundary animal disease and market access: future options for the beef industry in southern Africa, Working Paper 6, Brighton: STEPS Centre, Institute of Development Studies.

Sierevogel, T., Carruthers, B., Llabres, J-P. and Mukamuri, B. (2007) *Elaborating an Adaptation Strategy in Zimbabwe in Light of Changes to the EU Sugar Regime, Zimbabwe Final Report*, Report for the EU and Government of Zimbabwe, Harare.

Smale, M. and Jayne, T. (2003) '*Maize in Eastern and Southern Africa: Seeds of Success in Retrospect*', EPTD Discussion Paper, no. 97, IFPRI, Washington, DC.

Sola, P. (2004) 'Palm utilisation for basketry in Xini Ward, Sengwe communal area, Zimbabwe', in T. Sunderland and O. Ndoye (eds) *Forest Products, Livelihoods and Conservation: Case Studies of Non-Timber Forest Product Systems, Volume 2, Africa*, CIFOR, Bogor, Indonesia.

Spierenburg, M. (2004) *Strangers, Spirits, and Land Reforms: Conflicts about Land in Dande, Northern Zimbabwe*, Brill, Leiden, The Netherlands.

Stack, J. (1994) 'The distributional consequences of the smallholder maize revolution', in M. Rukuni and C. Eicher (eds) *Zimbabwe's Agricultural Revolution*, University of Zimbabwe Publications, Harare.

Stanning, J. (1989) 'Smallholder maize production and sales in Zimbabwe: some distributional aspects', *Food Policy*, vol 14, no. 3: 260-67.

Stoneman, C. (2000) 'Zimbabwe land policy and the land reform programme', in T. Bowyer-Bower and C. Stoneman (eds) *Land Reform in Zimbabwe: Constraints and Prospect*, Ashgate, Aldershot, UK.

— (ed.) (1988) *Zimbabwe's Prospects: Issues of Race, Class, State and Capital in Southern Africa*, Macmillan, London.

Sukume, C. (2009) *Improving Input and Output Markets for Smallholder Farmers in Zimbabwe*, World Bank, Harare.

Tandon, Y. (2001) 'Trade unions and labour in the agricultural sector in Zimbabwe', in B. Raftopoulos and L. Sachikonye (eds) *Striking Back: The Labour Movement and the Post-Colonial State in Zimbabwe, 1980-2000*, Weaver Press, Harare.

Tawonezvi, P. and Hikwa, D. (2006) 'Agricultural research policy' in Rukuni, M., Tawonezvi, P. and Eicher, C. with Munyuki-Hungwe, M. and Matondi, P. (eds) *Zimbabwe's Agricultural Revolution Revisited*, University of Zimbabwe Press, Harare, pp. 197-216.

Tevera, D. and Chikanda, A. (2009) *Migrant Remittances and Household Survival in Zimbabwe,* Idasa, Cape Town.

Tibaijuka, A. (2005) *Report of the Fact-Finding Mission to Zimbabwe to assess the Scope and Impact of Operation Murambatsvina in Zimbabwe*, UN Habitat, Nairobi.

Toulmin, C. and Quan, J. (eds) (2000) *Evolving Land Rights: Policy and Tenure in Africa*, Institute for Environment and Development, London.

Tschirley, D., Poulton, C. and Labaste, P. (eds) (2009) *Organization and Performance of Cotton Sectors in Africa: Learning from Reform Experience*, World Bank, Washington, DC.

United Nations (1951) *Economic Development of Under-developed Countries. Land Reform: Defects in Agrarian Structure as Obstacles to Economic Development*, United Nations, Economic and Social Council, New York, NY.

United Nations Development Programme (UNDP) (2008) *Comprehensive Economic Recovery in Zimbabwe: A Discussion Document*, UNDP, Harare.

— (2002) *Zimbabwe Land Reform and Resettlement: Assessment and Suggested Framework for the Future – Interim Mission Report,* UNDP, Harare.

Utete, C. (2003) *Report of the Presidential Land Review Committee on the Implementation of the Fast Track Land Reform Programme, 2000-2002 ('The Utete Report')*, http://www.sarpn.org.za/documents/d0000622/P600-Utete_PLRC_00-02.pdf.

van der Ploeg, J. (2008) *The New Peasantries: Struggles for Autonomy and Sustainability in an Era of Empire and Globalization*, Earthscan, London.

Vincent, V. and Thomas, R. (1961) *Agricultural Survey of Southern Africa*, Government Printers, Harare

Waeterloos, E. and Rutherford, B. (2004) 'Reform in Zimbabwe: challenges and opportunities for poverty reduction among commercial farm workers', *World Development,* vol. 32, no. 3: 537-53.

Walker, C. (2003) 'Piety in the sky? Gender policy and land reform in South Africa', *Journal of Agrarian Change,* vol. 3, no. 1 and 2: 113-48.

Weinrich, A.K.H. (1975) *African Farmers in Rhodesia: Old and New Peasant Communities in Karangaland.* Oxford University Press: Oxford.

Weis, T. (2007) *The Global Food Economy: The Battle for the Future of Farming,* Fernwood Publishing and Zed Books, Halifax and London.

Wekwete, K.H. (1991) 'The rural resettlement programme in post-independence Zimbabwe', in N.D. Mutizwa-Mangiza and A.H.J. Helmsing (eds) *Rural Development and Planning in Zimbabwe,* Avebury: Aldershot.

Werner, W. and Odendaal, W. (2010) *Livelihoods after Land Reform. Namibia Country Report.* Land, Environment and Development Project, Legal Assistance Centre, Windhoek.

Whitehead, A. and Tsikata, D. (2003) 'Policy discourses on women's land rights in sub-Saharan Africa: the implications of the re-turn to the customary', *Journal of Agrarian Change,* vol. 3, no. 1 - 2: 67-112.

Willems, W. (2004) 'Peasant demonstrators, violent invaders: representations of land in the Zimbabwean press', *World Development,* vol. 32, no. 10: 1767-83.

Wilson, K. (1989) 'Trees in fields in southern Zimbabwe', *Journal of Southern African Studies,* vol. 15, no. 2: 369-83.

Wolmer, W. (2007) *From Wilderness Vision to Farm Invasions: Conservation and Development in Zimbabwe's South-east Lowveld,* James Currey, Oxford.

Wolmer, W. and Scoones, I. (2000) 'The science of "civilized" agriculture: the mixed farming discourse in Zimbabwe', *African Affairs,* vol. 99, no. 397: 575-600.

Wolmer, W., Chaumba, J. and Scoones, I. (2004) 'Wildlife management and land reform in southeastern Zimbabwe: a compatible pairing or a contradiction in terms?', *Geoforum,* vol. 35, no. 1: 87-98.

Wolmer, W., Sithole, B. and Mukamuri, B. (2002) 'Crops, livestock and livelihoods', in I. Scoones and W. Wolmer (eds) *Pathways of Change: Crops, Livestock and Livelihoods in Africa: Lessons from Ethiopia, Mali and Zimbabwe,* James Currey, Oxford.

Worby, E. (2003) 'The End of Modernity in Zimbabwe? Passages from development to sovereignty,' in A. Hammar, B. Raftopoulos and S. Jensen (eds) *Zimbabwe's Unfinished Business: Rethinking Land, State and Nation in the Context of Crisis,* Weaver Press, Harare.

World Bank (2008) *World Development Report 2008: Agriculture for Development,* World Bank, Washington, DC.

— (2006) *Agricultural Growth and Land Reform in Zimbabwe: Assessment and Recovery Options,* Report No. 31699-ZW, World Bank, Harare.

— (2003) *Land Policies for Growth and Poverty Reduction,* World Bank and Oxford University Press, Washington, DC and Oxford.

— (1991) *Zimbabwe Agriculture Sector Memorandum: Volume II, Main Report,* Southern Africa Department, Agriculture Operations Division, World Bank, Washington DC

— (1975) *Land Reform. Sector Policy Paper.* World Bank, Washington, DC.

Zimbabwe (Government of) (2001) *Land Reform and Resettlement Programme, Revised Phase II,* Government of Zimbabwe, Harare.

— (1998) *The Land Reform and Resettlement Programme, Phase II (Policy Framework and Project Document),* Government of Zimbabwe, Harare.

— (1981) *Zimbabwe Conference and Reconstruction and Development, ZIM-*

CORD, Report of Conference Proceedings. Government of Zimbabwe, Harare.

Zimbabwe (Ministry of Lands, Resettlement and Rural Development) (1984) *Report on Results of the First National Survey of the Normal Intensive Resettlement Programme,* Government of Zimbabwe, Harare.

—(1980) *Resettlement Policies and Procedures,* Government of Zimbabwe, Harare.

Zimbabwe (Ministry of Local Government, Rural and Urban Development) (1995) *Review of the Land Resettlement Programme, 1980–95,* Government of Zimbabwe, Harare.

Zimbabwe (Ministry of Public Service, Labour and Social Welfare) (2006) *2003 Poverty Assessment Study Survey: Main Report,* Government of Zimbabwe, Harare.

— (1997) *1995 Poverty Assessment Study Survey: Main Report,* Government of Zimbabwe, Harare.

Zumbika, N. (2006) 'Agricultural finance, 1990-2004', in M. Rukuni, P. Tawonezvi and C. Eicher with M. Munyuki-Hungwe and P. Matondi (eds) *Zimbabwe's Agricultural Revolution Revisited,* University of Zimbabwe Publications, Harare.

INDEX

145, 167, 214; management 137-8, 144-5, 224; permanent 131-7, 140-2 *passim*; relations with employer 130-41 *passim*, 146
Lahiff, E. 2, 254-6 *passim*
Lambert, R. 246
Lan, D. 197
Lancaster House Agreement 14, 17
land 1-2, 5, 10-31, 34-8, 43-58, 77-93, 189-207 *passim*, 221, 234-6, 241-3, 252-6; ceilings 11, 17, 22, 24, 25, 95; use 15, 19, 25, 34, 37, 89, 98, 189, 191, 192, 194, 201, 204, 212, 241
Land Commission 17, 202, 242
Land Reform and Resettlement Programme 21-2, 24
land-to-the-tiller 10, 13, 107, 235
landless 5, 20, 23, 129, 221; People's Movement 254
Larsen, M. 160, 162
Lavigne-Delville, P. 201
Leach, M. 238
Learning and Innovation project 21
leases/leasehold 36, 37, 86, 88, 90, 201, 202, 221, 243, 246
Le Bel, 37
Lehmann, D. 233
liberalisation, market 18, 97, 126, 151, 160-2 *passim*
linkages, economic 12, 27, 41-2, 126, 165, 167, 215-25 *passim*, 227, 240, 247-8
Lipton, M. 3, 10, 11, 13, 107, 123, 124, 130, 143, 145, 165, 167, 187, 233, 235, 242, 248, 254
livelihoods 2, 6, 9-14, 59-69 *passim*, 76, 130, 145, 166-87, 213-36 *passim*, 249-50, 255; off-farm 169-73; straddling 90-1, 227; strategies 9, 11, 12, 130, 215, 226-31, 239, 246; typology 60, 226-31
livestock 57, 61, 91-3 *passim*, 95, 117-23, 125, 128, 153-6, 200, 223-4, 239, 250, *see also individual entries*
loans 17, 18, 23, 82, 83, 98, 101, 103, 111, 201, 246-7, 250
Lodge, T. 254
Loewenson, R. 129, 131
Lonely farm 42, 46-7, 56, 61, 62, 66-8 *passim*, 78, 138-9, 194, 204, 207, 208
Longhurst, R. 124
Luckert, M. 86
Lund, C. 201

Mabugu, R. 241
MacGaffey, Janet 163

Mahofa, 161
maize 2, 5, 15, 95, 97, 98, 103-12 *passim*, 117, 122-4 *passim*, 147-52, 158, 164, 216, 219, 222, 223, 235, 239, 240, 243, 244
Makhado, J. 245
Malawi 128, 200, 244
Manicaland 7, 176
Mantasa, 124
Manyama, M. 2, 25, 189
Manzungu, E. 245
Maphosa, F. 181
Maponga, 89
Mariga, I. 160
marketing 35, 111, 114, 122, 125, 147, 149, 152-62 *passim*, 167, 213, 216, 219
markets 13, 18, 26, 111, 147-65, 169, 216-19 *passim*, 234, 235, 242, 244, 248, 249, 256; black/parallel 26, 27, 98, 101, 152, 159, 165, 178; informal 216; 'vernacular' 202
Marongwe, N. 24, 25, 88, 178
Masakure, O. 244
Mashonaland 7, 28, 60, 67
Masiiwa, M. 24
Masvingo cluster 38, 40, 42, 44, 47-8, 56, 62-3, 87, 96, 101-3 *passim*, 107, 112-14, 128, 140, 142, 143, 174, 175, 185, 195, 199, 239
Matabeleland 7, 35, 60
Matarira, 124
Matondi, P. 60, 237
Mavedzenge, B.Z. 122, 154, 156
Maxwell, S. 12
Mbiba, B. 177
McGregor, J. 177, 210
Mearns, R. 238
mechanisation 99, 196, 197, 211, 224; Farm – Programme 99
Melber, H. 254
methodology 38-43 *passim*, 60
Mharapara, I. 112
'middle farmers' 12, 93, 215, 220, 232, 234, 238-40 *passim*
Mighot-Adholla, S.E. 200, 242
migration 10, 17, 114, 115, 128, 129, 141, 145, 166, 176-83 *passim*, 185, 186, 214, 217, 223, 224, 231, 254; cross-border 177-80, 185; illegal 177-8, 180
millet 124, 147, 149, 150
minerals 175-6
mining 25, 247
Mkwasine sugar estates 36, 115, 157, 159
Mlambo, A. 20, 156, 157

Printed and bound by CPI Group (UK) Ltd, Croydon, CR0 4YY

10/06/2025

14686698-0001